What is Constructive Theology?

Rethinking Theologies: Constructing Alternatives
in History and Doctrine

Edited by
Marion Grau
Susannah Cornwall
Steed Davidson

Volume 3

What is Constructive Theology?

Histories, Methodologies, and Perspectives

Edited by
Marion Grau and Jason Wyman

LONDON • NEW YORK • OXFORD • NEW DELHI • SYDNEY

T&T CLARK
Bloomsbury Publishing Plc
50 Bedford Square, London, WC1B 3DP, UK
1385 Broadway, New York, NY 10018, USA
29 Earlsfort Terrace, Dublin 2, Ireland

BLOOMSBURY, T&T CLARK and the T&T Clark logo are trademarks of
Bloomsbury Publishing Plc

First published in Great Britain 2020
This paperback edition published in 2022

Copyright © Marion Grau, Jason Wyman and contributors, 2020

Marion Grau and Jason Wyman have asserted their right under the Copyright, Designs and Patents Act, 1988, to be identified as Editors of this work.

Unless indicated otherwise, all Scripture quotations are from New Revised Standard Version Bible, copyright © 1989 National Council of the Churches of Christ in the United States of America. Used by permission. All rights reserved worldwide.

Cover design: Terry Woodley
Cover image © Markus Schieder / Alamy Stock Photo

All rights reserved. No part of this publication may be reproduced or transmitted in any form or by any means, electronic or mechanical, including photocopying, recording, or any information storage or retrieval system, without prior permission in writing from the publishers.

Bloomsbury Publishing Plc does not have any control over, or responsibility for, any third-party websites referred to or in this book. All internet addresses given in this book were correct at the time of going to press. The author and publisher regret any inconvenience caused if addresses have changed or sites have ceased to exist, but can accept no responsibility for any such changes.

A catalogue record for this book is available from the British Library.

A catalog record for this book is available from the Library of Congress.

ISBN: HB: 978-0-5676-9515-4
PB: 978-0-5676-9654-0
ePDF: 978-0-5676-9516-1
eBook: 978-0-5676-9518-5

Series: Rethinking Theologies: Constructing Alternatives in History and Doctrine, volume 3

Typeset by Newgen KnowledgeWorks Pvt. Ltd., Chennai, India

To find out more about our authors and books visit www.bloomsbury.com
and sign up for our newsletters.

Contents

Introducing Methods in Constructive Theology *Marion Grau and Jason Wyman*   1

Part I Reflecting on the History, Genre, and Theory of Constructive Theology   7

1 Constructive Theology: History, Movement, Method *Jason Wyman*   9

2 Constructive Theology as Theopoetics: Theological Construction as Divine–Human Creativity *John J. Thatamanil*   31

3 Methodological Themes and Patterns in Constructive Theologies *Marion Grau*   53

Part II Body, Text, Interdisciplinarity, and Practice   75

4 Embodied Knowing: Body, Epistemology, Context, and Hermeneutics *Heike Peckruhn*   77

5 Constructive Biblical Hermeneutics: History and Its Afterlife *Shelly Rambo*   103

6 Blessed Snakes in the Basket: Comparative Theology and the Constructive Theological Turn *Holly Hillgardner*   123

7 Constructive Black Theology in Britain: Participative–Methodological Praxis *Anthony G. Reddie*   145

Part III Postcolonial Reconstructions   165

8 Starting with the Land under Our Feet *Laurie Cassidy*   167

9 Ransomed by Money? Toward an African Constructive Theology *Lawrence N. Nwankwo*   191

10 The Evidence of Ghosts: Constructive Theology as Apologetic Theology in the Making *Judith Gruber*   213

Notes on Contributors   239
Index   241

Introducing Methods in Constructive Theology

Marion Grau and Jason Wyman

In 1975, theologian David Tracy wrote, "That the present situation in theology is one of an ever-increasing pluralism is by now a truism. That such a pluralist condition enriches the possibilities for theology would seem at least equally clear and true. For a theologian to accept the present pluralism as a state of pure enrichment, of gratuitous and untarnished blessing, is another matter entirely."[1] After the breakdown of liberalism's hegemony and neo-orthodoxy's dispersion, progressive Christian theologians in the second half the twentieth century, in particular in the United States, found themselves facing a plurality of methods, as well as an explosion of voices in the United States and around the world that demanded to be heard in academic theological conversation: black liberation theology emerged after James Cone's foundational 1969 *Black Theology and Black Power*; feminist theologians critiqued and expanded upon new waves of feminism, incorporating their insights into Christian theology; SGLBTQ theologies were bubbling forth; and around the world oppressed, poor, and disenfranchised people were beginning to have more and more of their perspectives represented in the academic theological world—a project that is still very much unfinished and ongoing. Liberalism, neo-orthodoxy, and liberationism each had their own starting points, weights given to sources, and overarching goals, even as particular theologians within each movement had even more specific projects. From a constructive point of view, Julian Hartt nicely asserted, again in 1979, that

> registration of despair over the departure of the theological giants of the age is not on the [constructive theological] agenda. It becomes us to be grateful for their achievements. This does not mean that theologians must somehow develop strength and pray for grace to perpetuate their work as well as their fame. Constructive work in theology is not an exercise in hero worship.[2]

Constructive theology, as exemplified here, is in many ways a challenge to embrace that difficult reality to which Tracy gestured, to "accept pluralism as a state of pure

---

[1] David Tracy, *Blessed Rage for Order* (Chicago: University of Chicago Press, 1996), 3.
[2] Julian N. Hartt, "The Workgroup on Constructive Christian Theology," Occasional Papers of the Collegeville Institute, no. 8 (March 1979): 1.

enrichment, of gratuitous and unvarnished blessing." The chapters in this volume are a celebration of the wide diversity of constructive theological work being done in Christian theology at present, a present that is so clearly in need of much engagement, deconstruction, and, most important of all, reconstruction with an eye to a more plural, more just world.

At this point in the theological academy, it is safe to say, at the very least, that "constructive theology" is a term embraced by many theologians. Every major theological school, divinity school, and seminary in the United States has at least one theologian who identifies as "constructive" on their faculty. Many of them are in leadership positions, including as chaired positions, deans, and presidents. Further, many of these constructive theologians have collaborated and worked together in various guises in different scholarly organizations and configurations. These theologians reference one another, critique one another, and build on each other's work. Again, at the very least, a community has been formed. Constructive theology is, nonetheless, a very broad heading. As an academic field that aims at rigor and intelligibility to those both within and without that constructive theological community, the question naturally arises as to what the particular "method" of constructive theology is. Of course, radical feminist theologian Mary Daly has rightfully critiqued the obsession with methodology found in the academy at large, including theology, as methodolatry, arguing that fetishizing method "kills creative thought" and is a circular construction and self-reinforcement of patriarchal, male-dominated normatizing in thinking and the academy.[3] Instead, she argues for "the free play of intuition in our own space, giving rise to thinking that is vigorous, informed, multi-dimensional, independent, creative, tough." Constructive theology, heavily informed by feminist theology, seems in some sense to have internalized Daly's call and has vigilantly resisted being consolidated to any single normative method, or to the policing of creative and playful theological engagement. It has refuted methodolatry.

Therefore, the method of constructive theology is pluralistic. Like many things, it is much more appropriate to consider constructive theology's methods multiplicitous. Its method is expressed as a mode, mood, framework, or set of concerns. Wyman has argued that its two overarching concerns are interdisciplinarity and a concern for justice, advocacy, or activism.[4] Other constructive theologians may not wholly agree, and that internal, open dialogue is itself part of what makes constructive theology and its method. The structure of the construct is laid bare, and the process of construction itself emphasized and put out to see. In its most basic form, constructive theology's method is to deconstruct and critique, creatively engage, reconstruct, and then, crucially, repeat. The openness to further reconsideration, further reconstruction, is a central feature of constructive theology. That openness is present throughout this volume, as each critical reconstruction leaves open the future reconsideration, critique, and reconstruction in light of previously unaccounted for perspectives and voices as well as critical discourses. This volume is important because it showcases constructive

---

[3] Mary Daly, *Gyn/Ecology* (Boston, MA: Beacon, 1990), 23.
[4] See Jason A. Wyman Jr., *Constructing Constructive Theology: An Introductory Sketch* (Minneapolis, MA: Fortress, 2017).

theology's method(s) in a parallel and dialogic fashion. It is important because it invites an indiscrete range of approaches to the theological conversation, to engage with, appreciate, critique, build upon, question, embrace, and generally construct with and alongside this diverse dialogue.

We offer this collection reflecting on constructive theology's method to demonstrate the breadth and width of its geographical dispersion and variety of approaches. Constructive theology has gained enough proponents and enough of a presence that it is worth claiming its space within the theological academy, and, in its interdisciplinary way, within the academy in a broader sense. It does so not through delimiting or cutting off from other forms of theological thinking, but by building upon, as well as departing from, other modes of theology. This volume can also serve, then, as a milestone marking nearly forty-five years of creative, organic, development of constructive theologizing.

The aims of this book are manifold. Jason Wyman has elsewhere given his historically based account of what constructive theology is and what its overarching method is.[5] One of the principal qualities of constructive theology, in that interpretation, is that it is done dialogically, that any sort of comprehensive, though not final or ultimately systematic, must be put together from a multiplicity of perspectives and voices weighing in on the same topics. This book does just that, bringing together a considerable group of theologians, each offering their own particular take on theological method, or some aspect of theological sources. Rather than prescribing any particular method, this book primarily lets theologians present their theological concerns and sources while allowing for a look below the surface, that is, making method more explicit. This methodological work is itself constructive because it recognizes that there is no given for how to do theology. Theology is not responsible to only itself, but to a great variety of communities: individuals of all sorts of types, groups, churches, in a sense the whole world as our collective destiny becomes more obviously and more direly intertwined. Each of the chapters contained in this book makes an argument for *a* way to do theology, not *the* way to do theology. Each theologian works both from the Christian tradition and in critical departure from it, each reflecting in and through a particular historical and geographical setting, with methods and thinkers that make sense and allow focus on what the kairos of that particular time and location may call forth. Another central feature of constructive theology is that it is honest and explicit about its contingency. Each chapter here makes an argument for an overlooked aspect of or approach to doing theology.

Another aim of this book is to recognize the expanding circle of constructive theological conversation and recognize and embrace the ways that expansion does or can change the constructive theological conversation. To this point, constructive theology has largely been a North American, and even more specifically US, conversation.[6] Those who explicitly do constructive theology outside of the United

---

[5] Ibid.
[6] A program exists in South Africa at the School of Religion, Philosophy, and Classics at the University of Kwazulu-Natal called the Centre for Constructive Theology. It also published a journal titled the *Journal of Constructive Theology*, which has since been renamed the *Journal of Gender Religion and Theology in Africa*. Many of the concerns between that and what are discussed here are shared, though the Centre takes as its primary aim educating ministers in South Africa who have not

States typically have had connections to US academics and institutions. But the term as well as the mode of constructive theology has spread. Therefore, this book takes as an aim to foster those emerging connections with constructive theology while minding the possibilities of academic colonialism or gatekeeping occurring. Constructive theology insists on the importance of context and starting points for doing any meaningful theology, and therefore lends itself easily to being used in all sorts of places. How that emerges in different places should be done reflectively so that dialogue can ensue and theological impositions avoided. We hope that this volume will inform, inspire, and encourage participation in the crucial work of constructive theology.

This volume is divided into three parts. The first, "Reflecting on the History, Genre, and Theory of Constructive Theology," deals with the whence of constructive theology as well as its form and informers. The second, "Body, Text, Interdisciplinarity, and Practice," highlights questions of lived experience and the use of outside disciplines. The third, "Postcolonial Reconstructions," closely examines different takes on postcolonial critiques and expressions in constructive theological work.

In Part I, Jason Wyman begins by offering a history of constructive theology, particularly in the United States. He also looks at the field as it stands and forward to its immanent development. Proposing stages of development, the chapter emphasizes the encounter between constructive theology, liberationism, and womanism, as well as its growing international compass.

Next, John Thatamanil keys in on the open-ended nature of constructive theology, focusing in particular on theopoetics as a creative partnership between the human and the divine. Theopoetics has an important role in the history of constructive theology work, and this chapter makes that undercurrent explicit, emphasizing the importance of imagination in creativity in the wake of collapsed traditional frameworks.

Marion Grau submits a thematic introduction to the potentials and limits of constructive theological work, examining the combination of historical and mythological work that constructive theology entails. Her exploration highlights the liberationist elements of constructive theology in the midst of a wide variety of theological tools that are employed by constructive theologians in (re)constructing theology.

Part II begins with Heike Peckruhn's consideration of the role of sense experience in constructing theology. Starting from the premise that all theological work follows experience, Peckruhn asserts that the senses provide a privileged site of knowledge, which feeds directly into our embodiment as meaning-making actors.

Shelly Rambo offers an analysis of the uses of the Bible in constructive theological work. Looking at different stages in the development of constructive theology, Rambo posits multiple biblical hermeneutics that have held sway in its trajectory. She ends by arguing for a turn to an affective understanding of the biblical text in its "afterlife."

Holly Hillgardner explores the potential of constructive theology for interreligious engagements. She uses a Hindu metaphor that emphasizes how the perceived threat of

> received formal theological training, especially those affiliated with African-initiated churches. The similarities between the two are important and worth investigating, but for all intents and purposes, to this point, constitutes a separate thing.

critical discourse, as incorporated into theology, can also be a salve for interreligious work. By using constructive theology's emphasis on interdisciplinarity, Hillgardner sees a theological way through the impasse regarding the fraught position of considering all religions as being fundamentally the same and all religions being irreconcilably and radically different.

Part II ends with a practical theological reflection by Anthony Reddie, who explores his use of what he terms "participative-methodological praxis" in Britain. A type of liberative constructive theology, Reddie's praxis encourages participants to come to theological insights through role playing, theater, and play.

Part III takes on postcolonial critiques specifically. Laurie Cassidy looks at settler colonialism and proposes using the materiality and history of land as a starting point for theology. By looking to the land and the "dangerous memories" it holds, Cassidy proposes pathways for overcoming the "amnesia" that has caused the United States to forget the political implications of Jesus's death.

Lawrence Nwankwo ventures to propose an entryway into an African constructive theology by examining the steriological concept of ransom as it is used in present-day Nigeria, where money, through the prosperity gospel, can be seen as a means of salvation against the backdrop of frequent kidnappings and the search for well-being. This chapter shifts the discourse to that of seeing the sociopolitical as a site of divine indwelling in believers.

The section, and volume, are brought to a close by Judith Gruber in a chapter wherein power-critical stance of constructive theology allows it to critically unsettle and creatively reconceive of established theological orienting principles. She illustrates this by looking to soteriology in the wake of postcolonial critiques, focusing on a discourse of the "refusal to be cured" as decolonial remembering.

Constructive theology is growing in its visibility and diversity. The chapters in this volume are by no means exhaustive, but they should give anyone interested in understanding or doing their own constructive theological work an abundance of threads to follow, methodological points of view to consider, and critical issues for theology to address. Ultimately, this volume invites emerging and established theologians to enter the conversation by finding points of resonance and dissonance for their own work: a theme, a method, a concern, a concept, a critique, a tradition. Constructive theology uses tradition and received insights creatively, open-endedly, and with an eye to the future agenda of theology for a planet in need of imagination and creativity, toward just and constructive ends. This volume is just one foray into that unfolding conversation and only finds itself more fully realized with each new voice and perspective that speaks up and joins.

Part I

Reflecting on the History, Genre, and Theory of Constructive Theology

1

Constructive Theology: History, Movement, Method

Jason Wyman

"Constructive" theology has worked its way into the common parlance of theological scholarship so subtly and over such a period of time that many haven't noticed how novel of a term and approach to theology constructive theology actually is. But, as everything else, the term, and its presuppositions, has a discrete history and carries with it many implicit and explicit expectations, themes, concerns, and communities. I have written a full narrative and analysis of the history of constructive theology elsewhere.[1] This chapter will incorporate much of that narrative but will specifically dive deeper into the developments and ironies that have led to the contemporary character of constructive theology, especially as it has negotiated interdisciplinarity, advocacy and liberation, and emergent crises in theology and in the world throughout the past fifty years.

Three major periods in the history of constructive theology can be helpfully identified: proto-constructive theology, constructive theology proper as codified by the Workgroup on Constructive Theology, and full-fledged and increasingly widespread constructive theology as it is done at present. Many might be surprised to learn that constructive theology as it is done today has such a short history that is in many ways so well defined, and ultimately that a relatively circumscribed tradition and method can be identified and described, even as constructive theology has often defined itself against traditions and prescriptions about how to do theology. Adding to the confusion, as the adjective "constructive" has become more accepted—there were times when it was hotly contested and fiercely resisted at theological hubs, and even today controversies and struggles arise as to whether theologians and their appointments can be in "constructive theology"—it has been used in such adjunct ways as "constructive" systematic theology,[2] "constructive dogmatic theology,"[3] "constructive

---

[1] Jason A. Wyman Jr., *Constructing Constructive Theology: An Introductory Sketch* (Minneapolis, MN: Fortress, 2017), especially chapters 1 and 2.
[2] As of the writing of this chapter, the Christian Systematic Theology Unit of the American Academy of Religion says in its Statement of Purpose, "This Unit promotes new constructive work in Christian systematic theology."
[3] As one example, a series published by Zondervan that arose out of an annual Los Angeles Theology Conference is named "Explorations in Constructive Dogmatic Theology."

Christianity," and at times as a substitute catchall for liberationist theologies and theologies that explicitly use context and identity as starting points, rejecting the abstracted theologizing from nowhere characteristic of so much historical theology. Constructive theology and constructive theologians have added to this ambiguity as the term "constructive" itself was worked out historically by theologians developing it, who had been trained in "systematic" theology and who encountered resistance to use of the term, or struggled to perceive what made constructive theology unique as it was coming into its own.

The term "constructive" has, in fact, gotten attached to many different theological projects with wildly different ends in mind. "Constructive" is a nondescript enough term, in many ways, and yet attractive enough in its ambiguity to be easily applied to things that may even in some deeper way be contradictory. Yet, constructive theology, as I use it here, and as has been solidified into a unique tradition, ultimately means something very specific. To begin with a basic point, self-naming is important, and whether the word "constructive" was chosen with much deliberation and reflection or not, the growth of the preference for, and at times insistence upon, doing "constructive" theology points to a development important enough to be named. Words and terms that are so persistent can't be easily overlooked or simply said to be a mostly superficial makeover of older traditions. Constructive theology implies a set of assumptions that took some time to cohere and come to light. It also implies differentiation from other ways of doing theology. In this case, the word "constructive" has most obviously replaced the terms "systematic" or "dogmatic," two more historically accepted modes of doing theology, and therefore must in some way be distinguishing itself from, and defining itself against, those modes. As a preliminary indication of what I argue distinguishes these ways of doing theology, dogmatic concerns itself with dogma, that is, what it sees as what Christians should confess to believe, and is ultimately responsible to the church itself and the church's standing before God;[4] systematic theology, arising out of the emerging modernist insistence on rationality and science in the 1600s, seeks to describe Christianity and its major doctrines in a rigorous, coherent, ultimately logically sound whole;[5] and finally, constructive theology emphasizes the contingent, transigent, impermanent, and ultimately constructed reality of any theological speech, insisting on foregrounding the imaginatively constructive work that is truly at the heart of theology.[6] Constructive theology certainly owes a debt to systematic theology and dogmatic theology and is related to them. Nevertheless, it does theological work in a novel way that is rooted in but distinct from either systematic theology or dogmatic theology.

All the same, constructive theology didn't emerge from nowhere and all at once. It took decades for an amorphous emergent mode of doing theology to become a

---

[4] Karl Barth, *Church Dogmatics: A Selection with Introduction* (Louisville, KY: Westminster John Knox, 1994), 85; Christopher Morse, *Not Every Spirit: A Dogmatics of Christian Disbelief*, 2nd ed. (New York: Continuum, 2009), 19.

[5] Wolfhart Pannenberg, *Systematic Theology*, vol. 1 (Grand Rapids, MI: Eerdmans, 1991), 19; Paul Tillich, *Systematic Theology*, vol. 1 (Chicago: University of Chicago Press, 1951), 10.

[6] Gordon D. Kaufman, *An Essay on Theological Method* (Missoula, MT: Scholars, 1975), 75; Sallie McFague in Carol J. Adams, ed., *Ecofeminism and the Sacred* (New York: Continuum, 1993), 85–6.

category, a trend, and ultimately an established and recognized theological community. Following its history, as it emerged and came to reinforce specific assumptions, sources, and ways of doing theology, helps to bring into focus the method that defines it as well as the historical needs and crises to which it responds. Further, understanding the history of constructive theology allows constructive theologians in the present to survey the "from whence" and the "to where" of constructive theological work today.

As a brief overview, theologians start to explore and consider the adjective "constructive," in limited ways, in the early twentieth century, with the earliest uses being around 1902.[7] An unknown figure named James Ten Broeke offered a book-length treatment of construction as a mode of doing theology in 1914.[8] That discourse grew, unevenly, until Bernard Eugene Meland solidified the term "constructive theology" as applied to his own multifaceted and difficult-to-pin-down work. In 1975, a group of theologians centered at Vanderbilt University Divinity School in Nashville formed what they called the "Workgroup on Constructive Theology," which pooled shared theological and ethical concerns and ended up codifying an approach to doing theology without ever explicitly naming what that methodology was. Through four iterations, which have included around one hundred leading Christian theologians and ethicists, it has employed an interdisciplinary and social-justice/activist/advocacy oriented methodology that has come to define constructive theology as a movement, both inside and outside the workgroup, wherever constructive theologians are found.

Proto-constructive Theology

Use of the term "proto-constructive" points to the fact that many of those who were responsible for the creation of what would become constructive theology were not so self-consciously. Like most meaningful movements, the motivation for founding constructive theology was not to create a new method of doing theology, but rather to engage significant cultural and intellectual shifts in the period in which it emerged. Repeated frequently throughout the history of constructive theology—and even through the present—is an attempt to negotiate a "paradigm shift" in the way the world is understood and engaged with. What makes these theologians and their theologies fall within the purview of the history of constructive theology is that they introduce the sustained use of the concept of construction to the project of theology, and they heavily inform and put in place the basic assumptions of what constructive theology becomes and is.

The first use of "constructive theology" occurs in a book published in 1902 out of Oxford, an unlikely place that nonetheless relates to what constructive theology becomes and helps as an initial foray into discovering the origin of constructive theology. It's an unlikely place because, barring very few exceptions, constructive theology has been a predominantly US tradition. The book, titled *Contentio Veritatis: Essays in Constructive*

---

[7] Wyman, *Constructing Constructive Theology*, 2. See Six Oxford Tutors, *Contentio Veritatis: Essays in Constructive Theology* (London: John Murray, 1902).
[8] James Ten Broeke, *A Constructive Basis for Theology* (London: Macmillan, 1914).

Theology, was put together by six tutors at Oxford University, with Hastings Rashdall being the one who would become the most well known. As the tutors put it in their introduction,

> Among younger men and women of fair education, there is a widespread unsettlement and uneasiness. There is a vague feeling that the old Orthodoxy is impossible; people suspect that much that was once commonly believed is no longer tenable, but they do not know how much, nor by what it is to be replaced ... The most [this] volume can do is call attention to the need of such a reconstruction, to show that the need is felt, and to indicate some of the lines which they believe it ought to take place.[9]

Anticipating later constructive theology, the book is done collaboratively, is built upon a structure of examining the current state of different theological doctrines and suggesting potential reconstructions, and is future focused and self-avowedly limited in its scope of finality. In the sole review of *Contentio Veritatis*, William Sanday, a theologian at Oxford, refers to the novelty of the term "constructive theology," writing,

> Two things have struck me more particularly in their book ... these are on the one hand a pleasing candor which gives the impression of great sincerity, and on the other hand a certain cheerful optimism which is everywhere more sensible of gain than of loss and which does not take pleasure in the mere act of destroying. The essays are described as "in constructive theology," and they really are constructive ... "Constructive theology," as the name implies, is a process and not a finished work. "Essays in Constructive Theology" is an appropriate title. What we have been discussing are essays or attempts, some of which really build—and the building has beauty as well as strength.[10]

It doesn't appear that the Oxford tutors or Sanday pursued developing "constructive theology" as a new field or movement in any sustained way, and it's unclear how the term made the jump to the United States. Interestingly, in any case, Rashdall was connected with Borden Parker Bowne,[11] an important theologian in the United States who is most well known for founding Boston personalism, and Sanday published, and his work was frequently reviewed in the *American Journal of Theology*, published by the University of Chicago and which would later become known as the *Journal of Religion*. Bernard Eugene Meland, an influential theologian at the University of Chicago Divinity School, as will be related later, is in many ways the first person to concretize the term "constructive theology" as it is used today.

The *American Journal of Theology* also includes the next clear indication of the emergence of constructive theology in its prototypical form, and the first in the

---

[9] Six Oxford Tutors, *Contentio Veritatis*, vi.
[10] William Sanday, "Review of *Contentio Veritatis: Essays in Constructive Theology*, by Six Oxford Tutors," *Journal of Theological Studies* 4, no. 13 (October 1902): 2.
[11] Gary Dorrien, *The Making of American Liberal Theology: 1900–1950* (Louisville, KY: Westminster John Knox, 2003), 300.

United States, five years after the publication of *Contentio Veritatis*. Herbert Alden Youtz, a theologian who studied with Borden Parker Bowne and taught at Auburn Seminary, in 1907, wrote a review of Clarence Augustine Beckwith's book *The Realities of Christian Theology: An Interpretation of Christian Experience* titled "Current Essays in Constructive Theology," in which he observed,

> Current essays in theology may be roughly classified in two groups: first those which are seeking for an "essence," a "finality," or an "ultimate principle of unity" which expresses an unresolvable *quantum* in all religion, or "essential religion" seen its lowest terms; second those which take current religious doctrines and try to translate them into the terms of the thought-life of today. They ask: What is the meaning or "reality" of this or that doctrine for this age and generation? Or, what form will this truth take, consistently with the scientific can philosophical convictions of today.[12]

Youtz's first category most closely describes systematic and, relatedly, dogmatic theology, seeking finality, essence, and unity, while his second accurately describes much of what makes constructive theology distinct, even through today. Constructive theology engages doctrines or crises individually, rather than in a larger system. Further, it sees its productions as contingent and limited. Of course, systematic theologians see their own work as being limited and contingent, but a critique that comes to fruition in the mid-twentieth century in early constructive theologians proper such as Gordon Kaufman and Sallie McFague is that systematic theologies nonetheless often lose sight of their own constructedness and contingent nature. This meaningful difference in mood and method was already being sensed by Youtz in 1907.

A further indicator of the emergence of a constructive, rather than systematic or dogmatic, sensibility occurred elsewhere in 1913 with the founding of the *Constructive Quarterly* by an Episcopal layperson, architect, and journalist of religion named Silas McBee. As McBee wrote in the introduction to the first issue of the *Quarterly*,

> The destructive method has had its full opportunity and will continue to have it and ought to have it. But it has developed no power to unite and is most effective at promoting division. The plan is to bring together members of all Communions who will write constructively of the Christianity they profess and practise in order that they may know their Communion as they themselves would desire to have it known.[13]

Such a mission reflects many of the same qualities of constructive theology today. It acknowledges the need for critique of Christianity, accepting the destructive, or later deconstructive, work of contemporary criticism. And yet it also acknowledges the

---

[12] Herbert Alden Youtz, "Current Essays in Constructive Theology," *American Journal of Theology* 11, no. 4 (October 1907): 694.
[13] Silas McBee, "Introduction," in *The Constructive Quarterly: A Journal of the Faith, Work, and Thought of Christendom*, vol. 1, ed. Silas McBee (March–December 1913), 1.

need for unified construction amid diversity. It doesn't seek a single normative stance, and it emphasizes speaking from one's context, vocational, confessional, geographic, or otherwise. It acknowledges the work of modernist and liberal projects, and yet points to a different method of confronting the problems left in their wake. Further, it speaks to the experienced crisis of disunity in the church and in the world, and yet denies the need for any finalized, unified theological pronouncements. In fact, in its mission statement, it affirms that plurality and different opinion are the hallmark of the journal itself. *The Constructive Quarterly* isn't yet full-fledged constructive theology, but its impressive number, variety, and quality of contributors indicates the level to which the need for a constructively based theology was felt. The *Quarterly* continued from 1913 through 1922, with McBee as its editor throughout.

An early question for constructive theology, which in some form continues through today, is whether "constructive" points toward construction or construal, words that share a common root. In the first issue and first article of the *Constructive Quarterly*, William Porcher DuBose, an academic, Episcopal bishop, and later founder and dean of the school of theology at the University of the South, wrote,

> Before venturing upon a construction, or even a constructive treatment, of Christianity, let me first carefully limit and define the term, as I purpose to use it. "Constructive" and "construction" may attach either to the verb to construct or to the verb to construe, and these two, though the same in origin, have a very different force in use. I do not undertake to construct but only to construe Christianity. Christianity *is*, and is what it is: I cannot conceive it as at this late day either needing to be or capable of being "made" or "made over."[14]

Several things are instructive about DuBose's squeamishness regarding the central term "constructive." First, it gestures toward the continuing unease, through today, of the academic theological community with the implication that constructive theology has become something separate from systematic theology. At this point in its development, I believe, it's difficult, if not impossible, to ignore the differences between the two. And DuBose, though he resists, had already sensed the implication that a split was occurring. Second, in considering whether there's some essential difference between systematic or dogmatic theology and constructive theology, DuBose puts his finger on the very issue at heart. For systematic and dogmatic theology, "Christianity *is*, and is what it is." Outside of constructive theology, reworkings of tradition are typically, at most, construals, self-conscious reinterpretations of what Christianity is already in some sense considered to be in essence. Constructive theology, however, assumes and engages with Christianity as a contingent and constructed phenomenon all the way down. Contrary to DuBose's insistence, constructive theology, ultimately, chooses "construction" over "construal." *The Constructive Quarterly* served, for nine years, as a place where the implications of such a new approach could play out in an ecumenical,

---

[14] William Porcher DuBose, "A Constructive Treatment of Christianity," in *The Constructive Quarterly: A Journal of the Faith, Work, and Thought of Christendom*, vol. 1, ed. Silas McBee (March–December 1913), 5; emphasis in the original.

fallible, open, good-spirited way. It waffles between construction and construal—even as some constructive theologians do today. It never reached the fullness of "imaginative construction" as would come to be definitive of constructive theology, but it allowed an open-ended, academic, pluralistic repetitive reconsideration of Christianity in its current religious and cultural moments. As the mission statement of the journal, printed at the beginning of every volume, summarizes, "The Constructive invites the free, living and deliberate statement of actual, operative belief." Such a goal is still central to constructive theology

Proto-constructive Theology Emerging in Book-Length Treatments: Newman Smyth and James Ten Broeke

Two figures, one who played a crucial role in making liberal theology part of the theological mainstream in the United States but who is generally less heralded than others of his time, and another who has for all intents and purposes been a mostly unknown fringe theologian, Newman Smyth and James Ten Broeke, respectively, offer the earliest monographs that connect an emerging constructive sensibility with theology. Smyth published *Constructive Natural Theology* near the end of his career and life, in 1913. Ten Broeke published *A Constructive Basis for Theology* in 1914. Both offer hints of qualities that have come to define constructive theology and begin the discourse of reframing the task of theology in the ways that constructive theology does, though neither fully fits what would become formalized constructive theology. Ten Broeke's, in particular, offers an extended look at what construction itself means for theology.

Neither Ten Broeke's nor Smyth's incorporations of "constructive" theology have been hugely influential books. Smyth's is something of a footnote on a much longer distinguished career, largely in liturgy and administration. Ten Broeke never reached much of an audience or had much influence, spending most of his career as an esteemed and widely loved teacher at McMaster University in Canada, serving as the successor of George Burman Foster.[15] What these books do show is the rising use of the word "constructive" and its legitimacy in theology, how it begins to unsettle established ways of doing theology, and some of the characteristics that would come to be definitive for constructive theology in its mature form. Smyth, in the introduction to *Constructive Natural Theology*, writes, "We should seek to understand anew what the Spirit hath to say to the churches in the progressive revealings of nature. The spoils of the natural sciences wait to be utilized by a new natural theology ... The reconstruction of systematic theology, which is desirable, requires a broad and deeply

---

[15] Charles M. Johnston, *McMaster University, Volume 1: The Toronto Years* (Toronto: McGill-Queen's, 2015), 231. Though Ten Broeke's lasting influence never grew much, it seems he was a remarkably well-connected theologian at the time. A small group of theologians, centered around the University of Chicago, increasingly employ language of "construction." These include Smyth, Foster (who Broeke considered a close friend and helped Broeke secure his position at McMaster), Clarence Beckwith (who was at Chicago Theological Seminary), Charles Birney Smith, and others. The language of "construction" and its location become even more important when considering University of Chicago theologian Bernard Eugene Meland's role in the history of constructive theology, related in this chapter.

laid foundation in natural theology."[16] Smyth and his work remain quite firmly in the realm of liberal theology. On the other hand, in this book at least, he introduces themes of "construction." Correlating it with the claims of the present chapter, Smyth works in an interdisciplinary way and argues for the ground up *reconstruction* of theology. Though Smyth certainly can't be considered a full-blown constructive theologian, in places his work hints at the emergence of a constructive way of doing theology, that is, one that rethinks all the way to the foundations the presumptions of any sort of eternal systematic essence to Christian theology. As Gary Dorrien relates, with Smyth's books, "liberal theology in a fully-orbed sense of the term took root in American mainline Protestantism,"[17] in the form of what he calls "progressive orthodoxy," itself prefiguring some of the ways constructive theology later runs up against a more typical liberalism. *Constructive Natural Theology*, written toward the end of Smyth's career, indicates emerging discourses and concerns in theology that would develop beneath the surface, breaking through definitively mid-century. Another early prefigural of constructive theology, incorporating an effort to completely rebuild the discursive foundations of Christian theology from the ground up, occurred with a more or less unknown figure named James Ten Broeke.

James Ten Broeke wasn't a great writer. He wrote two books and a handful of articles, mostly reviews. He was, however, relatively active in a conversation that was growing in the first half of the twentieth century that would lead to the category of constructive theology. As a marginal figure, he remains important for the history of constructive theology because he proposed a constructive method as the foundation of doing theology completely. What others may have read as an inconsequential sidepiece in the liberal theological tradition gives a glimpse into the paradigmatic shift in thinking about the way theology should be done that comes to be encapsulated within constructive theology. He serves primarily as an indicator of an emerging sensibility rather than as a standout figure himself. Nonetheless, Ten Broeke nicely relates features of his constructive basis for theology that have become normative for constructive theology more broadly:

> Let it be remembered ... that every meaning is necessarily the personal interpretation of some thinker reflecting upon what is given for constructive thought ... In the nature of the case, Christianity, as a system of objective judgments called theology is man's product; it is even a personal construction, serving as a guide, primarily of the individual, but also of the religious community.[18]

Ten Broeke proposes that there is no essential reality to Christianity or the doctrinal assertions of Christian theology. Theology always deals with the interpretation of things encountered in the world and the modes of thought available at any given moment. Ten Broeke's project is largely preoccupied with offering a justification

---

[16] Newman Smyth, *Constructive Natural Theology* (New York: Charles Scribner's Sons, 1913), 32.
[17] Gary Dorrien, *The Making of American Liberal Theology: 1805–1900* (Louisville, KY: Westminster John Knox, 2001), 282.
[18] Ten Broeke, *A Constructive Basis for Theology*, 74.

for why contemporary philosophical systems can serve as an equally good, if not better, basis for constructing a Christian structure than the ancient modes that are most usually relied upon. He continues to use "systematic" in describing what needs to be constructed, but he ultimately rejects that there is a system to be revealed and described. What Christianity is and what its doctrinal assertions are is fundamentally contingent and in many ways instrumental.

While the prevailing attitude at the time was one of being unmoored and uncertain where to go next, or questioning whether Christianity would simply be destructed out of existence, Ten Broeke sees an opportunity. He writes,

> Shall we simply continue to pull down the old house without being sure that we are able to build a better? Or shall we make not too radical changes and live in the hold house still? It seems as though the most one may reasonably hope to do is to form some temporary abode, using whatever material is at hand. In the present condition of things, it is to be expected that a good working hypothesis serviceable in the conduct of the individual and social religious life is about all that can be obtained without becoming dogmatic. Whether theology can ever be more than such an hypothesis is itself a problem. There is also good ground for expecting that the present affords much that is favourable to the construction of a theological view that will serve the religious life of the present, for those theology of each generation springs out of its complex life, and that life itself is largely the fruit of what has gone before.[19]

The metaphors of building a house and cartography (which Ten Broeke also employs) are frequent ones for constructive theologians. Structures, in this view, are meant to be taken as things with moveable parts, which can be swapped out, replaced, taken down entirely, and something completely new put in its place. Likewise, maps are never themselves completely true and serve to supply the information needed to any given wanderer at the time they are needed. Different maps can convey different information, and they can lose their usefulness or become irrelevant.

Two primary features are established by Ten Broeke that persist throughout the rest of constructive theology's history. First is the insistence on the fact that there is no essential system of Christianity to be uncovered. Although constructive theology, to this point, hasn't abandoned the traditional doctrines of Christian theology, it also firmly rejects the assumption that there is any final, true account of Christianity as a whole or even any particular doctrine. Constructive theologians tend to hold that while the doctrines are useful, they are not fixed, and some constructive theologians have advocated for moving beyond the doctrines to a more free-flowing, imaginatively constructive place altogether. The second is that Christian theology needs to be rethought in a constant, ongoing way so as to speak to new moments, problems, and thoughts. Constructive theologies, through the present, tend to be theological engagements with specific contexts and problems, employing insights from outside disciplines, and toward the end of making the world better or more just. The concern

[19] Ibid., 248–9.

of justice in the way it is often thought of in contemporary constructive theology, for Ten Broeke, was still a stretch. Yet he insists that doctrines and theologizing must serve those who live with it, or it might as well be dispensed with completely.

Ten Broeke made the term "constructive" a central part of his theological project. His influence never really grew, but the term "constructive" can be spotted with greater and greater frequency as the twentieth century continued. Bernard Eugene Meland, putting a heavy emphasis on culture and mythology, consolidated trends in disparate places to establish what resembles formal constructive theology, though his legacy and use of the term are still ambiguous. Connections between the earliest appearances of "constructed" in relationship to theology, Ten Broeke, and Meland remain yet to be surfaced—though I suspect a triangulation may be discerned between Ten Broeke and his connections in the northeast United States, Foster, who Ten Broeke replaced at McMaster and who was an anchor figure at the new University of Chicago Divinity School, and the later coalescences of the constructive mood of doing theology at Chicago (such an archival project remains for a future endeavor).

Bernard Eugene Meland

Bernard Eugene Meland is in many ways a theologian who stands on the cusp of divergent but connected movements. He bridges a divide between liberalism and what has often been called neo-orthodoxy, provides a line of connection between two generations of Chicago school theologians, and serves as a hinge between liberal theology and constructive theology. Meland began his career largely working with and in line with his mentor Henry Nelson Wieman. But Meland had a distinct break with his mentor, and his mature work moves away from Wieman's Chicago school liberalism and naturalism. Rejecting empiricism and the cultural obsession with science and scientific accounts of the universe—like that of Wieman and Smyth discussed earlier—Meland sought a more intentionally imaginative and constructive mode of doing theology. In *The Reawakening of Christian Faith*, Meland characterizes Christian theologizing as an "imaginative adventure," anticipating later emphases on the imagination in doing theology within the constructive theological tradition. Further, he rejected the unchastened idealism and faith in progress of liberal theology later in his career, trying to navigate between the liberalism he'd been trained in and what he found to be the compelling correction offered by neo-orthodoxy that burst through after the World Wars. What Meland settled upon was neither liberalism nor neo-orthodoxy, but rather a creative variety of theology rooted in an emphasis on the importance of understanding the interplay between theology and culture that manifests itself through myth. Myth, in Meland, foreshadows what later constructive theologians, such as Gordon Kaufman and Sallie McFague, as well as many others, might call a "model." The emphasis on language, narrative, unearthing myths, and models that become naturalized to the point of their contingent nature being forgotten remains a central conceit of constructive theology throughout its history. Finally, Meland, drawing upon neo-orthodoxy, centralizes the category of "crisis" for constructive theology. In its interdisciplinarity, its rethinking of models, it is compelled to deal with the crises that emerge as a result of and in response to culture and history at any given moment.

Meland was a transitional figure with respect to constructive theology. Later interpreters have tried to force Meland into different categories, and he himself, mostly uncomfortably, tried to situate himself within liberalism. Tyron Inbody, professor of theology who wrote the definitive book on Meland's work titled *The Constructive Theology of Bernard Meland*, nonetheless settled on the term "postliberal," while also meandering around liberal and neo-orthodox strands in Meland's work. Meland's work, however underappreciated and in many ways under-known, is a cornerstone in constructive theology and the first to use the term and the mood in an extended way that can be identified as having brought together all of the central concerns of what constructive theology becomes. Meland is still a proto-constructive theologian. But he leads up to and anticipates the distinctive developments that make constructive theology its own coherent movement. A small group of what I call "prolegomena" formalize the method of constructive theology around interdisciplinarity, an emphasis on recognizing and deconstructing models, an imperative to confront contemporary crises in the world, and to embrace a pluralist, dialogic mode of doing theology that is fallibilist and regenerative as it examines and critiques its own theological claims in an ongoing way.

Kaufman, Farley, Tracy, McFague

Gordon Kaufman, Edward Farley, David Tracy, and Sallie McFague serve as "prolegomena" to constructive theology because they both precede it and are adamantly a part of it. In the mid-1970s a number of theologians in different places were considering what was left of methodology in theology generally, looking for new ways to do systematics. Karl Barth's and Paul Tillich's influence on doing theology were enormous, and constructive theology itself inherits some of the concerns of each. From Barth it takes the rejection of systematization as idolatrous and hubris as well as the critique of liberalism's historicism. From Tillich it takes a concern with crisis and the fact that theology must answer questions posed by culture—Tillich's method of correlation, which Farley explicitly engages with and reworks for a constructive perspective. Kaufman, Farley, Tracy, and McFague each offer an element to the method of constructive theology that would be normative for the tradition once it becomes solidified and formalized by the Workgroup on Constructive Theology, of which all four were a part.

Gordon Kaufman, a long-standing professor of theology at Harvard Divinity School, insisted upon theology being "imaginative construction." Drawing upon a Kantian philosophical perspective that emphasized the unknowability of God to direct experience or reason, Kaufman argued that all theology is contingent and constructed. While theologians may recognize as much when pressed, they have a tendency to forget as much in arguing for a systematic completion of theology.[20] Such a tendency is at best dishonest and at worst hubristic and destructive. Recognizing the constructed

---

[20] Kaufman, *An Essay on Theological Method*, 4–5.

nature of all theology opens up a number of possibilities in theology. It rejects the idea that there is any essential structure of Christianity to unearth and describe, as is the propensity in systematic theology. It emphasizes the humanness of theological constructs and, as a result, prioritizes the fact that theologians must hold *themselves* responsible for the flaws in theology, both academically and in terms of the damage bad theology does in the world. The latter point Kaufman famously emphasized in his presidential address at the American Academy of Religion Annual Meeting titled "Theology for a Nuclear Age," which was expanded to a book and which had a profound effect on Sallie McFague. Kaufman's key insight, for constructive theology, is indeed the constructed nature of Christian theology itself. Such a view has actually always been endemic to the tradition of Christian theology, but theologians and Christians more generally tend to forget the distance between theological claims and the true nature of God and God's work. Kaufman radically centers the constructed, creative nature of doing theology and insists upon the need, in light of such an insight, to rethink and reconstruct theology that is intellectually rigorous and responsible, as well as efficacious in a world facing innumerable existential crises, such as the possibility of nuclear extinction.

Edward Farley, who was a professor of theology at Vanderbilt Divinity School, where the Workgroup on Constructive Theology was founded, emphasized what he termed the fall of the "house of authority." Basing his approach in the phenomenological experience of current Christians in the ecclesia, Farley argues that the underlying constitutive elements of the Christian faith are ultimately inaccessible to cognition, a posing of what he calls the "question beneath the question."[21] Farley's suspicion regarding essential, persistent structures underlying Christianity doesn't run as deep as Kaufman's. He entertains the idea that such structures may or do exist. However, Farley's phenomenological stance proposes that those structures aren't directly accessible, but that one only gets glimpses of them through the lived reality, at any given time, of the ecclesia, the body of faith. He asserts that it may seem natural to turn to historical authority to supplement the gaps in knowledge created by the inaccessibility of the underlying structures of Christian faith, which indeed has been a reflex for theology throughout much of its history. Farley, dissatisfied with that alternative, points out that if the reality underlying Christian faith is indeed inaccessible to human cognition in a direct way, appealing to older limited human cognitions that would have suffered the same shortcoming is ultimately fallacious. The house of authority falls because those who lived in it and made it are conditioned by the same limitations as those who experience Christianity and intend to say something about it today.[22]

In turn, therefore, Farley promotes the necessity of engaging other disciplines, both theological and more broadly academic, in order to interrogate and understand the experiences of the ecclesia. He, like other constructive theologians, also asserts the importance of constantly revisiting theological assertions in order to reconsider them and offer reconstructions in light of fresh experience. The question beneath

---

[21] Edward Farley, *Ecclesial Man: A Social Phenomenology of Faith and Reality* (Philadelphia, PA: Fortress, 1975), 6.
[22] Ibid., 16.

the question, brought forth by other academic disciplines against theology, ends up realigning theological investigation horizontally rather than vertically. Human cognition cannot directly apprehend the mysteries of faith, the structures of Christianity, as they truly exist in themselves, if such a thing even exists. Therefore, a variety of tools, meant to engage and construct from the lived reality of the ecclesia, over and against the house of authority, becomes the means of making sense of how Christians in any age connect with and live out the faith, whether that entails any truly existent substructure or not. Farley brings the insights of other disciplines, employed phenomenologically, to bear on questions with respect to the meaning of Christian experience and Christian theology in the current moment, respecting but not ultimately deferring to the house of authority, the historically normative assertions of past canonical theological figures.

Constructive theology, while ecumenical in nature, has in large part been a Protestant phenomenon. Nonetheless, a number of Catholic voices stand out as holding a special place in the history of the tradition. One such figure is David Tracy, an influential theologian who worked at the University of Chicago Divinity School. Tracy champions pluralism in his addition to the emerging ethos of constructive theology. Beginning not from an argument for pluralism, but the simple acceptance of its factuality,[23] Tracy makes the case that such pluralism is a powerful potentiality to be embraced rather than something to be feared or disowned. Like Farley, Tracy points out that the traditional authorities of theology have been undercut by a scientific worldview and Enlightenment reason. He argues that contemporary theology is torn by two allegiances: to the church and theological tradition on the one hand, and the modern academy on the other. Tracy, argues, then, that theology doesn't need or have one *single* legitimate methodology. Instead, what is needed is a clearly articulated methodology for any given theologian and a commitment to constructing theology from that point of view.[24] Different disciplines and different constructive projects can contribute to effective theological construction in the contemporary world, short-circuiting the need to hold up one single method as authoritative for all Christian theology. While Tracy admits that such openness to pluralism rightly makes theologians nervous, especially because of their allegiances to authority and tradition, it in fact opens up an opportunity for a much more wide-reaching, inclusive frame of mind in theological work. Theology is pursued in the spirit of open critical inquiry.

Given its relationship with extra-theological discourses and culture, Tracy's proposed method naturally resonates with Paul Tillich's method of correlation (Tracy even calls his method the "correlative method"). Tracy clarifies, however, that "Tillich's method does not call for a critical correlation of the results of one's investigations of the 'situation' and the 'message.' Rather, his method affirms the need for a correlation of the 'questions' from one source and 'answers' from the other."[25] Tracy sees a more critical two-way interaction and process of revision happening. With no obvious or defensible essential reality to Christianity, but rather contingent constructions, the space for a

---

[23] David Tracy, *Blessed Rage for Order* (Chicago: University of Chicago Press, 1996), 3.
[24] Ibid.
[25] Ibid., 46.

deeper rethinking of what makes up Christianity is created. For Tillich, a system that is Christianity answers the questions posed to it by culture. For Tracy, the interaction is more mutually critical. Christianity is in need of revision even while it needs to offer serious critique of culture. Tracy coined the term "revisionist theology," which was used for some time by other similarly minded theologians (including Kaufman and Farley). Ultimately, their methodological terms echo, resonate, and in some ways alter one another, and what emerges are the methodological consistencies that come to define constructive theology.

The three theologians Kaufman, Farley, and Tracy were in conversation around theological method before the formation of the Workgroup on Constructive Theology, which codified and cultivated what constructive theology is today. The workgroup was founded in 1975. As it happens, Kaufman, Farley, and Tracy held a roundtable, the subject of which was theological method in the same year. It seems that between the book-length treatments and the literal conversation happening, a certain critical mass around the question of theological method had accrued. Correlating their insights, what emerges is an engagement with theology that assumes its fully constructed nature, which questions received authority and insists theology in the present must have its own contributions to make, that anything theology puts into the world must be done in a pluralistically constructed way, and that theology must effectively speak to crises in the contemporary world, both produced by Christianity itself and in the world more broadly.

The occasion for bringing these insights together, and for introducing the final of what I've called prolegomena of constructive theology, was the appointment of Sallie McFague as the dean of Vanderbilt Divinity School, again in 1975. Like other origin stories, the beginning of the workgroup has something of a mythological quality built into its history. According to oral accounts, the dean prior to McFague, Walter Harrelson, a distinguished Bible scholar, suggested that theologians' work suffered from a lack of ongoing dialogue between individual theologians. At his suggestion, a gathering was planned around the appointment of feminist theologian Sallie McFague to be his successor. The workgroup, in different iterations, has met yearly since, most often still at Vanderbilt Divinity School, as well as the Collegeville Institute in Minnesota, and occasionally at other seminaries and institutions. McFague's appointment as dean and the first meeting that accompanied it offer a significant and easy to point to originating event for fully fledged constructive theology as it takes shape. McFague's own methodological commitments offer a final element to the prolegomena of constructive theology.

McFague, a feminist theologian who had a sustained interest in the importance of language and metaphor in theology, starting with its connection with the Bible and specifically parable, later came to embrace an ecologically oriented theology that built upon her earlier methodological insights. McFague was influenced by Kaufman, as well as by literary theory and theories of language/symbol/meaning, like those of Paul Ricoeur. McFague argued that the Bible might better be viewed as the "classic" of Christianity, a text with a surplus of meaning and deep truths embedded within its primarily narrative framework. Attending to the symbolism and metaphor found within the Bible, profound religious truths could be encountered. Significantly,

McFague argued that the conceptualization of that religious language into theological claims necessarily entailed a loss. Her primary example is the parables of Jesus. She argues that Jesus's parables are themselves already religious, or theological, language. They make claims about the nature of humanity, of God, of the Kingdom of Heaven, of Jesus's own person already, in narrative form. What parables, and metaphor, have that is special is the ability to keep religious thoughts "in solution," that is, with a greater well of meaning embedded in them in such a way that we intuit them. To try to explain the nature of those truths inherently involves a loss of some of that truth. Theology is ultimately interpretive, and theological claims are always fallible and contingent; they could always be otherwise She reacts against systematizing theology, claiming, "If theology becomes overly abstract, conceptual, and *systematic*, it separates thought and life, belief and practice, words and their embodiment."[26] The contingency and incompleteness of theology is a strength rather than a liability for McFague. Emphasizing its imagistic, creative, imaginative qualities ensures a more relevant and ultimately more honest theology.

McFague criticized the systematization of theology throughout her career. Much later, she told of a fundamental shift in her own understanding of the theological task and gestures toward some key features of constructive theology:

> Until the rise of liberation theologies, theology was more concerned with having intellectual respectability in the academy than with forging an alliance with the oppressed or particular political and social attitudes and practices. There was a convenient division between theology (concerned with the knowledge of God) and ethics (a lesser enterprise for action oriented types). Theologians were also usually "solo" players, each concerned to write his (the "hers" were in short supply) magnum opus, a complete systematic theology. As the deconstructionists have underscored, these theologians also strove to assert, against different voices, the *one* voice (their own—or at least the voice of their own kind), as the truth, the "universal" truth.[27]

By paying close attention to the language of the Bible, to the ways that parables resist systematization and conceptualization, and later tracking metaphors and models and how they become naturalized in theology, McFague makes the point both that theologies are always constructed, specifically through language, and that theology can be in conversation with the creative theological modes of history, even while proposing new metaphors and models. The key is to never sublimate those models in such a way that the particular imaginative endeavor of any theologian responding to a specific question or situation becomes confused with the one correct view. Contingency, constructedness, reconstruction, pluralism, imagination, interdisciplinarity—all of these characteristics interweave and connect the prolegomena for constructive

---

[26] Sallie McFague, "Parable, Metaphor, and Theology," *Journal of the American Academy of Religion* 42, no. 4 (December 1974): 630; emphasis in the original.

[27] Carol J. Adams, ed., *Ecofeminism and the Sacred* (New York: Continuum, 1993), 85–6; emphasis in the original.

theology and reach a potent moment of intermingling with the Workgroup on Constructive Theology.

The Workgroup on Constructive Theology

I have written fuller histories of the Workgroup on Constructive Theology elsewhere.[28] Over the course of four decades, to this point, the workgroup has been a low-key but highly influential collective of theologians that meets yearly and takes as its project to produce collaborative books that capture something of the moment of theology in which they are written. As mentioned earlier, the group began meeting loosely and informally at the suggestion of Walter Harrelson and reached a higher level of organization and formality upon the appointment of Sallie McFague as dean of Vanderbilt Divinity School. All of the "prolegomena" noted earlier—Kaufman, Tracy, Farley, and McFague—were part of the workgroup from its beginning, as well as a number of others. First gathering in 1975, members presented thoughts and papers to one another and eventually settled on writing a textbook together, which led to a tradition of textbook writing that has continued under each new iteration of the workgroup (through even its most recent configurations). The first textbook, *Christian Theology: An Introduction to Its Traditions and Tasks*, edited by Peter C. Hodgson and Robert H. King, was published in 1982 and was wildly successful. With such a mandate and the proceeds from that publication, the workgroup has since followed a cycle of dormancy and activity, with each new iteration expanding its membership and providing cross-generational mentorship for each new rising cohort. As summarized in its third textbook, *Constructive Theology: A Contemporary Approach to Classical Themes*, its stages through the 2000s can be usefully summarized as critical liberalism (with the caveat that in this chapter and elsewhere I have argued that "liberalism" doesn't quite capture what constructive theology is, given its thoroughgoing resistance to many of the features of theological liberalism), an attempt to reconcile and incorporate liberationist voices in response to crises, and a new constructive theology. Without going into the depth I have elsewhere, the stages, including the most recent, of the workgroup are worth outlining in brief. First, a behind-the-scenes note will help to foreshadow where I will complete this chapter, with a look at the challenges and promise diversity has presented to the workgroup, and thus to constructive theology as a whole—constructive theology is in many ways a home for many theologians of color, feminist theologians, and theological perspectives that resist the historically prioritized and unacknowledged distant white male perspective. But it came to that state through a series of frustrations and suspicions that betray a more complex history than may be readily apparent.

From its very beginnings, the Workgroup on Constructive Theology realized it had a problem, which it wished to address, with its demographic makeup. The group was almost entirely made up of white men, the two exceptions early on being Sallie McFague and Dorothee Soelle. According to an unpublished history of the group, which

---

[28] See Wyman, *Constructing Constructive Theology*, chapter 2.

documents some of the inner workings of its first two iterations, this homogeneity was acutely felt. Soelle criticized the early workgroup for being too standoffish about liberation theology—and indeed, the group didn't attempt to reconcile with liberation theology until the 1990s, and even then it required levels of justification that wouldn't be fully abandoned until its publication of *Awake to the Moment* in 2017. Through a combination of distance and tension, Soelle left the group relatively early on, leaving McFague as the only woman, and no voices of color or international voices. Even McFague threatened to leave the group for fear of being tokenized, according to the unpublished history. I have elsewhere tracked how black liberation theology and constructive theology came to approach one another. In this chapter I would like to pay special attention to how black women, especially, form connections with constructive theology, and how black women's voices have been so crucial ever since the second iteration of the workgroup.

The first textbook and its companion volume, which includes selections from historical theologies, was published in 1982 and introduces a common ongoing theme of constructive theology from the very beginning: an ambivalent attitude toward doctrine. On the one hand, each new constructive theological project admits that doctrines seem antiquated and backward-facing in a way the project of constructive theology seems uncomfortable with. At the same time, each textbook—and for that matter, the majority of stand-alone, single-author monographs produced by constructive theologians—is anchored to the organizing framework of doctrine. While not producing a *systematic* and coherent doctrinal statement, the first workgroup textbook does employ doctrines in order to demonstrate the method of historical examination, deconstruction and critique, and reconstruction. Despite its discomfort with the traditional nature of doctrine and its echo of "orthodox" or conservative types of theology, constructive theology has nevertheless remained moored to doctrines as, at the very least, a convenient entry point into engaging with the traditions it seeks to reconstruct.

Further, *Christian Theology* identifies itself to be in the business of agenda setting.[29] It proposes that engagement with the Christian theological tradition is important, while also arguing that deconstructing and reconstructing in response to its contemporary context is the heart of contemporary theological work. It does so in a purposefully and explicitly collaborative way. While the format of the book resembles a systematic theology, incorporating the primary doctrines of Christian theology in a scheme that echoes systematic theologies that come before, it does so in a way that puts alternative takes side by side in a way that doesn't try to obscure the process of elaborating theology. The tensions within the text, between authors, are maintained, and their own interests preserved in each chapter. The effect, as a textbook, is to bring students of theology into the ongoing dialogic process of constructing theology in collaboration. As a statement on theological method, it prioritizes focused, interdisciplinary, historically aware but not bound theological innovations. While not appearing particularly radical and leaning heavily on established voices in theology, the format and underlying

---

[29] Peter C. Hodgson and Robert H. King, eds., *Christian Theology: An Introduction to Its Traditions and Task* (Minneapolis, MN: Fortress, 1982), ix–x.

contention of the first workgroup textbook signals a shift in theological mood and method that has been developed and refined ever since.

Reconstructing Christian Theology, the second textbook of the Workgroup on Constructive Theology, is a book of a different kind that nonetheless expands on the constructive project begun by the founders of the workgroup. While the first book offers a steady tone, noting the anxieties of its moment in history without being preoccupied by them, the second textbook speaks from beginning to end in the language of "crisis." The book states that it intends to engage and incorporate liberationist thinking, confront crises in its contemporary world around sexism, racism, and colonialism, and internalize the postmodern paradigm shift that had become impossible to ignore.[30] The book employs a schematic of analysis/reconstruction that serves to expose injustice in the world in which the book was written and to attempt to deconstruct and reconstruct Christian doctrine in light of that unveiling.

A close examination of *Reconstructing Christian Theology* brings forth a deep contradiction running throughout the text, which is representative of a longer thread present throughout constructive theology's history. This tension deserves its own excursus. While *Reconstructing Christian Theology* names encountering and taking seriously liberation theology as one of its primary tasks, and while the workgroup had brought in a large number of justice-oriented feminist theologians, only one of its contributors, James H. Evans Jr., a black liberationist, is a person of color. Yet this fact belies the workgroup's efforts to incorporate diverse voices, in terms of gender, race, denominations, and so on. Coordinating between the unofficial history mentioned earlier, which immediately preceded the publication of *Reconstructing Christian Theology*, and subtle indications in the book like the acknowledgments, it's possible to discern that the workgroup had made great efforts to diversify its ranks. That effort was very successful with respect to bringing in feminist voices. The appeal proved to be much harder to sell to emerging liberationist discourses around race. Earlier in its history the workgroup had attempted in vain to attract James H. Cone and Cornel West.

In fact, black women, in particular Sheila Briggs and M. Shawn Copeland, were the first black participants in the workgroup. For reasons still unclear, while they were consulted, acknowledged, and given credit for their non-written contributions to *Reconstructing Christian Theology*, neither made a direct written contribution to the volume. The result is that while *Reconstructing Christian Theology* is forthright about its intention to engage and employ liberationist thinking, it fails in itself to do so with respect to the United States' foundational liberation theology, black liberation theology. Most fundamentally, it appears that the first generation of black liberation theologians were intrigued by, but ultimately deeply suspicious of, the emerging constructive theological project. Cone accepted the workgroup's invitation but later balked, even though he began to use the term "constructive" in much of his later work. In the wider constructive theological tradition, the contributions of black women can be felt keenly. Womanist emphases on experience, holism, and proclamation are highlighted in constructive work. Black theological

---

[30] Rebecca Chopp and Mark Lewis Taylor, eds., *Reconstructing Christian Theology* (Minneapolis, MN: Fortress, 1994), 6–7.

considerations of what it means to be human, from both men and women and in view of the discourse of intersectionality, arise as a much needed expansion of the constructive theological concern with injustice and crisis. Later iterations of the workgroup would certainly incorporate a much wider scope of human experience than the first, and in many ways the second, cohort of the workgroup. Briggs and Copeland, as well as Evans, in any case, made it possible to envision theology that took race critique, and intersectional critique along lines of race and gender together, possible within the constructive tradition. Perhaps arguably, constructive theology has become a primary mode of doing black theology, womanist theology, and other race-, power-, and gender-informed theologies in response to the crises of injustice in the contemporary United States and broader world today.

Ultimately, the second textbook fell short of the success of the first, and never had quite the effect that was intended for it. Nonetheless, if the first textbook introduced a dialogic approach and a concern for engagement with other disciplines with an agenda-setting tone, the second centers what perhaps becomes constructive theology's main defining feature and preoccupation: an interest in engaging injustice and trying to deconstruct and reconstruct Christian theology in such a way that minds its destructive tendencies and creates something that attempts to effect greater justice in the world—a sense of theological activism. The language of "crisis" remains throughout its history and reemerges as its central discourse in the workgroup's latest collaborative text.

If the workgroup encountered frustrations in its attempt to diversify through the production of its first two books, the composition of the group by 2005 and the third textbook, *Constructive Theology: A Contemporary Approach to Classical Themes*, had changed dramatically. The group had also expanded in size notably. At its peak, the group included more than eighty members. By its third iteration, the group included black liberation theologians, womanist theologians, Latinx and mujerista theologians, Roman Catholics, crip theologians, and continued its strong tradition of feminist voices. M. Shawn Copeland, who had participated in the workgroup in its second iteration but hadn't been a contributor, is represented, alongside a wide range of others (Sheila Briggs continued to participate in the workgroup but still didn't contribute to *Constructive Theology*). At the same time, the tone of the book is walked back considerably from that of *Reconstructing Christian Theology*. Constructive theology, throughout its history, has oscillated between a more radical, crisis-engaged rhetoric and something more moderate in its tone. The third book engages unapologetically with the current moment, including cultural and global crises. But it does so in a way that is more self-reflectively rooted in the history of theology. Structurally, the workgroup, while still somewhat conflicted, seems more comfortable with the doctrinally based framework and employs it explicitly, using the metaphor of cartography to describe the doctrines as landmarks along the way to understanding Christianity's textures in the contemporary world. *Constructive Theology* also offers a preliminary consideration of just what "constructive" theology means:

> We gather as teachers of Christian theology to *work* to put our creative energies together and make theology. We do so as a *group*; it is a collective endeavor from its beginning to its end. And our goal is to be *constructive*. We are not interested

in merely describing what theology has been; we are trying to understand and construct it in this present, to imagine what life-giving faith can be in today's world. In doing so, as with any construction job, we are attempting to build a viable structure. In our case, that structure is inhabitable, beautiful, truthful *theology*. Our biggest hope in writing this book is that those who read it might be inspired to do the same: to collaborate in writing new scripts for the deep wisdoms that live in your faith.[31]

By this point, constructive theology had come to hold a number of principles that are seen everywhere constructive theology is done, although those features hadn't yet been extensively articulated. Constructive theology, in its fruition, is interdisciplinary, justice-oriented, and geared toward active life-giving change in the world, done dialogically and without a pretense to complete internal coherence or comprehensiveness, and ultimately is fallible in its imaginative constructions. It recognizes the constructed nature of Christianity and seeks to engage the constructed aspects of the faith in order to reconstruct in a way that is more just, more relevant, and yet in connection with the historical tradition. Constructive theology has moved beyond revision. It is more fundamentally reimaginative, working on the premise that theology has always been so. The metaphor of the map suggests that we are never dealing with the thing itself of Christianity; rather we are dealing with fallible and flattened representations of things that can never be fully encapsulated in any reductive work.

The most recent production of the Workgroup on Constructive Theology, *Awake to the Moment*, recenters the language of "crisis" and shifts the audience it intends to engage. As the needs of theological education shifted, specifically as students came to seminaries and divinity schools with less of a background in the basics of Christian theology, the workgroup had already shifted the focus of *Constructive Theology*. *Awake to the Moment* seeks to speak directly to undergraduates and serve the needs of those constructive theologians teaching in undergraduate, rather than graduate, contexts. The result is a text that confronts doctrine in a looser way, is more in tune with popular culture, and begins with questions of hermeneutics, relevance, and again, the goal of bringing Christian theology in contact with crises in the contemporary world. *Awake to the Moment* asserts:

> Constructive theology is a distinctive form of Christian theology that does not separate heavenly concerns from worldly ones. Some theologians see their work to be a careful stewardship and reiteration of sacred doctrines handed down by church authorities, and they strive to keep those doctrines as pure as possible of the messy world of politics and social struggles. But constructive theologians see religious ideas as inseparable from the fabric of human existence. We are theologians because we are convinced of the significance of religious ideas in the *whole* tapestry of human and creaturely life, and we are constructive theologians

---

[31] Serene Jones and Paul Lakeland, eds., *Constructive Theology: A Contemporary Approach to Classical Themes* (Minneapolis, MN: Fortress, 2005), 2; emphases in the original.

because we apply a critical lens to the many ways that Christian ideas participate in making the world, both for good and bad.[32]

By this point, and even earlier, through *Reconstructing Christian Theology* and especially through *Constructive Theology*, the concept of "constructive" theology had spread far and wide in academia. Constructive theology had developed a pretty clear, if implicit, method: around a point of injustice or crisis, deconstruct Christian thinking, usually engaging doctrine and using interdisciplinary critical tools, tracking the ways Christianity has often been complicit in historical suffering and destruction. Second, imaginatively reconstruct, with an awareness of the constructed nature of all theology, in an attempt to foster a more just Christian faith, and with the humility to accept that all Christian theology is ultimately fallible and must be rethought again and again. Further, *Awake to the Moment* is forthright in its internalization and support for liberation theology without further attempts to justify it. In its present forms, constructive theology is deeply diverse, in disciplinary conversations, demographics, geography (within the United States for the most part), and religious/denominational perspective.

Constructive theology today has grown well outside the Workgroup on Constructive Theology. The workgroup serves as a finite collection of theologians whose work and development can be traced to identify what have become normative methodological concerns. Constructive theology is still dispersed enough that exceptions can be found to any proposed static principle—in fact, such a resistance is itself characteristic of constructive theology—but nonetheless, by and large, a community and way of thinking about and doing theology has emerged. Constructive theology is done dialogically, with the aim of making the world more fair and just, in conversation with other academic disciplines, in connection with but not synonymous with either liberal theology or liberation theology. It rejects systematization of theology more or less outright. Constructive theology has been hesitant to recognize itself as a distinct mode of theology, and yet at this point that distinctiveness is hard to overlook. To this point, constructive theology has primarily been a phenomenon in the United States. But international instances are beginning to emerge (several instances are represented within this volume itself). Use of the term and identification as a constructive theologian has become more common in European, African, Asian, and Latin American contexts. In part this is due to theologians who were outside the United States having pursued theological degrees at institutions in the United States and returning to their earlier contexts. But such affinities have been bolstered by the fact that similar concerns and motivations have already emerged in different geographies around the world. What remains to be seen is how different locales and contexts—including other religious contexts—will continue to shape the presuppositions and concerns of constructive theology in ways that make sense in those places. Such openness is one of constructive theology's cornerstones, and such an expansion of the conversation can only serve to make constructive theology more authentic to its own mission.

---

[32] Stephen G. Ray and Laurel Schneider, eds., *Awake to the Moment: An Introduction to Theology* (Louisville, KY: Westminster John Knox, 2016), 12; emphasis in the original.

Bibliography

Barth, Karl. *Church Dogmatics: A Selection with Introduction*. Louisville, KY: Westminster John Knox, 1994.
Broeke, James Ten. *A Constructive Basis for Theology*. London: Macmillan, 1914.
Chopp, Rebecca, and Mark Lewis Taylor, eds. *Reconstructing Christian Theology*. Minneapolis, MN: Fortress, 1994.
Dorrien, Gary. *The Making of American Liberal Theology: 1805–1900*. Louisville, KY: Westminster John Knox, 2001.
Dorrien, Gary. *The Making of American Liberal Theology: 1900–1950*. Louisville, KY: Westminster John Knox, 2003.
DuBose, William Porcher. "A Constructive Treatment of Christianity." *Constructive Quarterly: A Journal of the Faith, Work, and Thought of Christendom* 1 (March–December 1913): 5.
Farley, Edward. *Ecclesial Man: A Social Phenomenology of Faith and Reality*. Philadelphia, PA: Fortress, 1975.
Hodgson, Peter C., and Robert H. King, eds. *Christian Theology: An Introduction to Its Traditions and Task*. Minneapolis, MN: Fortress, 1982.
Johnston, Charles M. *McMaster University, Volume 1: The Toronto Years*. Toronto: McGill-Queen's, 2015.
Jones, Serene, and Paul Lakeland, eds. *Constructive Theology: A Contemporary Approach to Classical Themes*. Minneapolis, MN: Fortress, 2005.
Kaufman, Gordon D. *An Essay on Theological Method*. Missoula, MT: Scholars, 1975.
McBee, Silas. "Introduction." *Constructive Quarterly: A Journal of the Faith, Work, and Thought of Christendom* 1 (March–December 1913): 1.
McFague, Sallie. *Ecofeminism and the Sacred*. Edited by Carol J. Adams. New York: Continuum, 1993.
McFague, Sallie. "Parable, Metaphor, and Theology." *Journal of the American Academy of Religion* 42:4 (December 1974): 630.
Morse, Christopher. *Not Every Spirit: Dogmatics of Christian Disbelief*, 2nd ed. New York: Continuum, 2009.
Pannenberg, Wolfhart. *Systematic Theology*, vol. 1. Grand Rapids, MI: Eerdmans, 1991.
Ray, Stephen G., and Laurel Schneider, eds. *Awake to the Moment: An Introduction to Theology*. Louisville, KY: Westminster John Knox, 2016.
Sanday, William. "Review of Contentio Veritatis: Essays in Constructive Theology, by Six Oxford Tutors." *Journal of Theological Studies* 4:13 (October 1902).
Six Oxford Tutors. *Contentio Veritatis: Essays in Constructive Theology*. London: John Murray, 1902.
Smyth, Newman. *Constructive Natural Theology*. New York: Charles Scribner's Sons, 1913.
Tillich, Paul. *Systematic Theology*, vol. 1. Chicago: University of Chicago Press, 1951.
Tracy, David. *Blessed Rage for Order*. Chicago: University of Chicago Press, 1996.
Wyman Jr., Jason A. *Constructing Constructive Theology: An Introductory Sketch*. Minneapolis, MN: Fortress, 2017.
Youtz, Herbert Alden, "Current Essays in Constructive Theology." *American Journal of Theology* 11:4 (October 1907): 694.

2

Constructive Theology as Theopoetics: Theological Construction as Divine–Human Creativity

John J. Thatamanil

Why "Constructive" Theology?

With the exception of Jason Wyman's book *Constructing Constructive Theology* (2017), a perplexing vacuum persists in theological literature around the notion of constructive theology: very few theologians, even those whose job title is something like "Professor of Constructive Theology," have written about what they take constructive theology to be.[1] What is constructive theology, and why must theology be constructive?

Foregrounding the adjective "constructive" signals a reluctance to adopt other well-worn descriptors such as "dogmatic" or "systematic." The term "dogmatic" has about it the musty smell of another era, of long-forgotten relics found in attics lacking proper ventilation. Do we still have confidence in dogmas? What can we feel sure enough to be dogmatic about? Meanwhile, the word "systematic" gives the impression not only of mathematical consistency between theological propositions but also of an ordering of those propositions into a tightly integrated system of a sort that many constructive theologians no longer believe possible. Those who find these adjectives neither palatable nor fitting turn to the term "constructive." But why is "constructive" the appropriate alternative?[2]

The term is commendable because it renders human agency explicit. Theology is done not by the angels but by human beings, all too fallible ones at that. Theological construction is an activity that theologians take up with deliberate intentionality.

---

[1] Jason Wyman, *Constructing Constructive Theology* (Minneapolis, MN: Fortress, 2017). Other than Wyman's work, my own thinking about constructive theology has been shaped by Edward Farley's work, particularly his *Ecclesial Reflection*, and Kathryn Tanner's groundbreaking book *Theories of Culture*. See Farley, *Ecclesial Reflection: An Anatomy of Theological Method* (Minneapolis, MN: Fortress, 1982); and Tanner, *Theories of Culture: A New Agenda for Theology* (Minneapolis, MN: Fortress, 1997). As the argument unfolds, my indebtedness to Catherine Keller's commitment to theopoetics will also become clear.

[2] That said, constructive theologians cultivate an irenic rather than oppositional temperament. I am not ruling out all theological work done within the genres of dogmatic and systematic theology as some who operate within those rubrics appear to be working as constructive theologians. For one recent example, see Rubén Rosario Rodríguez, *Dogmatics after Babel: Beyond the Theologies of Word and Culture* (Louisville, KY: Westminster John Knox, 2018).

Constructive theologians own up to the fact that they are "making it up as they go along." All too right we are! A charge that is, in any case, leveled at theologians, we unabashedly embrace. The central categories, loci, themes, and structures of theological thinking needed in this contemporary moment are not available prefabricated in the past only to be bequeathed to us unmediated by the divine or by sacred authorities but are instead generated by specific historically situated acts of human creativity, though perhaps not only by human creativity (more on this in a moment). Whatever constructive theology is taken to mean, at least this explicit acknowledgment of creative human agency is central; constructive theologians forthrightly name that theology is a work of human production.

But then who doesn't? Who else is around to do theology? Are not all good theologians creative and constructive regardless of what name they give to theological labor? Is not "wise creativity" the mark of all theological production that we might wish to consider worthy?[3] Well, yes, but there is in much theological labor a propensity to elide or obscure the status of theologian as creative agent. Gordon Kaufman puts the matter plainly:

> Although it may be obvious to us that the constructive work of the imagination has in this way always been constitutive of theological activity, theologians have seldom understood themselves to be engaged primarily in imaginatively constructing a theistically-focused worldview; on the contrary, they have largely regarded themselves as attempting to express in human words and concepts what the divine King had objectively and authoritatively given the church or synagogue in revelation. The fact that their work was thoroughly imaginative and constructive in character was simply not recognized.[4]

In much dogmatic and some systematic theology, written by even the most creative of theologians, readers can be forgiven for garnering the impression that theology is *recuperative* in character. In such theological styles, some exemplary theological formulation, whether expressed in creedal form or in the writing of a classical theologian or a transhistorically deep grammar found "everywhere and at all times," remains adequate to theological needs of every historical moment.[5] Contemporary refinements may be necessary, but Thomism, let's say, will do. Still more, unquestionable authority

---

[3] David Ford, "Where Is Wise Theological Creativity to be Found? Thoughts on 25 Years of Modern Theology and the Twenty-First Century Prospect," *Modern Theology* 26, no. 1 (January 2010): 67–75.

[4] This snippet is taken from Jason A. Wyman, Jr., *Constructing Constructive Theology* (Minneapolis, MN: Fortress, 2017), Kindle locations 370–7.

[5] Kathryn Tanner makes the point directly:

> Contrary to the famous opinion of Vincent of Lerins, all Christians have not everywhere and at all times believed the same things. This opinion is certainly empirically untrue if it means that all the claims to which one's Christian allegiances commit one are shared by all other Christians, in all times and places. But it is even untrue for the case of some purported crucial subset-some core deposit or fundamental articles of the faith-if it implies shared conceptions of any depth.

See Kathryn Tanner, *Theories of Culture: A New Agenda for Theology* (Minneapolis, MN: Fortress, 1997), Kindle locations 1844–7.

is ascribed to some such past formulation whether it be the literally inerrant scripture, Spirit-inspired conciliar statement, or the like.

Hence, a fully adequate and divinely inspired wisdom is available in the past, which needs only to be rearticulated for the contemporary moment. On such accounts, the task of theology is akin to refurbishing a functional and inhabitable home. The abode of theology is livable as is even if it might need a new coat of paint and cosmetic flourishes here and there. The house won't sell if the 1970s wood paneling is left in place, but nothing is structurally compromised. The creativity called for is a limited matter of expressiveness, of style not substance, and so hardly entails a foundation to roof rehabilitation as might be suggested by the moniker "constructive theology."

Constructive theologians insist that no past theological formulation can be put back into contemporary circulation. Speaking and writing of any kind presuppose a communicative situation, a scene of exchange, between those who speak/write and those who listen/read. When the language of tradition is removed from past communicative situations in which that language was birthed, old vocabularies become obscure, unmusical, and, therefore, unintelligible. Therefore, Christian discourse must be renewed if it is to remain meaningful or even comprehensible. That work of renewal is a matter of human agency, that is to say, of deliberate reconstruction. Constructive theology requires the labor of creative imagination as there is no question of repeating past formulations.

True, theologians do face a host of complicated questions about continuity and creativity, reception and production.[6] Theology, at least Christian theology, is bound by fidelity to the encounter with the specific historical person of Jesus, an encounter whose articulation is found in languages of scripture and Christian traditions. That historicity is why Christian theology must maintain a recuperative posture. Something of soteriological importance happened just then during a particular set of historical dates to which Christian theology is compelled to return. Constructive theologians are bound to affirm this truth as vigorously as dogmatic theologians do. What differs is that constructive theologians refuse to posit that the meaning of what is disclosed in the event of Jesus the Christ is inextricably tied to *just one* specific scriptural idiom or cultural-linguistic logic that must simply be repeated. Hence the need for construction and reconstruction.[7]

With respect to the question of ethics, what if the house of tradition is not in fact inhabitable as is at least not for all its inhabitants? The term "constructive" signals the need for more drastic rehabilitation. Weight-bearing joists may need to be replaced, and even the foundation might require attention. The house of Christian theology may be both unfit for its current occupants and a threat to those on the outside. There may be asbestos in the walls, toxicity that threatens inhabitants and neighbors. Consider the way in which anti-Judaism seems to be writ into the fabric Christian

---

[6] Arguably, the most important relatively recent book on this question is Christine Helmer's *Theology and the End of Doctrine* (Louisville, KY: Westminster John Knox, 2014).

[7] Consider, for example, both the fidelity to the past and the radical creativity displayed in Sallie McFague's rethinking of the core motif of incarnation but now as expanded to the world itself as the body of God for the sake of ecotheology. See Sallie McFague, *The Body of God: An Ecological Theology* (Minneapolis, MN: Fortress, 1993).

faith and even strands of scripture itself.[8] Or consider the arguments by feminist thinkers who suggest that Christian readings of the maleness of Jesus and his disciples have inscribed marginalization and misogyny into the heart of Christian traditions.[9] Ponder the enormous and genocidal burdens that missionary theologies have inflicted on First Nations communities.[10] Consider also the sexual theologies generated by the church, which continue to violate the dignity and worth of LGBTQI+ Christians.[11] And what of those who belong to other religious traditions whose traditions have been demonized as leading to perdition?[12] For women, the colonized, persons of color, the queer, and persons of other religions, we must take up genuine (re)construction to create expressions of Christian tradition in which Christians and others can safely live and breathe.

Constructive theologians take on the name because we wish to make transparent that what human hands have made, other human hands can and must remake. For some, this might prove to be a destabilizing truth. Not so for the constructive theologian. Constructive theologians forthrightly acknowledge their creative agency because they are suspicious about strategies that seek to minimize the role of human creativity in theological production. When human creativity goes unnamed or is elided altogether, then all-too-human theological formulations are granted unquestionable divine authority; they can no longer be interrogated. Deconstruction and reconstruction are rendered impermissible, and the role of human creativity is hidden from view. The theologian is thereby figured as mere humble commentator, translator, or interpreter of the received and authoritative sacred past into the present moment.

If such radical implications follow from the term "constructive theology," constructive theologians have an obligation to say it plain, and so they do. They must seek to articulate why even the central theological categories and loci from past formulations may stand in need of creative reconstruction.[13] Is such root and branch creativity taking place among theologians who do not understand themselves to be constructive theologians? Most certainly. What distinguishes constructive theologians from their near kin who reject the term is the matter of being explicit: constructive theologians perform creative theological reconstruction self-consciously. And such self-consciousness brings in its train a sense of fallibility. If my constructions are

---

[8] While not itself an exercise in constructive theology, Adele Reinhartz's recent book gives an urgent account of the sort of problem that constructive theologians must directly confront rather than make naïve recourse to the "authority of scripture." If strands of scripture are anti-Judaic, what then? See Reinhartz, *Cast out of the Covenant: Jews and Anti-Judaism in the Gospel of John* (Minneapolis, MN: Fortress, 2018).

[9] Consider, for example, the groundbreaking work of Rosemary Radford Ruether, *Sexism and God-Talk: Toward a Feminist Theology* (Boston, MA: Beacon, 1993).

[10] See the indispensable work of George E. Tinker, *Missionary Conquest: The Gospel and Native American Cultural Genocide* (Minneapolis, MN: Augsburg Fortress, 1993).

[11] Linn Tonstad, *Queer Theology: Beyond Apologetics* (Eugene, OR: Cascade Books, 2018).

[12] For a vital attempt to survey, critique, and move beyond Christian exclusivisms, see Paul Knitter's *Introducing Theologies of Religion* (Maryknoll, NY: Orbis, 2002).

[13] On how easy it is for constructive theologians to overstate the degree and measure of theological creativity, see again, Jason Wyman. Wyman rightly notes that, ultimately, constructive theologians do not entirely reconstruct Christian traditions and often return to the same key doctrinal loci. Chastened by his observations, I shall try to be mindful of not overstating the creativity of constructive theology.

mine—however much they aspire to be faithful responses to divine initiative—they remain provisional, historically conditioned, and culturally contextual. We know we are making it up as we go along, and we have the humility, courage, and, I might add, playfulness to say so.

But *only* human creativity? Is there no role for divine creativity in theological construction? Here, constructive theologians differ among themselves and markedly so. On the one hand, we find figures like Gordon Kaufman and Sallie McFague for whom the production of theological language and models appears to be a human project alone. As Wyman has shown, for Kaufman, theology is cultural construction, assessment, and reconstruction of models of God and the God–world relationship that is subject to criteria developed and defended by the theologian. In his own words, "If faith is a gift of God, as it has been traditionally understood, theology is clearly human work, and we must take full responsibility for it. But it is human work that emerges out of faith's own need for more adequate orientation and symbolization. Such theological activity may reinforce—or it may weaken further—the religious stance."[14]

In contrast to the Kaufman lineage, one might point to the phenomenological theology of Edward Farley in which the rejection of the "household of authority" nevertheless leaves room for envisioning theological generativity as emerging from and out of divine–human collaboration. For Farley, the line between faith and human reflection about faith is not nearly as stark or impermeable as it appears to be for Kaufman. Farley manages to find a way to affirm both human fallibility and the contingency of all theological construction but nonetheless leaves human creativity open to divine agency. Theology takes its bearings from God's "coming forth as God" in redemption. It attends to and follows upon thinking what is disclosed in and through redemption.[15]

In what follows, I name a third trajectory that can be said to follow in Farley's wake but one that finds in imagination the possibility of a more than human creativity. We can speak of this vein of constructive theology as the theopoetic trajectory. Articulated most vibrantly in the work of Catherine Keller, *theopoiesis* dances along the edge of a fertile ambivalence in the notion of "*poiesis*," namely, "making." In the bringing together of "*theos*" and "*poiesis*," this ambivalence is not just doubled but multiplied. God-making—is the theopoet making God up? Or is the agent of *poiesis* the divine itself? Is God doing the making? Or might it somehow be *both*? Might it be possible to imagine that the divine participates in the very human activity of imagining God? This latter doubling is what I myself affirm.

I shall say more about Keller later. What will suffice for now is to suggest that Keller opens the door to the fertile possibility of the both-and, of a trajectory that holds open the possibility that we might *make up* the divine and *be made by* the divine, troubling

---

[14] Quoted in Wyman's *Constructing Constructive Theology*, 38; Kindle ed.
[15] On the difference between Kaufman and Farley, see again Wyman's *Constructing Constructive Theology*, 45. See also Edward Farley, *Divine Empathy: A Theology of God* (Minneapolis, MN: Fortress, 1996), chapter 5. For another phenomenological theology that begins by affirming the phenomenological givenness of divine disclosure, see Ray Hart's classic *Unfinished Man and the Theological Imagination: Toward an Ontology and a Rhetoric of Revelation* (New York: Herder and Herder, 1968).

the temptation to posit a tidy duality between human fallibility, which exiles divinity from theological creativity tout court, on the one hand, and accounts of theological generativity in which the divine somehow does theology for us in some pristine and privileged textual or traditional site, on the other. What if God participates in our work of making God up and yet, nonetheless, that work remains also human and thus fallible?

Any act of theological creativity—a prayer, a sermon, a liturgical act, a classroom lecture, a journal article, or theological book—will of necessity be a modest intervention; but if such activities are understood to be part of divine and worldly unfolding, constructive theology takes on theopoetic import. Theology at its best is/is like prayer. Theologians confess in a Pauline key, "We do not know how to [theologize] as we ought but that very Spirit intercedes in us with sighs too deep for words."[16]

But then words do come. After all, to speak of "sighs too deep for words" is itself a Spirited expression. It is a manifestation of a triple creativity: it is the work of the *Spirit* effecting *worldly* transformation through *Paul's* theopoetic creativity. New possibilities are opened to and for the world through Paul's prayer, which is simultaneously Paul's work and the Spirit's as well. This peculiar theological *coincidentia oppositorum* is also found in Paul's urging, "Work out your own salvation with fear and trembling; for it is God who is at work in you, enabling you both to will and to work for his good pleasure" (Phil. 2:12-13). We constructive theologians might again wish to reword Paul here to have him say: "Work out your own [theologies] with fear and trembling for it is God who is at work in you enabling you to both to will and work for God's good pleasure." That God is at work in us does not relieve Paul or his community of fear and trembling. The same holds true for us; we remain erring creatures. But the very real possibility of error does not negate the presence and operation of divine creativity. It is this doubling inseparability that I have in mind when I call for a theopoetic understanding of the theological project.

Nonetheless, I want also to articulate another more rudimentary understanding of theopoetics, a sense that is prior to the specifically participatory meaning that I am commending. Constructive theologians are convinced that when theological vocabularies lose traction, they do so because the imaginative framework that sustains those vocabularies is no longer appealing, credible, or even intelligible. Such imaginative frameworks are composed of the core metaphors, symbols, and narrative constructions within which theological concepts are embedded. Should these imaginative frameworks collapse—the imaginary of sacrificial atonement, for example—the concepts that articulate the meaning of such frameworks are put out of commission, perhaps irretrievably. Despite the lingering appeal of the Anselmian theory of atonement, a case can be made that the entire poetics of substitutionary sacrifice is no longer appealing or intelligible to a growing many. Theo*logical* arguments that offer defenses of Anselmian teaching are futile for those to whom any notion of substitutionary sacrifice no longer makes poetic sense. Under such circumstances, constructive theologians cannot tinker on the conceptual edges but must engage in

---

[16] My paraphrase of Romans 8:26.

genuine (re)construction at the level of *imagination*. The framing metaphors that structure a given theological proposal must be rehabilitated or replaced. Theological labor at this imaginative level is what I mean most basically by *theopoetics*.

When I teach constructive theology, I define "constructive theology" as the labor of faithful innovation that seeks to enrich, deepen, and grow the tradition's wisdom in meaningful and creative continuity with the past but without repetition. We study tradition to be tutored, disciplined, and inspired by past exercises in creative fidelity. The study of tradition is a study of the enormous fecundity of Christian imagination, an imagination that has never ceased to grow and learn from its interlocutors and even its opponents. Constructive theologians do not operate under the assumption that all the wisdom we need is already available. Creativity is far more than finding a new shell for an already established and immutable wisdom. At its best, constructive theology is motivated by the faithful conviction that God is neither done with the world nor the theological communities in whose name the theologian writes.

Constructive theologians, thus, have a great deal in mind when they speak of theological construction. I suggest that theology is compelled to be creatively constructive for at least the following several reasons: (1) the theopoetic character of theology; (2) the wide, nearly inexhaustible, internal diversity of tradition; (3) tradition's complicity with injustice; (4) theology's obligation to answer new questions that have never before been put to it; (5) a sense of truth as process and event-like in character; (6) theology as invested in a critique of authority; and (7) theology's calling to attend to new sources of wisdom *extra ecclesiam*.

The Primacy of Theopoetics

Thus far, I have announced the possibility that constructive theology can take an apparently paradoxical form, one that affirms that theological construction can be both a human and divine activity. Theological utterances can be marked by a kind of Pauline character—speech that is mine and yet not mine, fallible and yet nonetheless generated by divine creativity. The result is a vision of theology as marked by divine *authoring* but without recourse to accounts of infallible divine *authority*. Explicitly refused here is the false alternative between a vision of theology as either done for human beings by God or merely by human beings about God.

Such a novel account might be developed out of a variety of Christian theological trajectories, but here I trace one contemporary trajectory that takes its bearings from Catherine Keller's account of theopoetics. For Keller, the discourse of contemporary theopoetics arises from the intersection of multiple streams of reflection, including ancient Christian thought—Athanasius's God becoming human so that the human might become divine (*theosis*, which is just *theopoiesis* "contracted"), death of God theology, and contemporary process theology being the most prominent. In Keller's reading, these discourses have in common a care for the mattering of meaning and meaning of matter. The God-Word (*logos*) is made flesh/matter so that flesh/matter can become divine. God through the incarnation is engaged in God-making (*theo-poiesis*). Keller appeals to Basil of Caesarea:

> When a sunbeam falls on a transparent substance, the substance itself becomes brilliant, and radiates light from itself. So too Spirit-bearing souls, illumined by Him, finally become spiritual themselves, and their grace is sent forth to others. From this comes knowledge of the future, understanding of mysteries … distribution of wonderful gifts … endless joy in the presence of God, becoming like God, and, the highest of all desires, *becoming God*.[17]

This gives a startling though antique meaning to constructive theology or, rather, constructive theo-poeisis! *Theopoeisis* is not, first, a human activity; rather, God does God-making first. God is engaged in constructive God-making. Where? In human beings or—and here we advert to process theology—in human becomings. The Word is being made flesh not only in Jesus but in human beings generally. Before turning to the wording of God—or *theopoeisis* as linguistic activity—Keller reminds us that the ancient Christian tradition articulates a profound intimacy between human wording and divine enfleshing, with priority granted to the latter. To my knowledge, Keller is among the first of contemporary constructive theologians to draw upon the intimate connection between the terms *theopoiesis* and *theosis*. She writes,

> The term theopoetics finds its ancestor in the ancient Greek *theopoiesis*. As *poiesis* means making or creation, so *theopoiesis* gets rendered as "God-making" or "becoming divine." *Theopoiesis* appears in the first centuries of Hellenistic Christianity, often and then later consistently in its contracted form *theosis*, normally translated as "deification." The term *theopoiesis* retains the fuller sense of "making divine," "making God." … Clement in the third century defines *theopoiesis* as "assimilation to God as far as possible."[18]

Keller points to a "mysticism of participation" at work in these root theologies of God-making and God-becoming. At play is also a peculiar paradox of intimacy and unknowability: the God who absolutely exceeds us is nonetheless also present as that which we ourselves are becoming. The mystery becomes ours as we become the mystery by the grace of mystery itself.

Keller is on the mark to say that *theosis* "can only be read in the context of ancient spiritual practices, ascetic and ecstatic simultaneously." What might be added is that the play of apophatic and cataphatic discourse is itself one of those ancient practices. To say and to unsay, to say again and unsay once more is to trace the path of the mind's ascent into the divine darkness, the cloud of unknowing. *Theopoeisis* is, therefore, simultaneously the name for a divine process of God-making/God-becoming and the human discursive processes by which that very becoming takes place. Be-coming and be-speaking are not two.

---

[17] Catherine Keller, *Intercarnations* (New York: Fordham University Press), Kindle locations 2194–8; emphasis in the original.

[18] Catherine Keller, *Intercarnations: Exercises in Theological Possibility* (New York: Fordham University Press, 2017), Kindle locations 2186–93.

As theology becomes more attuned to the mystery of God, of God's nature as exceeding all language and thought, the more we intuit that theology must of necessity aspire to be evocative and not, primarily, descriptive. Speech about God is always a multipurpose activity, an activity that is meant to make God present, felt, and experienced. Theological language *invokes* and *evokes*, and that work is not performed by appeal to univocal conceptual language. We must make recourse to poetry, including the poetry of liturgy and prayer, if we are to be responsive to the animating presence of divine Spirit. Let us call such theological discourse first-order theology. First-order theology is God-talk understood as God's speaking *to* us and our responsive speaking *to* God. Two more prepositions seem crucial: namely, "through" and "in." Such God-talk is also God-making, *theopoiesis*. Such God-talk/God-making can be simultaneously God speaking to us and *through* us as well as *in* us, but not, I would hasten to add, without us. Second-order theology follows upon and attends to the entailments of first-order *theopoeisis*. Here, theology enters into a second speculative moment that seeks to excavate the meanings of first-order theological becoming and bespeaking. Also, here, we traffic in concepts that seek to explicate what remains excessive in theopoetic discourse.

Any particular *theo-logos* lives off the power and plausibility of a *theopoiesis*, which offers the living womb within which it is homed. Should a given theopoetic frame die, theologies that found their being and well-being within that particular framework will become implausible and enfeebled. At the most fundamental level, constructive theologians are called to be constructive because they must participate in the generation of these new theopoetic matrices within which future theologies stand a chance of finding life.

Consider, finally, another reason why theopoetics has to it a primacy that goes unrecognized. The appeal to *theopoiesis* as *theosis* expanded and *theosis* as *theopoiesis* contracted introduces a register of discourse in which the human and the divine are permeable to each other. Divinity is communicable, a communicable wellness, that creatures can catch by the initiative of divine grace. These ways of speaking may well be articulated in a particular metaphysics of divinity and humanity, but the primacy of this particular linguistic register has to it an aesthetic density that precedes, exceeds, and sustains any metaphysical explication and unfolding thereof. The appeal of this discourse is prior to any metaphysical or theological articulation and defense of the same. Hence the priority I grant to theopoetics for constructive theology. Constructive theologians will have to be constructive theopoeticians first, birthing or retrieving imaginative possibilities within which particular theological proposals can implant and be nourished. That is the first obligation of contemporary constructive theology in a historical moment in which a great many extant ways of imagining divinity are dying out.

But how? How are these new theopoetic frames to be generated? Thus far, I've said little about that question directly. And with good reason—the question is incalculably complex most especially because there are no formulae or algorithms for theological generativity. Of the making of theological argumentation, there is no end. But the generation of theopoetic frames operates in an altogether otherwise manner. Here, theopoetics is at least as mysterious and as complex as the creativity of any kind whatsoever. How are poems and artworks generated? In the case of theopoetic generativity, however, there are also additional and vexing questions about how human creativity can participate in and wait upon what Tillich would call theonomony; what is sought for is a generativity that is not merely an autonomous human project but creativity in which something more than the human shines through, something revelatory. To give a full account and defense of the possibility of such generativity would require nothing less than an ontology of revelation and an account of the role of imagination in such revelation. These are tasks well beyond the scope of this or any other chapter.

But this much can be said by way of summary and anticipation of next steps. (1) Theopoetic creativity is like any other act of artistic creativity, whether it be musical, literary, theatrical, or otherwise. (2) Such creativity cannot be produced according to any algorithms or formulae as none exist. (3) As a religious genre of creativity, new theopoetic frames depend upon disciplined waiting, which is one way of speaking about such spiritual disciplines as contemplative prayer and meditation. Here, we return to an Evagrian understanding of the theologian: "The theologian is one who prays truly; the one who prays truly is a theologian." (4) Such creativity must also attend/pay attention to the idioms, intuitions, concrete needs, and demands of the particular communities and historical exigencies by which theologians and their communities are claimed. What kinds of language feel tired, worn out, and unmusical? What are the situations that demand a new imaginative theopoetic frame?

To enumerate these four observations is not yet to spell out a concrete answer to the "how" question, but it does begin to describe what constructive theopoetics might be and the obligations that fall to constructive theopoeticians/theologians: what new modes of religious imagination are necessary if religious life as such (and secondarily religious reflection) is to be revivified as older primary religious vocabularies lose their appeal? In what follows, I will try to answer this rather broad question by focusing on specific situations, contexts, and theological tasks that give concrete content to the general claims advanced thus far.

The Inexhaustible Diversity of Tradition

In the remainder of this chapter, I seek to articulate other reasons why constructive theology must live up to its name and how theopoetics plays a role throughout. To begin with, the breadth and internal diversity of tradition place constructive and creative demands on the theologian. Constructive theologians find propositions of the following sort disingenuous: "Theology must be faithful to *the* Biblical worldview." Such claims are counterfactual and are usually disguised attempts to impose theological convictions by fiat. Such strategies attenuate the range of options available to the theologian by narrowing the boundaries of orthodoxy by assertion rather than by argument.

In truth, the history of tradition is a history of debate and diversity. You know you belong to a tradition not when you agree with it, but when you are claimed by the argument the tradition is having. A tradition is not an agreement but an argument conducted over the long historical haul. Take just one illustrative example: at no point in the history of Christian tradition has the church universal advanced a single account of what we are compelled to believe about salvation. So, we see widely different accounts of salvation as healing, as *theosis*, as substitutionary atonement, as *Christus Victor* atonement, as justification by grace through faith alone, and so on. Moreover, each of these positions can find grounding in the Bible, and hence we must recognize that the Bible too speaks with anything but one voice.

Crucially, each of these accounts is grounded in very distinctive theopoetic imageries. The image of Christ as triumphant victor is quite different from Christ as sacrificial lamb, even when these metaphors are cast together in the pages of scripture. Tradition is replete with a remarkable array of theopoetic possibilities many of which remain uncultivated in theological construction.

Kathryn Tanner has persuasively shown that given the profound internal diversity of tradition and Bible, theologians inevitably exercise creativity in selecting from the vast storehouse of scripture and tradition, a storehouse that I often characterize as a pantry together with a spice cabinet. Put simply, you cannot cook with everything; if you did, the result would be unappetizing. Selection is inescapable. Theologians and communities must then defend their selection as compelling for the communities for which they write and faithful to some major mother lode(s) of the tradition.

But the principle of selection hinges also on the uses you mean to make of what you have selected. Every theological project is, therefore, a work of cooking up a meal that is meant to be nourishing, healing, life-giving, and even beautiful, within a given context. Every theologian, indeed every reflective Christian, is a cook. Even when a standard dish is being prepared, Christian recipes permit of great variation and improvisation, making theological creativity inevitable.

Over the course of cumulative global Christian history, the storehouse of the Christian repertoire has grown beyond any single theologian's or theological community's capacity for mastery. We select because we must. We offer grounds for why these selections are ethically, aesthetically, epistemologically, and ontologically defensible. Nor do we fear that diversity may lead to conflict or failure of Christian practice. Rather, with Kathryn Tanner, we affirm that,

> diversity results not so much from a failure to internalize Christian culture as from proper socialization into the kind of practice Christianity is. The position does see that the universalizing tendencies of a Christian life-propensities, that is, to make a Christian way of life cover everything-prompt diversity. The effort to be Christian in changing cultural contexts prompts diversity in theological judgments, as would, it might be added the Christian penchant to live in a Christian way throughout the whole of one's life-all its dimensions-at any one time and place.[19]

Tanner offers an array of arguments that demonstrate that Christians who pursue faithful reflection even in the same time and place are likely to come to different

---

[19] Kathryn Tanner, *Theories of Culture: A New Agenda for Theology* (Minneapolis, MN: Fortress, 1997), Kindle locations 2377–80.

and, indeed, often divergent judgments about what follows for Christian thought and practice in those sites. Diversity cannot be safely contained at arm's length by suggesting that it is derived from cultural variation alone. There is no escaping decision and theological judgment. Such decisions and judgments are unavoidably exercises in theological creativity.

No recent movement within constructive theology has more robustly welcomed the internal diversity of Christian tradition than the assemblage of thinkers who have come together under the banner of "polydoxy." The term is meant to hallow multiplicity and refuse the all-too-neat and destructive dichotomy between orthodoxy, one the one hand, and heterodoxy, on the other. Catherine Keller and Laurel Schneider celebrate polydoxy to herald the vibrancy and multiplicity of theology in this unlikely moment. They rightly hold that theology has always already been multiple. In their words,

> "Christianity" was never merely One to begin with. Internally multiple and complex, it has always required an agile and spirited approach to theological reflection. We sense that the current resilience of theology in its becoming multiplicity of relations is a sign and a gift of that Spirit. From the start, the plurality of canonized gospels accompanied by the ancestral Hebrew library and the shadows of the excluded gospels made multiplicity manifest. Any durable unity that Christians achieved in texts, theology, or community was not just debatable but hotly debated. The debates display the manifold genius of Christian orthodoxy and the creative tenacity of dissent.[20]

Turning from the general to specific, given the immense variety internal to Christian traditions, we might well ask why we continue to be so very provincial in our theological selections. Given the plethora of soteriological options available to Christians, why do substitutionary theories continue to linger? That question is urgent for feminist theologians who worry about the risk to women and children of a punitive male God who seems to require the death of His Son before He can forgive. More recently, Catholic feminist ecotheologian Elizabeth Johnson has asked about what, if anything, substitutionary atonement theories have to say to broader ecological questions.

The unending Western repetition of Anselm can make it seem as though there are no other viable soteriological options available within Christian traditions. That foreclosure of theological possibilities by repetition ad nauseum is dangerous, especially when the broader theopoetic frame of sacrifice—which lived, in part, by proximity to the logic of animal sacrifice—fails now to capture the imagination. When that theopoetic matrix collapses, defending any atonement theology that has emerged from within it becomes a losing game. Wedding Christian faith to an obsolete theopoetic frame is to court the death of Christian life itself.

---

[20] Catherine Keller and Laurel Schneider, *Polydoxy: Theology of Multiplicity and Relation* (London: Routledge, 2010), 2; Kindle ed.

Tradition and Injustice

Yet another impulse that motivates constructive theology is recognition of the tradition's troubling complicity with injustice. The crux of the matter here is not that Christian communities have contravened the divine call to justice but that features of the tradition, long taken to be central, are bound up with injustice. So thoroughgoing is this entanglement that Christian confidence in the tradition might be shaken were it not for the fact that constructive theology is grounded in the conviction that the tradition can continue to evolve and grow. That is the very point of discourse about *constructive* theology. Constructive theology's call for theological creativity recognizes the need for real leave taking from past toxicities. Tradition need not repeat itself especially in its discursive and material acts of violence. Sadly, such leave taking cannot be easily accomplished as traumatizing features of the tradition leave genetic and epigenetic traces within the Christian body even as we work to remediate for past errors.

Consider the tradition's two-thousand-year-old complicity with anti-Judaism, which in recent centuries provided the fertile soil for anti-Semitism both inside and outside the church. Theologians at the heart of the tradition, including giants such as Justin Martyr and Martin Luther, held to noxious convictions about the Jews and found grounding in such texts as the Gospel of John's poisonous utterances placed in Jesus's mouth, such as "You are from your father the devil, and you choose to do your father's desires. He was a murderer from the beginning and does not stand in the truth, because there is no truth in him" (John 8:44). This statement is especially troubling in the light of those who hold scripture to be inerrant and infallible. Given the centrality that Gospel texts have for Christians, particularly those statements ascribed to Jesus himself, anti-Judaism flows right through the beating heart of Christian tradition.

There is no honest way to wish away such statements as marginal to tradition. Constructive theology must be guided by a rigorous will to truth that engages in honest stocktaking before it proceeds to the painstaking work of reconstruction. Such reconstruction is a far-reaching project as it requires nothing less than a Christian theology of Judaism. Only such a comprehensive venture will do if the following questions are to be addressed: "Has God only one blessing?"[21] Is God's covenant with Jews now abrogated? If not, how are we to understand the soteriological function of the Christ? These and many other questions must be tackled if Christian tradition's long legacy of anti-Judaism is to be overcome.

And so it goes in a host of other areas in which Christian theology stands in need of radical reconstruction: race, gender, sexuality, ecotheology, and the like. In all of these cases, it is insufficient to say only that Christian practice has erred. In every case, errors in Christian *practice* are inseparable from errors or omissions in Christian *reflection*. Now, it surely must be possible to cease and desist from a wounding practice before our theologies are remediated, but it is hard to see how new practices can be secured when prevailing theological convictions serve to sanctify an old status quo.

---

[21] Here, I cite the title of a groundbreaking book by my colleague Mary Boys, *Has God Only One Blessing: Judaism as a Source of Christian Self-Understanding* (Mahwah, NJ: Paulist, 2000).

Extinguishing violating practices requires rooting out the theological errors in which they are grounded. Talk of *constructive* theology is motivated by an appreciation for the gravity and complexity of the work before us. If anti-Judaism can so easily be read off Christian scriptures, then immense labor will be required to quarantine these toxicities, including, of course, reframing how Christians understand the nature of scripture and the question of authority.

Here too, theopoetic labor looms large. Earth-wounding dispositions and practices are not so much prescribed by theological arguments as they are inscribed in core metaphors that shape Christian imagination so that we come to see ourselves as the great exception, the one and only ensouled creature made in the image of God. What central metaphors and symbols serve to undergird human exceptionalism, deny human animality, and so set the conditions for the violation of animals and the natural world as a whole? The restricted application of the symbol of *imago Dei* to humans alone—and that too in their rationality alone—is a theopoetic constraint that leads to the construal of the animal as instrumental and beneath human beings in the great chain of being. A direct interrogation of the symbolic logic operative in the human-versus-animal dichotomy and the birthing of new metaphors are essential to a new anti-exceptionalist theopoetics. Here, we come to see that the theopoetic work of imaginative repair is essential to the work of birthing justice.[22]

The Power of New Questions: Theology and the Unforeseeable

Throughout this chapter, I have maintained that constructive theologians embrace the term "constructive" because theology is always done under circumstances that call forth creativity. Nowhere is this more evident than in the constant emergence of unanticipatable questions that demand theological answers. Consider the contemporary ecological turn. While a host of thinkers have blamed Jewish and Christian scriptures and theologies for the despoliation of the earth, Christian inattention to ecological questions cannot be classified either as outright error or as omission. Christian theology has until quite recently failed to consider matters ecological because ecological thinking, as we now know it, is largely unprecedented. The notion that all species, including homo sapiens as one among them, are bound together in a tangled network of co-belonging does have metaphysical antecedents in various traditions, but the specifically biological and climatological entailments of that co-belonging have not been thought prior to late modernity, indeed not for much longer than six decades. Even traditions that have deep resources to recognize the sacrality of the earth have engaged in wanton disregard of earth as ecological network. Consider the contradiction between Hindu reverence for the Ganges as sacred and life-giving mother and its abysmally polluted waters.

---

[22] For an important recent book that is taking on such work, see Eric Daryl Meyer's *Inner Animalities: Theology and the End of the Human* (New York: Fordham University Press, 2018).

Rosemary Ruether, in particular, has well recognized the novelty of these questions. That human beings could pose a threat to the entire planet became thinkable only after Hiroshima and Nagasaki. She writes,

> The radical nature of this new face of human ecological devastation means that all past traditions are inadequate in the face it. Whatever useful elements may exist in, for example, Native American or Taoist thought, must be reinterpreted to make them useable in the face of both new scientific knowledge and the destructive power of the technology it has made possible.[23]

Profound resources yes, ex nihilo creativity no, but nonetheless, reinterpretation requires constructive imagination.

In such cases, the questions raised drive constructive theologians to address root *theopoetic* matters that demand reframing theological imagination. Questions about the possibility of intelligent life on other planets, Artificial General Intelligence, and the vast trillion-year timescale of cosmic evolution require transforming an obsolete three-story mythic infrastructure that continues to lumber along in Christian religious discourse. Under the pressures of such new knowledges, conceptual tinkering will not suffice. Our entire imaginative picture of the universe must be refurbished. Theological writing by Brian Swimme, Thomas Berry, Mary Evelyn Tucker, and John Haught proposing a new universe story is engaged in just this kind of theopoetic undertaking. The labor of constructing more adequate theological concepts requires first that we construct a richer theopoetic cosmology within which such concepts can find life.

Truth as Process

Theology is also constructive in another crucial sense. Constructive theologians hold that truth cannot be understood as located in a fixed deposit of faith (*depositum fidei*) but instead is something that emerges through conversation. Although parties hold cherished antecedent convictions, in real conversation, they arrive at insights that exceed what they already knew; new insights emerge that defy anticipation.

This dialogical and emergent conception of truth is commended by Gordon Kaufman who contrasts this model against truth understood on "the model of property, something that is owned by one party, and thus is not directly available to others, but which can be passed on or given over to others if the owner so chooses." Kaufman offers an alternative: "If we move away from this property model of truth, however, to a model based on the experience of free and open conversation, a quite different conception comes into view."[24]

In contrast to "authoritarian" models in which truth is possessed by experts alone and then transmitted passively to those who lack truth as property, in authentic dialogue,

---

[23] Rosemary Radford Ruether, *Gaia and God: An Ecofeminist Theology of Earth Healing* (New York: HarperCollins, 1992), 206.

[24] Gordon Kaufman, *God, Mystery, Diversity: Christian Theology in a Pluralistic World* (Minneapolis, MN: Fortress, 1996), Kindle locations 2774–6.

what unfolds is marked by creativity. Kaufman writes, "For the interchange may have developed a life of its own, and it may have moved in directions no one anticipated and led to new insights and ideas which none of the participants had previously considered ... Thus, conversation is itself sometimes the matrix of significant creativity in human life."[25]

Here we have yet another reason for understanding theological labor as constructive rather than recuperative. Truth is not available in prefabricated proclamations because it is not "a property of particular words or propositions or texts that can be learned and passed on (more or less unchanged) to others-it is identified as a living reality that emerges within and is a function of ongoing, living conversation among a number of different voices."[26]

Historical theologians will not regard such claims as news. When they try to teach the meaning of a milestone text, say the Nicene Creed, they seek to reconstruct the contestations taking place in the fourth century so that the meaning of the text can be reconstructed. The Creed is incomprehensible apart from the conversational matrix in which it came to be. Constructive theologians seek to reconstruct that conversational matrix, albeit with a critical difference: they do so not out of antiquarian interests alone but for the sake of advancing contemporary conversations.

No creedal claim or dogmatic dictum can be abstracted from its emergence and intelligibility within processes of creative interchange. Indeed, propositional accounts of truth wedded to authority claims that take certain utterances to be infallible are likely to halt the flow of ongoing conversation through which meaning is carried forward into the future. When we keep talking, meaning continues to be replenished precisely because the intelligibility of older moments in the conversation is neither lost nor absolutized. We correct, elaborate, amplify, and, when necessary, reformulate and even retract what, in historical light, seems mistaken. Truth fossilized in the static amber of authority and isolated from the creative flow of conversation no longer lives.

An account of truth as calcified proposition is limited for another reason. Propositions can provide *information* but not *transformation*, which is the wellspring of religious life. An account of truth as dialogical and emergent comes closer to the primary evocative and transformative intentions of first-order religious discourse. Finally, need we state here the obvious theopoetic point that in just this discussion, two central metaphors play a crucial role, truth as deposit and truth as conversational disclosure? The constructive theologian decisively embraces the latter. Vital piety demands nothing less.

Critique of Authority

Sprinkled throughout this chapter has been a recurrent interrogation of classical conceptions of theological authority. Constructive theologians are wary of extant conceptions of authority. No theologian has played a greater role in troubling those

---

[25] Ibid., Kindle locations 2779–83.
[26] Ibid., Kindle locations 2810–12.

conceptions than Edward Farley. Farley imagines "the household of authority" as a circular habitation composed of many rooms, each of which props up the other. To understand the questionable logic of this household, we must quote him at length:

> If we ask why Ezra's words are true, we are told they are a divine communication. If we ask how they are given that status, we are told that they occur in a permanent record of a divinely authored work, the canonical Scriptures. If we ask why this collection of human writings is to be regarded as divinely authored, we are told that the *act of canonizing* on the part of the church is divinely authored. If we ask why ... this particular set of events in history is divinely authored, we are told that the church has declared it so and its declarations are divinely authored. If we ask how it is that the church's declarations are divinely authored, we are told that such are *necessary* to the certainty needed for salvation and its historical perpetuation. If we ask why ... such "necessity" is actually operative and not just a logical ideality, we are referred to salvation history and the logic of triumph. If we ask why we are to regard the logic of triumph and its attendant notions as an unquestionable criterion, something which is both a priori to Christianity itself and true, we are told that the overall interpretive framework of Scripture, dogma, and the church has never questioned it. So the circle, a vicious one is complete. The questioner has been referred from one room to another in the house of authority only to find himself or herself back in the original room.[27]

By "logic of triumph," Farley has in mind the argument that salvation history and ecclesial history are underwritten by God imagined as sovereign monarch. So, the dogmatic formulations that happened to win out have done so not through the hurly-burly contingencies of historical conflict, but because these triumphs were underwritten by God; here, the last possible loophole is closed, and the house of authority is sealed tight.

Some version of this vicious circularity is operative in classical accounts of theological authority. Once this circularity has been exposed, the pretensions of the house of authority stand unmasked. What comes next is the difficult work of case making, argumentation in the midst of historical flux without a divinely warranted skyhook. Constructive theologians have given a variety of accounts of what such theological labor will look like, including Farley himself, Gordon Kaufman, Sallie McFague, and David Tracy, among others. But in every case, there is no attempt to escape fallibility but, therefore, also the corrigibility of constructive theological proposals.

Here too, there is a theopoetic shift away from God construed as omnipotent monarch who establishes within history special sites of unquestionable truth. Unless and until named, this metaphor may remain undetected. Once interrogated, the contestability of this metaphor is exposed and other possibilities suggest themselves, including the central possibility of divine–human participation in the generation of

---

[27] Edward Farley, *Ecclesial Reflection: An Anatomy of Theological Method* (Minneapolis, MN: Fortress, 1982), 165–6.

truth, truth that nonetheless remains susceptible to correction and transformation—divine-human authoring but without conceptions of inerrancy.

Wisdom *Extra Ecclesiam*

A final reason[28] why theology must be constructive is that Christian theologians now recognize a diversity of sources of truth outside the church. Having given up on the old Roman Catholic notion, *extra ecclesiam nulla salus*—outside the church there is no salvation—Christian theologians display a new openness. Whether truth be found in secular movements or other religious traditions, Christian theologians no longer assume that God has spoken only to Christians. The world has in it powerful, compelling, and even holy truth, and the theologian must exercise creativity in *receiving* as well as offering truth, whether that truth be derived from Marx's socialist vision, contemporary physics, Judith Butler's gender theory, or Buddhist wisdom.

But if what is to be received is to be meaningful for those who are receiving, those who receive must be transformed. To be transformed by what we receive is a mark of learning and accountability rather than irresponsible misappropriation. This obligation falls heavily upon those who work with other religious traditions. Within the context of interreligious engagement, theologians must do more than speculate about religious others or acquire bits of information about them. What is called for is instead learning *with* and *from* our religious neighbors.

Given the reality of globalization, religious others are no longer on the other side of the planet but on the other side of the bed. Given the intimate proximity of religious neighbors, older models of interreligious engagement in which learning about other traditions was restricted to only (1) those who had specialist philological expertise and (2) those who could travel to the field no longer obtains. Specialist learning remains as urgent as ever, but now it must be supplemented by new modes of learning from religious neighbors, friends, and partners. Such learning can take the form of meditation with the Roshi in the local Zen community, joint social service projects to address the needs of the town in which one lives, or joining in interreligious nonviolent protest. Expert learning can exist alongside and support interreligious learning as a larger project incumbent upon all Christians who live alongside neighbors of other religious traditions.

Such learning becomes imperative now that religious communities and individuals are becoming religiously multiple. Woe to Christian preachers who believe that the work of interreligious engagement begins only *after* Sunday worship! Given the presence in the pews of intermarried families, every word spoken within Christian worship is at least implicitly an interreligious word. What are Jews present with their Christian partners to make of derogatory Christian preaching about the Pharisees? In our context, such challenges must be addressed collaboratively with the communities whose lives are being affected by the complex problems that attend navigating pluralistic

---

[28] Of course, I am not aiming to generate an exhaustive list here. Other constructive theologians will want to recognize other tasks as falling within the ambit of constructive theology.

public life. Interreligious conflict generated by anti-Semitism and Islamophobia has theological roots and, therefore, naturally requires theological solutions.

How does learning from religious neighbors become theological knowledge proper? After all, one can imagine comparative religionists and ethnographers also prizing collaborative learning. Interreligious learning becomes properly theological when what is learned enriches or transforms antecedent theological commitments, convictions, and practices. Such learning is the distinctive labor of comparative theology that engages in constructive theology through learning with and from neighbors of other religious traditions. Comparative theologians draw the conclusion that follows from inclusivist and pluralist theologies of religious diversity (TRD). For some decades now, theologians of religious diversity have argued that religious truth and transformation is present outside the church and in the religious scriptures, traditions, and practices of other traditions and not just in righteous persons. If one concludes that knowledge of ultimate reality, world, and human being is available in other religious traditions, no rational justification exists to delimit theological inquiry to Christian sources alone.

Indeed, genealogists of religion have dismantled the notion of impermeable boundaries between Christianity and "other religious traditions"; they have taught us that world religions discourse is no older than the nineteenth century. To hold that the world contains a set of discrete "world religions," each with its own tightly integrated religious grammar that makes interreligious learning impossible or nonsensical—including wisdom from other traditions in mine would be like incorporating elements of football into chess because both are games—is part of a recent historical project of creating world religions to rank order them. This recent discourse belies the long historical process of learning between Jews, Christians, and Muslims, not to mention early Christian learning from Hellenistic philosophical and religious traditions. In sum, despite a long history of interreligious learning, Christian theologians have become beholden to a questionable discourse about world religions that has erected boundaries between religions. The rupture of world religions discourse and the reality of globalized religious diversity has brought about a new situation for constructive theology.[29]

Here, constructive theology faces some of its most demanding challenges as it moves forward into uncharted territory. Heretofore, Christian theology has proceeded by appeal to internal sources and norms. Of course, the challenge to "the household of authority" has unmoored and complicated Christian theological deliberation. Still, the introduction of new sources and norms now derived from non-Christian traditions further complexifies theological labor. What is the status of non-Christian scriptures for Christian theology? What is the status of knowledge claims derived from experiences of ultimate reality reported by practitioners of other religious traditions? None of these questions has prefabricated answers. No appeal to the Christian past as establishing definitive precedents can be persuasive given the relative novelty of these questions. Constructive theologians must venture proposals that require testing in communities of conversation.

---

[29] For a full book-length defense of these claims, see my *Circling the Elephant: A Comparative Theology of Religious Diversity* (New York: Fordham University Press, 2020).

How? Again, no simple answer exists given the scale of the questions at stake. An entire theological subdiscipline, comparative theology, is aborning to meet the challenge. Most comparative theologians commend a turn to specificity: proceed piecemeal by focusing on particular themes, texts, and figures. Pick a theme such as the human predicament, and explore it in the thinking of two thinkers. Read two concrete texts together and track the transformations that take place in the theologian and the theologian's community. Undertake disciplined practice in a tradition other than one's own and write theology that emerges as a fruit of such practice. Engage in close ethnographic study of local religious communities and write theology thereafter. Engage in specific projects of interreligious learning but without ever losing sight of the liberative goals of emancipatory movements such as feminist theology and Dalit theology. These are among the compelling possibilities articulated by comparative theologians who also understand themselves to be constructive theologians.

The implications for theopoetics of the interreligious turn defy description. Perhaps the greatest gift to be offered by other religious vocabularies are bold new symbolic possibilities. Christian traditions have largely operated by way of theistic symbols that configure ultimate reality as personal agent. Theism has been the de facto and de jure setting for much of Christian discourse despite routine eruptions of ground of being discourse. Engagement with religious traditions of South and East Asia and indigenous traditions vastly expands the theopoetic possibilities beyond personal agent theism. The promise of this expansion is beyond imagining.

Conclusion

The variety and scope of the challenges facing contemporary theologians should suffice to show why the adjective "constructive" is fitting. It should also signal that constructive theology is a vast assemblage of projects bound together by a recognition of the unfinished and ongoing nature of theological reflection. What binds constructive theologians together are certain orientations and habits rather than a fixed set of methods. These orientations and habits include commitments to contextuality, experimentality, fallibility, and creativity. After all, no single "method" can tie together the constructive work of comparative theologians working on Buddhist-Christian dialogue, theologians working on the meaning of AI, or theologians considering animal suffering across millennia of evolutionary history. Therefore, constructive theologians seem by disposition not to be doctrinaire about how theology ought to be done. If contesting strong accounts of theological authority is a hallmark of constructive theology, how could it be otherwise?

My particular contribution to thinking about constructive theology in this chapter has been attention to theopoetics both in the general sense of attending to framing metaphors and in the special sense of divine–human collaboration. Theological concepts are enlivened by the undergirding metaphoric and symbolic structures within which they are housed. No amount of conceptual labor can restore concepts that are animated by and take their meaning from dead symbols that are no longer musical. Attention to and then a hopeful, faithful, and creative participation in the divinely initiated coming of the new is what marks theology as constructive.

Bibliography

Boys, Mary. *Has God Only One Blessing: Judaism as a Source of Christian Self-Understanding*. Mahwah, NJ: Paulist, 2000.
Farley, Edward. *Divine Empathy: A Theology of God*. Minneapolis, MN: Fortress, 1996.
Farley, Edward. *Ecclesial Reflection: An Anatomy of Theological Method*. Minneapolis, MN: Fortress, 1982.
Ford, David. "Where Is Wise Theological Creativity to Be Found? Thoughts on 25 Years of Modern Theology and the Twenty-First Century Prospect." *Modern Theology* 26:1 (January 2010).
Hart, Ray. *Unfinished Man and the Theological Imagination: Toward an Ontology and a Rhetoric of Revelation*. New York: Herder and Herder, 1968.
Helmer, Christine. *Theology and the End of Doctrine*. Louisville, KY: Westminster John Knox, 2014.
Kaufman, Gordon. *God, Mystery, Diversity: Christian Theology in a Pluralistic World*. Minneapolis, MN: Fortress, 1996.
Keller, Catherine. *Intercarnations: Exercises in Theological Possibility*. New York: Fordham University Press, 2017.
Keller, Catherine, and Laurel Schneider. *Polydoxy: Theology of Multiplicity and Relation*. London: Routledge, 2010.
Knitter, Paul. *Introducing Theologies of Religion*. Maryknoll, NY: Orbis, 2002.
McFague, Sallie. *The Body of God: An Ecological Theology*. Minneapolis, MN: Fortress, 1993.
Meyer, Eric Daryl. *Inner Animalities: Theology and the End of the Human*. New York: Fordham University Press, 2018.
Reinhartz, Adele. *Cast Out of the Covenant: Jews and Anti-Judaism in the Gospel of John*. Minneapolis, MN: Fortress, 2018.
Rodríguez, Rubén Rosario. *Dogmatics after Babel: Beyond the Theologies of Word and Culture*. Louisville, KY: Westminster John Knox, 2018.
Ruether, Rosemary Radford. *Gaia and God: An Ecofeminist Theology of Earth Healing*. New York: HarperCollins, 1992.
Ruether, Rosemary Radford. *Sexism and God-Talk: Toward a Feminist Theology*. Boston, MA: Beacon, 1993.
Tanner, Kathryn. *Theories of Culture: A New Agenda for Theology*. Minneapolis, MN: Fortress, 1997.
Thatamanil, John. *Circling the Elephant: A Comparative Theology of Religious Diversity*. New York: Fordham University Press, 2020.
Tinker, George E. *Missionary Conquest: The Gospel and Native American Cultural Genocide*. Minneapolis, MN: Augsburg Fortress, 1993.
Tonstad, Linn. *Queer Theology: Beyond Apologetics*. Eugene, OR: Cascade Books, 2018.
Wyman, Jason. *Constructing Constructive Theology*. Minneapolis, MN: Fortress, 2017.

3

Methodological Themes and Patterns in Constructive Theologies

Marion Grau

In *Braiding Sweetgrass: Indigenous Wisdom, Scientific Knowledge, and the Teachings of Plants*, the American environmental botanist Robin Wall Kimmerer proposes that the creation story of her ancestral Potawatomi people, Skywoman Falling, adds a crucial element to weaving together indigenous wisdom and scientific knowledge, threading together mythos and logos. Skywoman survives her fall only with the courageous and self-sacrificing love and care of turtle and muskrat, other species that allow her to begin to develop an ecosystem to feed her people. The principle of reciprocity and the understanding that all living things are mutually dependent on each other are central in the world of this creation myth. Wall Kimmerer reconstructs the myth of Skywoman Falling as humanity faces climate change, saying that from "the very beginning of the world, the other species were a lifeboat for people. Now, we must be theirs."[1] She then compares the myth of Skywoman to that of Eve and how these female characters are framed. "Look at the legacy of poor Eve's exile from Eden: the land shows the bruises of an abusive relationship."[2] In a similar way, constructive theologians have been engaged in "re-story-ation,"[3] in reconstructive theological work engaging with the founding myths and histories of Christian theological traditions, critically analyzing where they have been deployed as weapons against other members of the human or creation community.

Theology as Mytho-logy and Theopoetics

Creation myths are told around the world. They describe the energies of the cosmos, the powers of deities or gods, the elements, or important ancestors and relationships. Communities retell ancestral stories to name what is sacred, what needs to be protected, and what is dangerous and provide guidance to new generations by offering guiding

---

[1] Robin Wall Kimmerer, *Braiding Sweetgrass: Indigenous Wisdom, Scientific Knowledge, and the Teachings of Plants* (Minneapolis, MN: Milkweed Editions, 2013), 8.
[2] Ibid., 9.
[3] Ibid.

principles. Creation myths map, tell, advise, shape, and indoctrinate communities through the power of myth. Theologies manifest as stories and narratives of the sacred and of divine action in the world. Constructive theologians are invested in tracing and mapping such histories, translations, and shifts in meaning, to give a more reflective account of narrations of the sacred. Understanding the historic location and obligations of theological thinking means coming to terms with the formative force of the conditions of empires past and present on images of God and power.

Myth as Genre and Resource of Theology

The Greek concepts mythos and logos have been central to understanding Christian theology. In Western philosophical traditions these terms have often been cast as opposites: mythos as nonfactual untruth and logos as factual truth.[4] They have been linked to hierarchical dualisms that can involve gender and ethnicity, associating certain forms of reasoning to one group and to another myth. The valuing and devaluing of certain forms of knowledge as mythological (and thus unsophisticated or unreliable) and others as logical and factual shapes (and sophisticated and reliable) sifts and sorts forms of knowledge and meaning-making in particular ways, including the danger of irresponsibility to certain voices considered to be less factual or logical.[5] Yet, neither form of expression should be summarily dismissed. Scientific and economic reductionisms—claims that technology or financial profit override all other human needs—are narratives that claim to be "factual" but are also matters of construction and ideology.

More helpfully, mythos and logos can be viewed as akin to different genres, making different kinds of truth claims rather than making either true or false claims. Myth is one way in which human communities reason and imagine through the values and beliefs that structure a community. This can allow a community to process and reorient beliefs and behaviors to ever-changing contexts, political and economic transitions, and migrations and constructively address crises they experience.[6]

Despite theology's dependence on the structures of mythos, it is Christ the Logos in Johannine constructions that was eventually positioned as the core principle of the structure of Christian history.[7] This logocentrism was also articulated as a colonial

---

[4] For a detailed account of this shifting relationship, see Ingolf U. Dalferth, *Jenseits von Mythos und Logos: Die Christologische Transformation der Theologie*, Quaestiones Disputatae vol. 142 (Freiburg: Herder, 1993).

[5] As a response to the challenges of post-Newtonian science and the questions raised by the development of the modern university, liberal theologians traced a path between anti-scientific, fundamentalist attitudes and the complete dismissal of religious and theological truth claims with changing forms of knowledge. One of the main points of contention was the way in which myth and mythological elements in sacred texts were to be read in the context of other modes of thinking and reading. That is, one of the key central issues in modern Western theological debates was a hermeneutical concern, the issue of the interpretation of mythos and logos. For a detailed account of this history, see Gary Dorrien, *The Word as True Myth: Interpreting Modern Theology* (Louisville, KY: Westminster John Knox, 1997).

[6] Jason Wyman, *Constructing Constructive Theology* (Minneapolis, MN: Fortress, 2017), 20.

[7] Dalferth, *Jenseits von Mythos und Logos*, 76.

supersession of the Christian logos over the pagan mythos. Myths were seen in a diachronic view as prehistoric, precivilized, prescientific modes of narration primarily originating from the Orient—and read in an orientalist fashion—that is synchronically by peoples that were considered inferior in their rationality.[8] Constructive theologians have contributed toward corrective theologies as mytho-logy that expands the ways of thinking mythos and logos in relationship.

Some modern theologians pursued a recovery of myth as a valid form of narrativity, indeed as "central for theology."[9] Paul Tillich wanted to retain myth not as an inferior disposable form of religious expression, but an essential component of human life and thought:

> If mythology is in its essence a cultural creation like science, art, law, it is difficult to understand why it should be destroyed, indeed it is impossible that it should decline, for it has its own proper and necessary place in the meaningful structure of life.[10]

Many constructive theologians agree with Niebuhr and Tillich in their critique of liberalism's rejection of myth. Tillich argued that myth, "far from having disappeared, has only altered its form" and that conflicts around what kind of discourse is reliable stand not between myth and a presumed bias-free factual account, but rather between different types of myths.[11] Thus, myths, far from being superseded along with the "primitive" prerationality that supposedly accompanied them—imagined in some enlightenment fantasies[12]—have proliferated, even (or especially) in seemingly rationalist, scientific, economistic settings.

Telling More Compelling Myths

A powerful myth can be highly resistant to rational counterarguments and may better be countered by another, more compelling myth.[13] Constructive theologians aim to deploy a combination of different, more compelling myths, historical contextualizations, and the best knowledge available in a contemporary context to reconstruct theological teachings. Some of the tools of constructive theology involve finding ways to speak of the divine that embrace a variety of forms of wisdom and knowing, but that develop fruitful and dynamic ways of critically discerning them. Some of these approaches include remythologization, the rearticulation of mythological layers of meaning

---

[8] Ibid., 109.
[9] Wyman, *Constructing Constructive Theology*, 19.
[10] Paul Tillich, "The Religious Symbol," in *Symbolism in Religion and Literature*, Rollo May (New York: George Braziller, 1960), 84.
[11] Ibid.
[12] Thus, it has been argued that tales of the supersession of mythos by logos correspond to the self-mythologization of certain forms of philosophy and its supposed accomplishments. Dalferth, *Jenseits von Mythos und Logos*, 25.
[13] Ibid., 24.

along with the scientific and the religious alongside the secular.[14] Serene Jones writes that theology is "a place and a story," a form of human storytelling about meaning, the world, and the possibility of God.[15] Weaving together different types of creation narratives, for example, is a time-honored practice found in biblical, apocryphal, and gnostic texts, and in the transcultural adaptations throughout history, such as in Wall Kimmerer's juxtaposition of Skywoman with Eve.

There is little to be won by giving up myth for historical accounts, or vice versa. Rather, the question that remains is of the kinds of productive relationships between history and myth that we can imagine. Constructive theology's task can be described as a "theopoesis of material solidarity," moving toward the dream of God for greater flourishing for all creatures and pushing the "edge of perpetual materialization."[16] Theopoesis then is a "matter not of believing but of making, materializing God."[17] This work cannot be done by any single theologian or any single group. It is critically enhanced by voices of many from across the globe to articulate within and across context. Critically aware of the power of their fraught traditions and the ways in which narratives of any kind, and perhaps in particular religious and mythological narratives, have been used to support forms of oppression, constructive theologians continue to seek the elusive Divine as a force of liberation rather than enslavement.

Constructive theologians offer reflective narrativity about faith in intercontextual, intercultural, and interreligious modes pointing toward a gospel that may be infinitely translatable but never "universal."

Engaging Classical Impulses and Sources

Constructive theologians tend to find Anselm's classic description of theology as *fides quaerens intellectum*, faith seeking understanding useful. This involves seeking to understand faith in context, probing both faith and doubt through people's experiences, narratives, and beliefs, as well as to communicate these to new generations, and if necessary suggest changes in speech and action. Like many theologians on the moderate to progressive continuum, constructive theologians draw—with varying emphases— on the four sources of theology: Scripture, Tradition, Reason, and Experience. Each theologian will have different emphases, depending on the weight a particular tradition lays on either scripture, tradition, or experience. Each of these four classical sources have to be read and interpreted. Thus theological work includes a number of complex hermeneutical actions. Seeking understanding includes the provision of credible accounts for the multiple narratives and religious traditions that flow together

---

[14] This has also been proposed by Teilhard the Chardin and Sallie McFague. Cf. Dorrien, *Word as True Myth*, 223; and Sallie McFague, *The Body of God: An Ecological Theology* (Minneapolis, MN: Fortress, 1993), 81.

[15] Serene Jones, *Call It Grace: Finding Meaning in a Fractured World* (New York: Viking/Random House, 2019), xi.

[16] For a genealogy of constructive theology as *theopoesis*, see chapter 6 in Catherine Keller, *Intercarnations: Exercises in Theological Possibility* (New York: Fordham University Press, 2017), 116.

[17] Ibid., 117.

in communities, while offering a resolute prophetic witness. Whether these efforts are considered credible to those that engage them depends on their historical, ethical, and theological accountability to flourishing of all lives on the planet.[18]

A Critical Historical Consciousness

In some sense, constructive theologians' assumption that history matters and that theology has a history, is rewritten, and has a historical context, is a commitment to historicism.[19] Through a critical historical account of theology with a constructive lens, it becomes quickly visible that critiques of empire are intermittent, and gender hierarchies and racial and ethnic biases are embedded both in method and content. Like contextual theology, historical critical readings insist on the importance of understanding history for understanding the present: "Historians began to place events into contexts and to seek to delineate networks of relations as a way to understand history."[20] History shapes nations, communities, and persons, and the study of theological history helps in understanding context, development, and power relations impacting a text or a doctrine over time.

Constructive theologians engage the past in critical ways, with the concerns of the ancient texts and ancestors in faith. Ignoring the history of theological thought would be akin to denying we share much of the DNA of our ancestors, physically and mentally. Ignoring those histories would put us in danger of repeating those patterns of thinking and acting. This commitment to critical history is generally borne out through a historicist inflection, understanding theology as a product of history in a particular place, while maintaining its ability to speak a cross-historical truth.

> Many constructive theologians employ the findings of historical criticism, or from the hermeneutic-literary standpoint, utilize historicist or new historicist modes of reading.[21]

Many constructive theologians thus engage biblical studies that use historical critical methods, not just a provincial, modern Western European preoccupation, but as a heritage and commitment at least back to Augustine, whose rhetorical education led him to use hermeneutical methods that look at text, context, and history of tradition.

Constructive theology stands in the tradition of the Western Latin extraction and picks up major theo-ethical impulses from the liberating traditions, abolitionists that sought to contest and end slavery and work for the equality of women, and later those theologians and activists that worked for the liberation of the poor and racialized

---

[18] Michelle Voss Roberts, ed., *Comparing Faithfully: Insights for Systematic Theological Reflection* (New York: Fordham University Press, 2016), 9.
[19] Sheila Greeve Davaney, *Historicism: The Once and Future Challenge for Theology* (Minneapolis, MN: Fortress, 2006), 1. See also Christine Helmer, "The Contemporary Constructive Task," *Dialog* 56, no. 3 (Fall 2017): 218–22.
[20] Davaney, *Historicism*, 13.
[21] Wyman, *Constructing Constructive Theology*, 96.

peoples. These theologies stand in tension with more conservative and authoritarian strands of the Christian tradition at least since the time the Christian faith was declared the imperial religion by Constantine.

In his account of constructive theology, Jason Wyman lists four typical characteristics of constructive theologies so far: They (1) are persistently open-ended, (2) share an understanding that theology is the work of human construction, (3) are predominantly doctrinally based, and (4) tend to be suspicious of the attempt to create coherent and conclusive systems.[22] To this minimal definition, many will want to add the dimension of constructive theology as a counterhegemonic and anti-oppressive discourse.

Ideally, constructive theologians seek to learn from other churches and religious traditions, are often involved in ecumenical and interreligious conversations, and develop theologies that seek a liberating and antidiscriminatory way of living within this ambivalent and often violent heritage. Seeking theological wisdom through discursive community and narrativity aims toward reconstructive imagining.

Constructive theologians tend to assume that many people and contexts can make valuable contributions to theology. Theological articulations are thus susceptible to changes of language, culture, politics, and economic-ecological conditions. Thus, in Keller's language, such "intercarnations" signal the "boundlessly entangled materiality," preoccupied with "theological bodies diversely female, animal, vegetable, mineral, religious, irreligious, cosmic and cosmopolitan."[23]

A Metaphorical Approach to Theological Hermeneutics

Sallie McFague's *Metaphorical Theology* helped frame one way in which constructive theologies are using theological language, how it functions, and how models of God frame the understanding of who God is.[24] Feminist theologians insisted that "many models of God are necessary, among them feminine models, in order both to avoid idolatry and to include the experience of all peoples in our language about God."[25] A metaphor has similarities but also dissimilarities and is used to describe what humans experience as recognizable from their own world of experience.

This variation on the theme of Thomas of Aquinas's analogy of being as the rule that guides theological language is offered as an alternative to understand how language about God relates to what it attempts to describe. McFague attempted to chart a middle course between the idea of an utterly transcendent and therefore unknowable God, and a natural theology that espoused a basic trust in human experience as an acceptable, if flawed, medium from within which to articulate language about God. She further proposed that such models and metaphors need to be multiple, alive, and open in order to continue to represent new forms of inspiration and insight and move

---

[22] Ibid., 67.
[23] Keller, *Intercarnations*, 2.
[24] Sallie McFague, *Metaphorical Theology: Models of God in Religious Language* (Philadelphia, PA: Fortress, 1982). Note also the contribution of Vanderbilt theologians Edward Farley and Peter C. Hodgson to the development of the discourse.
[25] Ibid., 10.

beyond the dominant masculine metaphors for God in main theological traditions. This multiplicity of images and openness to expressions includes the rejection of limitations to how God can be named or described.

Apophatic Hermeneutics

A number of constructive theologians consider themselves to be in the legacy of apophatic, or negative, theology, admitting to the impossibility of ever knowing the Divine fully. Keller, for example, asserts that "theology is *riddled* with uncertainty"[26] that "takes responsibility for its own constructions" while facing "the glowing darkness of a puzzling unknowability."[27] This double commitment, to uncertainty and responsibility, shapes constructive theology. The sense of divine unknowability is hardly new—*apophasis* has been a reminder of the insufficiency of all theological articulation at least since Pseudo-Dionysius and Gregory of Nyssa. And it contains a warning to not fall into the temptation to take our own conclusions for the word and will of the Divine. This quality, which is hardly unique to constructive theological approaches, may be related to the resistance to the creation of a system, though not identical with it and not generally considered to be in tension with the commitment to metaphorical theology. Rather, it represents a constant reminder of the limitations of all theological metaphors and images.

Theology Has Political Implications

Many constructive theologians assume that all theological utterances have political implications and there is no such thing as a politically neutral theology. Theologies have helped shaped ideas about the relationship between church and state, about justice and law, about political and economic systems in both Western and Eastern Christian contexts. More recently, conservative political and religious actors have worked to influence elections, governments, and law in Latin America, the United States, and other places. These actors have countered and undermined the influence of theologies that support democracy and human rights, as well as liberation theologies, and have sided with right-wing candidates exhibiting misogynist toxic masculinity in several political processes, including but not only Brazil, Australia, and various locations in Asia and Africa. Even a theology that supports the status quo or a quietist theology has a political effect, that of supporting the powers that be.

Images of God as king who has to be obeyed can tend to reinscribe such use of power as normative. They can be countered such as by claiming that God is the real king over against any worldly authority, but often even there, the image of God is of a unilateral agent, without a sense of mutuality and care.[28] What form of power God

---

[26] Keller, *Intercarnations*, 113; emphasis in the original.
[27] Ibid., 114.
[28] Thanks to the work of Mary Daly, Elizabeth Johnson, and James Cone, following generations of theologians have a clearer idea of how the symbol of God functions. See Mary Daly, *Beyond God*

has, and what kind of government humans should espouse is indeed still, even after supposed secularism, a highly relevant question in many settings, including those where nationalist and reactionary forces are using ancient religious traditions as tools to legitimate their grasp for power. Theologies manifest as either counterhegemonic or hegemonic, complicit in maintaining the status quo, or questioning the powers that be. For even when theologies appear "neutral," they generally either support the status quo or hide or deemphasize their political implications. Politicians and rulers regularly use religious wedge issues to divide and conquer and distract from other concerns. Narrowing ethical concerns to the issues of abortion and homosexuality have been employed to distract from larger issues such as the climate crisis and the power of fossil fuel interests that have often been associated with religious conservativism where petroleum industry funded climate denialism has flourished.[29] These wedge issues have been promulgated over the course of several decades, especially among Christian conservatives, and it seems hard to counter certain theo-political narratives, especially as moneyed interests heavily fund petroleum interests.[30]

The Commitment to Liberation

The insistence that theologians must take into consideration the suffering of people and other members of the creation community and consider what their theological and ethnical response to that suffering is stands at the core of liberation theology. From Batholome de Las Casas's critical report on Spanish colonial forces' treatment of indigenous peoples in the Americas, to Martin Luther's insistence that the Bible be accessible to the people of the land so that they can hear, understand, and interpret in their own language, to abolition, suffrage, counterimperial, and civil rights struggles, and the Latin American liberation theologians Ernesto Cardenal and Gustavo Gutierrez, theologies that have challenged authorities have taken many forms.[31]

Often, such theological expressions involve a hermeneutic shift in how the texts of the tradition are read. In their introduction to liberation perspectives on systematic theology, Sobrino and Ellacuria suggest that the German historicist critical method of reading biblical texts helped to rediscover the reign of God as the central message

---

the Father: Toward a Philosophy of Women's Liberation (Boston, MA: Beacon, 1973); Elizabeth A. Johnson, She Who Is: The Mystery of God in Feminist Theological Discourse (New York: Crossroad, 1992); and James Cone, God of the Oppressed (Maryknoll, NY: Orbis, 1997).

[29] See, for example, Darren Dochuk, Anointed with Oil: How Christianity and Crude Made Modern America (New York: Basic Books, 2019).

[30] Scholars that have documented these connections are, among other, Randall Ballmer, Jeff Sharlet, and Robert P. Jones. See in particular Randall Balmer's article on the connection between white supremacy, antiabortion, anti-LGBT sentiment among American conservative Christians. Randall Balmer, "The Real Origins of the Religious Right: They'll Tell You It Was Abortion. Sorry, the Historical Record's Clear: It Was Segregation," Politico, May 27, 2014, https://www.politico.com/magazine/story/2014/05/religious-right-real-origins-107133.

[31] This promoted literacy and people's own potential access to sacred texts. It was of course no accident that slaves were often forbidden to learn to read, for the Bible was generally the major text used to teach reading. More women and more slaves were able to read, leading to the struggles of abolition and suffrage, and against abuses of power from wherever they came.

of Jesus of Nazareth.[32] In his reflection on the method of liberation theology, Clodovis Boff suggests that the perspective of the liberation of the poor affects all angles of theology, that this particular viewpoint accompanies all theological deliberation.[33] It does this not to the exclusion or in opposition to other theological concerns but in "critical complementarity" to other theological ventures.[34] It is the concrete historical experience of the poor and particular forms of injustice rather than the more abstract terms and concepts that are key in the work of liberation theology.[35] Such theology must emerge from action and lead to action, Boff argues.[36] Others have argued that this move toward the theology of experience "politicized the churches" while it democratized theology as the work of the people.[37]

The early constructive theology group felt a more natural affinity to liberal theology than liberation theology.[38] Composed initially of all white men and no women, it took a while for other social locations and forms of embodied experience to find room within the discourse.[39] Indeed, it took several incarnations of the Constructive Work Group to more fully embrace the principles of liberation theologies. The Workgroup on Constructive Theology named several issues that are key to the future development of theological work: ecological theology, economic and structural violence, gender, race, countering the colonial legacy of theology, and authoritarian tendencies in historic and contemporary politics.[40] With a new set of members, though primarily European American, who were already committed to liberation agendas, this began to shift and it became apparent that liberation theologies often contain aspects of a critique of liberal theology.[41]

The sources of Black liberation theology are black people's lived experiences of God's presence in suffering and liberating exodus acts.[42] Yet, for Delores Williams and other black women, the exodus was not a liberative metaphor. Instead, surviving as sisters in the wilderness was.[43] At times, survival is the key metaphor, rather than liberation. Black Women may need to name the black Christ in different ways than black men.[44] Or, in the case of disability theology, surviving rather than being healed or

---

[32] Introduction to Jon Sobrino and Ignacio Ellacuria, eds., *Systematic Theology: Perspectives from Liberation Theology* (Maryknoll, NY: Orbis, 1993).
[33] Clodovis Boff, "Methodology of the Theology of Liberation," in *Systematic Theology: Perspectives from Liberation Theology*, ed. Jon Sobrino and Ignacio Ellacuria (Maryknoll, NY: Orbis, 1993), 1.
[34] Ibid., 5.
[35] Ibid., 6.
[36] Ibid., 20.
[37] Elaine Graham, Heather Walton, and Frances Ward, *Theological Reflection: Methods* (London: SCM, 2005), 3.
[38] Wyman mentions the case of Gordan Kaufman, who maps out the basic premises of constructive theology, but falls short of going the route into a larger space of liberation. Wyman, *Constructing Constructive Theology*, 40.
[39] Ibid., 36.
[40] Susan Abraham, "Decolonizing Christianity," in *The Task of Theology: Leading Theologians on the Most Compelling Questions for Today*, ed. Anselm K. Min (Maryknoll, NY: Orbis, 2014), 180.
[41] Wyman, *Constructing Constructive Theology*, 36, 70.
[42] Cone, *God of the Oppressed*.
[43] Delores Williams, *Sisters in the Wilderness: The Challenge of Womanist God-Talk* (Maryknoll, NY: Orbis Books, 1993).
[44] Kelly Brown Douglas, *The Black Christ* (Maryknoll, NY: Orbis, 1994).

paternalized by the world around.⁴⁵ Metaphors need shifting and reinterpretation, or have to be challenged by others. The different perspectives can both enrich and focus too narrowly. None of them alone can fully describe people's experiences of divine presence and agency. These perspectives become richer, wiser, and perhaps truer, one might discover, if held in conversation with each other.

If liberation theologies have played a part in the history of constructive theologies, it is, however, also important to consider the way in which Latin American liberation theologies have changed and been challenged over the decades. Nancy Bedford, Ivan Petrella, and Marcella Althaus-Reid each represent the challenges to classical Latin American liberation theology.⁴⁶ In Europe, the Roman Catholic theologians Stefan Silber,⁴⁷ Judith Gruber,⁴⁸ and Sebastian Pittl,⁴⁹ among others continue to foster European engagements with liberation and postcolonial theologies in Latin America and elsewhere. Liberation theologies themselves have evolved, are being formulated across the world, and are increasingly sensitive to the danger of paternalisms and more open to postcolonial and intersectional approaches that look at interlocking forms of oppression, such as the way in which race, gender, and class interact to compound oppression.⁵⁰

Constructive Theologizing: Polydox, Contextual, and Intercontextual

The term "polydoxy"⁵¹ refers to the fact that even expressions of faith that are considered credally "orthodox" room multiple rather than singular theologies, and thus contain a breadth of expressions of faith, rather referring to merely one correct articulation. Thus "multiplicity itself," Keller and Schneider write, "has become theology's resource" as a "responsible pluralism of interdependence and uncertainty" can function as

---

[45] Nancy Eiesland, *The Disabled God: Toward a Liberatory Theology of Disability* (Nashville, TN: Abingdon, 1994).
[46] Nancy Bedford, "Little Moves against Destructiveness: Theology and the Practice of Discernment," in *Practicing Theology: Beliefs and Practices in Christian Life*, ed. Miroslav Volf and Dorothy C. Bass (Grand Rapids, MI: Eerdmanns, 2002), 157–81; Marcella Althaus-Reid, *Indecent Theology: Theological Perversions in Sex, Gender and Politics* (London: Routledge, 2001).
[47] See, for example, Stefan Silber: "Poscolonialismo. Introducción a los estudios y las teologías poscoloniales (El tiempo que no perece 3)," Cochabamba: Itinerarios/CMMAL 2018; or Stefan Silber and José María Vigil, eds., "Liberation Theology in Europe/La Teología de la Liberación en Europa," *Voices* 40 (November–December 2017) 2.
[48] See Judith Gruber, *Intercultural Theology: Exploring World Christianity after the Cultural Turn* (Vandenhoeck: Göttingen, 2017).
[49] See Sebastian Pittl. *Geschichtliche Realität und Kreuz: Der fundamentale Ort der Theologie bei Ignacio Ellacuría*, Ratio fidei 67 (Regensburg: Pustet, 2018); and "Alma mater pauperum? Ein fiktives Gespräch zwischen Berlin und El Salvador zur gesellschaftlichen Verantwortung sowie zu einer möglichen Option für die Armen an der Universität heute," in *Theologie der Befreiung heute, Herausforderungen–Transformationen–Impulse*, ed. Franz Gmainer-Pranzl, Sandra Lassak, and Birgit Weiler (Innsbruck: Tyrolia, 2017), 547–70.
[50] Patricia Hill Collins and Sirma Bilge, *Intersectionality* (Cambridge: Polity, 2016), 2.
[51] Catherine Keller and Laurel Schneider, eds., *Polydoxy: Theology of Multiplicity and Relation* (London: Routledge, 2010).

a baseline requirement for theology, rather than a detriment to its integrity.[52] This includes constructive theology's transdenominational and ecumenical qualities. Constructive theologians include a variety of traditions that learn from and challenge each other: Roman Catholics, Lutherans, Presbyterians and other Reformed traditions, Anglicans and Episcopalians, Wesleyans and Methodists, Baptists, to just name a few.[53]

To call any form of theology contextual is increasingly a tautology. The argument that all theology is contextual and the history of theology a "series of local theologies" (Schreiter) was articulated within missiology by the likes of Schreiter and Bevans. Bevans, for example, argues that "every genuine theology is a contextual theology."[54] The argument is so compelling that it has become the consensus among many.

A comparative, translational activity stands at the crossroads of religious and cultural worlds. Some compare to conquer, some to understand, some to engage and transform. In some ways, more so than so-called classic systematic theology, mission studies have had to consciously cross borders of language, perception, and conceptuality. It is thus perhaps no surprise that missiologists such as Robert Schreiter, Stephen Bevans, and Andrew Walls have considered the layering of contextual theologies, the structuring of local theologies in ways that have brought the "center" and "margins" of theological thinking closer together and made them more relatable to each other. Constructive theologies tend to be explicitly contextual, that is, they work from, critically engage, and analyze their context. While all theologies arise from and refer to their context, constructive theologies make themselves accountable to communities that tend to be excluded or marginalized.

At the same time, constructive theologies can be relevant beyond the immediate context in which they are formulated, though they make no claim to universality. The relevance of theological thinking to more than one context can be described as intercontextual. Stephen Bevans has used the term "intercontextual" to talk about the need that contexts inform each other mutually.[55] Perhaps in a parallel to intersectionality, intercontextuality might, for example, mean that each community works to dismantle antiblack racism, whether they are white, Asian, or Hispanic. There is great value to be drawn from both intercontextual and intersectional reflection in the work with local theologies. Whether theological frames are formulated in North or South, East or West, resisting authoritarian images of God and hence challenge authoritarian political theologies is a common feature.

The experiences of several communities can be relevant and make a claim on our own theological context. The suffering of others may be an impetus for changing a theology that has ignored, justified, or even legitimized the suffering of others. This means that even if a particular concern does not affect my community directly, there may be a prophetic claim that the suffering of others must matter to my community and therefore may be a moral obligation to change a local theology.

---

[52] Catherine Keller and Laurel Schneider, "Introduction," in *Polydoxy: Theology of Multiplicity and Relation*, ed. Catherine Keller and Laurel Schneider (London: Routledge, 2010), 1.
[53] Wyman, *Constructing Constructive Theology*, 159.
[54] Stephen B. Bevans, *An Introduction to Theology in a Global Perspective*, Theology in Global Perspective Series (Maryknoll, MN: Orbis, 2009), 52.
[55] Stephen Bevans, *Essays in Contextual Theology* (Leiden: Brill, 2018), 178–9.

Intersectional Critical Analysis

Intersectional analysis[56] of a context and theological locus heightens the possibility that the theological framing allows for an expansive approach to socially transformative thought and action. This might mean, for example, that a reconstruction is not fully liberating if it only included gender, but ignores questions of race/ethnicity, class, or sexuality. This does not necessarily mean every reconstruction must address all possible angles equally. But it may suggest that a methodological exploration of the reconstruction should consider what particular approaches enhance or limit liberating potential. What the particular intersecting angles of a constructive theological project may be can differ widely, but the understanding that liberation and transformation are necessarily intersectional is an important point of learning of the past decades of theological conversations and practice.[57] Discernment of what the crucial and relevant intersectionalities for a project may be is a key part in going about constructive theological work.[58] In systematic and constructive theology, intersectional framing is often still unsatisfactory or entirely absent and thus an area of desired growth.

In the early years of the Workgroup on Constructive Theology, some theologians engaged in feminist theology and ecofeminist approaches, especially as a growing number of women entered. Liberation theological approaches appeared somewhat later as a larger concern for the workgroup.[59] While liberation theologians Sobrino and Ellacuria suggest that the historical critical reading of texts on the kingdom of God together with the historical suffering of the poor motivates their liberation theology, Wyman proposes that at least some black constructive theologians do not find historical approaches to theology "sufficient to account for contemporary Black experience."[60] Further developments are ongoing as the group goes through successive incarnations.

The term "constructive theology" is not restricted to the works of the US-based Workgroup on Constructive Theology, or those employing the term as a substitute for systematic of dogmatic theology. Scholars in practical theology, for example, can use the term to talk about methods of narrative theology. Some global ecumenical theologians use the term for their own work. That is, rather than beginning to think

---

[56] The term "intersectionality" was framed and popularized by Kimberlé Crenshaw in a 1991 article that was able to break through decade-long attempts to think race, gender, and class together. An intersectional approach is generally characterized by the understanding that several issues are connected in the fight toward greater social justice. That is, the way in which power is mapped and functions across individual and group identities, gender and race, sexism and sexuality, race and class, gender, race, and colonialism, etc. See Kimberlé Crenshaw, "Mapping the Margins: Intersectionality, Identity, Politics, and Violence against Women of Color," *Stanford Law Review* 43 (1991): 1241–99; and Collins and Bilge, *Intersectionality*, 81–7.

[57] See, for example, Grace Ji-Sun Kim and Susan M. Shaw, eds., *Intersectional Theology: An Introductory Guide* (Minneapolis, MN: Fortress, 2018).

[58] These learnings date back at least to the difficult interactions between Audre Lorde and Mary Daly around how gender and racial oppression intersect, or Musa Dube's key move in combining postcolonial and feminist analysis. Musa W. Dube, *Postcolonial Feminist Interpretation of the Bible* (St. Louis, MO: Chalice, 2000).

[59] Wyman, *Constructing Constructive Theology*, 121.

[60] Ibid., 132.

about inviting more scholars across the globe into the shared work of constructive theology, some have been using the term for themselves, and yet others are employing analogous methods without using the term. Contributions to constructive theology are not limited to the workgroup and subsequent theologians proceed to envision forms of community that transcend the barriers of historical prejudice, intergenerational trauma, and exclusionary thinking that mark all of our communities. The use of postcolonial and decolonial perspectives can function as prophetic contextualization. These perspectives offer theologies that engage biblical texts, history, that work intercontextually and seek wisdom from many places, especially from less prominent voices.

Interreligious and Comparative Theological Thinking

Some scholars working in comparative theology are associated with constructive theology, doing work that is relevant and useful to constructive theology. Michelle Voss Roberts has gathered a collection of essays by comparative theologians toward a "constructive comparative theology"[61] that aims to break through rigid institutional expressions and the growing hunger for spiritual depth by providing a greater understanding of the importance of interreligious thinking and the complexity of religious belonging and practice.[62] A key skill and practice for many whose identities are already being shaped by a reality of religious diversity is the holding of religious commitment with and appreciation of religious difference.[63] Comparative theology as constructive work participates in the interdisciplinarity through its own mix of disciplines, theories, and textual archives.[64] Like constructive theology, comparative theologies can appear unruly rather than firmly ordered, "rhizomatic" rather than a system.[65] The presence of a religious other can both destabilize theologies and hold accountable, while questions come from both sides in a world where complex relations require neighborliness that manifests as more than superficial familiarity.[66] These comparative constructions may also be part of the polydox nature of constructive theologies.

Resisting Christian Triumphalism and Supersessionism

Christian supersessionism and theological anti-Semitism have been long-standing tendencies endemic to much Christian theology. Constructive theologians ideally work in ways that dismantle rather than repeat anti-Judaistic stereotypes in critiquing

---

[61] Roberts, *Comparing Faithfully*, 3.
[62] Ibid., 1.
[63] Ibid., 4, 6.
[64] See also John J. Thatamanil, *Circling the Elephant: A Comparative Theology of Religious Diversity* (New York: Fordham University Press, 2020).
[65] Roberts, *Comparing Faithfully*, 13.
[66] Ibid., 11.

and reconstructing theological narratives. The legacy of Christian anti-Judaism and anti-Semitism continues to haunt the texts of the tradition, and therefore also many of the theologies that build upon these texts. This work is crucial for any anti-imperialist critiques of Israeli politics.[67] The anti-Semitisms of the political right and left flare up intermittently and careful attendance to the intergenerational trauma of Holocaust and anti-Semitism must be taken into consideration even as critiques of policies of the acts of government officials of Israel are formulated. Theological anti-Semitism is at times unconscious and often stems from religious illiteracy and other forms of religio-cultural ignorance, and uncritically repeated prejudices, conspiracy theories, and thought patterns. Jewish scholars and Christian exegetes have done much work on these issues, and constructive theologians have access to a wealth of good work by biblical scholars and historians.[68] This means that constructive theologies at their best are also aware of and counteracting the dangers of Christian supersessionism in their critiques of doctrine and in the process of reconstruction.

Indigenous Wisdom and Ecotheologies beyond Anthropocentrism

Some of the least represented voices in Western theologies for centuries dominated by Western European and European American voices are indigenous voices. Indigenous voices are, however, crucial for a post-/decolonial impetus that many constructive theologians are committed to.[69] Indigenous peoples suffer especially under exploitative and authoritarian regimes and have been targeted for their resistance against environmentally destructive projects, or just for their existence and desire to survive on the land they belong to, culturally and in their way of life. Important interruptions and critiques have come from North-American indigenous theological work by Vine Deloria Jr., George Tink Tinker, Jace Weaver, Stephen Charleston, and Richard Twiss, to name just a few.[70] If traditional theist discourses make much of the "religion–science" conversation, constructive theologies can also learn from indigenous science

---

[67] Such as, for example, offered by Mark Ellis or Santiago Slabodsky. Santiago Slabodsky, *Decolonial Judaism: Triumphal Failures of Barbaric Thinking* (New York: Palgrave, 2014).

[68] See, for example, John Dominic Crossan, *Who Killed Jesus? Exposing the Roots of Anti-Semitism in the Gospel Story of the Death of Jesus* (San Francisco, CA: HarperSanFransisco, 1995), and Amy-Jill Levine, *The Misunderstood Jew: The Church and the Scandal of the Jewish Jesus* (New York: HarperCollins, 2006) for exegetical approaches; and Clark Williamson, *A Guest in the House of Israel: Post-Holocaust Church Theology* (Louisville, KY: Westminster John Knox, 1993), and Kayko Driedger Hesslein, *Dual Citizenship: Two-Natures Christologies and the Jewish Jesus* (New York: Bloomsbury, 2015) for two constructive approaches to doctrine.

[69] Vine Jr. Deloria's *God Is Red: A Native View of Religion* (Golden, CO: Fulcrum, 1994) challenged and deconstructed white theology from an indigenous US perspective. See also constructive theologian Laurel Schneider's use of indigenous sources in Laurel C. Schneider, *Beyond Monotheism: A Theology of Multiplicity* (London: Routledge, 2008).

[70] For example, Deloria, *God Is Red*; Richard Twiss, *Rescuing the Gospel from the Cowboys: A Native American Expression of the Jesus Way* (Downer's Grove, IL: Intervarsity, 2015); and Steven Charleston and Elaine Robinson, eds., *Coming Full Circle: Constructing Native Christian Theology* (2015).

and wisdom, pedagogy and methodology.[71] This could be a counterforce to the legacy of anthropocentric and colonialist theologies that fail to see humans as part of a larger chain of cosmic relations.

The reality of environmental destruction and climate change brings home the need for truly transformative theologies, pedagogies, and practices of action and activism aligned with them. Ecotheologians such as John Cobb, Sallie McFague, Mark Wallace, and Catherine Keller were important contributors to the Workgroup on Constructive Theology, where ecological theologies were part of the fabric. The importance of transdisciplinary work in environmental theologies is only becoming more dramatic. Climate activist Naomi Klein has challenged readers by arguing that climate change "changes everything."[72] If one takes this seriously, it will affect theology produced in a constructive mode as it responds to the civilizational crisis we face, the climate being a primary material reality that affects all human endeavor and existence, as well as the contexts from which theological thinking emerges. Even more than before, constructive theologians are challenged to be more than merely contextual, that is, responsible to one's own context, but be able to formulate and map the great complexity of intersecting realities and interlocking contexts. One can argue that climate change and ecojustice ought to be some of the primary points of intersectionality in constructive theologies.

Decolonizing Theology: Deconstructing Divine Sovereignty and Other False Universals

Constructive theological work may be focused on a particular geography or a relatively homogenous population. Even so, it is possible to ask what the aspects of a counterimperial power analysis would be for a given project, or whether, in Habermas's phrasing, theologians use theology with "an emancipatory intent."[73] An account of Schleiermacher's theology, for example, would change if one considered his placement in a colonialist society where women were not fully empowered subjects, but some Jewish women converts were able to host salons that gathered the intellectuals of the day for the discussion of changing knowledge and thought regimes.

Yet many of these theological systems contained frameworks for exclusion and repression, with heavy biases against women, Jews, other ethnicities, and religions. Despite its basic constructive methodology, these theologies ultimately became engaged in the "monopolization of theology as a Eurocentric male field with the distinctive aim of building a system representing the totality of reality" and critiqued for the "implied universalizing imperatives."[74] This universalizing tendency, intended

---

[71] See, for example, Gregory Cajete, *Native Science: Natural Laws of Interdependence* (Santa Fe, NM: Clear Light, 2000), or Kimmerer, *Braiding Sweetgrass*. Constructive theologies may also be further broadened by making room for indigenous and decolonizing research methodologies, such as those proposed by Linda Tuhiwai Smith. See her *Decolonizing Methodologies: Research and Indigenous Peoples* (London: Zed Books, 1999).
[72] Naomi Klein, *This Changes Everything: Capitalism against Climate* (New York: Simon & Schuster, 2014).
[73] See, for example, Habermas's *A Communicative Theory of Action* (Boston: Beacon, 1985).
[74] Helmer, "The Contemporary Constructive Task," 221.

to make Christian theology more accessible to the "cultured despisers of religion" in Schleiermacher's context, created its own forms of exclusion even as it sought to include.[75] Universalism and exceptionalism both represent an inherent misalignment between local phenomena and other contexts. Likely, we are no wiser today, and critical reflection on insufficiently liberating constructive theologies remains necessary.

Postcolonial thinkers began remarking on how the colonial logic and reality of the British Empire makes an appearance in Jane Austen's seemingly harmless novels about women and their fortunes and loves.[76] Biblical scholars were the first who brought postcolonial discourse analysis into their field, and later constructive theologians adopted it as a useful tool for examining the imperial commitments of biblical texts and historical theologies.[77] After the publication of Marcella Althaus-Reid's *Indecent Theology*, a while after biblical scholars had already worked with postcolonial theories for some years, some constructive theologians began to read and engage postcolonial theory.[78] Thus, for example, the colonial history and context of many theologians can be made visible by shaping our understanding of their work and its dependency on colonial power relations.[79]

The point here is not to eradicate or erase Western traditions, but rather to look at the plurivocality of traditions and their fluidity. Thus, an effort to "provincialize Europe"[80] in theological thinking would include a deconstruction of claims to the universality and uniqueness of Western traditions, at the same time as reclaiming their specificity and interwovenness across continents to counter the ways in which some traditions and thinkers have been assigned universal value, while others have not. This does not mean that it makes sense to claim that various contexts are entirely irrelevant to each other, but that part of the work of constructive theology may consist in assessing the mutual relevance of texts, thinkers, theologians, and approaches for contexts not only in one direction but potentially in multiple ones. Thereby one might argue that a theologian's work can be utilized in the work to construct transforming theologies that are counterimperial and work to dismantle structures of oppression, even if their historical position and context are less than ideal. Martin Luther remains one important example for this ambivalence in theological thinking. Various theologians

---

[75] Helmer argues that "comprehensiveness thus is to be criticized as both a methodological impossibility and a false universal. The theological system with its pretensions to universalizing claims and comprehensiveness has thus been replaced by theologies expressing distinctive realms of experience and history that explore topics of resistance from areas of oppression." Ibid.

[76] Gayatri Spivak and others have been key here.

[77] See, for example, Catherine Keller, Michael Nausner, and Mayra Rivera, eds., *Postcolonial Theologies: Divinity and Empire* (St. Louis, MO: Chalice, 2004); and Pui-Lan Kwok, Don Compier, and Joerg Rieger, *Empire and the Christian Tradition* (Minneapolis, MN: Fortress, 2007).

[78] The first results of this are represented in Keller, Nausner, and Rivera, *Postcolonial Theologies*.

[79] This has been done beautifully by Joerg Rieger and Kwok Pui-Lan. See Joerg Rieger, "Schleiermacher," in *Empire and the Christian Tradition*, ed. Pui-Lan Kwok, Don Compier, and Joerg Rieger (Minneapolis, MN: Fortress, 2007), 271–82; Joerg Rieger, "Power and Empire in the Study of Nineteenth-Century Theology: The Case of Schleiermacher," in *Papers of the Nineteenth-Century Theology Group*, ed. James Swan Tuite and Todd Gooch (Eugene, OR: Wipf & Stock, 2012), 102–21; and Pui-Lan Kwok, *Postcolonial Imagination & Feminist Theology* (Louisville, KY: Westminster John Knox, 2005).

[80] Dipesh Chakrabarty, *Provincializing Europe: Postcolonial Thought and Historical Difference* (Princeton, NJ: Princeton University Press, 2000).

associated with the Workgroup on Constructive Theology have contributed to this work: Stephen Ray, Kwok Pui-Lan, Mary McClintock Fulkerson, Laurel Schneider, Darby Ray, Monica Coleman, Mayra Rivera, and Shannon Craigo-Snell, to name just some.

Interdisciplinary Genres and Styles: Pedagogical, Therapeutic, and Apologetic

A historical overview of the discipline of systematic theology shows that much of the written record begins with texts that are of an occasional nature, often answering controversial contextual questions, responding to current events and pressing theological issues, letters answering particular inquiries. The history of theology is thus less "systematic" than is often claimed, and numerous theologians have expressed a dislike of the term. The genres of theological writing are multiple throughout history: liturgical poems, letter, gospel, treatise, sermon, hagiography, interpretations of biblical books, refutation of heretics, mystical visions, and, so often excluded from theological discourse, the pictorial art on church walls, altars, and so forth. If one includes those expressions, another picture appears: Sojourner Truth's creative reconstructions, abolitionists and the first wave of feminists, the proponents of the social gospel or the social initiatives of Pietists, those that articulate theology in resistance to oppression by reclaiming tradition and different narratives. If one looks for the engagements and concerns that are common to many constructive theologians, an expanded map emerges.

It is resistant engagement with authoritative theological statements that does not merely talk about concepts such as, say, salvation, but strives to weave narratives that aim to aid healing and transformation. Theologians know well the mode of unsaying that is the movement of apophatic theology.[81] The inability to grasp, perceive, and know the divine Other extends in many ways also to the nonhuman Other part of the same cosmic fabric but remains strangely unknown unless described in terms, metaphors, images, and basically in anthropocentric terms of the relations we know—if partially—as we are part of the fabric of the cosmos. If we are always already "becoming with," it behooves us perhaps to remain "with the trouble" that will be "making kin" as climate change occurs.[82]

Where to, Constructive Theology?

In many of its North-American and European contexts, theological study and work is a discipline that has been weakened in its foundations, experiencing challenges

---

[81] Catherine Keller has recovered apophasis for the constructive theology in a number of her writings. See, for example, Catherine Keller, *Cloud of the Impossible: Negative Theology and Planetary Entanglement* (New York: Columbia University Press, 2015).

[82] Donna J. Haraway, *Staying with the Trouble: Making Kin the Chthulucene* (Durham, NC: Duke University Press, 2016).

in a time of disarray, confusion, and fragmentation and facing increased levels of economic insecurity and endangered institutional sustainability. Under the guise of neoliberal economic efficiency, increasing religious disaffiliation, and the rule of the so-called hard sciences, a number of disciplines of inquiry are under attack in contemporary higher learning. Together with other humanities, theology is being progressively marginalized at universities and institutions of higher learning. This type of external pressure makes it perhaps even more important to account for and describe viable methods of doing theology, and in particular in a constructive mode. It also makes the work of future generations of constructive theologians more precious and important, especially as there are fewer permanent and stable academic appointments available.

Indeed, it is precisely in these times and places, where in many locations theology is becoming dislocated from many academic contexts, reduced, shrunk away, downsized, secularized into oblivion, and disappeared into the bible school incubators of often uncritical faith, that constructive theologians are challenged to engage in the deepest, most radical, and most ground-breaking work yet, especially as we are facing the threat of autocratic governments and climate change. Since religious illiteracy appears only to be increasing under regimes of secularism and anti-intellectual moods, and dominant forms of authoritarian religion and biblical illiteracy are rampant even among those who profess to be "Bible-believing," constructive theology is ever more important, done within and without the actual boundaries of discipline. Thus it helps counter the Babylonian captivity of Christian content through authoritarian, patriarchalist, anti-liberationist, white supremacist structures in the United States and Europe, as well as the right-wing sympathies and agendas of ultraconservative Christian presences in the global South and to support the work of constructive theologians in the South.

More than one contributor to the discourse has noted that much of the work of constructive theology so far appears to be deconstructive rather than constructive.[83] It is indeed often monumental work to challenge the dominant historical narratives and to counter its theological manifestations. That work in itself can take much of the energy that would otherwise go into a reconstruction. Other times, the very point of constructive theology might be to avoid replacing the just deconstructed singular narrative with another singular narrative. The work of constructive theology then is also a process that can go through several phases: raising awareness and critiquing dominant narratives, often with detailed critiques. After such critical interventions, it can be difficult to replace these narratives with simple solutions or singular alternatives. Constructive theologies often resist proposing singular alternatives or other seemingly coherent accounts claiming to offer a final solution. What is more, alternatives to worn doctrinal grooves ought to be constructed from and within particular contexts, which means they will be multiple, not singular. Thus, some constructive theologians have suggested that their work can be useful in analyzing the theological patterns operating in the reader's own context,[84] thus opening spaces

---

[83] Wyman, *Constructing Constructive Theology*, 76.
[84] Marion Grau, *Rethinking Mission in the Postcolony: Salvation, Society, and Subversion* (London: T&T Clark/Continuum, 2011), 25.

for the construction of counter-constructions from which prophetic intercontextual theologies may emerge.[85]

Many theologians favor open-ended approaches over attempts to provide a conclusive approach to theological issues and use a variety of methods, reading whatever disciplinary discourse provides useful angles to articulate a relevant, critical, and constructive approach to theology. Some see themselves as inheritors of the theologies of liberation, working with additional and expanded theories, critiques, and methods. Not all will want to claim the term "constructive," but many see themselves doing related forms of revitalizing, liberating work.

Aspects of constructive theological work can appear in many places and will manifest inside or outside traditional academic or church institutions. Constructive theological intentions and methods can thus be found in many contexts and are constantly evolving. There are traces of constructive theology in many locations around the globe, groups of theologians that value the engagement of ancient biblical and historical traditions, even as they are working against the oppressive tendencies in history and contemporary society. They are theologians in Africa, Europe, Asia-Pacific, North and Latin America, working in ecumenical and interreligious settings, struggling to articulate theologies for the liberation for indigenous peoples, women, and sexual and ethnic minorities. And so, in spite of the challenges, a growing number of people continue to construct theologies, critically rethinking the ecumenical traditions of the past for the lives of today and for the purposes of building faith communities that contribute toward more just and equitable societies. We will need these voices to reimagine interspecies relations through the deluge of climate change, to imagine what faith, love, and hope may remain.

Bibliography

Abraham, Susan. "Decolonizing Christianity." In *The Task of Theology: Leading Theologians on the Most Compelling Questions for Today*, edited by Anselm K. Min, 167–81. Maryknoll, NY: Orbis, 2014.

Althaus-Reid, Marcella. *Indecent Theology: Theological Perversions in Sex, Gender and Politics*. London: Routledge, 2001.

Balmer, Randall. "The Real Origins of the Religious Right: They'll Tell You It Was Abortion. Sorry, the Historical Record's Clear: It Was Segregation." *Politico*, May 27, 2014. https://www.politico.com/magazine/story/2014/05/religious-right-real-origins-107133.

Bedford, Nancy. "Little Moves against Destructiveness: Theology and the Practice of Discernment." In *Practicing Theology: Beliefs and Practices in Christian Life*, edited by Miroslav Volf and Dorothy C. Bass, 157–81. Grand Rapids, MI: Eerdmanns, 2002.

Bevans, Stephen. *Essays in Contextual Theology*. Leiden: Brill, 2018.

---

[85] Ibid.

Bevans, Stephen B. *An Introduction to Theology in a Global Perspective*. Theology in Global Perspective Series. Maryknoll, NY: Orbis, 2009.

Boff, Clodovis. "Methodology of the Theology of Liberation." In *Systematic Theology: Perspectives from Liberation Theology*, edited by Jon Sobrino and Ignacio Ellacuria, 1–21. Maryknoll, NY: Orbis, 1993.

Cajete, Gregory. *Native Science: Natural Laws of Interdependence*. Santa Fe, NM: Clear Light, 2000.

Chakrabarty, Dipesh. *Provincializing Europe: Postcolonial Thought and Historical Difference*. Princeton, NJ: Princeton University Press, 2000.

Charleston, Steven, and Elaine Robinson, eds. *Coming Full Circle: Constructing Native Christian Theology*. Minneapolis: Fortress Press, 2015.

Collins, Patricia Hill, and Sirma Bilge. *Intersectionality*. Cambridge: Polity, 2016.

Cone, James. *God of the Oppressed*. Maryknoll, NY: Orbis, 1997.

Crenshaw, Kimberlé. "Mapping the Margins: Intersectionality, Identity, Politics, and Violence against Women of Color." *Stanford Law Review* 43 (1991): 1241–99.

Crossan, John Dominic. *Who Killed Jesus? Exposing the Roots of Anti-Semitism in the Gospel Story of the Death of Jesus*. San Francisco, CA: HarperSanFransisco, 1995.

Dalferth, Ingolf U. *Jenseits von Mythos und Logos: Die Christologische Transformation der Theologie*. Quaestiones Disputatae vol. 142. Freiburg: Herder, 1993.

Daly, Mary. *Beyond God the Father: Toward a Philosophy of Women's Liberation*. Boston, MA: Beacon, 1973.

Davaney, Sheila Greeve. *Historicism: The Once and Future Challenge for Theology*. Minneapolis, MN: Fortress, 2006.

Deloria, Vine Jr. *God Is Red: A Native View of Religion*. Golden, CO: Fulcrum, 1994.

Dochuk, Darren. *Anointed with Oil: How Christianity and Crude Made Modern America*. New York: Basic Books, 2019.

Dorrien, Gary. *The Word as True Myth: Interpreting Modern Theology*. Louisville, KY: Westminster John Knox, 1997.

Douglas, Kelly Brown. *The Black Christ*. Maryknoll, NY: Orbis, 1994.

Dube, Musa W. *Postcolonial Feminist Interpretation of the Bible*. St. Louis, MO: Chalice, 2000.Eiesland, Nancy. *The Disabled God: Toward a Liberatory Theology of Disability*. Nashville, TN: Abingdon, 1994.

Graham, Elaine, Heather Walton, and Frances Ward. *Theological Reflection: Methods*. London: SCM, 2005.

Grau, Marion. *Rethinking Mission in the Postcolony: Salvation, Society, and Subversion*. London: T&T Clark/Continuum, 2011.

Haraway, Donna J. *Staying with the Trouble: Making Kin the Chthulucene*. Durham, NC: Duke University Press, 2016.

Helmer, Christine. "The Contemporary Constructive Task." *Dialog* 56:3 (Fall 2017): 218–22.

Hesslein, Kayko Driedger. *Dual Citizenship: Two-Natures Christologies and the Jewish Jesus*. New York: Bloomsbury, 2015.

Johnson, Elizabeth A. *She Who Is: The Mystery of God in Feminist Theological Discourse*. New York: Crossroad, 1992.

Jones, Serene. *Call It Grace: Finding Meaning in a Fractured World*. New York: Viking/Random House, 2019.

Keller, Catherine. *Cloud of the Impossible: Negative Theology and Planetary Entanglement*. New York: Columbia University Press, 2015.

Keller, Catherine. *Intercarnations: Exercises in Theological Possibility*. New York: Fordham University Press, 2017.
Keller, Catherine, Michael Nausner, and Mayra Rivera, eds. *Postcolonial Theologies: Divinity and Empire*. St. Louis, MO: Chalice, 2004.
Keller, Catherine, and Laurel Schneider. "Introduction." In *Polydoxy: Theology of Multiplicity and Relation*, edited by Catherine Keller and Laurel Schneider, 1–15. London: Routledge, 2010.
Keller, Catherine, and Laurel Schneider, eds. *Polydoxy: Theology of Multiplicity and Relation*. London: Routledge, 2010.
Kim, Grace Ji-Sun, and Susan M. Shaw, eds. *Intersectional Theology: An Introductory Guide*. Minneapolis, MN: Fortress, 2018.
Kimmerer, Robin Wall. *Braiding Sweetgrass: Indigenous Wisdom, Scientific Knowledge, and the Teachings of Plants*. Minneapolis, MN: Milkweed Editions, 2013.
Klein, Naomi. *This Changes Everything: Capitalism against Climate*. New York: Simon & Schuster, 2014.
Kwok, Pui-Lan. *Postcolonial Imagination & Feminist Theology*. Louisville, KY: Westminster John Knox, 2005.
Kwok, Pui-Lan, Don Compier, and Joerg Rieger. *Empire and the Christian Tradition*. Minneapolis, MN: Fortress, 2007.
Levine, Amy-Jill. *The Misunderstood Jew: The Church and the Scandal of the Jewish Jesus*. New York: HarperCollins, 2006.
McFague, Sallie. *The Body of God: An Ecological Theology*. Minneapolis, MN: Fortress, 1993.
McFague, Sallie. *Metaphorical Theology: Models of God in Religious Language*. Philadelphia, PA: Fortress, 1982.
Rieger, Joerg. "Schleiermacher." In *Empire and the Christian Tradition*, edited by Pui-Lan Kwok, Don Compier, and Joerg Rieger, 271–82. Minneapolis, MN: Fortress, 2007.
Roberts, Michelle Voss, ed. *Comparing Faithfully: Insights for Systematic Theological Reflection*. New York: Fordham University Press, 2016.
Schneider, Laurel C. *Beyond Monotheism: A Theology of Multiplicity*. London: Routledge, 2008.
Slabodsky, Santiago. *Decolonial Judaism: Triumphal Failures of Barbaric Thinking*. New York: Palgrave, 2014.
Smith, Linda Tuhiwai. *Decolonizing Methodologies: Research and Indigenous Peoples*. London: Zed Books, 1999.
Sobrino, Jon, and Ignacio Ellacuria, eds. *Systematic Theology: Perspectives from Liberation Theology*. Maryknoll, NY: Orbis, 1993.
Thatamanil, John J. *Circling the Elephant: A Comparative Theology of Religious Diversity*. New York: Fordham University Press, 2020.
Tillich, Paul. "The Religious Symbol." In *Symbolism in Religion and Literature*, edited by Rollo May, 75–98. New York: George Braziller, 1960.
Twiss, Richard. *Rescuing the Gospel from the Cowboys: A Native American Expression of the Jesus Way*. Downer's Grove, IL: Intervarsity, 2015.
Williams, Delores. *Sisters in the Wilderness: The Challenge of Womanist God-Talk*. Maryknoll, NY: Orbis Books, 1993.
Williamson, Clark. *A Guest in the House of Israel: Post-Holocaust Church Theology*. Louisville, KY: Westminster John Knox, 1993.
Wyman, Jason. *Constructing Constructive Theology*. Minneapolis, MN: Fortress, 2017.

Part II

Body, Text, Interdisciplinarity, and Practice

4

Embodied Knowing: Body, Epistemology, Context, and Hermeneutics

Heike Peckruhn

Our bodies matter. It is how they come to matter in and as the stuff of our theologies that I shall explore in this chapter. Making the body an object of concern is not new to the project of theology. It is *whose* bodies, *how* they materialize for us, and in which way bodies are plausible sources, even *agents*, of meaning-making that we need to account for when drawing on experiences as authoritative source to communicate on things human and divine.

Bodies Always Mattered in Theology

The incarnation of Jesus as Christ puts the human body at the center of Christian theological concerns, though not without complications. The body has been an ambiguous pivot point for salvation throughout historical Christian proclamations. There is the flesh as the matter that leads us to temptation, susceptible to sin and decay and thus as impediment to salvation, and yet it was conceived to be the home of the divine in Jesus. The body was imagined as temple or tomb, as spouse or prison of the soul, differentiated from flesh by Paul, considered enemy or ally in the quest for spiritual advancement—Christian theology manifests a preoccupation with the body's role in doing theological work for us. The soul, the will, or the mind were often commissioned to control the body's precarious conditions; ascetic renunciation is a vivid example of experiences that conceptually link body and soul in a quest to master physicality in order to transcend it toward salvific ends.[1]

Now as then, bodily experience is a contested and paradoxical space: It is sociopolitical *and* intensely personal, unavoidable *and* problematic, foundational *and* suspicious. It is a space for reflection that connects the deeply personal, unique, and embodied with avenues for analyses of culture, theology, and the ideological structures maintained in bodily interactions. The focus can be on the sociocultural dynamics of oppression to

---

[1] Michelle Mary Lelwica, *Shameful Bodies: Religion and the Culture of Physical Improvement* (New York: Bloomsbury, 2017), 17–30.

analyze experiences of persons with certain kinds of bodies and to emphasize prejudices and injustices bestowed on bodies marked a certain way. And it can be on giving attention to the physical realities of flux and deterioration of our bodies and the undeniable embodied effects of living in/as a body considered different from "normal."[2]

I will begin this chapter by first reviewing some of the most common ways in which the body and bodily experiences have been integral to theological projects. Responding to some of the challenges and drawbacks in their approaches, I will explore some crucial concepts from the field of phenomenology that will enable a more complex body methodology. When explicitly employed as source, bodies and experiences have been approached in a variety of ways, from mapping theology onto bodies, utilizing bodies to make subversive claims, and constructing body metaphor theology, to constructing meaning with textual bodies, and even conceiving of bodies themselves as theological tools. By showcasing a few common approaches to bodies in contemporary theology, I will describe the explicit or implicit assumptions about what a body is and the theological "product" made hereby available. This will allow me to discuss the inherent challenges that result from particular body methods and to highlight how in these approaches, perception is given a particular role in the theological task. In the second part of this chapter, I will explore select phenomenological concepts that help to frame perception as the space of theology, the space in which self–world–divine intermingle and hence where meaning is created and potentially subverted. I will conclude with a proposal for a method for body theology that allows for greater nuance and complexity when theologizing with bodies in mind.[3]

Mapping Theology onto Bodies

A very common approach is to take theological reflection and *put it onto* bodies and from there to articulate the moral implications for bodily behavior. An explicit or implicit theological anthropology is applied to a (often generalized, not particular) body, and in a closed hermeneutic loop the body serves as evidence for predetermined revelation. The particular truth a body is made to speak is constructed, measured, and evaluated against an already certain meaning as detected in scripture or interpretative tradition. This approach often presumes an ontology of the body that is sexed and gendered in a universal, binary male–female fashion.[4]

---

[2] Christopher Newell, "On the Importance of Suffering: The Paradoxes of Disability," in *The Paradox of Disability: Responses to Jean Vanier and L'arche Communities from Theology and the Sciences*, ed. Hans S. Reinders (Grand Rapids, MI: Wm. B. Eerdmans, 2010), 174–5.

[3] An in-depth theological and philosophical exploration of the brief discussion offered in this chapter, as well as a comparative investigation for a proposal of body theology principles, can be found in Heike Peckruhn, *Meaning in Our Bodies: Sensory Experiences as Constructive Theological Imagination* (New York: Oxford University Press, 2017).

[4] The binary sexed and gendered body is neither a biological given nor a universal presumption, but rather a modern concept. The ancient body only had one sex with both male and female aspects, with humans conceived of on a continuum on which they could move depending on how much maleness of femaleness a body would exhibit at a given time. See Thomas Laqueur, *Making Sex: Body and Gender from the Greeks to Freud* (Cambridge, MA: Harvard University Press, 1990), 8.

For example, one of the most popularly known works in this vein is John Paul II's collection of teachings on marriage, family, and Catholic sexual ethics—published as *Theology of the Body*.[5] In it, revelation gleaned from scripture and tradition is read into human embodiment, the body a revelation of the divine into our visible reality. Because the male–female binary is presumed as the most basic and important experience of being a human body, John Paul II's theological anthropology essentializes a sexed and gendered binary and associated biological functions as interpretive grid for social roles and theological messages. Binary sexed bodies reveal a "perennial 'man-woman' relation" and emanate an inherent "spousal meaning."[6] The pressing issue at hand for John Paul II is to utilize meaning originating from the outside of the body to construct moral guidelines for proper bodily behavior and provide correction where needed. He envisions reciprocal, mutual, self-giving love within the divine trinity that can and ought to be channeled and expressed by binary sexed bodies in particular binary gendered ways—male bodies conveying the mature giving of love, and female bodies living responsive love.[7]

When predetermined truths are mapped onto the body, a very generic and universalized conception of the body comes to symbolize and stand in for all actual embodiment. Bodies are merely the medium for channeling truth about the divine and human existence, though it is inherently vulnerable and imperfect as receptor and conductor of this transcendent meaning. Theological issues emerge in "problem bodies": those who are capable, but fail to be proper corporeal gendered messengers are in need of moral correction; those impaired and thereby limited to communicate their humanity in "normal" ways may be gendered feminine (passive, receptive, submissive), or their agency located in the soul rather than their passively constructed body as conductor for divine truths (whence it is up to the agentic capable theologian to perceive the soul/humanity in the other).[8] This kind of method, especially when it presumes and focuses on binary sexed and gendered bodies, has difficulties going beyond a prescriptive moral approach. Body theology generated like this is too restrained to speak to ideologies maintaining oppressive socioeconomic systems that position sexed, gendered, disabled, or raced bodies inequitably and thereby enable and inflict violence. With this method, the theologian often remains limited to prescriptions for marital/familial life and perhaps a general call to compassion for all persons.

Utilizing Bodies for Subversive Theological Claims

For theologians who are concerned with social structures that create inequities and inflict harm on bodies different from the universalized white, male, able-bodied/able-minded norm place, it makes sense to place (bodily) experience at the center

---

[5] Karol Wojtyła (John Paul II), *The Theology of the Body: Human Love in the Divine Plan* (Boston, MA: Pauline Books and Media, 1997). Based on audiences given from 1979 through 1984.
[6] Ibid., 105, 365.
[7] Ibid.
[8] Ibid., 66–8.

of reflection.⁹ The radical methodological move is to draw on *particular* embodied experiences, for example, *as* women, *as* othered humans in terms of race, sexuality, ability, and so on, for primary resources to critically utilize others (scripture, tradition, what passes as "reason")—and positing this kind of theologizing as equal to and even *more* inclusive and objectively constructed than universalizing theologies from "nowhere." Within this concern for validating particular experiences, the significance of the body and embodied differences then needs to be addressed. Why and how does it matter to my experience what my body actually is like in terms of race, gender, ability, and other differences? And even if embodiment makes a difference to experiencing, what difference does it make to theologizing?[10]

One way to tackle these questions is to start with the presupposition that the body, any body, is *the* source of revelation and experience of god and then extract what truths might be gleaned from it. Divine incarnation in Jesus can provide the methodological door: if the divine still embodies, affirms, permeates, and reveals in bodily experiences today, then the body theology project can move to revalue specific experiences. This kind of construction can focus on marginalized bodies and experiences that have been denied the possibility of being sites of divine revelation to counter existing harmful messages denying them full humanity and agency. The task is to overcome hierarchical perceptions of our embodied world that render certain bodies and experiences abject from consideration, and to recognize how *all* experiences reveal divine truth in embodied particularity.

Two theologians, whose works read quite differently from each other, exemplify this kind of approach, and both focus on sexual experiences: James Nelson, who is credited with coining the term "body theology," and Marcella Althaus-Reid, the liberation theologian renowned for her "indecenting" of theology. To Nelson, participating in the reality of god as body-selves requires overcoming the destructive effects of heterosexual patriarchal male alienation from bodies, which turned masculinity into a negative/negating identity (formed as not-feminine), and finding authenticity in relationships. His approach is to engage and discover divinely created need for embodied intimacy in generalized male experiences of sexual performance anxieties and loneliness. For example, he points to growing older as an undesirable reminder of fragility and loss and highlights the gendered marginalization of elderly adults particularly in terms of experiences of sexuality and intimacy.[11] Nelson's concept of embodiment in some ways

---

[9] Theologically, this is not a new method, nor reserved for those challenging white male pronunciations masking as universally applicable knowledge. Modern German liberal theologian Friedrich Schleiermacher, for example, conceived of religion as inward human experience accessed through embodied feelings.

[10] *How exactly* the body makes its way into theological construction often depends on where one is positioned in the theological field (e.g., biblical studies, systematic theology, pastoral theology), which often also determines which kinds of bodies and experiences are utilized (i.e., their own, that of others, historical, contemporary, specific, generalized experiences). Conceiving of what the body *is* and *does* is often informed via other intellectual disciplines at the theologian's disposal (psychology, discourse analysis, literary theory, etc.).

[11] James B. Nelson, *Body Theology* (Louisville, KY: Westminster John Knox, 1992), 79–90. He traces connections between sexual performance, youthful manliness, and the desire to preserve virility with aging, and points to confusing cultural messages of denying and shaming sexual agency, desire, and potency in older adults outside procreative norms.

parallels that of John Paul II as he also presumes a body that is sexed and gendered in binary ways, but he argues against ideologies of gender complementarity (which necessitates a completeness of human experience via coupling with the binary opposite sex-gender) and for the wholeness of the single, un-coupled person.[12] Yet in his exploration of the connection between sexuality and spirituality, Nelson becomes increasingly dependent on illustrative employment of generalized bodily experiences. Doing so, he often defaults to a biological essentializing of sex and gendered experiences to articulate metaphors with theological meaning.[13]

Marcella Althaus-Reid makes the sexual experiences and desires of the poor and marginalized in Latin America the embodied epistemological standpoint and explicit center of her queering hermeneutic circle.[14] When Althaus-Reid draws on experiences of sexually and economically marginalized bodies, she implies that these embodied experiences reveal particular perceptible truths.[15] With taboo-ized experiences, such as those of the poor racialized transvestite who strives to survive multiple oppressions through engaging in sex work in the nightclubs of Buenos Aires, Althaus-Reid unmasks ideological constraints within theologies and seeks to unveil not only the divine *in* those experiences, but *as* that experience. When the divine is immanent in *all* bodies, what do indecent bodies tell us that subversively signifies god? What does god the Faggot, god the Voyeur at the Orgy, or god the Whore who empties herself in a brothel tell us about human and divine relationships?[16] Althaus-Reid establishes the sexual as integral to critical theological analysis, but she, like Nelson, invokes an almost immediate metaphorical connection between sexuality and economics, politics, culture, and colonialism. The lemon vendors on the street of Buenos Aires, who can "tell you a few things about postmodernism," are her "living metaphors."[17] But it is the *image* of the lemon vendors more than the actual vendors speaking, it is the *interpretation* of their embodied location and subject position that Althaus-Reid creates and utilizes, what she makes to be the metaphor rather than what might be their

---

[12] Nelson utilizes the example of Jesus, who is incarnate as sensuous, intimate, passionate human body in touch with his eros, and thus a model of genuine wholeness of single persons. See ibid.

[13] For example, in the orgasmic sexual experience of men, Nelson sees

> hard and explosive phallic achievement [that] becomes in an instant the soft, vulnerable tears of the penis. Both are fully male. Both are deeply grounded in a man's bodily reality. Both dimensions of life are fully present when a man is most human. And to be fully human is to know the Christ—not as supernatural invader but as that reality truest to our own natures, and as that reality which intimately connects us with everyone and everything else. (Ibid., 110–11)

Reducing men to those humans by nature endowed with a penis, Nelson then employs what he frames as holistic bodily biology (hardness *and* softness, explosion *and* vulnerable "tears") metaphorically as truest reality, in other words, truest knowledge of Christ.

[14] Marcella M. Althaus-Reid, *Indecent Theology: Theological Perversions in Sex, Gender and Politics* (New York: Routledge, 2000), 2, 17, 22–6. Liberation theologies, Althaus-Reid charges, have idealized a gendered model of the poor that excludes sexual experiences, desires, and preferences. Gendered expectations and regulations regarding sexuality and sexual behavior mask a multitude of oppressions regarding gender, sex, race, and economical arrangements and make theological projects complicit with this multilayered oppression.

[15] Ibid., 7, 22–6, 32–3, 34–5, 85–6, 112–14, 136–7.

[16] Ibid.; see also Marcella M. Althaus-Reid, *The Queer God* (New York: Routledge, 2003).

[17] Althaus-Reid, *Indecent Theology*, 3, 7.

embodied lived experiences.[18] She considers bodily sites as *the* epistemological site for doing theology, but it is the bodily metaphor she invokes that drives her hermeneutics of the divine.[19]

Constructing Body Metaphor Theology

Explicit metaphorical approaches to body theology examine the connection between language and experience to emphasize for us why constructing new/body metaphors is important: language qualifies our embodied human reality, and metaphors are models that irreducibly structure our knowing—grounded in, expressing, and *producing* our experiences.[20] Because metaphors mediate our bodily experiences and guide their interpretation, theological construction employing this method focuses on providing metaphors that help us to reinterpret and reread our experiences and engage our contexts toward liberation.

Sallie McFague's corpus is well known for its pioneering linguistic body method. She constructs metaphors to express radical relationality between all that lives, which will bring about positive relations in the world to overcome the effects of alienation from our intrinsic relationality (which to her is the root of social ills).[21] Urging us to "think and act as if bodies matter," to affirm all life imbued with value, and to instill a sense of urgency for the planet, McFague's metaphors for god (such as the world as body of god) emphasize and affirm human embodiment and radicalize divine transcendence-immanence.[22] The body enters here to illustrate lived experience as dependent, liable to contingencies, vulnerable, susceptible to pain. She stresses that

---

[18] Womanist ethicist Emilie Townes critiques Althaus-Reid's descriptions as reinforcing voyeurism, maintaining the object status of the lemon vendors, and falling short of engaging with their materiality, nakedness, sex, race, class, and so on. Emilie M. Townes, "Marcella Althaus-Reid's *Indecent Theology*: A Response," in *Dancing Theology in Fetish Boots: Essays in Honour of Marcella Althaus-Reid*, ed. Lisa Isherwood and Mark D. Jordan (London: SCM, 2010), 64.

[19] For example, the "Bi/Christ" is a hard-to-pin-down marginalized and misunderstood body straddling and opening borders and categories of heteronormativity, heteropatriarchy, and their sexual and economic divisive arrangements. Althaus-Reid, *Indecent Theology*, 114-18. Other theologians whose theologies constructively build on/from erotic bodily experiences typically made invisible or indecent in heteropatriarchal structures are Mary E. Hunt and Lisa Isherwood. See, for example, Mary E. Hunt, *Fierce Tenderness: A Feminist Theology of Friendship* (New York: Crossroad, 1994); and Lisa Isherwood, *The Power of Erotic Celibacy: Queering Heteropatriarchy* (New York: T&T Clark, 2006).

[20] George Lakoff and Mark Johnson, *Philosophy in the Flesh: The Embodied Mind and Its Challenge to Western Thought* (New York: Basic Books, 1999), 31-6. See also George Lakoff and Mark Johnson, *Metaphors We Live By* (Chicago: University of Chicago Press, 1980; reprint, 2003).

[21] McFague is particularly concerned with the global ecological crisis and seeks to theorize unity and diversity to fashion a theology of nature that can (re)shape Christian identity and practice toward increased ecojustice. Sallie McFague, *Models of God: Theology for an Ecological, Nuclear Age* (Philadelphia, PA: Fortress, 1987), 45-6; and *Metaphorical Theology: Models of God in Religious Language* (Philadelphia, PA: Fortress, 1982), 26, 39, 51.

[22] With the metaphor of the world (all life) as the body of God, she constructs salvation inclusive of the natural world; all life is interdependent as one body and requires envisioning and enacting mutual flourishing on the planet, which is home to all beings (not exclusively belonging to humans). Sallie McFague, *The Body of God: An Ecological Theology* (Minneapolis, MN: Fortress, 1993), viii, 18, 168, 171-3; McFague, *Models of God*, 72-4.

when constructing embodiment metaphors, we ought to recognize mundane *and* diverse bodily experiences that shape our expressions of meaning, such as the different experiences based on race, class, gender, sexual orientation, disability. It is this diversity of particular embodiment that must ground the reflection on the world as body of god.[23] Yet her own hermeneutic remains limited to acknowledging embodied difference rather than thinking through and from it. She shortchanges theological possibilities by not further elaborating or reflecting on the diversity of human embodiment, even dismissing particularity as significant to experience when assuming a healthy generic body to be normative, and ascribing experiences of difference to the randomness of life and, as such, unimportant for analysis and reflection. While her method has constructive potentiality for theologizing *through* bodies in their particularities, her ontologically and epistemologically conceived body as model quickly becomes generic, even abstract, and differences in contexts and experiences within embodied life do not offer her particular insights.[24]

What is required of body theologies then is to include articulating how experiences are real matters within systems of social relations enmeshing bodies, language, and cultural power structures.[25] Nancy Eiesland addresses this challenge in her body metaphor work *The Disabled God*, in which she deliberately positions the disabled body as locus for reflection to explicitly deconstruct notions of "normal" embodiment. She attends to the physical body and its representations and utilizes multifaceted bodily experiences and knowledges for grounding symbols and metaphors. When we consider particular experiences of bodies marked "other" to be significant occurrences, central and indispensable to the theological project, and raising epistemological questions and concerns for us, we need to begin by representing the body "as flesh and blood, bones and braces, and not simply the rationalized realm of activity."[26] The hermeneutical focus is on nonconventional bodies as source for the *imago Dei*, because embodied experiences from particular social locations determine perceptions of the social and physical world that do not conform to the norm and provide new categories and models of thinking and being.[27] Eiesland insists that theological construction that liberates disabled bodies—not from their impairment, but from social and theological abjection—must be done *by* disabled bodies, because the experience of disablement is a particular epistemological standpoint and thereby offers new creative ways of resistance to forms of exclusion.[28] Yet it remains unclear *how* exactly it is that "we discern *in* our bodies ... the ravages of injustice and pain [and] the reality of surviving with dignity."[29]

---

[23] McFague, *The Body of God*, 47–8.
[24] Deborah Beth Creamer, *Disability and Christian Theology: Embodied Limits and Constructive Possibilities* (New York: Oxford University Press, 2009), 66–9.
[25] Mary McClintock Fulkerson, *Changing the Subject: Women's Discourses and Feminist Theology* (Minneapolis, MN: Fortress, 1994), viii.
[26] Nancy Eiesland, *The Disabled God: Toward a Liberatory Theology of Disability* (Nashville, TN: Abingdon, 1994).
[27] Ibid., 31.
[28] Ibid., 86.
[29] Ibid., 243; emphasis mine.

Constructing Theology with Textual Bodies

Another way to go about theological body business is to utilize the tools of literary/textual disciplines. As in body metaphor theologies, "body" is conceived of as entangled with and limited by discursive systems, and specific bodily experiences are brought to us in narrative accounts and are explored for the particular insights gained from particular bodily locations. In terms of methodology, poststructuralist themes of subject, language, and social constructions of identity often inform scripture/textually based reading and interpretative strategies. Here, what a body "is" and, therefore, what experience specific to certain bodies is is analyzed as a social construct—the sociocultural practices and interpretive lenses that produce definitions and "facts" about what counts as particularized experiences (e.g., that of "woman"). Presumed then is that there is no knowledge, no experience that is outside of language, hence, particular bodily experience cannot be universalized outside the contexts and linguistic codes that give it meaning.[30]

Delores Williams, for example, ascribes the triple inscriptions of racialization, masculinization, and sexualization to black women's bodies. Central to her constructive task is critical reflection on experience (embodied and narrated), often by analyzing stereotypes and cultural images of black women. In *Sisters in the Wilderness*, she draws on novels that describe and ground the historical experiences of race and class intersecting with gender to articulate African American women's experience then and now.[31] She utilizes experience (e.g., motherhood, surrogacy, ethnicity, wilderness experience) particular to specific bodies for hermeneutic purposes, analyzes how their bodies and experiences have come to be presented in theological discourse, and develops reading strategies for biblical texts and other literary sources supporting full moral agency of black women.[32]

In this approach, our embodiment is already given to us with particular meanings, which is constituted by and accessible in language. Embodied subjects are always made meaningful (to others and to ourselves) *as* a specific kind of person with identity *by* and *through* our experiences, for example, as a black woman. The methodological

---

[30] Mary McClintock Fulkerson's critique is directed at the failure to account for the ways in which discourses already restrict subjects and meanings. Differences in women's experiences based on social location might be acknowledged in theologies, but how these differences are signified through bodies is not addressed. Retaining the signifier "woman" for theological purposes reinforces anatomical boundaries and binaries that define two orders of bodies and their relation. See Mary McClintock Fulkerson, *Changing the Subject: Women's Discourses and Feminist Theology* (Minneapolis, MN: Fortress, 1994), 83–91.

[31] Delores S. Williams, *Sisters in the Wilderness: The Challenge of Womanist God-Talk* (Maryknoll, NY: Orbis Books, 1993). Another example is the work of Renita J. Weems, for example, *Just a Sister Away: Understanding the Timeless Connection between Women of Today and Women in the Bible* (New York: Warner Books, 1988, 2005).

[32] Many of the more recent theologies—womanist, postcolonial, mujerista, etc.—take some cues from poststructural theories, describing and analyzing the inscriptions of bodies and bodily performances connected to experiences of, e.g., land, space, citizenship, ethnicity, etc. See, for example, Kwok, Pui-Lan, ed., *Hope Abundant: Third World and Indigenous Women's Theology* (Maryknoll, NY: Orbis Books, 2010); Rita Nakashima Brock et al., eds., *Off the Menu: Asian and Asian North American Women's Religion and Theology* (Louisville, KY: Westminster John Knox, 2007); Ada María Isasi-Díaz, *Mujerista Theology: A Theology for the Twenty-First Century* (New York: Orbis Books, 1996).

challenge of this body approach is to not fix the meaning of a (now more particular) body and social realities of bodily experience provided in narrative. The questions emerging are: Who are we (made to be) in our particular experiencing within our sociocultural structures? How do we avoid excluding unfitting or contradictory meanings and affirm the instabilities of meaning inscribed on particular bodies as well as the generalities articulated as "experience" by women in specific locations and contexts? This openness to multiple meanings and change can be teased out, for example, in approaches informed by reading strategies of oral traditions, which address the needs of specific audiences in order to lift up suggestive, not definitive or exhaustive, themes for construction of redemption, liberation, and god.[33] Yet bodies are not reducible to language. There are other sign systems that discursively order and create subjects through bodily experience (e.g., music, dance, fashion). Textual methods in this vein can inadvertently maintain a materiality/ideas dichotomy, placing the task of theological construction external to the matters of our embodiment.

Conceiving of (the Theologians') Bodies Themselves as Theological Tools

A different approach from what I featured so far is to frame the body itself as theological agent. It is not necessarily new or uncommon, it is a frequent way to lay claim to our bodily experiences and often framed in terms of "spirituality"—the discerning of the divine in our here and now and reflecting on what our felt experiences (our emotions, our feelings arising in a situation) might mean and how we draw on it to articulate beliefs and values. "Trusting our bodies" when it comes to touching, smelling, hearing, seeing, and therefore knowing the divine/god is an endowment of our feelings and sensations with agency and epistemological authority.[34] Here, the body, particularly sensory capacities, is conceived as central space for theological construction, as sort of original contact point with and access to divine meaning or messaging about the world. Hence, we ought to (re)develop our sensory intelligence to "feel it out."[35]

Theoretically and methodologically, this position is explored in Carter Heyward's work. She posits all knowledge as being sensorially grounded and created, yet also limited by our embodied particularities and social context.[36] As humans, we are

---

[33] See Kwok Pui-Lan, *Postcolonial Imagination and Feminist Theology* (Louisville, KY: Westminster John Knox, 2005), 36n24.

[34] Constance Classen. *The Color of Angels: Cosmology, Gender, and the Aesthetic Imagination* (New York: Routledge, 1998), 30–5.

[35] This epistemological privileging of feelings is not without critics, especially when it is relegated to the realm of (women's) spirituality over against theology proper. For example, historical accounts and retrievals of "women's spirituality" are often characterized as bodily affective, maintaining stereotypes of "feminine" modes of theologizing, neglecting the cultural construction and gendering of particular religious activities in medieval times. See Anke Passenier, "Der Lustgarten Des Leibes Und Die Freiheit Der Seele: Wege Der Mittelalterlichen Frauenspiritualität," in *Sources and Resources of Feminist Theologies*, ed. Elisabeth Hartlieb and Charlotte Methuen (Mainz, Germany: Matthias-Grünewald Verlag, 1997), 196.

[36] Carter Isabel Heyward, *Touching Our Strength: The Erotic as Power and the Love of God* (San Francisco, CA: Harper & Row, 1989), 3–13.

"bodyselves," doubly intertwined in our existence as body–mind and as self–others/world. Epistemologically, bodily feelings are then a source of "objective" knowledge of real-life experiences and embodied realities. But, Heyward asserts, we are prevented from being familiar with and trusting our sensory capacities by structures of oppression that separated the material from the spiritual, and the individual from relations in community.[37] Sin and evil are lack of mutuality in relationships and drive destructive structures of alienation, such as compulsory heterosexuality or white male patriarchy. The sacred, and with it, liberation, is found in rediscovering and fostering our mutual relationality, in understanding our being a person as social relationship.[38] Our bodyselves are the sites of social inscriptions and of our experiences of oppressive forces, yet a reawakened wielding of our sensory intelligence will enable us to do theology, the "critical, creative reflection on the patterns, shape, and movement of the sacred in our life together."[39]

Like other theologians discussed here, Heyward grounds divine revelation in incarnation, particularly relational aspects (not exclusive to interhuman relationality). She, too, stresses the divine character of traditionally undervalued and dismissed corporealities. As social creatures we are alienated from our truth-channeling bodily tools that we need to incorporate again into our bodyselves to experience holistic liberation. Yet she draws a distinction between social inscriptions on our bodies/experiences and our perceptual capacities, which appear as inhibited yet untainted bodily channels for meaning emanating in situations.

Bodily Perceptions

When constructing body theology in the manner reviewed this far, it is not always made explicit that the theologian themselves is embodied, and thus their work is not simply that of an intellect brought to bear on other bodies. And if the theologian is explicitly conceived as corporeally involved—in experiencing, seeing, interpreting—it is not made clear how exactly the body is at work. A closer look at perception and how it is implicitly or explicitly conceived of is useful to pinpoint the methodological

---

[37] Ibid., 187. Heyward leans on Audre Lorde in defining the erotic as "yearning to be involved," and hence turns to bodily, sensual, erotic bodily experiences as sources for theological constructions of right relations.

[38] Ibid., 56, 91, 191. Heyward's work on mutuality, intimacy, and forging connections through erotic power is not without critics, especially those concerned with abuse in relationships of differential power. Much of the criticism can be traced to differences in how "mutuality" is read, defined, and applied to specific myriad relationships, but especially relationships of institutionalized power and authority. For overviews and critical investigations on the controversy set off by some of Heyward's work in the psychotherapeutic professional community, see these representative discussions and critical applications: Roy Herndon Steinhoff Smith, "The Boundary Wars Mystery," *Religious Studies Review* 24, no. 2 (1998): 131–42; Bonnie Miller-McLemore, "Sloppy Mutuality: Just Love for Children and Adults," in *Mutuality Matters: Family, Faith, and Just Love*, ed. Herbert Anderson, Edward Foley, Bonnie Miller-McLemore, and Robert Schreiter (New York: Rowman & Littlefield, 2004), 121–35; Cristina L. H. Traina, *Erotic Attunement: Parenthood and the Ethics of Sensuality Between Unequals* (Chicago: University of Chicago Press, 2011), 220–40.

[39] Carter Isabel Heyward, *Our Passion for Justice: Images of Power, Sexuality, and Liberation* (New York: Pilgrim, 1984), 7; Heyward, *Touching Our Strength*, 22.

dilemma. In the select theologians I highlighted, explicitly or implied, perception is an essential theological act. Some theologians have a "mixed use" of perception as both activity of the body and the mind, but in most projects, perception ends up as evaluative-interpretive judgment of a critically informed mind and it is its intellectual dimension that is emphasized as central to theology.

John Paul II utilizes his senses to see the *imago Dei* in the other and measures what he perceives of the other against divinely inspired, transcendent doctrine (when he looks around he discerns how what he sees corresponds with what he already knows of god's vision of humanity). Elevating the intellectual work of the theologian over the matter of our bodily experiences contributes to maintaining violent structures based on bodily hierarchies. Nelson concedes that the act and content of sensory perception is not biologically determined, but that our biological bodily givens lead to tendencies toward particular perceptions of reality.[40] In this conception, a liberated consciousness takes the form of holistic perception, which will help us uncover and recognize the "naturally" embodied truths in all bodies, and theological construction is in large part the work of offering a "true" (liberating, nondualistic, holistic) perception-(re)interpretation of our bodily experiences.

In Sallie McFague, our communication as human bodies is grounded in our sensuous experiences, which are the basis for metaphors and the symbolic system central in our knowledge acquisition. Because language qualifies our human reality, there is no unmediated sensory access to raw data about the world. Our sensory impressions, affects, and bodily impressions are our most primordial level of experience and provide the basis for metaphors and symbol systems. Yet McFague's theological task is of a "higher" order, the (intellectual) analysis of our bodily perceptions in order to effect new experiences via re-symbolization. This process involves recognition and evaluating of how our language guides our perception, because we do not have access to an unmediated experience of being our bodily selves (we always already experience through the references given to us in language).[41] Sensory perception puts us in touch with/in the world that offers us meaning, but thought and judgment is an evaluative task of bodily acts of perception, coordinating sensory input with critical reflection. In Nancy Eiesland, that the privileged—disabled—epistemological standpoint provides critical perceptive ability to the theologian seems taken for granted. Different embodiment and differential consciousness appear linked, but the processes of discernment seem to remain in the theologian's consciousness and somehow based in particular embodied experiences—how one leads to the other is uncertain.

Theologians like Delores Williams and Marcella Althaus-Reid employ discursive analysis of how particular kind of bodies come to be and evaluate how they have been

---

[40] For example, framed in psychoanalytic theories of sexual development, he asserts that men are inclined toward a typically male perception of the world, that is, they perceive reality via a zero-sum, unilateral, linear, aggressive, domineering consciousness. James B. Nelson, *The Intimate Connection: Male Sexuality, Masculine Spirituality* (Philadelphia, PA: Westminster, 1988), 21–4, 100–103.

[41] McFague, *Metaphorical Theology*, 34–8; McFague, *The Body of God*, 53; McFague, *Models of God*, 26. The availability of linguistic references is not simply a matter of linguistic taxonomy, but reflects cultural necessity for differentiation of experience and in turn inevitably informs experience and imbued available meaning.

culturally inscribed, and construct liberating narratives in order to bring about new body experience (stories) into our reality. Methodologically, it is storied experiences and metaphors from particular social locations against which interpretation needs to be tested, which requires a critical consciousness that originated in a breakthrough experience of suspicion.[42] Thus constructing body theology heavily depends on consciousness formation, the ability to "correctly perceive" and discern structures of oppression and the shape of liberation.

And while Carter Heyward situates perception most explicitly in the body as the sensory knowing of the theologian, it is analogous to receiving information about the world via bodily sensor-tools. Carter Heyward conceives of perception and our bodily senses as our access to meaning, as *the* way to make the world intelligible to us, for example, to alert us to danger or injustice. While she stresses that being embodied in our particularity (actual physicality and social contexts) brings certain limitations to which kind of sensory data/material we are receptive to, sensory perception itself is bodily access to unmediated material, knowledge untainted by sociocultural forces that we only need to learn to tap into to then utilize/interpret theologically (implied to be task of the mind). In the attempt to revitalize the active role of the body in the constructive task of theology, sensory perception is rendered a passive, mechanistic bodily function.

The act of perception in these theological projects is presented as either a bodily sensation within the realm of experience itself, and thus shaped by social structures, so that the theologian's intellectual task is to analyze and evaluate what and how bodies perceive from the outside; or bodily sensation is conceived of as distinct from social formation, an ontological corporeal ability to access and retrieve information in the world, and the theologian's task is to process this raw material, again an intellectual task.[43] More often than not then bodies make an appearance as theological objects and experiences become raw materials to be accessed, apprehended, and turned into text and metaphor to be utilized theologically.[44] Rarely is sensory experience itself conceived of as theologizing act, as bodily movement that materializes, maintains, and possibly shifts what is known and knowable in our context.

---

[42] See, for example, Elisabeth Schüssler-Fiorenza, *But She Said: Feminist Practices of Biblical Interpretation* (Boston, MA: Beacon, 1992), 21, 34.

[43] This is the empiricism–intellectualism spectrum of theorizing perception. Broadly speaking, empiricists understand this world to exist in itself imposing meaning on the perceiver and allow for the possibility of absolute objectivity. Intellectualists frame the world as immanent end of knowledge, in which a consciousness sustains the objective world constructed by empiricists. Empiricism frames the perceptual process by rendering the subject ignorant (because consciousness is denied a role in the process, though invoked for other functions). Intellectualism theorizes a subject completely cognizant of what is perceived. On this spectrum, perception is either a causal link in a mechanistic bodily process or an event/state in the mind. Despite some of our actual sense experiences being ambiguous or vague, both approaches theorize perception as determinate and corresponding to a (self-evident) objective world. Maurice Merleau-Ponty, *Phenomenology of Perception*, trans. Colin French (New York: Routledge, 1962), 29, 35–9.

[44] Part of our epistemological confinement can be based in language: In English, I "have" a body, I see "with" my eyes, I touch you with my hands, and so on, and there are no linguistic expressions available that make explicit that I *am* a body and that I *am* eyes seeing. Hence, some of the theologians mentioned earlier offer us conceptions of ourselves as bodyselves or bodyminds.

To prevent reinstating the body and bodily experience as an object of inquiry detached from (disembodied) intellectual tasks, theologians need to move from asking whether, or which and whose, bodily experience is to be a valuable/valid resource, toward inquiring how our existence as experiencing beings situates us in the world and how our perception is implicated herein. When claiming bodily experience as significant for theological construction, it requires accounting for how exactly it is that bodies are open to the world through the senses, how the world materializes and makes sense because of bodily perceptions. This will allow for a conceptualization of bodily perception itself as locus of theological imagination, as the space where self–world–divine engage in knowing and being known.

Being Bodies Perceiving

When experiences are sourced for theological work, then theologians need to begin with the premise that *any and all* experiences are essentially *bodily* experiences. Being in the world as body is my fundamental experience of myself: I read with my eyes or type with my fingers to record a theologically significant experience; I tell the story with my voice shaped by sounds in my throat and mouth; I analyze my experiences of being shaped by social expectations and resulting emotions often revisited (an intellectual exercise that itself depends on my actually being a thinking-breathing-feeling body); I engage in the act of remembering and thinking about experiences, and this is a shaping of and living engagement in and through my own embodiment, past and present.

Our *bodily* acts of hearing from, thinking about, remembering as, writing of, and so on are always experiences in the threshold space of me–others–world–divine. Theology as the work of interpreting and (re)crafting meanings that emerge at this hinge between worlds is then situated as embodied work in the most fundamental way: it is constructive not only in terms of sourcing bodily experiences, it is bodily constructive activity and theological movement in itself, and as such structured and constituted by what shapes this interrelated body–world–divine space. A closer look at our senses will allow us to conceptualize and explore the body, and particularly perception, as *the* space of crafting and (re)orienting messages about the divine–world relation.

My "body is my point of view of the world."[45] Merleau-Ponty theorized bodily perception as space and process of how we make sense to the world and of the world, and frames a way beyond conceiving our meaning-making solely as intellectual act (as thoughts or as mindful grasp on the world). I can only experience myself and/in the world insofar that I am a body that relates in/to the world. This essential bodily capacity is perceptual: how and what I feel, touch, smell, think, dream, learn, see, and so on *is* my experiencing in the world. "*I am bodily perceiving*" is my minimum condition of being. To *be* is to experience, to experience is to bodily perceive, and to perceive is to

---

[45] I can never have a perspective in and on the world that is not already derived from a perspective based in my specific embodiment. Merleau-Ponty, *Phenomenology of Perception*, 70.

be oriented in the world engaging in bodily sociocultural acts.[46] What exactly does that mean and imply? Perception is at work in all dimensions of my embodied existence. All experiencing of/in the world is to experience through and with my senses, the world I experience is always shaped in/through my perceptions, and in a reverse manner, how and what I perceive with my senses is also already shaped by the world.

I perceive myself in/and the world in reference to my body: that food over there is something I really want right now; the cabinet in the kitchen that holds bowls is too high for me to reach. Rather than passively channeling data about the world for me, my bodily senses imbue my experiencing with *intentionality* ("about-ness"), so that in being perceptually, I am actively reaching into and engaging the world. My seeing food on the counter while listening to music on the radio is my active *transcendence*, my outward movement into the world. My experiential references are bodily and come already charged with significance, the world already means something and makes sense to me in as I perceptually reach into it.[47] I already have tacit knowledge of how "I can" in my environment: the food that I would like to eat is made by me and for me, I hope it will not be too spicy, its aroma is heavenly to me, and to properly (according to my cultural norms) consume it I know I will need silverware, and use that particular stool to reach that upper cabinet, and if I move like this I will be able to get that bowl with just one hand.[48]

Every act of perception directs me toward and into the world, yet in perceiving I am embedded with a sense of relationship and participation in the world, and through perception, the world also reaches toward me.[49] Our bodily existence is organically interrelated with that of the world, in an *intertwined dependency of becoming*. The world, my environment, and other bodies engage me and make me meaningful, but not in universal or arbitrary ways. I move within and as part of a world in which cultural contexts provide a set of seemingly inescapable meanings. What the world means to me-as-specific-body is constituted in my movements in the world, and I am also constituted by the world acting upon me. A depository of collected repeatedly emerging meanings, the *sediment of perceptual habits*, subtends my sensory experiences in and of the world.[50] Habits are neither universal nor naturally inherent to our bodily existence, but we acquire and change them through repetition: "That's what your people like to eat, girls don't sit like that, people like you need to speak up more, bodies like yours don't look like they should be in the pulpit or get to go into this particular bathroom" are messages through which the world is acting upon me, indicating how I perceptually

---

[46] Ibid., 346.
[47] Ibid., 106.
[48] This is Merleau-Ponty's "body schema," the specific way of being in the world in a given environment, something necessary to subjective self-perception as bodily whole, and for perception of the world as a coherent whole, rather than a conglomerate of parts. David Morris, "Body," in *Merleau-Ponty: Key Concepts*, ed. Rosalyn Diprose and Jack Reynolds (Stocksfield, UK: Acumen, 2008), 116.
[49] Paul Rodaway, *Sensuous Geographies: Body, Sense and Place* (New York: Routledge, 1994), 8.
[50] Merleau-Ponty argues that certain meanings appear inescapable because cultural contexts are a depository, the *sediment*, of collected repeatedly emerging meanings. This sedimentation of habits is a condition of our mutual existence and subtends my experience (without conscious efforts to connect to it). Sedimentations of habit are changeable repositories of meaning that respond to cultural flux.

emerge to the world, how and what bodies like mine come to mean, and which spaces and bodily movements are available for bodies (not) like mine. And in each repetition, I participate in this sedimentation of habits while also possibly expanding, subverting, and changing its perceptual horizon of possible meanings.[51]

The minimum condition for my existence is that I am a body perceived/ing, and in perception, meaning emerges in the body–world interrelation. My physical body and capacities as well as the repeated and culturally settled perceptual habits of, for example, gendered, raced, and ableist norms and restrictions aligned with bodies like me determine what perceptually emerges as literally and figuratively too high for me to reach (or not) and desire (or not) in social spaces. My body may belong in the kitchen or in the board room, I may emerge meaning-fully as out of place, or I may perceptually appear in a specific space as desirable or threatening, sounding agreeable or repulsive to others. There is no neutral gaze, no objective touch shaping me: I am formed and classified by socio-bodily perceptual habits that construct what my perceived sex, gender, race, ability come to mean, and that determine my bodily possibilities here and now. Sensory habits establish and maintain social ordering through, for example, racialized and socioeconomic mechanisms that enforce habitually perceiving, controlling, and enforcing what particular bodies mean and how/where they can move in particular contexts.[52]

Sara Ahmed theorizes this intertwined body–world shaping of bodily senses as *perceptual orientation*. Perceptual orientation creates *alignments* in space: I only know which way to turn once I know which way I am facing. When I see, touch, feel, hear others in relation to myself in the world, I determine if they are left, right, front, behind, near, far—but in this perceptual act others also emerge as desirable, approachable, graspable, or even perceivable (and thus conceivable), and others may not perceptually exist at all in particular ways.[53] I am directed toward objects, positions, certain bodies that I habitually perceive as subjects of desire; other bodies may be aligned as objects of knowledge for me; some bodies emerge in my perception as out of line in regards to a specific privilege, and so on. And, in perception, spaces align me in regards to desire, knowledge, and privilege: perceptual orienting lines direct how I as particular body can move in this space, how I line up with objects of desire, and which of my

---

[51] Iris Marion Young describes this in *Throwing Like a Girl*. A woman's sense of "I can" is also an "I cannot"—an inhibited and ambivalent bodily intentionality: a tacit understanding of a general "I can" that is not within *her* possibilities, within her particular female bodily movements and self-transcendence. Iris Marion Young, *On Female Body Experience: "Throwing Like a Girl" and Other Essays*, Studies in Feminist Philosophy (New York: Oxford University Press, 2005), 27–45. See also Gayle Salamon's investigation of the construction of trans selves, describing an intersubjectively produced body schema, the felt sense of a trans(itioning) body, a body that might not "be" one's material substance. Gayle Salamon, *Assuming a Body: Transgender and Rhetorics of Materiality* (New York: Columbia University Press, 2010). Judith Butler articulates on the repetition and potential for subversion in "Performative Acts and Gender Constitution: An Essay in Phenomenology and Feminist Theory," *Theater Journal* 40:4 (1988): 519–31.

[52] Mark M. Smith, *How Race Is Made: Slavery, Segregation, and the Senses* (Chapel Hill: University of North Carolina Press, 2006). This sensory history of race in the United States describes the mediation of racial identities through sound, smell, taste, and touch, particularly when racially mixed populations made clearly defined and visually discernable racial identities unstable.

[53] Sara Ahmed, *Queer Phenomenology: Orientations, Objects, Others* (Durham, NC: Duke University Press, 2006), 54.

movements may cross the line of how to "makes sense" of someone like me, who emerges with a body that already—perceptually—feels queer, looks brown and able-bodied, and sounds foreign. Such lines of orientation are sediment perceptual habits, social investments toward a certain way of perceiving things. For example, bodies emerging in spaces in which colonization and patriarchy reinforce orienting lines perceptually face whiteness, individual wealth, heteronormative relationships as that which is desirable, though not necessarily achievable for just any body.

Because of our socially habituated orientations, what is meaningfully perceived emerges already arranged along certain lines and stands out against a background.[54] This background is precisely that which gives rise to my perceptions as always already meaningful. As a perceiving being, I already bodily conform to the "logic of the world," to the kinds of ways my particular cultural context already provides the possibilities and conditions of my perceptual emergence. And my cultural context shapes my bodily interactions in the world and orients me toward certain possible interpretations, so that particular meanings appear inescapable.[55] My senses are socially shaped, oriented, and regulated along certain lines of desire that become compulsory, so that I see myself and others as sexed and gendered bodies, bodies that have a race, are associated with a nation, are disabled, and so on, without noticing that this emergence can only be meaningful against a background in which whiteness, nationalism, ableism, and heteronormativity aligned our perceptions to enable such recognitions.[56]

For example, race as bodily feature is not an independent, universal, natural occurrence in the world. Bodies are racialized in/through habits of perception. The fantasy of biologically established racial hierarchy is an orientation device that gathers on a background of colonialism and works with orienting lines of blackness/whiteness to generate a direction of perception, namely, seeing/experiencing raced bodies, bodies that emerge already being a race and moving into the world that imbues them with value. Racial identities were and are mediated and articulated through sound, smell, taste, and touch. "Knowing" what embodied blackness sounds like, what black hair feels like, what black bodies smell like, that blackness is dangerous and signifies evil, and so on serve as a sensory tool to align and segregate bodies in space, and lend legitimacy to segregation and its enforcement based on racially charged sensory qualifications.[57] This kind of sensory education into racial perception and coming-to-experience

---

[54] Background is a term appropriated from Gestalt psychology, denoting the context against which a figure comes to "stand out" and into perceptual focus, which gives meaning to the perceived figure, but which remains "out of focus."

[55]
> There is a logic of the world to which my body in its entirety conforms, and through which things of intersensory significance become possible for us ... A thing is, therefore, not actually *given* in perception, rather it is internally taken by us, reconstituted and experienced by us in so far as it is bound up with a world, the basic structures of which we carry with us, and of which it is merely one of many possible concrete forms. (Merleau-Ponty, *Phenomenology of Perception*, 326; emphasis in original)

[56] Or, for example, that the past is "behind me" and the future "ahead of me" is not a universal perceptual orientation to time, nor has chronological temporality always been sensory alignment.

[57] Smith, *How Race Is Made*, 48–62. Odor, sound, tactile differences supported an alignment of morality with particular bodies and within perceptual grasp of those bodies only. Segregation, legal decisions, social activities, and so on were based on sensory qualifications that were racially charged.

race depends on sedimented habits that shape backgrounds and orienting lines, and sociocultural technologies or perceptual orienting devices do the work of providing the continuity for perceptual orientations to habituate and become coherent over time. For example, particular immigration laws and law enforcement practices (by government ordained as well as vigilante bodies), voting laws and regulations, and so on become orienting devices and create and reinforce which bodies can emerge meaningfully as full and desirable citizens (not foreign, not hyphenated) along lines of race, and our sensory habits and tacit knowledges are aligned in our perceptions.[58] When and where the male, straight, white, and Christian body emerges aligned as desirable and in line with that which we are habituated to face as, say, desirable leader of a particular community, then the perceptual work provided in backgrounds of whiteness, patriarchal heterosexuality, US American nationalism, and Christian supremacy, which constantly reinforce this alignment of certain bodies with inherent moral, social, religious superiority, is relegated out of sight.

The space of theological construction, in this threshold of body–world–divine interrelation, is already inherently structured by a "perceptual grid" of gender, race, and other bodily orientations. I am already exposed and vulnerable to the bodily effects and alignments in the world, though in my bodily experience I also embody choice and creativity, opacities of meaning, and resistances in how I-as-body live out these social and bodily perceptual habits. Potential reorientations, *resistance to the structures of meaning*, sensed dissonances in our bodily perceptions may become new habits of movements with each other, but they do depend on being recognizable, if only marginally/peripherally. A black Jesus, god as mother, god incarnated in the sexual experiences of a queer unhoused youth—in my own personal religious sensorium, these are configurations that my own religious upbringing aligned with sin, indecency, "other" from the holy. As theologically "failed alignments," failures to be in line or in tune with the dominant perceptual orientation, they have the potential for reorientations toward new experienced meanings only because they are already recognizable as failures, ambiguities, or paradox within a specific cultural matrix.[59] "Jesus," "god," "black," "queer" already are part of my world of meanings that can perceptually emerge in my experiences; thus they are not newly created meanings, but realigned meanings emerging out of perceptually reorienting and facing bodies

---

[58] See, for example, the exemplary analysis and theological work by Kelly Brown Douglas, *Stand Your Ground: Black Bodies and the Justice of God* (Maryknoll, NY: Orbis Books, 2015). Douglas traces the myth of white racial supremacy through its productions and reproductions via Manifest Destiny, American exceptionalism, and the habituation into racialized discourse and institutions that glorify and sanctify the protection of whiteness and white bodies at all cost, especially at the expense of nonwhite bodies, and from it, constructs the theological meaning of faith, sin, and freedom.

[59] I am borrowing here from Judith Butler's work on subjectivity, which she describes in her earlier works as irrevocably produced and shaped by discourse. Agency is possible insofar as discourse and social technologies shape the subject, but it is essentially a subjected agency. In later works, the Butlerian subject gains more moral agency through acts of deviance, though it is dependent on intersubjective recognition to be constituted as moral agent. Judith Butler, *The Psychic Life of Power: Theories in Subjection* (Stanford, CA: Stanford University Press, 1997); Judith Butler, *Giving an Account of Oneself* (New York: Fordham University Press, 2005). For an account of the development of Butler's account of agency, see Kathy Dow Magnus, "The Unaccountable Subject: Judith Butler and the Social Conditions of Intersubjective Agency," *Hypathia* 21, no. 2 (2006).

in different alignments. Or to use gender as an example: If god is male or female, or beyond such alignment with one or the other gender, if god is made meaningful only in complementary binary human embodiment, or if god emerges in genderqueer potentiality, any of these alignments already depend on a context in which our structures of meaning provide perceptual possibilities of how gender can emerge as a human bodily feature. Different cultural contexts may provide different perceptual possibilities, from multiple gender options to different sensory alignments, which then form a different perceptual background against which the divine can be aligned.[60] Such realignments of meanings, such reorientations against the grain of what is "normally" perceived, can give the world a new, sense-able shape—but it takes (sensory) work. The embodied acts of tending toward an indecent or abject divine have to be repeated to become sustainable and habitual, and this repetition often takes place in the face of discrimination and violence.[61]

Being Perceptually Theologizing Bodies

We exist in the world as bodies experiencing through and with our senses in an interdependent body–world relation that is fundamentally perceptual. I experience a world that emerges in cultural, sexed, raced, religious, and socioeconomic manifestations, among others, and this experience coincides and depends on my own emerging, being, and transcending in a situation as cultural, sexed, raced, religious, normal-able, socioeconomic body. I am a body perceiving, and I know the world as sensorily, and the world knows what I mean as I materialize to their senses. Even my thinking, imagining, dreaming, speaking are bodily experiences and thereby perceptual acts, constituted and performed in just the way we explored the body–world relation earlier. What I perceive as I move in the world and as part of the world, what is meaningful and imaginable to me, is aligned for me through my sensory education. When I engage in theological construction, what is imaginable, thinkable, sense-able of the divine, the salvific, the redemptive, always already builds on bodily experiences in which the world and I are made together in perception according to a given contextual logic to which we conform. In terms of theological method, a foundational presumption for body theology then needs to be: I don't simply have a body, but AM a body, and I am always a perceptual body experiencing; thus, my bodily sensory experience *is* me. My senses are educated into always already perceiving meaningfully, and thus, *my bodily experiences are my theological imaginations* that emerge as I move in the world and am shaped in it. In other words, the threshold of me–others–world–divine is the space of my bodily sensory experiences; therefore, my theological imaginations *are* in/my bodily experiences, what I imagine as truth about

---

[60] Constance Classen, *The Color of Angels*, 46–50, describes how odors of sanctity and the stench of sin and hell aligned persons and places along religious hierarchies, and sensory specialists emerged who had particular olfactory skills or heightened (in)tolerance. See also David Howes, *Sensual Relations: Engaging the Senses in Culture and Social Theory* (Ann Arbor: University of Michigan Press, 2003).

[61] Ahmed, *Queer Phenomenology*, 101–3.

myself and others, how I experience despair and what is aligned with my desire for freedom, what and where I imagine hope and salvation emerge in bodily experiences that is my knowledge of the world.

Hence, body theology needs to be a query into our perceptual experience to trace the structures of our bodily theological imagination. For example, a body theology method conceives of my experiences of the divine as my sensory transcendence and part of coming into being perceptually. As my vision, my touch, my smell, my hearing extend me into the world to see the hand of god at work and hear the word of god in the moment, I cannot grasp/fix the divine in my perception as object of my experience. Rather, my perceptual intentionality, the about-ness and for-me-ness of my experiences, is part of an intertwined relationship of meaning-making—the divine and I come to be meaningfully in this relationship. What god and I come to mean in a specific context is neither universal nor arbitrary. My cultural context provides the meanings available, which depend on sedimented habits. What and how my senses will recognize and therefore experience as divine is culturally shaped and oriented. For example, my European Protestant cultural upbringing has shaped my sensory life in ways to imbue superiority to intellectualized seeing/reading and speaking/hearing of god, expressed in our language and recognized in preaching of The Word and written dissemination of Divine Truth.[62] So "naturally," my experiencing of the divine is aligned in such a way that meaningful knowledge of god is perceptually transmitted to me in those particular sensory ways, so that growing up, I tended to privilege hearing god over sensing odors of the divine throughout my day.[63] Immersed in an aforementioned background of white, colonial, heteronormative Christianity, my experience of the divine was also oriented in perceptually facing god in the male, white, straight savior Jesus. And because the emergence of my own meaning and that of the divine is perceptually intertwined, and some kind of bodies emerged as more closely aligned with divinity, my emergence as female, brown, queer self, too often came to mean as other-than-divine to myself and others.

Theological (bodily–sensory–imaginative) resistance to experiencing the divine as legitimizing oppressive social structures (of whiteness, Christian supremacy, able-bodied and able-mindedness, etc.) is possible and is itself a perceptual disorientation and realignment of our senses. Other cultural contexts provide examples of different ways of sensing-knowing often foreclosed where vision, speech, and rational inquiry are privileged.[64] Feeling and knowing the divine in the singing, stomping, and sweating of the circle dance, or experiencing the message of god as real and true only because sweat can be felt on the human messenger's body are different ways of imbuing epistemological authority. This kind of resistant, disorienting theological sensorium is

---

[62] A note on not capitalizing god throughout this chapter—capital G God is already a sensory performance of meaning and sedimentation of (reading) recognition habits that make a (Christian) monotheistic god superior to other gods. Enforced in grammar rules that can be adhered to by Christians and non-Christians alike, the power of sensory habits is noticeable when a small g god "pops out" to readers in English reading as "off."

[63] Classen, *The Color of Angels*, 36–7.

[64] See the works in sensory anthropology, such as David Howes, ed., *The Varieties of Sensory Experience* (Toronto, Canada: University of Toronto Press, 1991). Or Howes, *Sensual Relations*.

shaped in cultural contexts realigning theologically what makes sense perceptually as liberation and freedom to particular bodies.[65] Heeding marginalized sensory ways of knowing in theological constructions is a way to integrate what is already, in our bodily experience, acting and making claims on bodily life.

Constructing Theology with a Body Method, Precariously

As a craft, theology more often than not is implicitly or explicitly the telling of stories/ the story of the divine in the (human) world, and it can be a challenge to realign/cross into spaces of suppressed and undervalued experiences: experiencing the mattering of bodies that do theology (in experiencing and communicating their experience), but which are commonly denied their "speaking" against that which has come to count as acceptable god-talk.[66] Without a concept of how we as bodies always already "speak" (transcend into the world) and make meaning, and without theological spaces in which this emerging meaning can be traced and accounted for, we will always be tempted to fall for speaking *about* and *for*, rather than *with* and *through* all our bodies, especially those without access to language proper (voice, language, and agency we are already culturally tuned into and we deem worth considering). Theology in this vein ubiquitously tends to worry about adequate representation of bodily experiences rather than actually allowing it to be present. In other words, we rush to represent the subject and narrate its moral agency, rather than letting the subject *be* and creating conditions that support our embodied presence and recognition of meaning-making differences.[67]

In theological anthropology, for example, when constructing human subjectivity and agency, certain bodies tended to be theologically "troublesome," as theologians wrestled with a sediment habit of overemphasizing rationality and intellectual capacities. A body methodology needs to embrace uncertainty and unknowing that emerges (to me as able-minded person) in the embodiment of persons with severe cognitive impairment: When I presume bodily perception as fundamental condition of being in the world, then *all* persons actively engage in interrelated meaning-making, because *all* bodies reach into and grasp the world sensorially. Not all persons tend

---

[65] See, for example, Rachel E. Harding, "YOU GOT A RIGHT TO THE TREE OF LIFE: African American Spirituals and Religions of the Diaspora," *CrossCurrents* 57, no. 2 (2007): 266–80. Or Anthony Pinn, "Sweaty Bodies in a Circle: Thoughts on the Subtle Dimensions of Black Religion as Protest," *Black Theology* 4:1 (2006): 11–26. It is not that in some contexts, certain senses are used while others are not, but how culturally some senses are privileged over others to be more "truthful." These are experiences of the cultural shaping and privileging of perception.

[66] Emilie Townes explores embodied knowledge found on the margins and points to the illusion of autonomous selves as moral agents. Different embodied experiences are different ways of knowing and bring about different ways of embodying and transmitting moral agency. Emily M. Townes, *Womanist Ethics and the Cultural Production of Evil* (New York: Palgrave Macmillan, 2006).

[67] Gayatri Chakravorty Spivak's often-cited essay "Can the Subaltern Speak?" discusses the dynamics of power and race as epistemic violence inflicted on subaltern consciousness and voice. Gayatri Chakravorty Spivak, "Can the Subaltern Speak?," in *Colonial Discourse and Postcolonial Theory*, ed. Patrick Williams and Laura Chrisman (New York: Columbia University Press, 1994).

to be perceived by able-minded normates as having a "conscious" grasp of their environment.[68] But no matter how my cognitive capacities may be perceived by others, I am part of the intertwined perceptual orientation in relationship; perceptually, I am part of sense-making activities in the world and extend as agent into my shared world. In a body theology approach that has conceptualized perception in the way outlined in this chapter, it is not the question of agency of subjectivity that needs to be theologically justified, because all persons are theologizing, meaning-making bodies. Rather, my task is to theologically explore the sensory alignments, the cultural training of our perception that orients me to conceive of certain persons as "just bodies" who are questionably human "without" full capacities of mind. And from there, the demand put to me is to engage in acts of sensory disorientation, seeing, touching, feeling the divine in my grandmother with late-stage Alzheimer's, or my student on the autism spectrum—all of us fully human, all of us bound up together and making each other.[69]

As body in the world with other bodies, I always already make theology, speak of what is god, even against my intellectual pronouncements. With body theology, bodily movements and actions are not merely more or less reliable expressions of intellectualized belief, but in itself manifest theology: I can trace whose bodies are made salvific, whose bodies are divine and too sacred to approach, and how. I can trace perceptual alignments through which bodies are sacrificed to make up the matter of ecological and economic priorities and privileges, of white supremacist surveillance, of hetero-patriarchal ableist arrangements. I can point to perceptual orientations that determine which bodies are legalized, sanctified, and safeguarded from and through the dangerous and disposable bodies made abject. A body theology method can expose the dissonance of pronouncements that all bodies are equal messengers of the divine with bodily movements and habituations complicit in racially segregated neighborhoods, school-to-prison-pipelines, and so on, which thereby continue to sediment sensory habits of sacred whiteness. The theologies—god-talk—emerging from social meaning-making contexts speak loudly through my everyday movements of what is sacred, whose bodies are perceived as imbued with sacred power, and who may enter spaces conceived of as holy and who is literally barred from them.

The strength of theological constructions that claim bodily experience as a source rests with attention to sensory meaning-making in all the dimension of bodily life: social/cultural habits, language, collective and individual bodily movements, perceptual alignments, sensory orientations, and perceptual devices. To do *theological construction with a body methodology* must not be restricted to making sense *of* bodily experience, but must include framing bodily experiences as making sense, making meaning, and always already informed by a logic within which meaning is

---

[68] "Normate" is disability scholar Rosemary Garland Thomson's term for the unmarked authoritative identity position, the imagined "normal person": self-determined, rational, able-minded, and able-bodied. Rosemarie Garland Thomson, *Extraordinary Bodies: Figuring Physical Disability in American Culture and Literature* (New York: Columbia University Press, 1997), 8.

[69] This kind of approach also would allow for a conception of the "natural world" as agentic. I do not have the space to elaborate on it here, but in this theological method utilizing perception, the nonhuman and even nonanimal world takes an active part in knowledge creation and changing meanings.

perceived bodily. Body theologies need to account for how bodily knowledge (which *is* our theological knowledge) emerges, how (theological) perceptions and perceivable possibilities are made meaningful, are ambiguous and open to change, and where perceptual tensions and contradictions may appear. Taking perception seriously raises the stakes of doing body theology. No matter which theological discipline I employ, when making embodiment explicitly central to our theology, we now ought to consider the following:

- *Bodily experience makes sense*: That is my sense-making in the world. To do body theology is to acknowledge that I actively create and make meaning as I bodily move with and within embodied contexts. To position bodily experience as resource in theology, I need to acknowledge that bodies always already make sense: there is already a logic to bodily experiences, and bodily experiences create and manifest meaning.
- *Perception grounds our existence*: Perception is embedded in sociocultural habits, languages, bodily movements, orientations and is open to change, to tensions and contradictions, ambiguity and paradox.
- *Theologically, I need to embrace ambiguity and paradox*: Bodily experiences, because of their perceptual nature, are ambiguous and paradoxical and there is no static meaning fixed to certain experiences. Body theology must remain open to disorientations, changing meanings, perceptual ambiguities, and movements. This can be a strength of body theology in that it allows for attending to cracks, fissures, and occlusions in our theological orientations.
- *Theological construction can remain epistemologically unsettled*: If I indeed acknowledge and even nurture ambiguity in my theological constructions, I cannot strive for certainty and full understanding. I might deepen my understanding of specific experiences, but it will always be contingent and momentary. Methodologically, this infuses body theology with a mobile constructivity: grounded in lived bodily experiences and continuously attending to new meanings emerging.

Body theology can theologize "impurely," in the ambiguous and paradox dissonance of what I might (profess to) believe and what my bodily perceptual orientation reveals (in other words, there may be many gods emerging in my bodily movements). Body theology, with its openness to multiple meanings, can constructively work beyond a Christian Logic of One that seeks to articulate a universal singular truth account.[70] Tracing the divine in perceptual movements and bodily meaning-making can enable me toward creative theologizing that recognizes that in experience god, indeed, is many, and the multitude of the divine as it emerges in specific contexts is not always pretty, reconcilable, or even good. I may not intellectually confess belief in a white hetero supremacist God, but I can trace how that God indeed does act in the world through my body, and I need to urgently recognize how I continue to materialize that God in my bodily experiences. Perceptual openness enables me to orient myself toward what

---

[70] Laurel Schneider, *Beyond Monotheism: A Theology of Multiplicity*. (London: Routledge, 2008).

demands flourishing in this messy, embodied world, and to align myself bodily with the work that brings about a god in whom truly all lives—queer, brown, trans, disabled, and so on—matter/materialize. I can disorient myself to theological business as usual and seek to foster theologizing the divine in the flesh, in the hinges of the speakable and unspeakable, in/as the connections that ground and enable life and change of bodies, worlds, and cultures. Because my bodily experiences *are* my theological imaginations, I am presented with a moral demand: to account for how my bodily experiences take on shape and meaning and to construct theology as visceral, embodied, sense-able movements. I may bodily theologize—move my body in ways that cross perceptual habits, move against the lines of what is "normal," "good," "worthwhile"—and let my articulated theological language continue to catch up with what bodies, ambiguously, precariously, fluidly, may already work to make meaningful in the world.

Bibliography

Ahmed, Sara. *Queer Phenomenology: Orientations, Objects, Others*. Durham, NC: Duke University Press, 2006.
Althaus-Reid, Marcella M. *Indecent Theology: Theological Perversions in Sex, Gender and Politics*. New York: Routledge, 2000.
Althaus-Reid, Marcella M. *The Queer God*. New York: Routledge, 2003.
Brock, Rita Nakashima, Jung Ha Kim, Kwok Pui-Lan, and Seung Ai Yang. *Off the Menu: Asian and Asian North American Women's Religion and Theology*. Louisville, KY: Westminster John Knox, 2007.
Butler, Judith. *Giving an Account of Oneself*. New York: Fordham University Press, 2005.
Butler, Judith. "Performative Acts and Gender Constitution: An Essay in Phenomenology and Feminist Theory." *Theater Journal* 40:4 (1988): 519–31.
Butler, Judith. *The Psychic Life of Power: Theories in Subjection*. Stanford, CA: Stanford University Press, 1997.
Carman, Taylor. *Merleau-Ponty*. Routledge Philosophers. Edited by Brian Leiter. New York: Routledge, 2008.
Carrington, Christopher. *No Place Like Home: Relationships and Family Life among Lesbians and Gay Men*. Chicago: Chicago University Press, 1999.
Classen, Constance. *The Color of Angels: Cosmology, Gender and the Aesthetic Imagination*. New York: Routledge, 1998.
Creamer, Deborah Beth. *Disability and Christian Theology: Embodied Limits and Constructive Possibilities*. New York: Oxford University Press, 2009.
Douglas, Kelly Brown. *Stand Your Ground: Black Bodies and the Justice of God*. Maryknoll, NY: Orbis Books, 2015.
Eiesland, Nancy L. *The Disabled God: Toward a Liberatory Theology of Disability*. Nashville, TN: Abingdon, 1994.
Eiesland, Nancy L. "Sacramental Bodies." *Journal of Religion, Disability & Health* 13:3–4 (2009): 236–46.
Fulkerson, Mary McClintock. *Changing the Subject: Women's Discourses and Feminist Theology*. Minneapolis, MN: Fortress, 1994.
Garland Thomson, Rosemarie. *Extraordinary Bodies: Figuring Physical Disability in American Culture and Literature*. New York: Columbia University Press, 1997.

Harding, Rachel Elizabeth. "YOU GOT A RIGHT TO THE TREE OF LIFE: African American Spirituals and Religions of the Diaspora." *CrossCurrents* 57:2 (2007): 266–80.
Heyward, Carter Isabel. *Our Passion for Justice: Images of Power, Sexuality, and Liberation.* New York: Pilgrim, 1984.
Heyward, Carter Isabel. *Touching Our Strength: The Erotics as Power and the Love of God.* San Francisco, CA: Harper & Row, 1989.
Howes, David. *Sensual Relations: Engaging the Senses in Culture and Social Theory.* Ann Arbor: University of Michigan Press, 2003.
Howes, David, ed. *The Varieties of Sensory Experience.* Toronto, Canada: University of Toronto Press, 1991.
Hunt, Mary E. *Fierce Tenderness: A Feminist Theology of Friendship.* New York: Crossroad, 1994.
Irigaray, Luce. *Speculum of the Other Woman.* Translated by G. C. Gill. Ithaca, NY: Cornell University Press, 1985.
Irigaray, Luce. *This Sex Which Is Not One.* Translated by C. Porter and C. Burke. Ithaca, NY: Cornell University Press, 1985.
Isasi-Díaz, Ada María. *Mujerista Theology: A Theology for the Twenty-First Century.* New York: Orbis Books, 1996.
Isherwood, Lisa. *The Power of Erotic Celibacy: Queering Heteropatriarchy.* New York: T&T Clark, 2006.
Jones, Serene. "Women's Experience between a Rock and a Hard Place: Feminist, Womanist, and Mujerista Theologies in North America." In *Horizons in Feminist Theology: Identity, Tradition, and Norms*, edited by Rebecca S. Chopp and Sheila Greeve Davaney, 137–53. Minneapolis, MN: Fortress, 1997.
Keller, Catherine. "The Apophasis of Gender: Fourfold Unsaying of Feminist Theology." *Journal of the American Academy of Religion* 76 (2008): 905–33.
Kwok, Pui-Lan, ed. *Hope Abundant: Third World and Indigenous Women's Theology.* Maryknoll, NY: Orbis Books, 2010.
Kwok, Pui-Lan. *Postcolonial Imagination and Feminist Theology.* Louisville, KY: Westminster John Knox, 2005.
Lakoff, George, and Mark Johnson. *Metaphors We Live By.* Chicago: University of Chicago Press, 1980; rpt. 2003.
Lakoff, George, and Mark Johnson. *Philosophy in the Flesh: The Embodied Mind and Its Challenge to Western Thought.* New York: Basic Books, 1999.
Laqueur, Thomas. *Making Sex: Body and Gender from the Greeks to Freud.* Cambridge, MA: Harvard University Press, 1990.
Lelwica, Michelle Mary. *Shameful Bodies: Religion and the Culture of Physical Improvement.* New York: Bloomsbury, 2017.
Magnus, Kathy Dow. "The Unaccountable Subject: Judith Butler and the Social Conditions of Intersubjective Agency." *Hypathia* 21:2 (2006): 81–103.
Marratto, Scott L. *The Intercorporeal Self: Merleau-Ponty on Subjectivity.* Contemporary French Thought. Edited by David Pettigrew and Francois Raffoul. Albany: State University of New York Press, 2012.
McFague, Sallie. *The Body of God: An Ecological Theology.* Minneapolis, MN: Fortress, 1993.
McFague, Sallie. *Metaphorical Theology: Models of God in Religious Language.* Philadelphia, PA: Fortress, 1982.
McFague, Sallie. *Models of God: Theology for an Ecological, Nuclear Age.* Philadelphia, PA: Fortress, 1987.

Merleau-Ponty, Maurice. *Phenomenology of Perception*. Translated by Colin French. New York: Routledge, 1962.
Merleau-Ponty, Maurice. *The Primacy of Perception and Other Essays on Phenomenological Psychology, the Philosophy of Art, History and Politics*. Evanston, IL: Northwestern University Press, 1964.
Miller-McLemore, Bonnie. "Sloppy Mutuality: Just Love for Children and Adults." In *Mutuality Matters: Family, Faith, and Just Love*, edited by Herbert Anderson, Edward Foley, Bonnie Miller-McLemore, and Robert Schreiter, 121–35. New York: Rowan and Littlefield, 2004.
Moltmann-Wendel, Elisabeth. *I Am My Body: A Theology of Embodiment*. New York: Continuum, 1995.
Morris, David. "Body." In *Merleau-Ponty: Key Concepts*. Edited by Rosalyn Diprose and Jack Reynolds, 110–20. Stocksfield, UK: Acumen, 2008.
Nelson, James B. *Between Two Gardens: Reflections on Sexuality and Religious Experience*. New York: Pilgrim, 1983.
Nelson, James B. *Body Theology*. Louisville, KY: Westminster John Knox, 1992.
Nelson, James B. *Embodiment: An Approach to Sexuality and Christian Theology*. Minneapolis, MN: Augsburg, 1978.
Nelson, James B. *The Intimate Connection: Male Sexuality, Masculine Spirituality*. Philadelphia, PA: Westminster, 1988.
Newell, Christopher. "On the Importance of Suffering: The Paradoxes of Disability." In *The Paradox of Disability: Responses to Jean Vanier and L'arche Communities from Theology and the Sciences*, edited by Hans S. Reinders, 169–79. Grand Rapids, MI: Wm. B. Eerdmans, 2010.
Passenier, Anke. "Der Lustgarten Des Leibes Und Die Freiheit Der Seele: Wege Der Mittelalterlichen Frauenspiritualität." In *Sources and Resources of Feminist Theologies*, edited by Elisabeth Hartlieb and Charlotte Methuen, 192–216. Mainz, Germany: Matthias-Grünewald Verlag, 1997.
Peckruhn, Heike. *Meaning in Our Bodies: Sensory Experiences as Constructive Theological Imagination*. New York: Oxford University Press, 2017.
Pinn, Anthony. "Sweaty Bodies in a Circle: Thoughts on the Subtle Dimensions of Black Religion as Protest." *Black Theology* 4:1 (2006): 11–26.
Rodaway, Paul. *Sensuous Geographies: Body, Sense and Place*. New York: Routledge, 1994.
Salamon, Gayle. *Assuming a Body: Transgender and Rhetorics of Materiality*. New York: Columbia University Press, 2010.
Schneider, Laurel. *Beyond Monotheism: A Theology of Multiplicity*. London: Routledge, 2008.
Schüssler-Fiorenza, Elisabeth. *But She Said: Feminist Practices of Biblical Interpretation*. Boston, MA: Beacon, 1992.
Silverman, Hugh J. "Merleau-Ponty and the Interrogation of Language." In *Merleau-Ponty: Perception, Structure, Language*, edited by John Sallis, 122–41. Atlantic Highlands, NJ: Humanities, 1981.
Smith, Mark M. *How Race Is Made: Slavery, Segregation, and the Senses*. Chapel Hill: University of North Carolina Press, 2006.
Smith, Roy Herndon Steinhoff. "The Boundary Wars Mystery." *Religious Studies Review* 24:2 (1998): 131–42.
Spivak, Gayatri Chakravorty. "Can the Subaltern Speak?" In *Colonial Discourse and Postcolonial Theory*, edited by Patrick Williams and Laura Chrisman, 66–111. New York: Columbia University Press, 1994.

Stuart, Elizabeth. "Experience and Tradition: Just Good Friends." In *Sources and Resources of Feminist Theologies*, edited by Elisabeth Hartlieb and Charlotte Methuen, 49–71. Mainz, Germany: Matthias-Grüenewald Verlag, 1997.

Townes, Emily M. "Marcella Althaus-Reid's *Indecent Theology*: A Response." In *Dancing Theology in Fetish Boots: Essays in Honour of Marcella Althaus-Reid*, edited by Lisa Isherwood and Mark D. Jordan, 61–7. London: SCM, 2010.

Townes, Emily M. *Womanist Ethics and the Cultural Production of Evil*. New York: Palgrave Macmillan, 2006.

Traina, Cristine L.H. *Erotic Attunement: Parenthood and the Ethics of Sensuality Between Unequals*. Chicago: University of Chicago Press, 2011.

Weems, Renita J. *Just a Sister Away: Understanding the Timeless Connection between Women of Today and Women in the Bible*. New York: Warner Books, 1988; 2005.

Williams, Delores S. *Sisters in the Wilderness: The Challenge of Womanist God-Talk*. Maryknoll, MN: Orbis Books, 1993.

Wojtyła, Karol (John Paul II). *The Theology of the Body: Human Love in the Divine Plan*. Boston, MA: Pauline Books and Media, 1997.

Young, Iris Marion. *Intersecting Voices: Dilemmas of Gender, Political Philosophy, and Policy*. Princeton, NJ: Princeton University Press, 1997.

5

Constructive Biblical Hermeneutics: History and Its Afterlife

Shelly Rambo

The Bible is a critical part of the architecture of Christian theology. Alongside tradition, reason, and experience, scripture is recognized as a key source of authority upon which theological work is carried out. From its earliest stages, constructive theologians take the Bible's authority as a question, not a given, in their work; they raise a host of questions about the history of the Bible, its transmission in history, and its contemporary readers. Theological interpretations of biblical texts can be weighty, liberating, damning, and transformative. From projects that analyze the transmission of biblical texts within particular communities, to those that vivify biblical images to shed light on contemporary situations and decipher the deployments of the Bible in contested political spaces, constructive theologians pay serious attention to how biblical interpretations map onto the lives of persons and communities—to harmful or healing ends.

In this chapter, I present three modes of constructive theological biblical engagement: authority, liberation, and testimony. These trace a history of biblical interpretation by constructive theologians (from the Workgroup in Constructive Theology to the present), but they also represent concerns and commitments operating when constructive theologians turn to sacred texts. Following this, I present a challenge unfolding for constructive theology and claim that constructive biblical work is uniquely positioned to track the subtle workings of biblical authority that sink below the surface of everyday life. I refer to this as the biblical "afterlife."[1]

Authority

Early constructive theologians grapple with claims about biblical authority and inspiration, in response to the epistemological revolutions of the eighteenth and

---

[1] Shelly Rambo, *Resurrecting Wounds: Living in the Afterlife of Trauma* (Waco, TX: Baylor University Press, 2017). In *Resurrecting Wounds*, I reframe the eschatological concept of the afterlife to describe a way of living beyond events of trauma. I develop this notion of a biblical afterlife at the end of this chapter.

nineteenth centuries. They embrace, rather than reject, the challenges that the Enlightenment brings to the traditional sources of authority. In the 1982 inaugural textbook by the Workgroup on Constructive Theology, Edward Farley and Peter Hodgson reflect this embrace by stating, "We want to understand how scripture and tradition can continue to function as criteria for church and theology outside the house of authority."[2] They accept that the Bible cannot be understood as a self-authenticating, divinely breathed, timeless document whose authority is immune to human touch. The critical consciousness of modernity rendered these views of the Bible naïve, contrary to scientific inquiry, and untenable grounds for human knowledge. They are aware of the need to articulate a view of the Bible that both affirms the project of modern historical biblical criticism and honors the normative status of the Bible for Christian communities. If the Bible is a source for theological work, the traditional claims to divine revelation in and through the scriptures need to be rethought. Knowing about the historical contexts in which biblical writings are produced challenges the notion that the Bible is a timeless document that can transcend history, even as it speaks about a particular history. With a new historical consciousness, the "biblical writings began to be seen as reflecting the particular outlook, assumptions, and attitudes of the people that produced them."[3] Christians do not need to retreat from this historical study, according to these theologians. Instead, they need new ways of understanding the relationship between the ancient world that birthed the Christian scriptures and the reception of these scriptures that follow from them. The critical inquiry into the history *does* present challenges to an understanding of the Bible as divinely inspired and revealed. But these challenges are inevitable and worth taking up—faithfully, yet on different grounds.

In turning away from revelationist understandings of the Bible's authority, Farley and King point to scriptural authority on other terms. They write: "Our task ... is to sketch an alternative sense in which biblical writings may be construed as 'scripture,' that is having a constitutive function in the shaping and nurturing of a community of faith."[4] One way of recasting authority is expressed through the term "functionalism." Attention turns from the book itself and, instead, to its function within Christian communities. Authority is discovered and discerned within the life of the community of interpreters—the *ecclesia*. It is not surprising that Hodgson and Farley identify David Kelsey's work as an important theological pivot in functionalist approaches. This move is influenced by theologians aligned with narrative theology and post-liberalism. Such theologians are not saying that the Bible is not authoritative. Rather, its authority is more properly found in the living, breathing communities who seek to interpret God's revelation in and among them.

The Bible can no longer be approached as self-authorizing. Theological engagements with the Bible are to be framed in terms of hermeneutics, meaning that all of the sources of theology are subject to the art of interpretation. Hermeneutics presumes that there is

---

[2] Edward Farley and Peter C. Hodgson, "Scripture and Tradition," in *Christian Theology: An Introduction to Its Traditions and Tasks*, ed. Peter C. Hodgson and Robert H. King (Philadelphia, PA: Fortress, 1982), 76.
[3] Ibid.
[4] Farley and Hodgson, "Scripture and Tradition," 62.

movement between texts and interpreters, texts and contexts, and theologians wrestle with the claims of the Bible's unique status without attributing its authority to a pure deposit of truth or to a divinely authored set of writings. The ancient setting of the Bible is brought into the context of present-day readers, and this interaction involves acknowledging the angle of the reader's vision.

Constructive theologians are aware of accusations by conservative theologians that they dismiss the Bible's authority altogether.[5] American evangelical theologian Carl Henry specifically targets "functionalism" in *God, Revelation and Authority*, deeming it important enough to dedicate a separate Appendix to refuting it.[6] The charges of Henry and others is that liberal theologians drain all authority from the Bible. If divine revelation and inspiration is contested, then theologians provide merely, Henry states, "creative reconstructions of divine revelation and its implications."[7] To this, constructive theologians might respond saying, "Yes—duly charged." But they would claim that these reconstructions are faithfully carried out in interpretive communities. Readings of scripture are mediated through the experiences of the readers and interpretive communities. Scripture is not an "objective authority," immune to human experience.[8] Rosemary Radford Ruether's now classic claim that human experience infuses all sources of authority, rendering the traditionally ascribed "objective sources"—scripture and tradition—themselves experientially constituted, is largely accepted by constructive theologians.

Constructive biblical work often seeks to counter the exclusions of persons and communities carried out in the Bible's name. This speaks to practices of invoking particular biblical texts in order to marginalize and exclude certain groups of people. When constructive theologians hear "the Bible says 'x,'" they are typically suspicious of the direct, simple, and authoritative appeal that this phrase tags, as if scripture justifies itself. What they hear in those statements is the authority of scripture located in scripture itself. They find themselves responding to what biblical scholar Mary Ann Tolbert calls a "doctrine of biblical authority" that comes into play in ecclesial communities when

---

[5] Joerg Rieger, "Constructive Theology," in *Encyclopedia of Sciences and Religion*, ed. Anne L. C. Runehov and Lluis Oviedo (Dordrecht, Netherlands: Springer Netherlands, 2013), 483–6. Constructive theologian Joerg Rieger notes that the *Evangelical Dictionary of Theology* "accuses constructive theology of unwittingly deconstructing and demolishing biblical faith, implying that biblical faith is only supported by more conservative theological models (Elwell 1984, 269, 271)."

[6] Carl F. H. Henry, *God, Revelation and Authority*, vol. III (Wheaton, IL: Crossway Books, 1999), 360.

> Functional analysis, for example, contrary to verificational analysis, approaches each sentence of religious discourse as a separate phenomenon; it stipulates no preconceived significance for the sentences and seeks the meaning of language in its use. To clarify the diverse uses of language, functional analysts resort to the paradigm case technique, and to what Ferré calls the significant comparison technique. Functional analysis inquires into the intention of the user in using language. This approach has resulted in different theories of the function of theological speech. Does theological language, it is asked, have a function all its own? What is the proper role of religious language? Is it sometimes used to fulfill an improper role?

[7] Carl F. H. Henry, "Inerrancy and the Bible in Modern Conservative Evangelical Thought," in *Introduction to Christian Theology: Contemporary North American Perspectives*, ed. Roger A. Badham (Louisville, KY: Westminster John Knox, 1998), 54.

[8] Rosemary Radford Ruether, *Sexism and God-Talk* (Boston, MA: Beacon, 1983).

issues of social liberation arise, she says.⁹ Tolbert writes: "It is not the Bible itself but the overt, often institutionally based appeal to an already formulated doctrine of biblical authority that displays this generally negative, exclusivistic pattern."[10]

Four elements are present in such invocations. First, the text is presented as transcendent and ahistorical. Second, the ancient worldview is directly applied to the contemporary worldview. Third, biblical texts are to be parsed, quoted, and used apart from its contextual realities. The words themselves hold authority as if they wield a certain power in and of themselves. The last is that there is a single meaning to which the text points. These comprise a "special hermeneutics" applied to the Bible.[11] She observes this in the theological classroom, in which the study of the Bible ("general hermeneutics") can be at odds with a piety nurtured within faith communities. Constructive theologians may invoke the normative and authoritative status of the Bible, but they would counter these four elements at each point, insisting that "the Bible is a historical text." The ancient worldview is not immediately translatable into our own setting. The context of the biblical writings must be considered. The Bible yields multiple meanings.

Liberation

Reworking biblical authority in response to Enlightenment challenges, many constructive theologians were attentive to the role of biblical interpretations in justifying the exclusion of persons and communities from full participation in religious life. Biblical work aimed to liberate the Bible from its interpretive exclusions. Sallie McFague's work on religious language bridges the first and second phases. In her analysis of metaphor, she explains how biblical concepts such as Father, Lord, and kingdom congealed with theological force to keep women in subordinate positions within Christian traditions. Because of their power to narrate God's relationship to the world, privileged metaphors convey a series and ordering of relations that support patriarchal systems. They are not simply ancient words; they offer worlds, shaping a vision of what the present world can—and should—be. Many feminist theologians consider McFague's work on metaphor as foundational for their theological diagnosis

---

[9] Mary Ann Tolbert, "A New Teaching with Authority," in *Teaching the Bible: The Discourses and Politics of Biblical Pedagogy*, ed. Fernando F. Segovia and Marry Ann Tolbert (Maryknoll, NY: Orbis Books, 1998), 171.

[10] Ibid.

[11] "Special hermeneutics" refers to the practices of invoking biblical authority to support and sacralize particular perspectives. Mary Ann Tolbert writes: "Thus, the 'special hermeneutics' of biblical authority or normativity is not the constant practice of any ecclesiastical community, but rather a practice employed in certain selected moments of division and debate" (ibid., 175–6).

> All readings are interested; that is, they are shaped by the advocacies and beliefs of readers, but this general rule becomes something much more dangerous in the "special hermeneutics" of authority. In that case, readers construct readings of the Bible according to their *own* perspectives and conventional practices and then endow those readings with transcendent and eternal authority over the lives of others—hiding from others, and sometimes even from themselves, the degree of personal interest shaping their readings. (182; emphasis in the original)

of women's exclusion from full participation in their faith traditions.[12] A central theme of feminist theological work is that the Bible is used as justification for women's subordination and, at that moment in history, justification against their ordination. Feminist biblical interpretation and the method of naming, retrieval, and recovery provided not only biblical method but a method that defined the work of feminist theology.[13]

These moves are still present in constructive theological work that employs biblical texts: to contest a particular reading, to point to ignored parts of the biblical story, and to contend with the texts that terrify or that are used instrumentally.[14] They expose the canon within the canon and affirm the expansion of noncanonical materials that are, themselves, products of exclusion, such as the Gospel of Mary and the Gospel of Thomas, both of which feature women as prominent disciples.[15] In this phase, constructive theologians actively work against theological interpretations that deny inclusion to particular groups of people, on the basis of race, gender, and sexuality. Working from inside, they forge other ways of interpreting passages continually used against particular communities—that is, endorsements of slavery or condemnations of homosexuality. They use their own exegetical and theological expertise to show that biblical passages affirm the very communities that other theological interpreters condemn. For example, in *God, Desire, and a Theology of Sexuality*, Dave H. Jensen rejects approaching the Bible as a moral guidebook for sexual behavior and, instead, invites Christians to view Scripture as providing readers with "glimpses (of) divine desire" that allow us to view our relationships in light of God's desire in and for the world.[16] Appealing to tradition, he present an affirmative Christian sexual ethic rooted in ancient Christian reading practices.

One of the central insights shared by constructive theologians, drawing from the rich resources of feminist and black liberation theologies, is that experience

---

[12] Laurel Schneider, *Re-imagining the Divine: Confronting the Backlash Against Feminist Theology* (Cleveland, OH: Pilgrim Press, 1999).

[13] Elisabeth Schüssler Fiorenza, "In Memory of Her," *Journal of Feminist Studies in Religion* 35, no. 1 (2019): 129–30.

[14] Phyllis Trible, *Texts of Terror: Literary Feminist Readings of Biblical Narratives* (Minneapolis, MN: Fortress, 1984), 3. "A third approach … recounts tales of terror *in memoriam* to offer sympathetic readings of abused women."

[15] Rosemary Radford Ruether, in *Sexism and God-Talk*, draws attention to the canonizing process. She writes:

> At a certain point a group consisting of teacher and leaders emerges that seeks to channel and control the process, to weed out what it regards as deviant communities and interpretations, and to impose a series of criteria to determine the correct interpretive line. The group can do this by defining an authoritative body of writings that is then canonized as the correct interpretation of the original divine revelation and distinguished from other writings, which are regarded either as heretical or as secondary authority. In the process the controlling group marginalizes and suppresses other branches of the community, with their own texts and lines of interpretation. The winning group declares itself the privileged line of true (orthodox) interpretation. Thus a canon of Scripture is established. (14)

Karen L. King, *The Gospel of Mary of Magdala: Jesus and the First Woman Apostle* (Santa Rosa, CA: Polebridge, 2003).

[16] David Hadley Jensen, *God, Desire, and a Theology of Human Sexuality*, 1st ed. (Louisville, KY: Westminster John Knox, 2013), 8.

shapes biblical interpretation. The Bible is a source for communities of faith. But the norm for reading the Bible is determined by the community. For African American communities, God is the God who liberates the enslaved peoples—the biblical vision of a God who situates Godself on the side of those who are oppressed and marginalized. James H. Evans writes: "One cannot do theology in and for the African American community without coming to terms with the influence of the Bible."[17] But he also notes that the experience of black communities with the Bible is unique and particular. This experience *conditions* biblical interpretation.[18]

Theological attention turns to those who are reading the Bible within their particular settings. The field of hermeneutics and works by Hans-Georg Gadamer and Paul Ricoeur proved helpful to theologians to claim that the truth of the Bible does not reside behind the text or in the text but, rather, in *front of the text*, "with the vicissitudes of flesh-and-blood interpreters."[19] Theologians from around the globe narrate the role that the Bible and biblical translation play in Western Christian missionizing-colonizing practices. Naming the Bible as a tool of Western expansionism, they expose the violent and deeply problematic legacy of Christianity outside of western Europe. Recognition of the Bible's fraught transmission and reception is central to the constructive biblical engagements. The Bible fueled a vision of mission, evangelization, and civilization.[20] There is a problematizing of the missionizing legacy of Christianity and a naming of practices of cultural erasure. Indigenous sources of revelation and traditions that provided identity and spiritual connection were replaced by the God of the Christian Bible and what Kwok Pui-Lan calls its "politics of truth."[21] Kwok captures the dynamics of theological appropriations of the Bible from non-Western contexts and directly rejects Christian claims to biblical authority—canon, sacred, norm—in light of colonial histories. To simply accept the Word as authoritative is a colonizing logic.[22]

Constructive theologians are interested in what happens to the Bible when it is situated within these cultural contexts. Communities subject to colonization appropriate biblical images and significantly reshape them. They find their experiences named with the narratives of the Bible, and the images of exile, exodus, and crucifixion

---

[17] James H. Evans, *We Have Been Believers: An African-American Systematic Theology* (Minneapolis, MN: Fortress, 1992), 33.

[18] Ibid. He writes: "It is still the case that the social, political, economic, and aesthetic marginalization of African-Americans—that is, the social dislocation of black people in the United States and elsewhere—conditions their approach to and use of biblical imagery, precepts, and motifs" (35).

[19] Paul Ricoeur, "The Model of the Text: Meaningful Action Considered as a Text," *New Literary History* 5, no. 1, What Is Literature? (Autumn 1973): 91–117. "Therefore, what we want to understand is not something hidden behind the text, but something disclosed in front of it" (113); Mark Lewis Taylor, "Reading from an Indigenous Place," in *Teaching the Bible: The Discourse and Politics of Biblical Theology*, ed. Fernando F. Segovia and Mary Ann Tolbert (Minneapolis, MN: Fortress, 2009), 120.

[20] For a compelling constructive theological work on missions, see Marion Grau, *Rethinking Mission in the Postcolony: Salvation, Society and Subversion* (London: T&T Clark, 2011).

[21] Kwok Pui-Lan, "Discovering the Bible in the Non-biblical World," in *Lift Every Voice: Constructing Christian Theologies from the Underside*, ed. Susan Brooks Thistlethwaite and Mary Potter Engel, revised and expanded ed. (Maryknoll, NY: Orbis Books, 1998), 278. Kwok expanded these reflections in a full-length manuscript, *Discovering the Bible in the Non-biblical World* (Maryknoll, NY: Orbis Books, 1995).

[22] Kwok Pui-Lan, "Discovering the Bible in the Non-biblical World," 276–88.

provide routes for liberation. Biblical texts not only became sites for reflection, they also provided authorization for protest against the colonial Christian Bible wielded against them. The belief that God is on the side of enslaved peoples and frees them from bondage to those in power is a biblical vision that supports movements for liberation across the globe. A newly alighted consciousness of the politics of interpretation brings together biblical scholars and theologians committed to projects of liberation.

Testimony

A wave of theological writings turns to biblical language and rhetoric to testify to the ethical failures of modern theological projects and imagine theology otherwise. Authors share deep concerns about the violent apparatus of modernity—war, violence, nuclear arms—and see this violence operating in theological systems, expressed in the textual traditions themselves. Although this theo-biblical work is carried out under different names—such as postcolonial, post-Shoah, theopoetics, trauma—it reframes the theological task in terms of *testimony*. Influenced by a range of critical theories, the work reflects careful and attentive textual work that contends with the limits of language, discursive systems of thought, and the dominant forms of theological writing and discourse.

Biblical scholars and theologians wrestling with the legacies of colonization beyond Europe begin to distinguish their method of interpreting biblical texts from a "liberationist hermeneutics."[23] In *Postcolonial Theologies: Divinity and Empire*, the authors (Keller, Nausner, and Rivera) note that a "liberation hermeneutics" attempted to name the imperial forces at play in biblical studies and Christian history and claimed, in scripture, an "anti-imperial thematics."[24] Postcolonial readings, by contrast, "operate with a more troubling ambivalence, tracing both decolonizing and colonizing themes within scripture."[25] These readings attest to the ambivalence of interpretations. Biblical scholars such as Musa W. Dube and Tat-siong Benny Liew provide models for reading biblical texts that emphasize the nuances of the biblical rhetoric under the conditions of empire.[26]

In another trajectory of testimony, biblical scholars and theologians within the West were taking account of the legacy of anti-Semitism within biblical studies and actively engaging post-Holocaust literatures. A wave of biblical scholarship emerged in

---

[23] Catherine Keller, Michael Nausner, and Mayra Rivera, *Postcolonial Theologies: Divinity and Empire* (St. Louis, MO: Chalice, 2004), 10. Keller, Rivera, and Nauser emphasize: "Postcolonial theory facilitates new readings of scripture and of the history of the interpretation of scripture, helping to uncover their complex ties to empire" (ibid.).

[24] Ibid.

[25] Ibid.

[26] Tat-siong Benny Liew, *Politics of Parousia: Reading Mark Inter(Con)Textually*, Biblical Interpretation Series, v. 42 (Leiden: Brill, 1999); Tat-siong Benny Liew, *Colonialism and the Bible: Contemporary Reflections from the Global South*, Postcolonial and Decolonial Studies in Religion and Theology (Lanham, MD: Lexington Books, 2018); Musa W. Dube, *Postcolonial Feminist Interpretation of the Bible* (St. Louis, MO: Chalice, 2000); Don H. Compier, Kwok Pui-Lan, and Joerg Rieger, eds., *Empire and the Christian Tradition: New Readings of Classical Theologians* (Minneapolis, MN: Fortress, 2007).

response to the Holocaust and the role that Christian biblical interpretation played in carrying out violence against Jews in Europe. The central question was: How can—and should—the Christian Bible be read in light of the genocide of the Jews? A stream of biblical scholarship confronted the problematic and potentially irreparable legacy of biblical interpretation. Tod Linafelt's *Strange Fire: Reading the Bible after the Holocaust*, published in 2000, brought together representatives of both Jewish and Christian thought to provide reflections on the biblical texts, yielding a critical interrogation into biblical theology.[27] Careful review of particular texts accompanied reflections on the traditioning and transmission of biblical texts. These writings unearthed the testimonial dimensions of both traditions, but it precipitated, for the scholars of Christianity, a posture of humility, reverence, and sobriety in interpretation—registered in the tone of scholarship.[28]

Rebecca Chopp weds this work of Holocaust testimony with projects of liberation and testimonies springing up from other communities. She sheds a spotlight on modern theology and its pursuit of truth. The modern pursuit of truth puts witnesses on trial, asking them to defend their testimonies in front of the judge of reason. The twentieth century, and its horrors, shows the limits of reason to judge truth. Modern theology has followed the rules of the modern courtroom. In the courtroom of modern theology, Chopp warns, the testimonies of survivors may be deemed irrational when voiced and brought under the judgment of theological reason. Chopp says that, moving forward, theology must reposition itself to hear the "moral summons" at the heart of witness testimonies. She names the new mode of theology in terms of a "poetics of testimony."[29] The appeals to imagination bear liberationist commitments in that they expose a mode of theological engagement in which reason was given ultimate value to determine the coherence or plausibility of religious expressions. Imagination is

---

[27] Tod Linafelt, ed., *Strange Fire: Reading the Bible after the Holocaust* (Sheffield, UK: Sheffield Academic Press, 2000). There was a subsequent collection: Tod Linafelt, ed., *A Shadow of Glory: Reading the New Testament after the Holocaust* (New York: Routledge, 2002).

[28] Timothy Beal, Yvonne Sherwood, and Tod Linafelt were among a group of biblical scholars who were involved in the discussions between biblical scholars and theologians about how to read the Bible in postmodernity. The "Bible, Theology, and Postmodernity" group of the American Academy of Religion served as a site of constructive biblical engagement, featuring biblical scholars and theologians grappling with the legacy of the Holocaust for Jewish and Christian scriptures. The group is now constituted under the title "Sacred Texts, Theory, and Theological Construction."

[29] Rebecca Chopp, "Theology and the Poetics of Testimony," in *Converging on Culture: Theologians in Dialogue with Cultural Analysis and Criticism*, ed. Delwin Brown, Sheila Greeve Davaney, and Kathryn Tanner, Reflection and Theory in the Study of Religion (Oxford: Oxford University Press, 2001). Chopp planted the seeds, in this invitational essay, for trauma-directed theologies. The work of Serene Jones, Flora Keshgegian, and others, including my own, takes biblical texts as witness texts depicting the early Christian community as witnesses to the trauma of crucifixion. The insights from trauma theory resonate with biblical testimonies and yield doctrinal innovations—salvation, resurrection, and the meaning of the cross as the central symbol of Christian faith. Christian theology has the capacity to witness difficult truths, but familiar paths of theological interpretation must set on a different course. Serene Jones, *Trauma and Grace: Theology in a Ruptured World* (Louisville, KY: Westminster John Knox, 2009); Flora Keshgegian, *Redeeming Memories: A Theology of Healing and Transformation* (Nashville, TN: Abingdon, 2000); Shelly Rambo, *Spirit and Trauma: A Theology of Remaining* (Louisville, KY: Westminster John Knox, 2010).

connected to practices of unearthing experiences of colonization detailed in strains of postcolonial discourse.[30]

Biblical writings provide a counterpoint to theological systematizing; the Bible is unsystematic, pluriform, and thus cannot be so simply folded into a system of thought. Systematic theologian Jürgen Moltmann opens the door to consider whether the very form and structure of systematic theology is implicitly coercive in totalitarian systems. He writes:

> Every consistent theological summing up, every theological system lays claim to totality, perfect organization, and entire competence for the whole area under survey. In principle one has to be able to say everything, and not to leave any point unconsidered. All the statements must fit in with one another without contradiction, and the whole architecture must be harmonious, an integrated whole.[31]

Thus, turning to biblical testimonies may provide a corrective to the modern theological enterprise.

Bringing together strains of feminist, liberationist, postmodern, and process theologies, Catherine Keller's biblical poetics gives way to a theopoetics that ripples across the theological landscape.[32] Her work demonstrates a sophisticated interplay between recognizable Christian terms and tropes and the wordplays and rhetorical dances of French philosophers. It revels in the uncertainties, the inconclusive, open, porous, oozing dimensions of religious language and imagery. Her biblical work captures a rhythm to theological inquiry that refuses the closed interpretive world of patriarchal interpretation. Concerned with how biblical authority is wielded against women, Keller urges feminist theologians to sustain engagements with biblical writings. "While unimpressed by the patriarchal 'authority of scripture,' I do understand my task here as a scripturally grounded narrative engagement, indeed a form of 'narrative theology.'"[33] Keller takes the apocalyptic genre of biblical literature and tracks its transmission, asking how a genre related to disclosure becomes, through the history of theological interpretation, a universalized Western narrative of closure.[34]

Recognizing that biblical texts are often employed to secure truth, Keller and others turn to biblical texts to do just the opposite—to release the hold of particular theological claims. Mayra Rivera theologizes the biblical concept of glory in order to resist claims to a dominant account of divine transcendence, one that envisions

---

[30] Theological work must take new form. Chopp's appeal to poetics aligns well with Kwok Pui-Lan's articulation of the importance of imagination in a postcolonial context. Kwok Pui-Lan, *Postcolonial Imagination and Feminist Theology*, 1st ed. (Louisville, KY: Westminster John Knox, 2005).

[31] Jürgen Moltmann, *The Trinity and the Kingdom: The Doctrine of God* (Minneapolis, MN: Fortress, 1993), xii.

[32] Catherine Keller, *On the Mystery: Discerning Divinity in Process* (Minneapolis, MN: Fortress, 2008); Catherine Keller, *Face of the Deep: A Theology of Becoming* (London: Routledge, 2003).

[33] Catherine Keller, *Apocalypse Now and Then: A Feminist Guide to the End of the World* (Boston, MA: Beacon, 1996), 25-6.

[34] Catherine Keller, *God and Power: Counter-apocalyptic Journeys* (Minneapolis, MN: Fortress, 2005).

God as radically separate from the world.³⁵ In Rivera's reading, kabod-doxa reveals a mode of engaging the world that is elemental and earthy. Her biblical work opens up a tightly bounded theological claim. In turn, I reclaim the Johannine term *menein*, that is, to remain, to speak of a certain vision of living in the aftermath of trauma. In *Spirit and Trauma: A Theology of Remaining*, the Johannine iterations of "remaining" bring the ancient witness of the Jesus followers to the cross into conversation with present-day communities gathered in witness to various forms of trauma in the present. The Johannine text contains a witness to survival.³⁶

This phase approaches the Bible for its testimonial function, seeking within the biblical writings a witness to historical violence. The biblical texts are important, even authoritative, for their capacities to witness the losses of modernity and the dissolution of binary ways of structuring thought and action. Theologians find linguistic routes around dogma; biblical literatures are not uniform and, thus, theology cannot be either.

The Future of the Bible in Constructive Theology

Whereas discussions of biblical authority have largely dropped out constructive theological texts, biblical authority is not a thing of the past.³⁷ Speaking within the US context, biblical authority lives on in the broader collective in unanticipated forms and occupies persons at a level that is yet to be theologically accounted for.³⁸ This authorizing is neither exclusively external nor internal. Instead, it operates through a constellation of images and biblical archetypes that form the fabric of American life.³⁹ Historian Jonathan Ebel describes this as the "theological substructure of American civil religion and its complexities as a lived religion."⁴⁰

The language in trauma literatures, and more recently in affect studies, is helpful in envisioning what I refer to as the "afterlife of the Bible." "Afterlife" refers to the ongoing

---

[35] Mayra Rivera, "Glory: The First Passion of Theology?," in *Polydoxy: Theology of Multiplicity and Relation*, ed. Catherine Keller and Laurel C. Schneider (London: Routledge, 2010), 169. Thus, my exploration does not aim to retrieve a univocal scriptural meaning of doxa at the intersection of Greek and Hebrew senses. Instead, it seeks to honor the term's complexity by keeping visible in doxa all of the associations named earlier—and thus its indeterminacy—and by attending to the cosmic winds and magnetic perturbations that afflict and lure us today, I seek to unsettle theological reifications of doxa and quicken the relationships latent in it.

[36] Rambo, *Spirit and Trauma*, 104. "Menein is a way of communicating a different kind of present that will be required in the wake of Jesus' death. It is a presence that takes the form of bearing with, of enduring, of persisting."

[37] Note this absence of specific attention in the 2016 book, produced by the workgroup. Laurel C. Schneider and Stephen G. Ray, eds., *Awake to the Moment: An Introduction to Theology*, 1st ed. (Louisville, KY: Westminster John Knox, 2016), 2.

[38] Although there are many theories of the secular/secularism, I am interested in the analysis provided by social scientists such as Courtney Bender and Wendy Cadge, who track the ways in which religion is operating in public spaces. Courtney Bender and Pamela Klassen, eds., *After Pluralism: Reimagining Religious Engagement* (New York: Columbia University Press, 2010); Courtney Bender, Wendy Cadge, Peggy Levitt, and David Smilde, eds., *Religion on the Edge: De-centering and Re-centering the Sociology of Religion* (Oxford, UK: Oxford University Press, 2013).

[39] Jonathan H. Ebel, *G.I. Messiahs: Soldiering, War and American Civil Religion* (New Haven, CT: Yale University Press, 2015).

[40] Ibid., 2.

traces of biblical authority and influence that continue long after visible structures are gone. The Bible inspires and triggers, but it often does this outside of authorized interpretive communities. Biblical texts continue to offer a repository for navigating life's rhythms, but religious leaders may be nowhere in sight. To assume that it has lost its status is a failure to account for how the Bible adheres to and the degree to which it has shaped the Western collective imagination, not simply within Christianity, but more broadly. The afterlife also captures the lingering impact of biblical teachings on those who no longer profess a relationship to a biblical faith tradition.[41]

The study of trauma provides a working vocabulary for conceiving of modes of biblical transmission that operate apart from traditional authorizing channels. Trauma researchers set out to assess the impact of violence on persons, communities, and even countries.[42] A central insight of trauma is that events are not over when they are declared, or even appear to be over. Speaking on an individual level, because of the impact of violence on human systems, adaptive processes shut down. The system goes offline. Because of this, a timeline of past, present, and future is altered. Traces of the event surface at other points in time, but it is difficult to directly trace a clear line back to it. The past occupies the present world; it is somehow alive in the present, though appearing in forms that are no longer directly tied to the places and persons in the past. Psychologically, these traces are described in terms of symptomology. Symptoms tell a story of trauma somatically. Triggered by the senses, the past flashes into the present, awakening the body to mobilize to respond to danger. The body rallies to protect, but this sensory vulnerability means that events can be reexperienced outside of the time and spaces in which they occurred.[43] These dynamics extend to the collective, in terms of social or political bodies.

Constructive biblical hermeneutics is well positioned to track the "substructural" theologies that thread through public speech and authorize particular political ends. This is present in early constructive biblical work, but its authorizations are less evident and no longer traced to explicitly religious institutions or representatives. One trajectory for imagining constructive biblical interpretation in the afterlife of biblical authority is to *approach the Bible as a repository of body memories*. While the Bible is composed of words and narratives, it offers rich images that target the senses and

---

[41] One potential route for exploring this is through Richard Kearney's conception of *anatheism*. Richard Kearney, *Anatheism: Returning to God after God* (New York: Columbia University Press, 2011).

[42] The interdisciplinary study of trauma began in the late 1980s and was named explicitly in Cathy Caruth, ed., *Trauma: Explorations in Memory* (Baltimore, MD: Johns Hopkins University Press, 1995). John Briere and Catherine Scott write: "As compared to other areas of psychology and behavioral science, the systematic study of the human response to trauma is relatively new. The new modern field of studying traumatic stress was born in the aftermath of the Vietnam War, and the term *posttraumatic stress disorder* (PTSD) was introduced into the mental health lexicon only in the mid-1980's." John N. Briere and Catherine Scott, *Principles of Trauma Therapy: A Guide to Symptoms, Evaluation, and Treatment*, 2nd ed. (Thousand Oaks, CA: Sage, 2014), 1.

[43] These are important books in the articulation of the impact of trauma on the body: Babette Rothschild, *The Body Remembers: The Psychophysiology of Trauma and Trauma Treatment* (New York: W.W. Norton, 2000); Peter Levine, *Waking the Tiger: Healing Trauma* (Berkeley, CA: North Atlantic Books, 1997); Bessel van der Kolk, *The Body Keeps the Score: Brain, Mind, and Body in the Healing of Trauma* (New York: Penguin Books, 2015); Pat Ogden, Kekuni Minton, and Clare Pane, eds., *Trauma and the Body: A Sensorimotor Approach to Psychotherapy* (New York: W.W. Norton, 2006).

attest to primary affective experiences of communities who are contending with life's vicissitudes: shame, guilt, envy, revenge, and so on. If these writings witness to root experiences of ancient communities, contemporary communities, by reading, receiving, and reenacting these biblical texts, are shaped across time. Something like collective memory is inscribed into the life of the community, but it is not done through oral or written means alone. Instead, it is transmitted, as well, as body memories. Hodgson writes: "In relation the potential radicality of all experience is thematized in central root experiences by which everything else is illuminated."[44] These root experiences are not anti-rational but may follow along other lines—other ways of knowing that were not, until recently, brought to light. The biblical texts transmit the collective memories of a people reckoning with God and with each other, wrestling with the vicissitudes of life. These are certainly recognizable through certain *events*, but the experiences conveyed are affective. The events narrate life's rhythms. The Bible is a living, breathing repository for our deepest affections. For these and others, affect, and affect theory, provides a route for constructive theologians to talk about the somatic dimension without separating it from words. Affect theory attempts to provide a corrective to the "linguistic turn" represented in much poststructuralist theory in order to resist the mind/body split that continues to be enacted in critical theorizing.[45]

As those working in the area of trauma envision what it looks like for persons who have experienced trauma to "come to life again," biblical texts spur visions of what it looks and feels like to do this.[46] Bodies hold memories of trauma. Various stands of trauma research suggest that memories process differently in experiences of trauma. They are not stored as declarative memories but as non-declarative ones; these cannot be accessed by talking-out trauma.[47] Instead, they store somatically as *sensations*. Traumatic memories can be transformed only by helping a person to reorient to the

---

[44] Peter C. Hodgson, "Constructive Theology and Biblical Worlds," in *Teaching the Bible: The Discourses and Politics of Biblical Pedagogy*, ed. Fernando F. Segovia and Mary Ann Tolbert (Maryknoll, NY: Orbis Books, 1998), 49. Hodgson writes: "Theology is a constructive activity that correlates root revelatory experiences, traditioned textual expressions, and contemporary social locations through the interaction of critical-interpretative and practical-appropriative thinking" (48). He acknowledges that claims to primary revelatory experiences are under scrutiny in postmodernity. The linguistic emphasis in poststructuralism made it difficult to speak about accounts of anything prior to language—anything "root." More comfortable with the claims of *mediated* knowledge, constructive theologians tended to emphasize textual expressions and social locations above claims to immediate experience. However, Hodgson wants to hold onto root revelatory experiences, arguing that there is something lost in removing these experiences from the data of theological work. In this sense, he shares concerns with affect theorists that there is something lost in folding everything under the umbrella of linguistic operations. Studies in affect could turn constructive theologians to biblical accounts of how experiences provide their own data for interpretation.

[45] Jennifer L. Koosed and Stephen D. Moore, "Introduction: From Affect to Exegesis," *Biblical Interpretation* 22 (2014): 382.

[46] Ronnie Janoff-Bulman, *Shattered Assumptions: Towards a New Psychology of Trauma* (New York: Free Press, 2002). Janoff-Bulman asks: "How can we understand the psychological impact and aftermath of these traumatic experiences? How do people come to terms with these events and go on with their lives?" (3). Studies in trauma often speak about the challenge of integrating experiences of trauma into what one knows of themselves as a process of death and rebirth. Living is not a return to a prior self but a process of coming into a new relationship with life.

[47] Although many trauma researchers describe this process, a helpful overview can be found in "Part Two: This Is Your Brain on Trauma," in Bessel van der Kolk's *The Body Keeps the Score*, 51–102.

world somatically—to work trauma out of the body. Restoring a person's capacity to regulate their breath and notice their sensations is a primary goal of trauma healing. Words and narratives are higher-level functions that are important for helping someone integrate the experience of trauma, but sensory work is first-order business.

When communities come to Christian worship spaces to receive a fresh word from God, this is not typically registered as an invitation to renew the senses and to generate, in neurobiological terms, new mirror neurons to create alternative pathways of bodily response. But interpreted affectively, we could think of the body's wisdom and creativity at play. Somatic work attempts to reroute the senses. Christian theologians often speak about salvation history as narrated in scriptures. This is a composite of biblical stories, thematized in order to tell a larger story of God's redemption of the world. This history is composed of root experiences of guilt, shame, anger, envy, grief, trust, empathy. When this salvation history is taught, it begins to shape certain affects. The sensorium in biblical texts guides and shapes the senses of those who receive and interpret these biblical texts. When communities read these passages, there is more than understanding and comprehension taking place. I have argued elsewhere that eschatology, the teachings about end things, targets the limbic system by fostering images of final judgment, periods of trial and tribulation, and high-stakes conditions for the securing of one's salvation.[48]

We can think of this in another way as well. Biblical phrases can trigger a host of memories. The biblical imaginary can be awakened with the simple recitation of a biblical phrase. The words can mobilize a host of sensations from the past. Consider these:

The wages of sin is death.
Wives submit to your husbands.
I am the way, the truth, the life.
Love is patient; love is kind.
Nothing can separate us from the love of God.
The Lord is my shepherd; I shall not want.

Sedimented body memories, they are messages engrafted onto the body. And they are not just words. They evoke worlds. They do not merely come to mind. They stir the affections. They can be tribal calls, sealing the contours of community identity. They can hold people in pain, with the assurance that they are not alone in the valley of their suffering. They can fill someone with terror, as the consequences of an action is mapped onto eternity. They can mobilize resistance, becoming platforms for assurance that the rulers of this world will not prevail. They stir the biblical imaginary in ways that cannot be written off. Biblical stories tell the accounts of our lives with a strange combination of proximity and distance. But it is their rhythm, their imagery, rather

---

[48] Shelly Rambo, "Salvation in the After-Living: Reflections on Salvation with Joshua Ralston and Sharon Betcher," in *Comparing Faithfully: Insights for Systematic Theological Reflection*, ed. Michelle Voss Roberts (New York: Fordham University Press, 2016), 296–315.

than their propositional force, that explains its sustaining hold on the imagination. They live within the imaginary at some level and do their work on and in us.

We can also see this in action when biblical images and tropes appear on public protest signs. For example, "Act Justly, Show Mercy, Walk Humbly," "If God is for us then who can be against us," "I am fearfully and wonderfully made," "Love your neighbor as yourself," or a statement like "God hates gays" that includes a biblical reference to Leviticus 20. These invoke biblical authority but in an afterlife mode; there is enough public recognition that they carry weight—but the weight circles around fundamental affirmations of rights, about life. They carry authority, but mobilized toward particular ends. They remain, as fragments of sacred traditions that can carry multiple meanings—for those with deep understanding of those traditions and for those with very little. Something lingers in the structures of society so that when they are used, they surface a biblical imaginary that resides below the surface of things. If we consider the impact of these biblical appropriations on the collective limbic system, it may explain a resurgence of interpretations that follow bloodlines and ignite tribal allegiances.[49]

Returning to the biblical texts over and over again, constructive theologians may want to think in line with a "carnal hermeneutics," about how biblical passages may be employed to reroute affects and move them forward differently.[50] The biblical texts feature characters and communities coming to terms with feelings of shame, desires for revenge, incalculable regret, wonder, guilt, and empathy. And practices emerge from these—practices of lament and restitution, commemoration and sacrifice. Interpretive communities can find resonance with these affects, express themselves through them, and also serve as cautionary tales. For example, awakening readers to the experience of the witnesses at the foot of the cross in the Christian gospels may be a way of training a community to work with disgust. Sharon Betcher purports this posture of biblical witness, suggesting that Christian bodily practice can orient Christians to behold what is disgusting. Christians are invited, through meditations on the cross, into practices of working through disgust—of practicing spiritual muscles that are essential for engaging in liberatory work.[51] Wendy Farley points to Buddhist practices as counterpoints to narratives of sin and guilt that can put moral freight on experiences of suffering. Operating with a different diagnosis of the human condition, these contemplative and meditative practices, she says, can orient persons in more helpful ways to suffering.[52] I revisit the gathering of disciples in the Upper Room, suggesting that it is an invitation

---

[49] See Vamik Volkan, *Bloodlines: From Ethnic Pride to Ethnic Terrorism* (Boulder, CO: Westview, 1998); Sebastian Junger, *Tribe: On Homecoming and Belonging* (New York: Twelve Books, 2016).

[50] Brian Trainor and Richard Kearney, eds., *Carnal Hermeneutics*, Perspectives in Continental Philosophy Series (New York: Fordham University Press, 2015).

[51] Sharon Betcher, *Spirit and the Obligations of Social Flesh: A Secular Theology for the Global City*, 1st ed. (New York: Fordham University Press, 2014), chapter 4.

> The images to which canonical Christianity returns again and again—to Christ as corpse or on the cross—suggest both a way of meditatively employing the images of the scorned, disfigured, abused, imperial torture victim, and a way to break through transcendentalist metaphysics. Religious images are but icons for redirecting our aversions so that we might more mindfully engage those bouts of aesthetic nervousness, unique to each of us, that grip us on the streets of our mongrel cities. (122)

[52] Wendy Farley, *The Wounding and Healing of Desire: Weaving Heaven and Earth* (Louisville, KY: Westminster John Knox, 2005).

to a new sensorium. The Upper Room narrative is a somatic scene in which the risen Jesus returns to train them in a way that has to do with bodies, breath, and touch.[53]

In light of this, *constructive biblical hermeneutics could be reframed as postmemory work*. In *The Generation of Postmemory*, Marianne Hirsch sets out on a theoretical journey to discover how she, as a second-generation Holocaust writer, can conceive of her place in history.[54] She is pressing beyond notions of survival and transmission to think about post-generational healing and how the work of subsequent generations may inscribe the past differently—to remember *forward*. Instead of viewing a historical rupture and repetition of the violence, Hirsch posits that the next generation can "create an opening in the present to something in the past that goes beyond their indexicality or the information they record."[55] Given the fact that intergenerational experiences of violence are rarely conveyed in straightforward narratives, postmemory work is often work done with material remnants (diaries, letter, photographs) or through engaging the senses. I imagine sorting through photographs, catching a whiff of perfume, noticing something that was always there but registers only decades later. Through the objects and materials that remain, children encountering these ask how they are positioned in relationship to history, not as passive recipients to this history nor disconnected from it, but as agents of healing the past. These modes of encounter are neither purely conceptual nor exclusively material.

Hirsch is talking about family memories, and she develops the term "affiliative" to conceive of the ways that families connect across generations. The mediations of memory assume that communication is disrupted and entangled. She imagines this family collective in an "organic web of transmission."[56] It is not unlike how theologians imagine Christian traditions. While not overlooking the damage enacted by Christianity, constructive theologians imagine the *ecclesia* as a family. They claim a thread of intimacy and belonging through attachment to the memory of Jesus, bonded by the Spirit in their differences. It is a family created through time that also cuts across time.

Considering constructive biblical interpretation as postmemory work is a way of witnessing the transmission of biblical texts forward. The concern with tradition, understood as repetition, is that it entrenches and secures the boundaries of Christian identity. But there is equal concern, on the other end, that connections and ties to the past are severed. The earlier interpretations do not go away and are not erased; instead, subsequent interpretations are superimposed and even carry the earlier interpretations into different contexts. The displacement and layering create something new out of the old without presuming to erase the earlier inscriptions.[57] Postmemory work is

---

[53] Rambo, *Resurrecting Wounds*, 80–4.
[54] Marianne Hirsch, *A Generation of Postmemory: Writing and Visual Culture after the Holocaust* (New York: Columbia University Press, 2012); Eva Hoffman, *After Such Knowledge: Memory, History, and the History, and the Legacy of the Holocaust* (Cambridge, MA; Perseus Books, 2004).
[55] Hirsch, *A Generation of Postmemory*, 74.
[56] Ibid., 36.
[57] This process of textual layering is known as palimpsest. Rita Nakashima Brock uses it to describe the experience of moral injury for military veterans. See Rita Nakashima Brock, "Moral Injury, Soul Repair, and Congregations," FCC Minneapolis, accessed August 12, 2019, http://www.fccminneapolis.org/wp-content/uploads/2016/05/Moral-Injury-Handout-May-2016-MN.pdf.

more like collage. It works in mixed mediums. It tracks the history, not simply as the history of ideas, but as the material practices of biblical transmission. This invites new partnerships with scholars working on provenance and manuscript curation and dissemination.[58] Such scholars highlight the relationships that people have through the texts, and the connectional pathways made possible or impaired by the Bible is a web of exchanges—second-hand, third-hand. The method, I think, is productive for conceiving of constructive biblical hermeneutics.

Hirsch refers to "aesthetic and ethical practices of postmemory, practices that situate themselves in the specific aftermath of historical catastrophe."[59] It is precisely because there is distance that a creative space can open up to receive that history for the "truths that it tells"[60] in that someone can meet it differently, potentially open it up to a different iteration. The alteration of past memories does not need to be received simply as distortions; instead, the positioning of another generation—intentionally and creatively—toward the past may produce an alternative future. There is critical distance from that history, enough to recreate the routes that those memories can travel.

We could say that constructive theologians have always been invested in tracking the traumatic reception of biblical texts; but it is provocative to think about tracking positively, with an eye toward reparation.[61] A hermeneutics of suspicion gives way to hermeneutics of repair and resilience. In interpreting biblical transmission, it may be productive to think about theological interpretation of biblical texts as a means of "working through" past trauma toward certain ends.[62] Venturing new readings is not, therefore, a departure from the past or a break from it but, instead, a gapped continuity that makes possible a different outcome. The ongoing reading and writing and ritualizing and liturgical offers opportunities to heal the past *forward*.

---

[58] Jennifer Knust, a scholar of the literary and history of ancient Christianity, is interested in the practices of provenance. She and other biblical scholars are also tracking how biblical history is employed in political projects, such as the creation of the Museum of the Bible. The museum is a good example of how, in contemporary public life, biblical authority is mobilized for particular ends—to tell a single uninterrupted story of Christian nationalism. See Jennifer Knust, "Editing without Interpreting: The Museum of the Bible and New Testament Textual Criticism," in *The Museum of the Bible: A Critical Introduction*, ed. Cavan Concanon and Jill Hicks Keeton (London: Lexington Books, 2019). See also Katherine Stewart, "The Museum of the Bible Is a Safe Space for Christian Nationalists," *New York Times*, January 6, 2018, https://www.nytimes.com/2018/01/06/opinion/sunday/the-museum-of-the-bible-is-a-safe-space-for-christian-nationalists.html.

[59] Hirsch, *A Generation of Postmemory*, 228.

[60] Caruth, "Preface," in *Trauma: Explorations in Memory*.

[61] Nod to Eve Sedgwick's notion of reparative readings. Eve Kosofsky Sedgwick, "Paranoid Reading and Reparative Reading, or, You're So Paranoid, You Probably Think This Essay Is About You," in *Touching, Feeling: Affect, Pedagogy, Performativity* (Durham, NC: Duke University Press, 2003), 123–52.

[62] Perhaps this is akin to the "counter-apocalyptic spatial therapeutics" that Catherine Keller was forecasting in *Apocalypse Now and Then*, in which she writes: "If I grew up apocalyptic, I have since had the luck or instinct to stay put and begin to heal from this dislocating spatiality, to revitalize bit by bit my numbed sense of habitat. Likewise, in the interest of counter-apocalyptic spatial therapeutics, this chapter will consider certain trans-historical, indeed transcontinental, dislocations of Western sensibility" (141).

Conclusion

Constructive theologians insist that the Bible is not one thing. It is not a single text with a single message to be received across time. They loosen the hold of damning interpretations, insisting on the multiplicity of modes and contexts of theo-biblical interpretations. But it is often experienced for its singular force, when tied to primary affections. It is not a single text, but it can be experienced as such. I suggest, here, that constructive theologians should consider more fully how biblical authority *lives on* affectively, often apart from explicit claims or visible religious practices. Old systems, old houses are not gone but, in fact, are returning—even resurging. The challenge is to account for its afterlife. The house returns in unexpected times, places, and forms. If theologians account for the adherence, attachments, they will think about how to work constructively with the ingredients of formation: bodies, affect, and imagination. The future may point beyond a focus on how biblical texts are explicitly functioning and attempt to account for the afterlife of the Bible that lives on in persons, communities, and nations. Building upon the three phases of constructive engagements with the Bible, the current moment may operate with all of the muscle memory of these previous modes to take account of the biblical remains.

Bibliography

Bender, Courtney, Wendy Cadge, Peggy Levitt, and David Smiled, eds. *Religion on the Edge: De-centering and Re-centering the Sociology of Religion*. Oxford, UK: Oxford University Press, 2013.

Bender, Courtney, and Pamela Klassen, eds. *After Pluralism: Reimagining Religious Engagement*. New York: Columbia University Press, 2010.

Betcher, Sharon. *Spirit and the Obligations of Social Flesh: A Secular Theology for the Global City*, 1st ed. New York: Fordham University Press, 2014.

Briere, John N., and Catherine Scott. *Principles of Trauma Therapy: A Guide to Symptoms, Evaluation, and Treatment*, 2nd ed. Thousand Oaks, CA: Sage, 2014.

Caruth, Cathy, ed. *Trauma: Explorations in Memory*. Baltimore: Johns Hopkins University Press, 1995.

Chopp, Rebecca. "Theology and the Poetics of Testimony." In *Converging on Culture: Theologians in Dialogue with Cultural Analysis and Criticism*, edited by Delwin Brown, Sheila Greeve Davaney, and Kathryn Tanner. Oxford, UK: Oxford University Press, 2011.

Compier, Don H., Kwok Pui-lan, and Joerg Rieger, eds. *Empire and the Christian Tradition: New Readings of Classical Theologians*. Minneapolis, MN: Fortress, 2007.

Dube, Musa W. *Postcolonial Feminist Interpretation of the Bible*. St. Louis, MO: Chalice, 2000.

Ebel, Jonathan H. *G.I. Messiahs: Soldiering, War, and American Civil Religion*. New Haven, CT: Yale University Press, 2015.

Elwell, W. A., ed. *Evangelical Dictionary of Theology*. Grand Rapids, MI: Baker Book House, 1984.

Evans, James H. *We Have Been Believers: An African-American Systematic Theology*. Minneapolis, MN: Fortress, 1992.

Farley, Edward, and Peter C. Hodgson. "Scripture and Tradition." In *Christian Theology: An Introduction to Its Traditions and Tasks*, edited by Peter C. Hodgson and Robert H. King, 61–87. Philadelphia, PA: Fortress, 1982.

Farley, Wendy. *The Wounding and Healing of Desire: Weaving Heaven and Earth*. Louisville, KY: Westminster John Knox, 2005.

Fiorenza, Elisabeth Schüssler. "In Memory of Her." *Journal of Feminist Studies in Religion* 35:1 (2019): 129–30.

Grau, Marion. *Rethinking Mission in the Postcolony: Salvation, Society and Subversion*. London: T&T Clark, 2011.

Henry, Carl F. H. *God, Revelation and Authority*. Wheaton, IL: Crossway Books, 1999.

Henry, Carl F. H. "Inerrancy and the Bible in Modern Conservative Evangelical Thought." In *Introduction to Christian Theology: Contemporary North American Perspectives*, edited by Roger A. Badham, 53–65. Louisville, KY: Westminster John Knox, 1998.

Hillgardner, Holly. *Longing and Letting Go: Christian and Hindu Practices of Passionate Non-Attachment*. New York: Oxford University Press, 2017.

Hirsch, Marianne. *A Generation of Postmemory: Writing and Visual Culture After the Holocaust*. New York: Columbia University Press, 2012.

Hodgson, Peter C., and Robert H. King. Preface to *Christian Theology: And Introduction to Its Traditions and Tasks*, edited by Peter C. Hodgson and Robert H. King, ix–xiii. Philadelphia, PA: Fortress, 1982.

Hoffman, Eva. *After Such Knowledge: Memory, History, and the Legacy of the Holocaust*. Cambridge, MA: Perseus Books, 2004.

Janoff-Bulman, Ronnie. *Shattered Assumptions: Towards a New Psychology of Trauma*. New York: Free Press, 2002.

Jennings, Willie. *The Christian Imagination: Theology and the Origins of Race*. New Haven, CT: Yale University Press, 2011.

Jensen, David Hadley. *God, Desire, and a Theology of Human Sexuality*, 1st ed. Louisville, KY: Westminster John Knox, 2013.

Jones, Serene. *Trauma and Grace: Theology in a Ruptured World*. Louisville, KY: Westminster John Knox, 2009.

Jones, Serene, and Paul Lakeland, eds. *Constructive Theology: A Contemporary Approach to Classical Themes*. Minneapolis, MN: Fortress, 2008.

Junger, Sebastian. *Tribe: On Homecoming and Belonging*. New York: Twelve Books, 2016.

Kearney, Richard. *Anatheism: Returning to God after God*. New York: Columbia University Press, 2011.

Keller, Catherine. *Apocalypse Now and Then: A Feminist Guide to the End of the World*. Boston, MA: Beacon, 1996.

Keller, Catherine. *Face of the Deep: A Theology of Becoming*. London: Routledge, 2003.

Keller, Catherine. *God and Power: Counter-apocalyptic Journeys*. Minneapolis, MN: Fortress, 2005.

Keller, Catherine. *On the Mystery: Discerning Divinity in Process*. Minneapolis, MN: Fortress, 2008.

Keller, Catherine, Michael Nausner, and Mayra Rivera. *Postcolonial Theologies: Divinity and Empire*. St. Louis, MO: Chalice, 2004.

Keshgegian, Flora. *Redeeming Memories: A Theology of Healing and Transformation*. Nashville, TN: Abingdon, 2000.

King, Karen L. *The Gospel of Mary of Magdala: Jesus and the First Woman Apostle.* Santa Rosa, CA: Polebridge, 2003.
King, Robert H. "Introduction: The Task of Theology." In *Christian Theology: An Introduction to Its Traditions and Tasks*, edited by Peter C. Hodgson and Robert H. King, 1–27. Philadelphia, PA: Fortress, 1982.
Koosed, Jennifer L., and Stephen D. More. "Introduction: From Affect to Exegesis." *Biblical Interpretation* 22 (2014): 382.
Kosofsky Sedgwick, Eve. *Touching, Feeling: Affect, Pedagogy, Performativity.* Durham, NC: Duke University Press, 2003.
Kwok, Pui-lan. *Discovering the Bible in the Non-Biblical World.* Bible & Liberation Series. Maryknoll, NY: Orbis Books, 1995.
Kwok, Pui-lan. "Discovering the Bible in the Non-Biblical World." In *Lift Every Voice: Constructing Christian Theologies from the Underside*, revised and expanded ed., edited by Susan Brooks Thistlethwaite and Mary Potter Engel, 276–88. Maryknoll, NY: Orbis Books, 1998.
Kwok, Pui-lan. *Postcolonial Imagination and Feminist Theology*, 1st ed. Louisville, KY: Westminster John Knox, 2005.
Levine, Peter. *Waking the Tiger: Healing Trauma.* Berkeley, CA: Sage, 2014.
Liew, Tat-siong Benny. *Colonialism and the Bible: Contemporary Reflections from the Global South.* Postcolonial and Decolonial Studies in Religion and Theology. Lanham, MD: Lexington Books, 2018.
Liew, Tat-siong Benny. *Politics of Parousia: Reading Mark Inter(Con)Textually.* Biblical Interpretation Series, v. 42. Leiden: Brill, 1999.
Linafelt, Tod, ed. *A Shadow of Glory: Reading the New Testament after the Holocaust.* New York: Routledge, 2002.
Linafelt, Tod, ed. *Strange Fire: Reading the Bible after the Holocaust.* Sheffield, UK: Sheffield Academic Press, 2000.
Moltmann, Jürgen. *The Trinity and the Kingdom: The Doctrine of God.* Minneapolis, MN: Fortress, 1993.
Nakashima Brock, Rita. "Moral Injury, Soul Repair, and Congregations." FCC Minneapolis, accessed August 12, 2019. http://www.fccminneapolis.org/wp-content/uploads/2016/05/Moral-Injury-Handout-May-2016-MN.pdf.
Ogden, Pat, Kekuni Minton, and Clare Pane, eds. *Trauma and the Body: A Sensorimotor Approach to Psychotherapy.* New York: W.W. Norton, 2006.
Outler, Albert C. "They Wesleyan Quadrilateral—in John Wesley." *Wesleyan Theological Journal* 20:1 (Spring 1985): 7–18.
Rambo, Shelly. *Resurrecting Wounds: Living in the Afterlife of Trauma.* Waco, TX: Baylor University Press, 2017.
Rambo, Shelly. "Salvation in the After-Living: Reflections on Salvation with Joshua Ralston and Sharon Betcher." In *Comparing Faithfully: Insights for Systematic Theological Reflection*, edited by Michell Voss Roberts, 296–315. New York: Fordham University Press, 2016.
Rambo, Shelly. *Spirit and Trauma: A Theology of Remaining*, 1st ed. Louisville, KY: Westminster John Knox, 2010.
Ricoeur, Paul. "The Model of the Text: Meaningful Action Considered as a Text." *New Literary History* 5:1, What Is Literature? (Autumn 1973): 91–117.
Rieger, Joerg. *Christ & Empire: From Paul to Postcolonial Times.* Minneapolis, MN: Fortress, 2007.

Rieger, Joerg. "Constructive Theology." In *Encyclopedia of Sciences and Religion*, edited by Anne L.C. Runehov and Lluis Oviedo, 483–6. Dordrecht: Springer Netherlands, 2013.

Rivera, Mayra. "Glory: The First Passion of Theology?" In *Polydoxy: Theology of Multiplicity and Relation*, edited by Catherine Keller and Laurel C. Schneider, 167–85. London: Routledge, 2010.

Rothschild, Babett. *The Body Remembers: The Psychophysiology of Trauma and Trauma Treatment*. New York: W.W. Norton, 2000.

Ruether, Rosemary Radford. *Sexism and God-Talk: Toward a Feminist Theology*. Boston, MA: Beacon, 1983.

Rutz, Cynthia Lillian. "*King Lear* and Its Folktale Analogues." PhD diss., University of Chicago, 2013.

Schneider, Laurel C. *Re-imagining the Divine: Confronting the Backlash against Feminist Theology*. Cleveland, OH: Pilgrim, 1999.

Schneider, Laurel C., and Stephen G. Ray, eds. *Awake to the Moment: An Introduction to Theology*, 1st ed. Louisville, KY: Westminster John Knox, 2016.

Segovia, Fernando F., and Mary Ann Tolbert. *Teaching the Bible: The Discourses and Politics of Biblical Pedagogy*. Maryknoll, NY: Orbis Books, 1998.

Tanner, Kathryn. *Reflection and Theory in the Study of Religion*. Oxford: Oxford University Press, 2001.

Taylor, Mark Lewis. "Reading from an Indigenous Place." In *Teaching the Bible: The Discourse and Politics of Biblical Theology*, edited by Fernando F. Segovia and Mary Ann Tolbert, 117–36. Minneapolis, MN: Fortress, 2009.

Thatamanil, John. *The Immanent Divine: God, Creation, and the Human Predicament*. Minneapolis, MN: Fortress, 2006.

Trible, Phyllis. *Texts of Terror: Literary Feminist Readings of Biblical Narratives*. Minneapolis, MN: Fortress, 1984.

Van der Kolk, Bessel. *The Body Keeps the Score: Brain, Mind, and Body in the Healing of Trauma*. New York: Penguin Books, 2015.

Volkan, Vamik. *Bloodlines: From Ethnic Pride to Ethnic Terrorism*. Boulder, CO: Westview, 1998.

Voss Roberts, Michelle. *Tastes of the Divine: Hindu and Christian Theologies of Emotion*. Comparative Theologies: Thinking across Traditions. New York: Fordham University Press, 2014.

Wiley, Tatha. "Paul and Early Christianity." In *Empire and the Christian Tradition: New Readings of Classical Theologians*, edited by Don H. Compier, Kwok Pui-lan, and Joerg Rieger, 47–62. Minneapolis, MN: Fortress, 2007.

Wyman, Jason A. *Constructing Constructive Theology: An Introductory Sketch*. Minneapolis, MN: Fortress, 2017.

6

Blessed Snakes in the Basket: Comparative Theology and the Constructive Theological Turn

Holly Hillgardner

As the field of contemporary comparative theology continues to come into its own, a story from the Hindu traditions may help us think about the ways in which the field has been constructed. As one version of the hagiography tells it, Mirabai, a sixteenth-century North Indian princess-poet, breaks her society's gendered norms to live in devotion to God. Refusing a traditional family life, she becomes an itinerant devotee of the god Krishna, whom she claims as her husband. Angry at her unconventional behavior, her relatives send her a two-faced present, a venomous snake disguised in a basket of flowers. Just as the snake rises from the petals to strike her, it turns into a Krishna icon! Miraculously defanged, the snake's transformation confirms Mirabai's countercultural life of love.

What almost destroys Mirabai instead transforms into the very force that fuels her life. What almost kills her instead strengthens her, and she writes, sings, and dances for Krishna with new vitality. In another version of the story, Mirabai and Krishna join forces to subvert the harm meant to her. Repurposing the dangerous snake, Mirabai wraps it around her neck, as it transforms into jewelry. She tells the story in one of her songs: "Mira folded the snake around her neck, it was a lover's bracelet, lovely!"[1] Defanged but not merely decorative, the former threat now speaks to the committed, complicated love she and Krishna share.

Comparative theology, too, has transformed its own specific threats—ideas that deconstructed the discipline, almost to the point of extinction—into something "lovely," that is, life-giving methodological lenses that revive and reshape the discipline. As we think with these stories about Mirabai, they can help us explore how constructive theological methodologies—postcolonial, feminist, interreligious, and ethnographic approaches, for example—might be viewed as snakes in the basket of comparative theology. In other words, critical tools that reveal the problems with comparative thought function also as gifts, spiritually and intellectually honest ways through comparative theology's morass of ethical and methodological challenges. These resources continue to move contemporary comparative theology toward a more

---

[1] Mirabai, *Mirabai Versions*, trans. Robert Bly (New York: Red Ozier, 1984).

dialogical, interdisciplinary, ethical practice, one that constructs itself differently than its earlier incarnations did.

With the help of Mirabai's metaphor, we first trace how the fledgling discipline of comparative theology emerged and interrogate the role of the "snakes in the basket" in its formation. To highlight current Hindu–Christian theology's continuing work with constructive methodologies, we focus on three recent comparative theologies: Michelle Voss Roberts's *Body Parts: A Theological Anthropology*, Neela Bhattacharya Saxena's *Absent Mother God of the West: A Kali Lover's Journey into Christianity and Judaism*, and Kristen Bloomer's *Possessed by the Virgin: Hinduism, Roman Catholicism, and Marian Possession in South India*. These books were chosen not just because they are current examples of the wide diversity of the field, but also because they each demonstrate important ways in which comparative theology is still constructing itself. The critical methodologies highlighted in these three texts constitute the growing edges of comparative theology; thus, they point to the future of what I am calling "constructive comparative theology."[2] In the last section, we zoom out from the three focus texts to consider more widely how such theology might best flourish. Proposing that comparative theology is best framed as constructive theology, we pinpoint strategies that best allow for constructive, comparative theological work.

A Look Back at Religious Comparativism

Comparative theology's development can be traced alongside an exploration of the near-death experiences of its sister discipline, comparative religion. In the late decades of the twentieth century, the intellectual and ethical challenges posed by postmodern and postcolonial theory effectively silenced the discipline of comparative religion, and scholars responded by retreating into highly specialized "area studies." After a spell of paralysis regarding comparativism, what Indologist Wendy Doniger calls the "second wave" of postmodernism, poststructuralism, and postcolonialism effectively breathed new life into the dry bones of comparative religion. This wave saved the discipline from a disconnected irrelevancy at best or an extinction at worst.[3]

Learning how to surf this second wave of thought, scholars continued to break away from modernist, "objective," view-from-above stances. Instead, they embraced metaphorical redescriptions of compared religious phenomena and more carefully constructed comparative categories. David Gordon White sums up the reconstructed task of comparative work: "We may legitimately compare *relations and aspects*

---

[2] Jon Paul Sydnor's *Ramanuja and Schleiermacher: Toward a Constructive Comparative Theology* (Cambridge, UK: James Clarke, 2012) is one of the first in the field to use the term "constructive theology" to describe comparative theology.

[3] Wendy Doniger, "Postmodern and -colonial -Structural Comparisons," in *A Magic Still Dwells: Comparative Religion in the Postmodern Age*, ed. Kimberley Patton and Benjamin Ray (Berkeley: University of California Press 2000), 63–74 (72). Doniger suggests that the "first wave" of postmodernism and postcolonialism disabled comparative religious studies, but the more nuanced "second wave" invigorated it.

rather than *things*."⁴ With this focus, comparativism now aimed for more complex, interdisciplinary representations of religious phenomena, descriptions that did not "other" and objectify the subjects. For example, to represent well the "polycentrism" of Hinduism, a famously complex religious construction, Richard King argued that scholars need to work constructively with indigenous Indian epistemologies, particularly those that existed before the advent of the Western academic discourse of religion.⁵ As such ideas took root, scholars began to tiptoe back into the waters of comparativism.

Not only did comparative religion revive in the wakes of postcoloniality and postmodern critical theory, but also the "new comparative theology" began to emerge from its primordial soup. Here, I use "new comparative theology" to differentiate this field, which Reid Locklin and Hugh Nicholson have traced to the late 1980s, from the early-nineteenth-century comparative theological genre, one that "epitomizes the universalist ideology that has since become so problematic."⁶ This earlier comparative theology often flattened out religious difference into universalist generalities. In other words, in a quest to harmonize religions with one another, complex religious phenomena were often ignored or misinterpreted, sometimes in supercessionist ways that occluded religious traditions. The new comparative theology takes a different approach: it "generally uses comparison to *unsettle and complexify* prevailing theological assumptions" rather than "*de-problematize* Christian commitment through various metonymical rhetorical strategies."⁷ The birth of this new comparative theology was made possible through comparative theology's engagement with interdisciplinary, constructive resources, ones that were also up to the task of answering the charges against comparativism.

Not just comparative theology, but all comparative fields had to answer these charges. Kimberley Patton and Benjamin Ray list the "substantial and often well-founded" arguments against the comparative method as "intellectual imperialism, universalism, theological foundationalism, and anti-contextualism."⁸ Efforts to remedy these issues, however, sometimes hindered the field in new ways. For example, when previous comparative studies had posited broad, cross-cultural similarities among religions,

---

⁴ David Gordon White, "The Scholar as Mythographer: Comparative Indo-European Myth and Postmodern Concerns," in *A Magic Still Dwells: Comparative Religion in the Postmodern Age*, ed. Kimberly Patton and Benjamin Ray (Berkeley: University of California Press 2000), 47–54 (53); italics mine.

⁵ Richard King, "Colonialism, Hinduism, and the Discourse of Religion," in *Rethinking Religion in India: The Colonial Construction of Hinduism*, ed. Esther Bloch, Marianne Keppens, and Rajaram Hegde (New York: Routledge, 2010), 95–113 (110). King goes on to name the "single most important task facing those who work with Indian traditions": the postcolonial goal of "extricat[ing] the history of the Indian tradition from its Eurocentric narration" (110).

⁶ Reid B. Locklin and Hugh Nicholson, "The Return of Comparative Theology," *Journal of the American Academy of Religion* 78, no. 2 (2010): 471–514 (481).

⁷ Hugh Nicholson, "Comparative Theology after Liberalism," *Modern Theology* 23, no. 2 (2007): 229–51 (244); italics mine. By metonymical strategies, Nicholson means the use of imprecise comparative categories with a wide array of associative and connotative meanings. For example, "religion" comes to stand in for "American," "Protestant," and "white Christianity."

⁸ Kimberley C. Patton and Benjamin Ray, "Introduction," in *A Magic Still Dwells: Comparative Religion in the Postmodern Age*, ed. Kimberly Patton and Benjamin Ray (Berkeley: University of California Press 2000), 1–22 (1).

the unique particularities of religious traditions often became one-dimensional. They flattened out the "other" religious tradition in favor of the dominant paradigm, namely, Christianity. In reaction to this destructive homogenization, comparativists began limiting their work to strict explorations of "difference." With this reactive move, they then found only worlds of incommensurability among religions, or "windowless monads" with each religious tradition in its own impoverished, "oversimplified box."[9] Now a new kind of ethical danger arose: the risk of isolationism with no way to bring these closed-off worlds together.

Here, we can see the irony of the "snakes in the basket" in action. Engaging the interconnected discourses of postcolonialism and postmodernism, the very tools that exposed the fissures of comparativism, also helped comparative scholars find ways out of the aforementioned universalism/incommensurability dualism. Because postmodernity and postcolonialism focus on "different aspects of difference," they each do valuable work helping the other discourse from falling into reductionisms that do violence to religions' complexities.[10] Postcolonial thought, for example, provides an impetus for understanding and working against unjust forces, a motivation that may get lost in some forms of postmodernism that overstate the implications of deconstruction. Of course, some deconstruction is necessary here: it helps prevent postcolonial thought from hardening into an essentialization of culture and what has been called the "idolatry of identity."[11] Interpenetrating streams of postmodern and postcolonial thought thus help prevent each stream from ossifying into a caricature of itself. To use our herpetological metaphor, they help defang each other: they open up space that allows both similarities *and* differences to exist. Then complex and ethical comparative religious work can emerge. Here, we see just one example of how constructive resources catalyzed the revival of a reconstituted comparative religion as well as the birth of constructive comparative theology. As the snake in the basket transforms into the force that saves and energizes Mirabai's life, these ominous discourses instead provided life-saving tools, resources for the deconstruction and reconstruction of comparative thought in multiple modes.

Using these constructive resources, comparative scholars relearned how to think comparatively. No longer able to rely on sui generis categories that reflected Christian bias, scholarship distorted by colonialist thinkers, and unexamined dualisms, comparative scholars needed new tools to construct a different kind of comparison, one that might better address the almost fatal critiques of the discipline. Since both comparative religion and comparative theology emerged from disciplines with a "loaded karma," to use interreligious theologian Raimundo Panikkar's apt term,[12] these disciplines need the continued help of critical methodologies, such as the

---

[9] Kimberley C. Patton, "Juggling Torches: While We Still Need Comparative Religion," in *A Magic Still Dwells: Comparative Religion in the Postmodern Age*, ed. Kimberly Patton and Benjamin Ray (Berkeley: University of California Press 2000), 153–71 (163).

[10] Doniger, "Postmodern and -colonial -Structural Comparisons," 72.

[11] Catherine Keller, Michael Nausner, and Mayra Rivera, "Introduction: Alien/Nation, Liberation, and the Postcolonial Underground," in *Postcolonial Theologies: Divinity and Empire*, ed. Catherine Keller, Michael Nausner, and Mayra Rivera (St. Louis, MO: Chalice, 2004), 1–21 (18).

[12] Raimundo Panikkar, "Forward: The Ongoing Dialogue," in *Hindu Christian Dialogue: Perspectives and Encounters*, ed. Harold Coward (Maryknoll, NY: Orbis Books, 1989), ix–xviii (vi).

aforementioned postcolonial and postmodern critical theory and others, for example, gender theory, which we will soon address. These tools collude for the ongoing defanging of comparativism's colonialist, modernist, and sexist histories—all poisons that were threatening the viability of the comparativist project.

Multiple constructive resources are thus necessary to defang comparativism. The best scholars of religion employ a diverse, flexible toolbox, so advised the late Buddhist feminist scholar Rita Gross: "Methodologies should be worn very lightly. If another method is proposed that better explains the material being discussed, switch, don't fight!"[13] Here, Gross does not underestimate the uses of theory, but argues that working with multiple, diverse methodologies creates more adequate scholarship that accounts for contending, not easily reconciled religious views and commitments. This is perfect advice for comparative theologians, and the toolboxes employed by the three scholars we discuss here are indeed diverse. Their work attests to the panoply of resources needed to write constructive comparative theology in light of the challenges we have discussed.

We now turn to an examination of three recent Hindu–Christian comparative theologies. With an eye to the ways in which they are respectively breaking new ground, we dive deep into the recent work of Michelle Voss Roberts, Neela Bhattacharya Saxena, and Kristen Bloomer, each of whom provides insight into how comparative theology continues to construct itself. As we locate the specific methodologies deployed in each of these texts, we also observe how comparative theology is currently constructing itself.

Comparative Theology's Present: Case Studies in Constructive Hindu–Christian Theology

Comparative Theology for All?

As one of the first female comparative theologians, Michelle Voss Roberts brought a desperately needed focus on gender into the field. In her first book, *Dualities: A Theology of Difference*, she brings us the female voices of Lalleswari and Mechthild, "outsider" Hindu and Christian women who also complicate stereotypes of "Eastern" and "Western" religious categories. Through this intersectional work, she illuminates the historical links between the postcolonial other and essentialized notions of femininity.[14] As postcolonial and feminist methodologies mutually inform each other in her work, comparative theology as a discipline shifts and becomes less encumbered by patriarchal and colonial assumptions.

Voss Roberts has also helped construct a more accessible discipline, one that takes laypeople and nonexperts seriously as doers of comparative theology. Written

---

[13] Rita M. Gross, "Response," in *How to Do Comparative Religion? Three Ways, Many Goals*, ed. René Gothóni (Berlin: Walter de Gruyter, 2005), 187–91 (164).

[14] Michelle Voss Roberts, *Dualities: A Theology of Difference* (Louisville, KY: Westminster John Knox, 2010), 22.

for divinity school students, her third book, *Body Parts: A Theological Anthropology*, explicitly invites a wider audience to join the work of constructive theology. Rather than gatekeeping comparative theology as an exercise for specialists only, Voss Roberts's book moves to democratize the field. In the process, she neither dumbs down the concepts nor condescends to her audience; instead, she welcomes and invites students, her named audience, as well as other nonexperts, into complex comparative thinking.

This invitation fits in with her larger project of moving comparative theology into the mainstream of theological study. Her vision for a comparative theology that might be used as a constructive theological textbook came to fruition with her edited volume *Comparing Faithfully: Insights for Systematic Theological Reflection*.[15] In soliciting contributors to this volume, Voss Roberts made an effort to include non-Christian voices. While such a methodological move may seem obvious for a discipline that purportedly values interreligious learning, much comparative theology proves insular; it is written *by* Christians *for* Christians. While this textbook, too, is written with a Christian audience in mind, it also includes the voices of a Muslim and a Hindu, who each do theology from their own perspectives and also respond to Christian theological voices.[16] A welcome and necessary move for the field, such dialogical, interreligious work must continue to find its way into constructive comparative theology.

In her latest book, Voss Roberts utilizes a feminist methodology of embodiment through her comparative framework of "body parts." Using these comparative categories she employs from a Hindu tradition, she actively works against the body/soul dualism that has impoverished Christian theology by privileging the soul over the body. For help in reclaiming the importance of Christian embodiment, she turns to the non-dual Saivism of Kashmir, specifically the categories of Abhinavagupta's "body of consciousness," which consists of thirty-six parts divided into four categories. This multipart system has many advantages, but one of the most important is its notion of multiplicity and diversity: if we can see the *imago Dei* as reflecting thirty-six surfaces of the human being, then the human being shines like a multifaceted jewel, rather than a flat surface. In this way, this set of comparative categories from a Hindu tradition "reopens the mystery of the embodied *imago dei*."[17]

To further encourage an embodied methodology, Voss Roberts designates the final section of each of her chapters for spiritual "practices of attention." In these sections, she offers suggestions—not just suggested readings, but practices—for further exploring the ideas she has presented. These practices are not in the service of simple cognitive knowledge; instead, they aim for a more thorough bodily knowing, even hoped-for transformations that will lead to "wise and compassionate ways of being in the world."[18] Indeed, Voss Robert reminds us, "metaphysics—detached from contemplative practice—tends toward domination."[19] Framed as a vital part of a

---

[15] Michelle Voss Roberts, ed., *Comparing Faithfully: Insights for Systematic Theological Reflection* (New York: Fordham, 2016).
[16] See Amir Hussain's and Jeffrey D. Long's contributions in ibid., 185–91 and 107–25, respectively.
[17] Michelle Voss Roberts, *Body Parts: A Theological Anthropology* (Minneapolis, MN: Fortress, 2017), xxi.
[18] Ibid., xlvii.
[19] Ibid., 22.

Christian anthropology, her "practices of embracing the limited body" prove crucial, especially for white, middle-class Christians who have often not understood how their privileges affect their theologies. As she explains, embracing limits allows Christians to "self-limit: to keep the presumed universality of one's experience in check, to adjust one's reality to accommodate others, and to use one's powers to remove unnecessary and disabling limits for others."[20] In this way, practices of acceptance of human limits combine with practices of healing, solidarity, lament, and protest with and for those who have been limited by structural sin.[21]

In her constructive comparative work, such a foregrounding of ethical concerns directly relates to her feminist methodologies. For example, in an earlier article, she traced the slow gendering of comparative theology and argued for the importance of critical gender studies for the field. If comparative theology can indeed find a multiply situated positionality that includes gender, she posited, then it is well placed to gain insights into oppressive power structures—boldly naming problems while also humbly questioning the field's own potentially hegemonic epistemological categories.[22] Functioning in this way, a constructive theology does not separate itself from ethical questions; they are inextricably bound. Laboring to define and characterize where constructive theology is today, Jason Wyman writes in his book *Constructing Constructive Theology: An Introductory Sketch*, "Constructive theology blurs the line between theology and ethics, especially when it comes to activist theologies."[23]

Since constructive comparative theology refuses to separate the theological from the ethical, *Body Parts* begins with an ethical and theological problem: "The United States has been caught up in the othering that Christ was supposed to have overcome: black and white, gay and straight, men and women, Christians and Muslims, 'real' Americans and immigrants."[24] With a nod to Sallie McFague's classic terminology, Voss Roberts aspires to "models of God" that can do better, ones that do not contribute to the othering and dehumanizing of others.[25] She names methodological plurality, religious plurality, and embodied theology as goods that Hindu–Christian comparative theology has at its disposal for these tasks. She also draws from other constructive resources—namely, disability studies and animal studies—that have not yet widely made their way into comparative theology.

Body Parts is also born out of divinity school students' practical concerns and questions. In a significant move toward what could be called the democratization of the discipline, she draws her comparative theological questions directly from her teaching. When exploring with a class how the *imago Dei* functions in different human situations, for example, she poses this question to her students: "How does a coma

---

[20] Ibid., 49.
[21] Ibid., 51.
[22] Michelle Voss Roberts, "Gendering Comparative Theology," in *The New Comparative Theology: Interreligious Insights from the Next Generation*, ed. Francis X. Clooney (New York: T&T Clark, 2010), 129–49.
[23] Jason A. Wyman, Jr., *Constructing Constructive Theology: An Introductory Sketch* (Minneapolis, MN: Fortress, 2017), 235.
[24] Voss Roberts, *Body Parts*, xix.
[25] Sallie McFague's classic book *Models of God: Theology for an Ecological, Nuclear Age* (Minneapolis, MN: Fortress, 1987) serves as one of Voss Roberts's primary conversation partners in *Body Parts*.

patient image God?" The characteristics of the *imago Dei* that her class had earlier brainstormed, including creativity, mutual relationship, and rational thought, had to be rethought. Of this process, she reports, "My students trust God's gracious love for all people, but the implications [of the *imago Dei*] now trouble them."[26] Inspired from these concerns, the book relates how students motivated her exploration of what it means to image God in diverse situations.

Voss Roberts also addresses the related issue of cultural appropriation, a serious concern that can be exacerbated when nonexperts begin to play with concepts and ideas from religious traditions that are not their own. She offers a helpful, alternative paradigm to combat the utilization of others' sacred concepts for one's own benefit: she encourages telling a larger story. To be sure, it is a risk to try to tell a story larger than one's own experience, Voss Roberts says, but when we tell our stories in conversation with other voices besides our own, we aim not only to include others but also to be responsible to them.[27] Her vision aims to address appropriation while not discouraging comparative work, even for nonexperts.

As a related practice, Voss Roberts encourages practices of imagination for comparativists. Connecting the previously discussed practices of limitation to imagination, she reminds us that imagination always starts from a place of limitation where we ask, "How might things be different?"[28] Imagination is also necessary for empathy, she argues; we must see and feel suffering, even if it is not our own.[29] With these practices, she names constructive tools that are appropriate for all levels of comparativists, including beginners. These tools do not eschew scholarly theoretical tools, but neither do they require expertise with them. She thus brings an inclusive spirit into the sometimes-rarified world of comparative theology. If comparative theology is indeed to be truly constructive, then it will need to construct with the voices of many. To this point, Wyman offers, "Constructive theology values collaboration like no other theological movement ever has."[30] Voss Roberts's Hindu–Christian theology aims to bring comparative theology to the seminary classroom, while being cognizant of the challenges involved. As she employs comparative theology with and for her students, she demonstrates that the field need not be relegated to a rarified subgenre of theology; instead, comparative theology can be housed in the field of constructive theology.

Comparative Theology by Non-Christians?

As mentioned previously, most works of comparative theology are written by Christians.[31] If those who are religious but not Christian do not feel inspired to write works of comparative theology, where does this leave the field? If the idea of comparative theology cannot be uncoupled from an ethic of mutual learning, as

---

[26] Voss Roberts, *Body Parts*, xxvii.
[27] Ibid., xxxiii.
[28] Ibid., 75.
[29] Ibid., 74.
[30] Wyman, *Constructing Constructive Theology*, 168.
[31] Some of my analysis first appeared as a review of Saxena's book in the *Journal of Hindu-Christian Studies* 30 (2017).

I propose, but the reality of who does comparative theology does not match that ideal, what is then to be done?

Of course, the history of Hindu–Christian relations has never truly been characterized by mutuality: at best, early comparative attempts were marked from their beginnings by biased representations of Hinduism and efforts to destroy and replace non-Christian culture, at worst. While progress has been made toward an ethic of mutuality in comparative religious studies, repeated misrepresentations of Hinduism by Christian scholars have long marred the field.

Theology, of course, has been one of the worst offenders, and it has been late in exploring and unraveling this history.[32] Skepticism is far from an unearned reaction when it comes to Christians claiming that they want to learn from Hinduism. Even as comparative theology values mutual learning and transformation, unless Hindus make the choice to engage more in the comparative theological community, this ethic alone will never offer the hoped-for corrective to the imbalances in Hindu–Christian comparative theology. If greater participation from non-Christian interlocutors does not happen in due time, so suggests Francis X. Clooney, then this disinterest may tell scholars something crucial about inhospitalities in comparative theology's categories and structures.[33] Christian comparative theologians may thus ultimately find that they are still peering at the religious other in a system with little space for the religious other to look at them.

Neela Bhattacharya Saxena, however, has written a book of comparative theology from a Hindu–Buddhist perspective. Not a theologian by training but a professor of English and women's studies, Saxena searches for the divine feminine in India and the West. An ambitious book, *Absent Mother God of the West: A Kali Lover's Journey into Christianity and Judaism* is woven through with diverse currents from literature, philosophy, and interreligious theology. She takes readers on a far-ranging pilgrimage, a communal search party for the goddess. Deeply poetic and philosophical, her interdisciplinarity opens up new vistas for comparative theology as it makes surprising connections among continental thought, esoteric religion, ecofeminist religion, and postcolonial thought, to name only some of her conversation partners.

The book thus reads as an interdisciplinary collage of the divine feminine, as understood across multiple religious traditions. Not only a cross-cultural description of the Mother God, this book also espouses Her ethical importance. For instance, she argues that the forgetting of the Mother God is implicated in the world's current state of environmental degradation: if we ignore the divine feminine, she proposes, we may be doomed to abuse Mother Earth. In a chapter called "Matricide," she details the connection between our theologies and our environmental ethics. Here, as is the case

---

[32] Sharada Sugirtharajah, "Complacencies and Cul-de-Sacs: Christian Theologies and Colonialism," in *Postcolonial Theologies: Divinity and Empire*, ed. Catherine Keller, Michael Nausner, and Mayra Rivera (St. Louis, MO: Chalice, 2004), 22–38 (22). See also Sugirtharajah's *Imagining Hinduism: A Postcolonial Perspective* (New York: Routledge, 2003), for a volume that explores early Indology in both its Christian missionary and orientalist representations from a postcolonial perspective.

[33] Francis X. Clooney, *Comparative Theology: Deep Learning across Religious Borders* (Malden, MA: Wiley-Blackwell, 2010), 82.

with Voss Roberts's work, this constructive comparative theology is an activist one; it is driven by ethical questions.

In search of a more just world suffused by the Mother God, Saxena searches for Her presence. She claims early in the book that her theological viewpoint is one of a "woman who has been miraculously free from internalized [psycho-spiritual] oppression" and wonders whether this freedom is a result of her "oneness with a black female deity."[34] Further speaking to the aims of the book, she notes that the voices of Indian women are often left out of the burgeoning conversation about goddesses in religious studies. As a woman of Bengali heritage, she wants to bridge that gap. She longs to help herself and readers enter into the feminine blackness of Kali, which she posits as a kind of spirituality without borders that is accessible to all. As she upholds Kali as her goddess, she embraces the model of Indic spirituality that allows one to find an *ishta devata*, a personal god; that is, she does not suggest that everyone, irrespective of culture and context, should embrace Kali. At the same time, she warns of a dangerous Western consumer mentality that might reduce such theological polydoxy to a cosmic shopping trip. Instead, she suggests a middle way that allows all to show respect to Kali and learn from Her.

She claims that she is not articulating theology, yet she also names herself as a Hindu–Buddhist and writes a confessional, personal text about the Mother God. Her sources are wide ranging: philosophical, literary, and, yes, theological. Notably, the god for which she searches is black and female, which is certainly a theological claim. The title, *Absent Mother God of the West*, turns out to be both a feminist and a postcolonial explanation of the Mother God's absence in the West. Even as the author maintains that she herself has experienced the Mother God, she notes how the "West" cannot seem to find Her. As she bridges these worlds, she longs to share the Mother God's presence and Her blessing with the whole world.

Comparative Theology and Ethnographic Approaches?

Almost ten years ago, Kristen Bloomer advocated for ethnography as an important method in comparative theology.[35] We see the fruits of this approach in her longitudinally researched book *Possessed by the Virgin: Hinduism, Roman Catholicism, and Marian Possession in South India*. As she tells the stories of three women in South India who experience Marian spirit possession, she employs methods not yet widely used in comparative theology. Up to this point, most comparative theology has been textual; that is, it emphasizes juxtaposed close-readings of ancient texts. Typically, the religious writings of one author from one religion are set in contrast to the writings of another from another religion. With this book, we see a dramatically different methodological approach, one reliant on the social sciences.

---

[34] Neela Bhattacharya Saxena, *Absent Mother God of the West: A Kali Lover's Journey into Christianity and Judaism* (Lanham, MD: Lexington Books, 2016), xiv.

[35] Kristen C. Bloomer, "Comparative Theology, Comparative Religion, and Hindu–Christian Studies: Ethnography as Method," *Journal of Hindu-Christian Studies* 21 (2008): 33–42.

Highlighting the importance of interdisciplinarity in constructive theology, Wyman offers, "Constructive theology opens theology from a primarily inward turned discipline, which holds its own judgment as normative for rigor and applicability, and accepts at least the techniques of other disciplines."[36] In this case, Bloomer's ethnographic methodology functions for multiple purposes, including assuaging postcolonial concerns about the tenuous connection of theory and texts to the real needs of persons and communities.[37] Toward this goal, she argues that comparative theology must evolve toward interactions "between real people living in real, specific, historical situations."[38] We cannot rely on traditional texts as the sole sources for this work. Theologian Delwin Brown has also mused on the imperatives of what he calls the "new ethnography":

Knowing the other is not discovering some given within the other. It is not finding the other's foundational logic. It is not knowing the other better, or even as well as the other knows himself or herself. Knowing the other is constructing the other in critical collaboration with the other and in the same joint venture being reconstructed oneself.[39]

Through the "new ethnography" that values transformation *by* and *with* the other, rather than simply knowledge *of* the other, comparative theology gains an important tool for its constructive work. In the past, such work has been framed as interreligious dialogue. Using methods new to comparative theology, Bloomer experiments with a different paradigm.

While Bloomer herself does not name *Possessed by the Virgin* as a work of comparative theology, I submit that it may be read this way. The inspiration for the book begins with her hearing about an Indian Catholic woman who views Mary as a goddess. As the author pursues this phenomenon, she finds other women who have had similar experiences that subvert traditional understandings of the religious boundaries of Hinduism and Christianity. Her ethnographic methodology offer inroads to doing comparative theology differently: by documenting these women's lives, she lifts up the stories and voices of women who—because of their gender, caste, marital status, and/or religion—have not been heard. She brings the persons whom she studies alive for the reader through animated storytelling, which results in some unexpected results for her personally:

---

[36] Wyman, *Constructing Constructive Theology*, 173.
[37] Postcolonial threats also emerge with the use of ethnographic data. For example, Kimberley Patton in "Juggling Torches" warns that if scholars show a predilection to read the reported religious experiences of people as "politically coded pretexts" for the real story of power that supposedly lies beneath their stories, then they "discount the very persons they endeavor to understand" (168).
[38] Kristen C. Bloomer, *Possessed by the Virgin: Hinduism, Roman Catholicism, and Marian Possession in South India* (New York: Oxford University Press, 2018), 5.
[39] Delwin Brown, "Refashioning Self and Other: Theology, Academy, and the New Ethnography," in *Converging on Culture: Theologians in Dialogue with Cultural Analysis and Criticism*, ed. Delwin Brown, Sheila Greeve Davaney, and Kathryn Tanner (New York: Oxford University Press, 2001), 49.

> These conventions and genres of storytelling, these voices that I narrate, facilitate another kind of possession—one slightly different, but perhaps only slightly, from the topic of this book. As a write I become, in a matter, possessed by the conventions, as well as by my memory of the people whose voices I represent.[40]

Here, subject matter and methodology collide: becoming animated by the very force she studies—possession, this experience informs her work on how possession functions in the world.

More than any other constructive methodology that comparative theology can use, an ethnographic approach grounds itself in the real lives of people. Rather than focusing on ideas expressed in texts, as comparative theology has traditionally done, such an approach views people's lives as texts. As Bloomer spends time with women and their communities, she concurrently explores ideas of social power, gender, agency, and excess. Reflecting on the extraordinary events she witnesses, she writes, "Places particularly ripe for this 'excess' are colonized places—places where Christianity has come into contact with other, indigenous forms of spirituality, places often far out of reach from the Vatican."[41] Through such an approach that combines ethnographic reports with postcolonial theory, theoretical ideas from comparative theology come to full and fantastic life. Using ethnography, Bloomer shows hybridized identity, for example, in all its complexity both as a liberating practice and also as one bearing the destructive marks of colonization and sexism. She writes of the women's experiences of resistance, dismantling hegemonies, and reconstructing realities as complex phenomena. For example, as women perform as "priestesses of the goddess," their statuses get raised *and* they often simultaneously collude with oppressive elements of their cultural situation. Spirit possession is disruptive in multiple ways—to theology, to the patriarchal hierarchies, to gender and caste distinctions, for example—and yet Bloomer treats these stories "not as easy stories of resistance but of struggle within complicated webs of power and meaning."[42] She remains ambivalent about whether these practices of possession are liberating for the women and their communities. Here, she explicitly engages questions of justice, as good constructive comparative theology should do.

As an aid to documenting the complexity of these cases of Marian possession, Bloomer frames most of her chapter subsections with similar titles. For example, sections are titled "What the Prayer House Said," "What Nancy Said Decorating My Hands," "What Money Said," or "What Her Sermons Said." This structure allows her not only to report on the lives of the women, but also to highlight the multiplicity of aspects that need to be heard to gain an adequate depiction of the women's experiences. For example, the section "What Gendered Bodies Said in the Quest for Respectability" allows her both space to tell the woman's story and also to suggest complicated interpretations in light of power and gender. With these structural choices, she allows for the complexity of each of the women's stories to emerge.

---

[40] Bloomer, *Possessed by the Virgin*, 25.
[41] Ibid., 7.
[42] Ibid., 19.

Near the end of the book, Bloomer explains these choices in terms of the women's powers of agency, and the theory (and theology) behind her structural innovations become even clearer: "Agency never consists of being a 'sole author,' nor is agency necessarily unidirectional. There is no such thing as a fully autonomous agent transcendent of historical circumstance. Even gods and goddesses, or any sense of divinity or 'something bigger' must pass through the web of history."[43] By framing the women's stories in ways that highlight this complexity, she performs the construction of her subjects.

Bloomer waits almost until the last chapter to do anything that could be considered theology though. In her penultimate chapter, she begins to explore the relationship between pain and spirit possession, and then she meditates—theologically, I argue—upon this connection. Then, in the final chapter, she uses the term "theology" when she names both phenomenological and theological options for explaining "What Many Marys Said."[44] Here, she ventures an answer to the question, "Why does Mary manifest in so many different ways in different places, but the persons of the Trinity do not?" Her answer: because Mary is a woman. Threading gender theory into this constructive theological claim, Bloomer interrogates the boundaries of Christianity and Hinduism and the ways they overlap in the three Indian women's lives. Then, near the end of the book, she turns the gaze from the three women to herself, offering a personal theological reflection: "Perhaps I was the one in need of redemption. Perhaps I needed spirits, having rejected them."[45] Here, she recounts the way her own subjectivity may have framed and influenced this work that introduces ethnography into the comparative theological world.

Strategies for a Constructing a Vibrant Hindu–Christian Comparative Theology

First, we explored comparative theology's past, a past challenged—like the history of other comparative disciplines—with interlocking intellectual and ethical difficulties. Next, we looked closely at three examples from comparative theology's present. Through these case studies, we paid attention to how comparative theology continues to construct itself. In this last section, we will look to the future of comparative theology, as we locate it within the hospitable borders of constructive theology. We will also name some of the crucial elements of constructive comparative theology that will enable its success.

Constructive theology offers constructive comparative theology a welcoming space for the future flourishing of the discipline. Good comparative theology *is* a form of constructive theology; it cannot exist well in any other mode. As we have seen in our three case studies, good constructive comparative theology has an activist focus,

---

[43] Ibid., 231.
[44] Ibid., 225.
[45] Ibid., 231.

for example. It is collaborative and interdisciplinary, as well. Such are the gifts of constructive theology to comparative theology.

As the young discipline of constructive comparative theology works toward a sustainable future, Christian comparative theologians must continue to cultivate relationships with those from other traditions. Traditionally called interreligious dialogue, such relationships are complicated by all sorts of power dynamics. Good interreligious dialogue though, Panikkar reminded us, is a postcolonial move itself; it can only take place in a postcolonial space.[46] Expressing a similar critical ethos, Diana Eck describes interreligious dialogue as "the discipline of thought that enables us to gain clarity about our own situatedness, our own form of questioning our own position—whether methodological, political, religious, secular, even antireligious—so that our own subjectivity, our own language, and our own categories are not privileged and universalized unwittingly in our work."[47] In contrast to colonial discourses, dialogical discourse, which takes both traditional and less traditional forms, helps to dismantle the webs of projections, bias, imperialism, and injustices of colonialism through a decentering of the theologizing subject. This is the ongoing work of constructive comparative theology.

We thus are holding together what I think are the twin aims of good comparative theology: careful, patient theological construction, and theology's responsibility toward the marginalized. Of course, for comparative theology, such a focus requires an important methodological move: liberation itself must be constructed comparatively, as Tracy Sayuki Tiemeier has proposed.[48] Scholars, she argues, cannot assume that they know exactly what liberation means in interreligious contexts. When we construct liberation across religious boundaries, when we listen to the voices of the oppressed, we build a better theology, one that listens to other voices in the service of a more just world. Constructive theology, Wyman asserts, "must also seek to effect real change in the world. That is, it has activist intentions."[49]

As such, constructive comparative theology necessitates relating to the other in a spirit of solidarity and hospitality. A deep encounter with the religious other is a hallmark of comparative theology that remains an end in and of itself. It is not a stepping stone to a better theology for oneself, Tiemeier reminds us. In fact, to use comparative theology as a stepping stone leads to a situation "dangerously close to imperialism," which she names as a sin for comparative theology to combat and a threat

---

[46] Panikkar, "Forward: The Ongoing Dialogue," xiii. While Panikkar did not work expressly with postcolonial theory, he recognized the ongoing vestiges of colonialism and offered intrareligious and interreligious dialogue as ways through the morass. Earlier than most in the field of interreligious theology, he recognized the shifting and permeable boundaries of religious identity, yet he usually avoided using the language of poststructural or postcolonial theory.

[47] Diana Eck, "Dialogue and Method: Reconstructing the Study of Religion," in *A Magic Still Dwells: Comparative Religion in the Postmodern Age*, ed. Kimberly Patton and Benjamin Ray (Berkeley: University of California Press, 2000), 133–44 (144).

[48] Tracy Sayuki Tiemeier, "Comparative Theology as a Theology of Liberation," in *The New Comparative Theology: Interreligious Insights from the Next Generation*, ed. Francis X. Clooney (New York: T&T Clark, 2010), 129–49 (130).

[49] Wyman, *Constructing Constructive Theology*, 174.

to comparative theology's highest goal of promoting "self-and-other-understanding in interreligious dialogue."⁵⁰

Because deep engagement is mutual, Christian theologians must be open to being looked at as the other as well as looking at the other. Regarding the *tout autrei*, the other, Kenn Liberman offers, "The point of the *tout autrei* is to keep the system open, to present the play of differences between the self and the other from settling into a system or totality, even an altruistic totality."⁵¹ Comparative theologians, if they retain all of the agency, block themselves and the other from being transformed by the other's subjectivity. Even if their intentions are benevolent, comparative theologians in this mode objectify the other, rather than relate to the other. Relating to the other honestly is difficult and vulnerable work. In his work on interreligious dialogue, Panikkar has famously said that one must be willing to be converted in dialogue.⁵²

While constructive comparative theology as practiced today has been made possible by thinking with critical resources from around the world, to be a complete constructivist is be part of a long tradition of Western arrogance. If there is absolutely no possibility for transcending one's constructedness, Richard King asserts, then there is no reason to think across religious boundaries.⁵³ If there is no chance at all, for instance, that one might have a direct experience into a state of Hindu liberation/*moksha*, to use his example, then there may be no impetus to take Hindu theological ideas seriously in a spirit of mutual learning. For this reason, constructive comparative theology must leave room for the possibilities of hermeneutical mutuality.

As good comparative theology thrives only in spaces of mutuality, we now ask, "What methodological tools and wider visions can comparative constructive theology offer the future of constructive theology?" In other words, what can comparative theology give back to the genre that nurtures it? Next, we focus on what constructive theology can gain from comparative theology. What methodologies can help it meet the challenges ahead? What sources should be used for this work? In this last section, I propose three giftsthat constructive comparative theology can offer to constructive theology at large.

The Gift of Widening Conversation Partners

Perhaps the most obvious of constructive comparative theology's contributions to constructive theology is its insistence that one cannot do theology inside the bubble of a single religion. The idea that one needs resources outside one's own religious tradition to understand God is a somewhat radical proposal, one that has long raised

---

⁵⁰ Tracy Sayuki Tiemeier, "Restless Hearts: A Comparative Asian American Woman's Theology" (PhD diss., Boston University, 2009).
⁵¹ Kenneth Liberman, "The Other in Tibetan Buddhism," in *Who, Exactly, Is the Other?: Western and Transcultural Perspectives*, ed. Steven Shankman and Massimo Lollini (Eugene: University of Oregon Books/University of Oregon Humanities Center, 2002), 41–7 (47).
⁵² Raimon Panikkar, *The Intrareligious Dialogue* (Mahwah, NJ: Paulist, 1999), 62.
⁵³ This is an important argument made by Richard King in *Orientalism and Religion: Postcolonial Theory, India, and "The Mystic East"* (New York: Routledge, 1999), 182.

eyebrows in theological circles. In response to such a concern, one might argue that Christian theology has always been comparative in a sense. As a religion initially formed from a Jewish sect's interactions with diverse Roman religions, Christianity constructed itself with and against other religious traditions. Two thousand years later, the challenge for constructive Christian theology is to unravel and not repeat its colonialist, triumphalist past.

Constructive comparative theology thus asserts that one must take differing religious voices into account and not just bolster one's own theological claims. Describing the genesis of constructive theology, Wyman writes, "It's not an exaggeration to say that constructive theology began fundamentally from an effort to make Christian theology, which has long been a project conflicted over its relationship with the world and other intellectual modes, thoroughly interdisciplinary."[54] Thus, while such interdisciplinary resources are a hallmark of constructive theology, these resources have not necessarily included those of diverse religious voices. If constructive theology gathers its tools widely and from multiple disciplines, then it should not be too much of a stretch to look to multiple religious voices as sources for our theological questions and answers.

Constructive theologians, I submit, will not find their questions and concerns adequately addressed if they do not engage with diverse religious traditions, that is, comparative theology. The textbook previously mentioned, *Comparing Faithfully: Insights for Systematic Theological Reflection*, functions as a call to students and others to try out comparative theology for themselves. Possessed of an accessible tone and structure, it argues—by its very existence as a textbook for introductory theology classes—that all theologians can (and should!) be comparative theologians.

The Gift of Messy Ambiguity

Comparative theology aims to compare different religious traditions that are not quite incommensurate, but not quite commensurate either. Comparative theology cannot even dream of making its loci and categories line up in a systematic, orderly manner. For example it does not insist on stable, unchanging comparative theological categories; instead, categories must be provisional and revisable. The aforementioned textbook also helps us understand the necessarily messy nature of the work. Cognizant that most seminaries teach introductory Christian theology classes with an eye to traditional loci, such as divinity, Christology, and soteriology, the text employs such loci. Constructive, comparative work then exposes these loci as slippery—both too much and not enough for the task at hand; that is, comparative theology both fulfills and subverts the traditional loci. In the "Christology" section of the book, for example, the figure of Lord Lao from the Daoist tradition is placed in conversation with Jesus, who has no peer in Christian theology.[55] In this slippery comparative categorization, we have both an affirmation of traditional Christology and a challenge to it.

---

[54] Wyman, *Constructing Constructive Theology*, 112.
[55] Bede Benjamin Bidlack, "What Child Is This? Jesus, Lord Lao, and Divine Identity," in *Comparing Faithfully: Insights for Systematic Theological Reflection* (New York: Fordham, 2016), 195–215.

When we unpack the connotations of *constructive* theology, we remember that construction is messy and communal. The construction of a house, for example, is most often the work of many people: plumbers, sheet rockers, roofers, electricians, and more. In the process, the roof may leak, there may be sawdust on the floors, and the walls may need to be moved. To meet the needs of the communities that the construction serves, there are always remodels and repairs and additions ahead. In comparative constructive theology, the constructive categories must be built and rethought each time; it is provisional and recursive work. As constructive theology can be differentiated from its sister discipline, systematic theology, by its embrace of the messy, non-systematic nature of theology, comparative theology adds its affirming voice to this "messy, but ongoing, in flux, revisable approach to theology."[56]

The Gift of Risky Creative Intuition

Comparative theology creatively juxtaposes religious ideas through careful, patient theological construction; at the same time, it must also allow for the flourishing of intuition. In my book *Longing and Letting Go: Hindu and Christian Practices of Passionate Non-attachment*, I identified my primary comparative category as passionate non-attachment, which I planned to explore through the texts of a medieval Hindu woman and a medieval Christian woman. As the book came together, something unexpected happened: an intuitive confluence of subject matter and methodological approach. Just as Mirabai and Hadewijch, my respective Hindu and Christian interlocutors, practiced their own kinds of longing and letting go, the process of writing this book exposed longing and letting go as a model for constructive comparative theology itself. In other words, a confluence emerged between subject matter and methodology.

A similar experience with convergence in the creative process is occurring with my new project on comparative pilgrimage. In this project, journeying with pilgrims is emerging as both the theme and the methodology. A reluctantly intuitive person, I am learning to see the comparative constructive theological project as a slow gathering up of clues. Of course, such an approach might also spur bad comparativism, characterized by sloppy, shallow work. Jonathan Z. Smith calls intuitive logic the "magic" of comparative work, but he uses "magic" derogatorily to describe the problematic and undisciplined mode of comparative thought that does not pay enough attention to difference.[57] In the edited volume *A Magic Still Dwells*, comparativist scholars of religion answer Smith's charge. As they take this accusation seriously—that comparison *is* indeterminate and unscientific—they also embrace and rehabilitate the concept of "magic." More an art than a science if that choice must be made, "comparison is an imaginative and critical act of mediation and redescription in the service of knowledge," they attest.[58] In constructive comparative work, intuition must be risked, despite the recognition that

---

[56] Wyman, *Constructing Constructive Theology*, xx.
[57] Jonathan Z. Smith, "In Comparison a Magic Dwells," in *Imagining Religion: From Babylon to Jonestown* (Chicago: University of Chicago Press, 1988), 19–35 (21).
[58] Patton and Ray, "Introduction," 4.

early Hindu–Christian comparative work was fueled by dangerous colonial intuitions claimed as Indological science. There is no guarantee that today's comparativists will not make similarly disastrous mistakes. There is, I submit, no constructive theology without considerable risk. The alternative—to be afraid to try to learn from each other—is riskier.

Those Snakes Again

We began this chapter with a metaphor about the ambivalence of constructive resources for comparative theology. Incisive as a way to describe the challenges of constructing a comparative theology, the metaphor of snakes in Mirabai's basket fails when applied in another way to comparative theology. The image of the snake speaks of danger, but for some of us, constructive resources unambiguously saved our theologies. As a teenager, I remember being so desperate to find feminist and interreligious theological resources that I sneaked into a seminary's theological library in high school. This was after raiding my friend's father's theological bookshelves, only to find sources that seemed to claim that God loved Christian men more than anyone else. Hiding in the university library stacks, I found constructive resources that were enormously life-giving to me. I am cognizant that many other sisters and brothers could also tell stories of their saved lives because of LGBTQ, black, Latinx, ecological, and other constructive theological resources, for example. As Mirabai boldly wore the snake around her neck, we, too, picked up these constructive resources and found tools of transformation.

At its best, constructive comparative theology results in greater interreligious empathy and understanding for an interconnected, pluralistic world. Along the way though, it unsettles theological assumptions and complicates theological questions and answers. Clooney reminds us that a tension exists in the very words "comparative theology"; that is, "if we do our work well and ground scholarly commitments in faith commitments, then we always be on the edge of failing in scholarship or failing in faith. Then we will be properly conflicted theologians, comparative theologians."[59]

These specters of failure constitute another risk; thus, constructive comparative theology needs to embrace what Sharon Welch calls an "ethic of risk." Facing squarely into the possibility of falling short, she takes seriously the chance that the vision will not be successful, not today and not even in our lifetimes. We may not get the results for which we long, and we may have to let go; but letting go does not mean letting go of love, of anger, and of resistance.[60]

We will always be in negotiation with these tensions; yet, in comparing religious traditions, constructive comparative theology does something that theology has always done in one way or another. The ideas that religious boundaries are porous and ever-changing, that comparison is always implicit in theology, and that theology has always borrowed from other cultures to develop its ideas are just a few constructive theological themes that comparative theology has employed to develop itself. Now,

---

[59] Clooney, *Comparative Theology*, 30.
[60] Sharon B. Welch, *A Feminist Ethic of Risk* (Minneapolis, MN: Augsburg Fortress, 1990), 20.

with the help of constructive methodologies, we can do it more adequately and more mindfully of the risks at hand.

Less than ten years ago, Tiemeier reminded us that the "new comparative theology," like almost all theology, is predominantly Christian, white, middle class, and male; however, comparative theology is still in its infancy, she further noted.[61] Remembering its constructive midwives as it now matures into adolescence, comparative theology must continue to draw upon diverse resources for an open, mutual, interdisciplinary, dialogical, intuitive, justice-centered praxis.

Bibliography

Bidlack, Bede Benjamin. "What Child Is This? Jesus, Lord Lao, and Divine Identity." In *Comparing Faithfully: Insights for Systematic Theological Reflection*, edited by Michelle Voss Roberts, 195–215. New York: Fordham, 2016.

Bloomer Kristen C. "Comparative Theology, Comparative Religion, and Hindu-Christian Studies: Ethnography as Method." *Journal of Hindu-Christian Studies* 21 (2008): 33–42.

Bloomer Kristen C. *Possessed by the Virgin: Hinduism, Roman Catholicism, and Marian Possession in South India*. New York: Oxford University Press, 2018.

Brown, Delwin. "Refashioning Self and Other: Theology, Academy, and the New Ethnography." In *Converging on Culture: Theologians in Dialogue with Cultural Analysis and Criticism*, edited by Delwin Brown, Sheila Greeve Davaney, and Kathryn Tanner, 41–56. New York: Oxford University Press, 2001.

Clooney, Francis X. *Comparative Theology: Deep Learning across Religious Borders*. Malden, MA: Wiley-Blackwell, 2010.

Doniger, Wendy. "Postmodern and -colonial -structural Comparisons." In *A Magic Still Dwells: Comparative Religion in the Postmodern Age*, edited by Kimberly Patton and Benjamin Ray, 63–74. Berkeley: University of California Press, 2000.

Eck, Diana. "Dialogue and Methos: Reconstructing the Study of Religion." In *A Magic Still Dwells*, edited by Kimberly Patton and Benjamin Ray, 133–44. Berkeley: University of California Press 2000.

Gross, Rita M. "Response." In *How to Do Comparative Religion? Three Ways, Many Goals*, edited by René Gothóni, 187–91. Berlin: Walter de Gruyter, 2005.

Hillgardner, Holly. *Longing and Letting Go: Hindu and Christian Practices of Passionate Non-attachment*. New York: Oxford University Press, 2017.

Hillgardner, Holly. "Review of *Absent Mother God of the West: A Kali Lover's Journey into Christianity and Judaism*." *Journal of Hindu-Christian Studies* 30 (2017): 120–1.

Keller, Catherine, Michael Nausner, and Mayra Rivera. "Introduction: Alien/Nation, Liberation, and the Postcolonial Underground." In *Postcolonial Theologies: Divinity and Empire*, 1–21. St. Louis, MO: Chalice, 2004.

King, Richard. "Colonialism, Hinduism, and the Discourse of Religion." In *Rethinking Religion in India: The Colonial Construction of Hinduism*, edited by Esther Bloch, Marianne Keppens, and Rajaram Hegde, 95–113. New York: Routledge, 2010.

King, Richard. *Orientalism and Religion: Postcolonial Theory, India, and "The Mystic East."* New York: Routledge, 1999.

---

[61] Tiemeier, "Comparative Theology as a Theology of Liberation," 129–49 (129).

Liberman, Kenneth. "The Other in Tibetan Buddhism." In *Who, Exactly, Is the Other?: Western and Transcultural Perspectives*, edited by Steven Shankman and Massimo Lollini, 41–7. Eugene: University of Oregon Books/University of Oregon Humanities Center, 2002.

Lochlin, Reid B., and Hugh Nicholson. "The Return of Comparative Theology." *Journal of the American Academy of Religion* 78:2 (2010): 471–514.

McFague, Sallie. *Models of God: Theology for an Ecological, Nuclear Age*. Minneapolis, MN: Fortress, 1987.

Mirabai. *Mirabai Versions*. Translated by Robert Bly. New York: Red Ozier, 1984.

Nicholson, Hugh. "Comparative Theology after Liberalism." *Modern Theology* 23:2 (2007): 229–51.

Panikkar, Raimundo. "Forward: The Ongoing Dialogue." In *Hindu Christian Dialogue: Perspectives and Encounters*, edited by Harold Coward, ix–xix. Maryknoll, NY: Orbis Books, 1989.

Panikkar, Raimundo. *The Intrareligious Dialogue*. Mahwah, NJ: Paulist, 1999.

Patton, Kimberley C. "Juggling Torches: While We Still Need Comparative Religion." In *A Magic Still Dwells: Comparative Religion in the Postmodern Age*, edited by Kimberly Patton and Benjamin Ray, 153–71. Berkeley: University of California Press, 2000.

Patton, Kimberley C., and Benjamin Ray. "Introduction." In *A Magic Still Dwells: Comparative Religion in the Postmodern Age*, 1–22. Berkeley: University of California Press, 2000.

Saxena, Neela Bhattacharya. *Absent Mother God of the West: A Kali Lover's Journey into Christianity and Judaism*. Lanham, MD: Lexington Books, 2016.

Sherman, Rita DasGupta, and Arvind Sharma, eds. *Hermeneutics and Hindu Thought*. New York: Springer, 2008.

Smith, Jonathan Z. "In Comparison a Magic Dwells." In *Imagining Religion: From Babylon to Jonestown*, 19–35. Chicago: University of Chicago Press, 1988.

Sugirtharajah, Sharada. "Complacencies and Cul-de-Sacs: Christian Theologies and Colonialism." In *Postcolonial Theologies: Divinity and Empire*, edited by Catherine Keller, Michael Nausner, and Mayra Rivera, 22–38. St. Louis, MO: Chalice, 2004.

Sugirtharajah, Sharada. *Imagining Hinduism: A Postcolonial Perspective*. New York: Routledge, 2003.

Sydnor, John Paul. *Ramanuja and Schleiermacher: Toward a Constructive Comparative Theology*. Cambridge, UK: James Clarke, 2012.

Taylor, Mark C. "Introduction." In *Critical Terms for Religious Studies*, edited by Mark C. Taylor, 1–20. Chicago: University of Chicago Press, 1998.

Tiemeier, Tracy Sayuki. "Comparative Theology as a Theology of Liberation." In *The New Comparative Theology: Interreligious Insights from the Next Generation*, edited by Francis X. Clooney, 129–49. New York: T&T Clark, 2010.

Tiemeier, Tracy Sayuki. "*Restless Hearts: A Comparative Asian American Woman's Theology*." PhD diss., Boston University, 2009.

Voss Roberts, Michelle. *Body Parts: A Theological Anthropology*. Minneapolis, MN: Fortress, 2017.

Voss Roberts, Michelle. *Comparing Faithfully: Insights for Systematic Theological Reflection*. New York: Fordham, 2016.

Voss Roberts, Michelle. *Dualities: A Theology of Difference*. Louisville, KY: Westminster John Knox, 2010.

Voss Roberts, Michelle. "Gendering Comparative Theology." In *The New Comparative Theology: Interreligious Insights from the Next Generation*, edited by Francis X. Clooney, 109–28. New York: T&T Clark, 2010.

Welch, Sharon D. *A Feminist Ethic of Risk*. Minneapolis, MN: Fortress, 1990.

White, David Gordon. "The Scholar as Mythographer: Comparative Indo-European Myth and Postmodern Concerns." In *A Magic Still Dwells: Comparative Religion in the Postmodern Age*, edited by Kimberley Patton and Benjamin Ray, 47–54. Berkeley: University of California Press, 2000.

Wyman, Jason A., Jr. *Constructing Constructive Theology: An Introductory Sketch*. Minneapolis, MN: Fortress, 2017.

7

Constructive Black Theology in Britain: Participative–Methodological Praxis

Anthony G. Reddie

Participative Black Theology as a Form of Constructive Theology

In analyzing the development of my scholarship in the context of "constructive" theology, I would define it as a mode of theological inquiry that seeks to rethink the propositional nature of Christian theology. Constructive theology, for me, is the attempt to create new theological frameworks, themes, and models of theological inquiry to respond to contextual and sociopolitical milieus in which the theologian is ensconced. It is the attempt to build theological ideas in a creative and eclectic fashion that provides more methodological and procedural freedom than what might be expected in "systematic" theology. Given constructive theology's greater attention to sociopolitical milieus, I would suggest that it is linked in this respect to contextual theology, the latter being a form of nomenclature with which I am more instinctively comfortable.

Participative-practical black theology involves the use of exercises and games that seek to enable participants to reflect critically on self, and through the enactment of the central activity, participants are enabled to explore aspects of the theory and practice of black theology in dialogue with others. In order to provide an embodied reality for the practice of performative action that lies at the heart of participative-practical black theology, I have created a number of experiential exercises through which adult participants can explore the dynamics of encounter within a safe learning environment. The thrust for this work has emerged from previous pieces of research.[1]

In using this approach, as a participative black theologian, my work differs from that of many other scholars working in the area of black theology as my underlying

---

[1] Extensive examples of this work can be found in the following works by Anthony G. Reddie: *Acting in Solidarity: Reflections in Critical Christianity* (London: DLT, 2005); *Dramatizing Theologies: A Participative Approach to Black God-Talk* (London: Equinox, 2006); *Black Theology in Transatlantic Dialogue* (Basingstoke: 2006); *Working against the Grain: Re-imaging Black Theology in the 21st Century* (London: Equinox, 2008); and *Is God Colour Blind?* (London: SPCK, 2010). See also *SCM Core Text: Black Theology* (London: SCM, 2012).

theological method is not provided by systematic theology or ethics. My particular methodological stance is one very much drawn from the field of practical theology. Leading scholars in the field of practical theology have theorized around the development of practical theology as a model of reflective activity in which the theologian interrogates the connections between the theory and practice of Christianity in a diverse range of contexts and settings.[2] Practical theology is the overall framework or approach to the Christian faith that uses different models of disciplines, such as psychology, counseling, education, and sociology, as ways of looking at God's action in the world. One of the central tasks of practical theology is to consider the relationship between how the church and individual Christians have considered the meaning of faith in light of what individuals and the church actually do in terms of religious practice, as opposed to the rhetoric of theological ideas and scholarly theorizing alone.

My work as a participative black theologian seeks to develop models of black theological reflection and learning that encapsulate the central tenets of black theology within a liberative pedagogical framework. My development as a scholar has been concerned with attempting to combine practical theology with black theology in order to provide an accessible framework for the radical reinterpretation of the Christian faith for the transformation of ordinary people. In effect, my work is concerned with the conscientization of ordinary people, shaping their Christian formation though an exposure to a black theological rearticulation of the central ideas and concerns of the Christian faith.

In talking about conscientization of ordinary people, I am speaking of two concurrent epistemological moves. The first is the attempt to enable ordinary people to become critically aware of their agency as historical subjects caught up within interconnecting webs of illegitimate power, discrimination, and injustice. Second, conscientization speaks to a process of radicalization and politicized self-understanding of the Christian faith, in which solidarity with the poor and the marginalized becomes the radical intent of faith as opposed to adherence to abstract doctrines and church dogmatics.

The ongoing development of this work is one that I have termed as a form of "performative action." Performative action requires that we creatively engage with the "other" in the socio-constructed space within the classroom, in which all participants promise to engage with the "other" in a fashion that affirms mutuality, cooperation, and a shared commitment to the production of new knowledge.[3] The production of new knowledge is not simply for the purpose of passing exams or writing term

---

[2] See Paul Ballard and John Pritchard, *Practical Theology in Action: Christian Thinking in the Service of the Church and Society* (London: SPCK, 1996). See also the more recent titles in practical theology: Helen Cameron, Deborah Bhatti, Catherine Duce, James Sweeney, and Clare Watkins, *Talking about God in Practice: Theological Action Research and Practical Theology* (London: SCM, 2010); and Kathleen A. Cahalan and Gordon S. Mikoski, eds., *Opening the Field of Practical Theology: An Introduction* (Lanham, MD: Rowman & Littlefield, 2014). See Duncan B. Forrester, *Truthful Action: Explorations in Practical Theology* (Edinburgh: T&T Clark, 2000). Also note Elaine L. Graham, *Transforming Practice: Pastoral Theology in Age of Uncertainty* (Eugene, OR: Wipf and Stock, 2002). See also John Swinton and Harriet Mowat, *Practical Theology and Qualitative Research* (London: SCM, 2006).

[3] See Jose Irizarry, "The Religious Educator as Cultural Spec-Actor: Researching Self in Intercultural Pedagogy," *Religious Education [The Vocation of the Religious Educator]* 98, no. 3 (Summer 2003): 365–81. See also Clark C. Apt, *Serious Games* (New York: Viking, 1970).

papers;[4] rather, the desire is to create new forms of knowing for the express purpose of changing behavior and developing better praxis in terms of the experiential skills of engaging with the "other." The central thrust of this work is the creation of anti-racist, anti-oppressive, and nondiscriminatory forms of Christian discipleship that see difference as a gift of grace and not as a problem to be avoided or solved.

In effect, this work combines ministry and scholarship, establishing the connection between the two by means of the attempt to create new knowledge while resourcing people in their ongoing attempt to live out their faith as progressive, anti-racist Christian disciples. The form of teaching and learning in this interactive, participative pedagogy is one that often occurs outside of formal classrooms, more often in workshop settings in local churches.

This process of performative action operates within safe, but often contested spaces in which religious participants are invited to adopt particular roles in various exercises as part of an imaginative role-playing framework, in order to test out their motives and positionality vis-à-vis the "other." In this constructive approach to black theology, I have used a variety of exercises and activities to enable participants to find a means of exploring their feelings and emotions in a safe space. The exercises allow them to adopt imaginary roles and "park" their experiences within a comparatively safe "rest area" where they can notionally ascribe responsibility for their anger, frustration, or tension to the fictional persona of the character they have been playing.

The use of performative action within the context of a participative approach to black theology has been developed for the purpose of encouraging adult learners to learn from this discipline in order that their concomitant Christian discipleship is committed to the practice of racial justice. The use of exercises and drama represents an invitation for adult learners to reflect within the hospitable and safe space of the classroom or the workshop setting. The topics and themes of participative exercises are drawn from the agenda set by black liberation theology, namely, those outlined in the thrust for radical "Black Christologies," expansive "theological anthropology," the analysis of power and what constitutes normativity, and the significance and import of experience as a criteria by which we undertake Christian theology. In this context, they can explore and commit themselves to working for and becoming a part of the collective spiritual, psychological, and praxis-based journey of the Christian church, toward the "promised land" of racial justice.

In the various exercises, participants, by means of conversation and interaction, have the opportunity to reflect on their action within the context of a central activity and assess their agency and responses to it for its truthfulness to God's gracious activity in Jesus Christ, when juxtaposed with the historical and contemporary experience of racism and oppression.

The participatory element of the work challenges learners to decide how they will inhabit particular spaces and places, in order to assess in what ways they are playing out learnt pathologies that are often informed by the specious binaries of "them"

---

[4] These training days are not assessed nor are students tested on the learning they have accrued during the day; therefore, this work is very much located in the affective development of ministerial students and not in their evaluated cognitive learning.

and "us."[5] What would happen if participants were enabled to take on the persona of the "other" in order to live out their realities and experiences within a participative exercise? To what extent would these experiences change their subjective self and their concomitant consciousness? The challenge of conscientizing participants is central to the intent of this constructive mode of black liberative theologizing, within formal and informal learning contexts. Black liberative theologizing is that which is committed to the human flourishing of all peoples, with the accent on human liberation, which is not compromised by a fixed adherence to the Bible or to neoliberal capitalism often found in prosperity forms of black Christianity. It is worth noting that my work operates within formal teaching and learning contexts for assessed degree awards and within informal contexts working with ordinary people in community, church-based settings.

In the methodological formulations of participative black theology, the pedagogical process is as important as the emerging theological content. In the context of performative action, one is constantly challenging students to question their assumptions about what is deemed to be "normative" and that which is termed as "aberrant" or "transgressive." The purpose of this approach to undertaking black theology to instill good practice in the quest for racial justice lies in the belief that internalized change (spiritual and psychological) can be a conduit for externally verified changes in behavior and practice. Both of these modes provide the subjective, experiential basis for liberation, at an individual, interpersonal, communal, and ultimately, systemic level.

In the various exercises, the different participants are challenged to determine their individual agency and positionality in this pedagogical process. How will they engage? To what extent can they deconstruct their past, with all its attendant learnt behaviors? In what ways will their resultant new learning have an impact on their subsequent Christian discipleship? What are the challenges of attempting to take any resultant learning into the practice of ministry, as it confronts them in their future work, be it within church or community?

An important element of my use of a performative, participative methodology for engaging with adult learners is the belief in the importance of practice as a legitimate basis for knowledge construction. In some respects, this is the key element of my scholarship in that, procedurally, my starting point as a constructive theologian is the significance of religious practice and the desire to attempt to refashion and rethink Christian praxis. In shaping my research and scholarship in this form, one is seeking to conscientize ordinary people, which can also create new forms of epistemology, which, in turn, can influence the academy. One of the established ways in which predominantly Western epistemologies have operated has been by means of a hierarchical and binary framework in which our knowledge of human affairs is often predicated on the notion of moving from theory to practice.[6] It is assumed that once we have our thinking or

---

[5] African American womanist theologian Kelly Brown Douglas demonstrates the extent to which binary notions of "in groups" and "out groups" within Christian communities can be traced back to the notion of a "closed monotheism" within Judeo-Christian theologies of the Hebrew Bible and the New Testament. See Kelly Brown Douglas, *What's Faith Got to Do with It?: Black Bodies/Christian Souls* (Maryknoll, NY: Orbis Books, 2005).

[6] See David Willows, *Divine Knowledge: A Kierkegaardian Perspective on Christian Education* (Aldershot: Ashgate, 2001).

ideas worked out, then we can move to applying them to the concrete areas of life at a later point.[7]

Performative action is a methodology that gives rises to a dramatic process of doing theology in which participants and the educator enter into a process of performance wherein there is an inherent dialectic and from which new truths can be discerned. The methodology is built upon exercises that challenge ordinary people to engage in activities in which reflective forms of role playing and group work assist in creating new forms of theological engagement, that is, a means of undertaking constructive theology.[8]

This practical-participatory black theology–led approach to conscientization is one that seeks to elevate the importance of practice as a means of creating new knowledge and critical insights into the transformative praxis of Christian ministry. This approach to critical learning arises from the embodied encounter between adult learners within the teaching and learning moment in workshops and also in the classroom.

The use of participative exercises seeks to embody the transformative elements of black theology within an experiential learning framework for the purposes of conscientizing ordinary people, in the hope that the latter will embody and give expression to anti-racist practices of Christian discipleship and ministry. The new knowledge participants accrue is not simply for the sake of epistemological innovation, but rather, such knowledge production is to institute necessary forms of Christian praxis that will give rise to the type of agency that makes for anti-racist discipleship and ministry.

Of course, it needs to be noted that I have no way of knowing whether my teaching will exert any such effect on the future practice of ministry of any of the learners with whom I have come into contact. The participants with whom I have worked have varied, but usually they are ordinary lay people; however, on occasions, I have undertaken minister's retreats, leading continued development in ministry events for the support of those in representative, authorized ministry. No form of pedagogical work can determine the praxiological outworking of Christian discipleship and ministry for ordinary people who have been participants in the performative action I have constructed.

This interactive, participative engagement with ordinary people, in which new epistemological insights are generated through the process of conscientization, is one that can be construed as an articulation of constructive theology. Participative black theology has emerged not solely as a pedagogical means of conscientizing ordinary people; rather, it has given rise to new ways of understanding the discipline. The constructive aspect can be seen in the following exercise where I outline a means of

---

[7] I have to acknowledge the development of "practical theology," which in its examination of the relationship between theory and practice seeks to outline a more reciprocal relationship between the two often competing realities. A useful guide to the development of practical theology can be found in James Woodward and Stephen Pattison, eds., *The Blackwell Reader in Pastoral and Practical Theology* (Oxford: Blackwell, 2000). See also Paul Ballard and John Pritchard, *Practical Theology in Action* (London: SPCK, 1996); and Kathleen A. Cahalan and Gordon S. Mikoski, eds., *Opening the Field of Practical Theology: An Introduction* (Lanham, MD: Rowman & Littlefield, 2014).

[8] See Irizarry, "The Religious Educator as Cultural Spec-Actor," 365–81.

reflecting on the legitimization of black theology that has perhaps stunted its growth as an expression of liberative praxis in terms of becoming a mass movement.

Participative Black Theology in Action

The following exercise has been created to help participants realize that one of the troubling aspects of black theology has been the way in which it has internalized its need for epistemological respectability and legitimation at the expense of the needs of ordinary people marginalized at the bottom of many societies in the world. It has been developed as a means of decolonizing black theology, building on the landmark work of Caribbean black liberation theologian Noel Erskine,[9] who first coined the term "decolonizing" black theology. This theme is significant for the ways in which black theology has directed its focus more on black middle-class professionals than ordinary poor black people.

One can see aspects of this neocolonial framework of black Christianity in terms of how "we" have all been manipulated into thinking of those who are different and therefore deemed transgressive, in very subtle ways that still emphasize their basic unacceptability.[10] Black theology challenges head-on any attempt to make blackness acceptable by stealth, that is, it critiques the notion that some of us can be deemed acceptable by adhering to white bourgeois middle-class social mores (what I have named the "Sidney Poitier syndrome").[11] Those who are different are identified as aberrant others, but there are some who might be deemed sufficiently fortunate to possess the magic ability to transcend their blackness in order to effect a semblance of normative sameness.[12] The legitimation of black theology has been critiqued, with great alacrity, by Elonda Clay, in a special issue of *Black Theology: An International Journal* dedicated to the legacy of James H. Cone. Clay's essay offers a respectful but critical assessment of black theology on the occasion of the fortieth anniversary of James Cone's groundbreaking text *Black Theology and Black Power*. Clay critiques the development of black theology in the United States as a static intellectual movement

---

[9] See Noel L. Erskine, *Decolonizing Theology: A Caribbean Perspective* (Maryknoll, NY: Orbis Books, 1983).

[10] See Almeda M. Wright, "Image Is Everything? The Significance of the *Imago Dei* in the Development of African American Youth," in *Albert Cleage Jr. and the Black Madonna and Child*, ed. Jawanza Eric Clark (New York: Palgrave Macmillan, 2016), 171–87.

[11] The Sidney Poitier syndrome as I have termed it takes its cue from his landmark 1967 film *Guess Who's Coming to Dinner*. In this film, Poitier plays a highly respected African American medical doctor of impeccable credentials who is engaged to be married to a young white woman. The drama of the film emerges when the latter brings her black fiancé home to meet her liberal white parents. While the film was a landmark production when it came out in 1967, one is still left with the clear sense that Poitier's character had to be saint-like simply to get to make it with a relatively unspectacular white woman (who lacks his great accomplishments).

[12] Lee H. Butler Jr., "Testimony as Hope and Care: African American Pastoral Care as Black Theology at Work," in *Living Stones in the Household of God: The Legacy and Future of Black Theology*, ed. Linda E. Thomas (Minneapolis, MA: Fortress, 2004), 24–32.

that has reified the tropes of liberation to a historic moment rooted in the 1960s religio-cultural and sociopolitical epoch.[13]

In a telling comment on the reified nature of black theology, Clay says,

> I posit that the original way in which the concept, heuristic, and signifier "liberation" functioned in U.S. Black Liberation Theology, has by both form and content, been un/consciously resignified into a discourse of cultural legitimation. That is to say, while the use of "liberation" had a particular importance for a specific historical moment (late 1960s), second- and third-generation Black theologians have seemingly failed to rethink the heuristic of "liberation" for changing conditions and contexts, which include postmodernity, post-Black Power/Civil Rights politics, post-industrialization, and the network society epoch.[14]

The antithesis of the legitimation of which Clay speaks is the commitment of black theology to reconnect with the popularist roots of the movement in the Garveyite era in the early decades of the past century and later in the black nationalism of Albert Cleage. While one can critique the bounded, black nationalist conceptualizations of the aforementioned movements that retain patriarchal, heteronormative models of belonging, they, nevertheless, attended to existential experiences of the urban proletariat in the United States and not those deemed as middle-class progressives.

The exercise works as follows:
The Meal Test
Ask each person to imagine the following scenario:

- You are a member of a club or organization. That club expresses its identity and togetherness by means of a weekly formal meal. Every member of the club is invited to the meal and has a major decision to make when they arrive at the entrance of the room where the meal is being held. You can now choose between two meals; and as a member, there is no difference in cost between the two. Everyone eats together.
  - On the one hand, you can choose the "set meal." This set meal is the standard accepted meal. It has already been prepared and is already on the menu.
  - Alternatively, you can eat your favorite meal. This favorite has been prepared for you in exactly the way you would want it and has been cooked to perfection.
- Which meal do you choose? The one everyone else might be eating, or your own special meal? You have absolute choice, and as a full member of the club, you are there at the meal on the same terms as everyone else. Which meal?

---

[13] Elonda Clay, "A Black Theology of Liberation or Legitimation?: A Postcolonial Response to Cone's *Black Theology and Black Power* at Forty," *Black Theology: An International Journal* 8, no. 3 (2010): 307–26.
[14] Ibid., 310–11.

Theological Reflections on the Exercise

The Meal Test has been performed on numerous occasions since it was first developed in the autumn/fall of 1995. In fact, this was the first ever experiential exercise I developed when I began my doctoral studies at the University of Birmingham. In developing it, I was concerned with finding an interactive and accessible means of enabling ordinary people of differing ethnic groups to reflect on issues of power, normativity, and acceptability within the "Body of Christ."

The exercise was created in order to find a means of replicating the dynamics of cultural exchange between peoples of differing ethnic identities, class, geography, and philosophical and ideological outlooks. The point of departure in the construction of any exercise, such as this one, is the pedagogical outcomes that one wishes the participants to imbibe as part of the learning outcomes. Being aware of the type of learning outcomes one hopes to derive from the exercise is what then gives rise to the construction of the activity in the first instance. The exercises represent the nexus of transformative pedagogy combined with liberative theological reflections, which gives rise to new forms of knowledge and conscientized models of Christian praxis.

In developing this exercise, it was my hope to create an activity that would address the impact of Christendom on the positionality of black people within the economy of the church, with acceptability predicated on those who are perceived at being best exponents at mimicking white middle-class social mores. Those who are most disadvantaged are those deemed as more working class, whose sexuality does not cohere to the constrictions of heteronormative frameworks. I witnessed firsthand the ways in which "race" remained a corrosive factor in the practice of the Christian faith among monocultural and even more pluralistic faith communities, and yet was rarely expressed or even acknowledged.[15] The thrust of the exercise, like the many others I have created, is to conscientize ordinary people and those also training for ordained ministry.

Growing up in a predominantly white church in the county of Yorkshire, UK, I remember quite clearly the rhetoric of "we don't see color" and yet seeing the ways in which "color" and in effect "race" so patently informed the very basis of how groups of people engaged with one another.

It should be the case that the *Meal Test* (in which the meal serves as a metaphor for church and the wider society) allows each person to choose their own individual meal and to enjoy it while sitting alongside their neighbor who is presently enjoying their own particular favorite meal. The Kingdom of God is a reality that embraces and celebrates diversity. God who has inspired all people to be themselves has created this diversity.[16] One can imagine the monotony of the meal if everyone chose the same standard meal! The lack of difference is a denial of the plural nature of humanity. There would be no variety or difference. The standard meal, for many black people in

---

[15] See David Joy and Joseph Duggan, eds., *Decolonizing the Body of Christ: Theology and Theory after Empire* (New York: Palgrave Macmillan, 2012).

[16] The African American black theologian addresses the question of diversity in his reading of the Kingdom of God in one of his more recent books. See Dwight N. Hopkins, *Being Human: Racer, Culture and Religion* (Minneapolis, MN: Fortress, 2005), 53–80.

postcolonial Britain, represents the axiomatic normativity of white, Euro-American mission Christianity that seeks to displace, subjugate, and disparage the metaphorical contextuality of the favorite meal.[17] The exercise seeks to embody the central theological claim that in God's kingdom *unity does not suggest we need to be uniform or homogeneous in our collective means of being human.* The affirmation of unity in diversity as a central motif of the Kingdom of God is one that needs to be reaffirmed at a time when increasing numbers of white evangelicals are opting for right-wing forms of white nationalistic politics in the United States and across Europe.[18] *The Meal Test* represents an embodied, constructive theological tool for developing a liberative, egalitarian ethic for communitarian Christian living that represents the formative ideal that is God's Kingdom.[19] The exercise of the meal enables participants to explore notions of sameness and difference, in which shared identities are located by the commitment of individuals to remain in the same space, dedicated to one another, while not having to eat the same meal.

The body of Christ is about recognizing difference. The body should be concerned with providing opportunities for all marginalized and oppressed peoples to have their choices, preferences, and identities recognized, and for the existing power structures to be overturned in order that those elements can be realized.[20]

For some, this conceptualization of the meal may seem at odds with the Eucharist, where participants share the same elements of bread and wine. I would argue, however, that the problem with this enacted idea is that the centralization of power in the hands of a priestly class can become the basis for notions of imperialistic centralism. That is, we all eat together under the control of the normative hands of the priest, this often being a white hand in many white-majority countries. That, in effect, whiteness, as the presence of Christ is effected through one, predominantly male hand. I am aware that comparisons between this metaphor and the enacted theological ideal of the Eucharist will be problematic for some, but I would argue that for black lay people, who are not part of the priestly class, the metaphor of the meal has its uses.

In taking the meal as a metaphor for the church, black Christians must seek to work in partnership with other agencies of faith and none, in order to proclaim the radical message of the Kingdom of God that is not reducible to personal piety and individual notions of "being saved." Beckford has identified the limited basis of this form of theological construction, critiquing the limitations of neo-Pentecostal spirituality as a mode for effecting black liberation.[21]

---

[17] David Joy, "Decolonizing the Bible, Church, and Jesus: A Search for an Alternate Reading Space for the Postcolonial Context," in Joy and Duggan *Decolonizing the Body of Christ*, 3–24.

[18] One can witness this in the rise of white evangelical support for Donald Trump, alongside the rise of white Christian-inspired nationalism in Hungary and other nations across Europe.

[19] The importance of contextual diversity as a hallmark of the Kingdom of God in which indigenous spiritualities of former colonized peoples is affirmed and celebrated is explored in Dwight N. Hopkins and Marjorie Lewis, eds., *Another World Is Possible: Spiritualities and Religions of Global Darker Peoples* (London: Equinox, 2009).

[20] R. S. Wafula and Joseph F. Duggan, *Knowledge Activism—Beyond Theory: A Worldwide Call to Action* (Alameda, CA: Borderless, 2016), 51–77.

[21] Robert Beckford, *Dread and Pentecostalism* (London: DLT, 2000), 193–6.

In many respects, the challenge to the spurious notion of white superiority is the easier of the pedagogical outcomes emerging from the exercise. Critiquing white hegemony is what one would expect of black theology. Black Christians need to learn to affirm their favorite meals in the *Meal Test*. They need to reclaim a radical black Christology first espoused with great eloquence by James Cone.[22] Cone writes of Jesus,

> It seems clear that the overwhelming weight of biblical teaching, especially the prophetic tradition in which Jesus stood unambiguously, is upon God's unqualified identification with the poor precisely because they are poor. The kingdom of God is for the helpless, because they have no security in this world. We see this emphasis in the repeated condemnation of the rich, notably the Sermon on the Mount ... Jesus' teaching about the kingdom is the most radical, revolutionary aspect of his message.[23]

The very intentionality of Jesus's praxis acts as a counterbalance to the non-contextual and often abstracted theologies of predominantly prosperity-led practitioners of black Christianity as seen in the likes of Creflo Dollar[24] in the United States and Matthew Ashimolowo in the UK.[25] Jesus engages with the context in which he is located, in a real and embodied way, and does not retreat into spiritual banalities as a means of avoiding being labeled "political."[26] The Jesus embodied in the *Meal Test* is one who confounds contextless abstractions that often work as a means of reinscribing the normativity of the status quo, in which heteronormative patriarchy remains in control at the expense of seemingly transgressive bodies.

Politics of difference is always at play in any historical context and demands an honest appraisal from adherents of the Christian faith. In using this term, I am speaking of the critical interplay of notions of "race," ethnicity, class, ideology, culture, and experience and the ways in which these facets of human life are often the fissures in which perspectives of difference get played out in societal and communitarian settings. By this, I mean that there are no contexts that are neutral and in which all bodies are seen as "normal" or deemed "acceptable." One can see this in evidence if we locate the radical respectability of the Civil Rights Movement, in which leadership was ensconced within heteronormative patriarchy, alongside that of the "Black Lives Matter" movement. The latter is a heterogeneous movement in which queer bodies are clearly in evidence, alongside that of black women and non-churched youth, within a nonhierarchical structure.[27] The Black Lives Matter movement has its own constraints and challenges, in terms of the extent to which it fully incorporates the perspectives

---

[22] See James H. Cone, *A Black Theology of Liberation* (Maryknoll, NY: Orbis Books, 1990).
[23] See ibid., 117.
[24] See http://www.creflodollarministries.org/ for further details of his ministry.
[25] See http://www.kicc.org.uk/ for further details of his ministry.
[26] See Robert Beckford, "Theology in the Age of Crack: Crack Age, Prosperity Doctrine and 'Being There,'" *Black Theology in Britain: A Journal of Contextual Praxis* 4, no. 1 (2001): 9–24.
[27] The famed South Africa liberation theologian Allan Boesak has written an excellent constructive theological work that explores the contrasting methodologies and generative embodiments of these respective movement. See Allan Aubrey Boesak, *Pharaohs on Both Sides of the Blood-Red Waters: Prophetic Critique of Empire* (Eugene, OR: Cascade Books, 2017).

and religio-cultural positionalities of all black people, particularly women and LGBTQ+ people, but there is no doubting the greater plurality in its modus operandi when compared to the Civil Rights Movement.

It can be argued that the radical nature of Jesus's praxis was the clear intentionality of his pedagogy when confronted with questions pertaining to notions of difference and acceptability. This was especially the case in terms of who is deemed "one of us"—and therefore acceptable—and those who are identified as "one of them"—and in oppositional terms are seen as an aberrant presence in the body politic of the collective whole.

In terms of epistemological insights, the exercise assists in the constructive task of creating new insights from and about black theology, for effective praxiological impact. The issue that arises from the exercise for black participants is the challenge to reflect on the tantalizing lure of respectability politics that has always been replete within black communities to which black theology has often colluded.

Reflecting on my subjective agency, I have considered the ways in which Britain, a predominantly white society, has a penchant for stigmatizing black males like myself. Black people in general and black men in particular are often perceived and treated as immoral degenerates. We are troublemakers and undesirables, but some of us, of course can be acceptable. If we have the right accent and can mimic the cultural mores of polite white bourgeois society, then we too can be invited to the meal and thereby pass the *Meal Test*. "Passing" means being able to mimic the social mores of the white bourgeoisie, which often leads to social and cultural advancement for black people. I have used the word "test" because those who are identified as transgressive bodies know how it feels to have to engage with the troubled nature of passing the respective religio-cultural social mores in order to be deemed sufficiently "civilized" so that we can gain access to the respectable metaphorical tables of white middle-class normativity. The issue at hand is whether we seek to pass the test or refuse to comply with its middle-class Eurocentric blandishments. The nature of the test is one that creates a standardized template in which aberrant bodies are asked to participate in order to assess whether they can be admitted to the club as respectable members. One can see aspects of this corporate-led, culturally acceptable version of blackness in the popularized images of the Huxtables as portrayed in *The Cosby Show* or the Banks family in their portrayal in *The Fresh Prince of Bel-Air*.

Both these highly successful shows (running from 1984 to 1992 and from 1990 to 1996, respectively, on NBC television) presented an aspiring image of black social mobility and acceptability. In both shows one witnesses idealized and, dare one say, acceptable notions of blackness—images of being black that can be considered sufficiently "good" to be invited to the "meal" of white corporate America! In my own life as a black male, I have witnessed how my acceptability to be welcomed in the meal, alongside the polite, the acceptable, the educated, the socially desirable, and the respectable middle class, has been in direct proportion to my social mobility by way of higher education and further study. My own ascent into the ranks of white, middle-class respectability has been accentuated by the fact that I am a "lay theologian" in whom academic respectability is reinforced by ordination and clergy hegemony.

My own acceptability within the formal meal, as one who is able to eat the standard meal as well as my favorite, is testament to the progress I have made in terms of social and occupational mobility.[28] What if my working-class Yorkshire accent had not taken on the trappings of middle-class modulation and university-educated sophistry? Would I still be so willingly embraced within the meal? Would the standard meal still be forced upon me as a mode of making me suitably civilized so that I can become an authentic part of the meal and the formal membership of the club that accompanies it?

For black Christians sitting at the meal, we must not only be sufficiently brave to argue for the eating of the types of foods that give us life and sustain us, we must also resist the temptation to be the "good black person" who will opt to eat the standard meal simply to become acceptable to others. Black theology has often unwittingly colluded with this push toward acceptability and legitimation in its formative development as a form of systematic theology, anchored firmly within the academy, with little agency in grassroots communities across the African Diaspora.

This struggle for legitimacy has to be put into its historical context in order to understand the reactionary struggles evinced by James Cone when attempting to establish black theology as a legitimate academic discipline.[29] Reading Cone's final published work is a reminder that the early critics of black liberation theology asserted that his scholarship was better understood as anthropology and sociology and not legitimate theology. Reading Cone's *I Said I Wouldn't Tell Nobody*, one is reminded of the neocolonial control of the definitional boundaries of theology as they existed in late 1960s America. The decision to locate black theology as a form of systematic theology, while establishing the legitimacy of the discipline within the academy, has had consequences in its connection to ordinary people. I have used this exercise as a means of seeking to develop a more informal, bottom-up form of discourse in which disenfranchised, transgressive bodies are given greater agency in the construction of theological discourse. For while I understand the theological form in which early, dare one say, traditional black theology emerged, this participatory model of the discipline utilizes the lived experiences of black people that are often reflected on and discussed, but engaged directly.

The exercise has demonstrated the ways in which the debate around the metaphor of the meal and who gets to sit at the table is one that is cognizant of class-based issues related to concerns surrounding respectability and acceptability of certain types of black people.

The exercise outlines the myopic vistas often adopted by black theology that have been explored in more experiential, participative ways in my own work, which has helped to provide a constructive critical challenge to existing epistemological insights in the discipline.[30]

---

[28] I address issues of my own development and social progress and mobility in a previous piece of work. See Anthony G. Reddie, *Black Theology in Transatlantic Dialogue* (New York: Palgrave Macmillan, 2006), 8–15.

[29] This issue has been put into clearer purview with the publication of James Cone's final memoirs. See James H. Cone, *I Said I Wasn't Gonna Tell Nobody* (Maryknoll, NY: Orbis Books, 2018).

[30] The importance of this work can be seen in two of my books in which the concerns I am addressing around the monolithic and myopic gaze of black theology have been addressed. See Anthony G. Reddie, *Is God Colour Blind?* (London: SPCK, 2010); and *SCM Core Text: Black Theology* (London: SCM, 2012).

Participative Exercises as a Means of Constructing Theology

In this and the other exercises I have developed as the conduit for carrying the substantive ideas of participative black theology, it is my contention that the reflections that emerge from it are alternatively generated forms of constructive theology. In the exercises that form the core of this approach to black theological reflection, one can see a critical interaction between the embodied, reflective insights of the participants that are juxtaposed with academic black theology–based work that seeks to give rise to methodological praxis by means of subjective change embedded within the lives of ordinary people.

In the development of this work, I have witnessed the ways in which the experiential reflections arising from the participative workshops help to mirror the new forms of thinking around how one perceives the central intent of black theology. One of the issues that has arisen from the *Meal Test* exercise is that of the limited prism often adopted by black theology, both in its depiction of black communities in the United States and the UK, and also within the historiographical development of the discipline itself.

One can see the aforementioned in terms of how black theology has reflected on black religious communities. In a great deal of the early black theology work, there was a tendency to see black communities as monolithic. Much of this early work takes little or no account of diversity within black communities, embodied in concerns such as class, gender, and sexuality.[31] The major lacuna in terms of the early development of black theology was undoubtedly gender and the existence of patriarchy, which led to the emergence of womanist theology.[32] Womanist theology emerged as a necessary corrective to the androcentric myopia of much that was black theology, which emerged in the late 1960s and the 1970s. It was not uncommon to find black male writers referring to "man" when wishing to talk about the plight of all black people. In effect, their androcentric thinking was no better than that of the white male theologians they were often critiquing. The formative notions of womanism include self-determination, self-definition, the love of oneself, a commitment to holistic living, solidarity with other women, and a respect for the experience and knowledge claims that arise from the reality of being a black woman.[33]

The critical failure in black theology in Britain has been the almost complete absence of black women as leaders and contributors to the development of the epistemology in this field. At the time of writing, there are no sole-authored books by a black woman in black theology in Britain.[34] In my own engagement with black theology

---

[31] An important addition to the lexicon of black and womanist theologies is by Pamela R. Lightsey, *Our Lives Matter: A Womanist Queer Theology* (Eugene, OR: Pickwick, 2015).
[32] For an excellent introduction to womanist theology, see Stephanie Y. Mitchem, *Introducing Womanist Theology* (Maryknoll, NY: Orbis Books, 2002).
[33] Alice Walker, *In Search of Our Mothers' Gardens: Womanist Prose* (Boston, MA: Houghton Mifflin Harcourt; rpt 2004), xi.
[34] In a previous book I have analyzed the comparative failure of black theology in Britain to produce significant input of black women in the construction of black knowledge. The best I could surmise

the androcentric and patriarchal complexion of the discipline and movement did not occur to me. It was only upon reaching the final chapters of the twentieth anniversary edition of *A Black Theology of Liberation*[35] and reading the critical response of Delores S. Williams[36] that I realized the inherent flaws in Cone's initial work (and those of his contemporaries).

It can be argued that black theology must show greater intent at deconstructing the inherent class bias between middle-class and working-class black people, particularly when it comes to respectability politics and who is affirmed and who is disparaged. The exercise highlights the need for solidarity among black peoples in that it challenges participants to reflect on the different meals that are evoked alongside the controlling normative positionality of the "Standard Meal."

The challenge for black theology is expressed in the extent to which it has reified the middle-class-based concerns at legitimation and respectability. Black theology has often worked on the presumption of homogeneity, often meaning black male bodies. Womanist scholars have long challenged the patriarchal construct of respectability and legitimation.[37] Much less effort has been spent looking at questions pertaining to class, gender, sexuality, or differences in political outlook, among a few of the concerns in this area. Black theology has often ignored class differences and the internalized, middle-class bias that is often secreted within the body politic of black communities in the UK and the United States. We can see this particularly in the case when scholars have spoken about black and black-majority churches.[38]

The lack of critical insight into the middle-class pretensions of black churches and the inherent anti-blackness and working-class prejudice remains prevalent in black theological discourse. One of the notable exceptions in this regard is Kelly Brown Douglas's monumental *Black Bodies and the Black Church: A Blues Slant*.[39] Brown Douglas's work provides an unflinching, critical gaze on the black church in the United States and the internalized racism of many of its leading branches, particularly those in the so-called progressive north. One can see this exemplified in her analysis of southern black Christianity, where the author establishes an existential tripartite,

---

was to outline the work of black men who have supported and encouraged black women to contribute to black theological thinking. See Anthony G. Reddie, *Black Theology in Transatlantic Dialogue* (New York: Palgrave Macmillan, 2006), 102–7.

[35] James H. Cone, *A Black Theology of Liberation*, twentieth anniversary ed. (Maryknoll, NY: Orbis Books, 1990).

[36] Delores S. Williams, "James Cone's Liberation: Twenty Years later," in ibid., 189–95.

[37] In more recent times, one can cite the work of M. Shawn Copeland, *Enfleshing Freedom: Body, Race and Being* (Minneapolis, MN: Fortress, 2009); Eboni Marshall Turman, *Towards a Womanist Ethic of Incarnation: Black Bodies, the Black Church and the Council of Chalcedon* (New York: Palgrave Macmillan, 2013); Stephanie M. Crumpton, *A Womanist Pastoral Theology against Intimate and Cultural Violence* (New York: Palgrave Macmillan, 2014); and Melanie L. Harris, *Ecowomanism: African American Women and Earth-Honoring Faiths* (Maryknoll, NY: Orbis Books, 2017).

[38] See Peter J. Parris, *The Social Teaching of the Black Churches* (Philadelphia, PA: Fortress, 1985); Dale P. Andrews, *Practical Theology for Black Churches* (Louisville, KY: Westminster John Knox, 2002); and the more recent Dale P. Andrews and Robert London Smith Jr., eds., *Black Practical Theology* (Waco, TX: Baylor University Press, 2015); and Crumpton, *A Womanist Pastoral Theology*.

[39] Kelly Brown Douglas, *Black Bodies and the Black Church: A Blues Slant* (New York: Palgrave Macmillan, 2012).

operational basis for black bodies in relationship to the black church, moving from aspirant middle-class orientated churches that eschewed the alleged emotionalism of southern black Christianity, to the religious formation of the latter in all its African retentive guises. The third formulation was the blues, which shared the unfortunate distinction of being hated by both sides of the black Christian divide.[40]

Perhaps the most telling example is the internalizing of racialized hierarchies, what Douglas calls "Colorism," that existed within many black churches, particularly those in the north. Consider this indictment on the sensibilities of churches supposedly providing an alternative socioreligious arena representing the countercultural values of the Kingdom of God. Douglas, writing on the absurdities of a pernicious colorism and the ingrained antiblack ethic that existed in some churches and states,

> Still other black congregations hung a fine tooth comb at the entrance to be used. If the comb could not pass through the potential black worshipper's hair, then he or she would be denied entrance.[41]

Our tendency to view black communities as monolithic has meant that the diverse range of experiences and values that exist within the overall whole tends to be either downplayed or ignored altogether. An uncomfortable truth that is noticeable in particular types of black religio-cultural discourse is the existence of a type of hierarchy of "blackness." This often takes its cue from the prevailing concerns in many black communities, themselves, where some people are judged as belonging in a more complete fashion than others.

There are many black people who have been accused of not "really being black" or not being "black enough."[42] Scholars such as Michael Eric Dyson[43] Kobena Mercer,[44] and, most notably, Victor Anderson[45] have challenged us to see beyond the often-straightjacketed interpretations we place on black cultural expression and their accompanying lived experience. Anderson, in particular, has challenged the way in which black religious, cultural critics have wanted to acknowledge only the "positive aspects" of black life, and have often sought to overlook or ignore those elements of which we are not so proud. As he reminds us, we cannot all be saints, heroes, and "trailblazers."[46]

One of the challenges that have faced a number of black communities in the African Diaspora is the sense of wanting to "put one's best on show" and draw a discreet veil over those aspects that cause an element of embarrassment and unease within

---

[40] Ibid., 61–85.
[41] Ibid., 97.
[42] See Isaac Julien, "Black Is, Black Ain't: Notes on De-essentializing Black Identities," in *Black Popular Culture*, ed. Gina Dent (Seattle, WA: Bay, 1992), 255–63.
[43] Michael Eric Dyson, *Reflecting Black: African American Cultural Criticism* (Minneapolis: University of Minnesota Press, 1993).
[44] Kobena Mercer, *Welcome to the Jungle: New Positions in Black Cultural Studies* (London: Routledge, 1994).
[45] Victor Anderson, *Beyond Ontological Blackness: An Essay on African American Cultural Criticism* (New York: Continuum, 1995).
[46] Ibid., 118–31.

the community itself. An example of this monolithically defined way in which black religio-cultural scholars have reflected on black religious identities can be seen in the visceral shock that first emerged when stories pertaining to the inherent humanity and frailty of Rev. Dr. Martin Luther King Jr. began to emerge.[47] I remember a black community activist with whom I was friends at the time lamenting, "Why did they have to reveal all this? The man didn't deserve this!" Michael Eric Dyson's honest account of the life of Martin Luther King is an important example of dealing with the wholeness of human experience, and not just the edited highlights,[48] but this work has still caused some anger and disappointment among some.

In a later book, the same author attempts a critical reassessment of the life of deceased rapper Tupac Shakur. Dyson opens up new possibilities for us to see beyond the limited binaries of "heroes" and "villains," "good people" and "bad" ones.[49] Life, culture, and cultural expression are complex and often contradictory for those kinds of simplistic binaries.[50]

I am conscious of the ways in black Christian communities have policed our internal lives, determining whose lives are worth celebrating and those who are to be overlooked and quietly ignored because of their transgressive presence within the larger edifice of black Christianity in Britain. The theological problematics of the aforementioned can be discerned in the specific plight of black LGBTQ people in Britain and the lack of support given them by all black churches in Britain, particularly within African and Caribbean Pentecostal churches. These restrictive and narrow forms of Christian social ethics are often in evidence in black churches in Britain. These forms of restrictions can usually be discerned in the areas concerned with acceptable sexual conduct, with promiscuous heterosexual behavior more readily tolerated than monogamous homosexual practices. What is often at play in many black churches and the myriads forms of black Christianity is a rigid forms of heteronormativity that is often predicated on such binaries between those who are deemed as righteous (and saved) and those who are not.[51] It is a form of Christianity that rigidly adheres to a "them and us" paradigm, which clearly makes judgments on the worthiness of particular people.

While the exercise I have described provides the experiential basis on which ordinary participants can gain insight into the cultural and sociopolitical issues replete within many black communities in the United States and the UK, its utility extends to the very historiography of black theology itself. *The Meal Test* challenges the push toward legitimation in black theology in terms of its identity as primarily a subset of systematic theology within the theological academy developed and controlled by white Euro-American hegemony.

---

[47] See Ralph D. Abernathy, *And the Walls Came Tumbling Down* (New York: Harper and Row, 1989).
[48] Michael Eric Dyson, *I May Not Get There with You: The True Martin Luther King, Jr.* (New York: Simon and Schuster, 1999).
[49] Michael Eric Dyson, *Holler If You Hear Me: Searching for Tupac Shakur* (Pittsburgh: University of Pennsylvania Press, 2002).
[50] See Robert Beckford, *God of the Rahtid: Redeeming Rage* (London: DLT, 2001), 47–65.
[51] Beckford, "Theology in the Age of Crack," 9–24.

In this regard, the work of Charles Howard and later Jawanza Eric Clark is hugely significant in providing a critical nexus between epistemological innovation and praxiological change.[52] Both scholars have sought to combine intellectual engagement in the furthering of the discipline with the commitment to root their ideas within the popular religio-cultural mass movements that represent the active engagement of ordinary black people in their respective milieus. In both of these respective studies, we see an expressed commitment to praxis-based contemporary movements that seek to move black theology beyond its often myopic reified obsession with its own intellectual status within the academy, rooted in the identity politics of the 1960s.

The Meal Test has been a means of generating black theology work via my participative methodology that reflects the wider literature of black theological reflection from more theoretical scholars. My participative work, which can be seen in several books that have been detailed, thus far, has given rise to creative and constructive ways of talking about God in light of black religious experience. *The Meal Test* is an example of a participative means of exploring and creating new ways of understanding Christian theology.

Conclusion

In conclusion, then, this particular approach to undertaking black theology is one that seeks to use creative interdisciplinary models for theological reflection, which is now common parlance within the broader arena of "practical theology,"[53] alongside the penetrating analysis and searing insights of constructive and systematic theology. This approach to undertaking black theology is one that is attempting to breach the gap between the academy and the church and grassroots believers and academics. It is a commitment to using the experiences and the agency of ordinary black people as raw materials for an interactive approach to constructive theology using the techniques and methods from practical theology. In effect, it is another way of "doing black theology." It is a form of constructive theology that creates new knowledge through a participative engagement that forms a link between experiential knowledge that gives rise to conscientized modes of Christian discipleship and epistemological insights that are synonymous with the academy. In this context, this work is a new approach to constructive theology that entails a commitment to methodological praxis. It is a form of constructive theology in that it is attempting to build original theological discourse, seeking to rethink how we understand this global phenomenon called Christianity, developing new perspectives and themes that respond to contemporary challenges as they emerge in specific sociopolitical milieus. What I am offering here is a radically modified approach to constructive theology in that I am adding a methodological

---

[52] See Charles Lattimore Howard, *Black Theology as a Mass Movement* (New York: Palgrave Macmillan, 2014); and Jawanza Eric Clark, *Indigenous Black Theology* (New York: Palgrave Macmillan, 2012).
[53] See *Contact: Practical Theology and Pastoral Care* 146 (2005) for an entire issue dedicated to the role of theological reflection within practical theology.

twist, utilizing insights from practical theology in order to create a participative model of black theology that operates as a form of constructive theology.

Bibliography

Abernathy, Ralph D. *And the Walls Came Tumbling Down*. New York: Harper and Row, 1989.

Anderson, Victor. *Beyond Ontological Blackness: An Essay on African American Cultural Criticism*. New York: Continuum, 1995.

Andrews, Dale P. *Practical Theology for Black Churches*. Louisville, KY: Westminster John Knox, 2002.

Andrews, Dale P., and Robert London Smith Jr., eds. *Black Practical Theology*. Waco, TX: Baylor University Press, 2015.

Astley, Jeff. *Ordinary Theology: Looking, Listening and Learning in Theology*. Aldershot: Ashgate, 2002.

Ballard, Paul, and John Pritchard. *Practical Theology in Action: Christian Thinking in the Service of the Church and Society*. London: SPCK, 1996.

Beckford, Robert. *Dread and Pentecostalism*. London: DLT, 2000.

Beckford, Robert. *God of the Rahtid: Redeeming Rage*. London: DLT, 2001.

Beckford, Robert. "Theology in the Age of Crack: Crack Age, Prosperity Doctrine and 'Being There.'" *Black Theology in Britain: A Journal of Contextual Praxis* 4:1 (2001): 9–24.

Boesak, Allan Aubrey. *Pharaohs on Both Sides of the Blood-Red Waters: Prophetic Critique of Empire*. Eugene, OR: Cascade Books, 2017.

Brown-Douglas, Kelly. *Black Bodies and the Black Church: A Blues Slant*. New York: Palgrave Macmillan, 2012.

Brown-Douglas, Kelly. *What's Faith Got to Do with It?: Black Bodies/Christian Souls*. Maryknoll, NY: Orbis Books, 2005.

Butler Jr., Lee H. "Testimony as Hope and Care: African American Pastoral care as Black Theology at Work." In *Living Stones in the Household of God: The Legacy and Future of Black Theology*, edited by Linda E. Thomas, 24–32. Minneapolis, MA: Fortress, 2004.

Calahan, Kathleen A. and Gordon S. Mikoski, eds. *Opening the Field of Practical Theology: An Introduction*. Lanham, MD: Rowman & Littlefield, 2014

Cameron, Helen, Deborah Bhatti, Catherine Duce, James Sweeney, and Clare Watkins. *Talking about God in Practice: Theological Action Research and Practical Theology* London: SCM, 2010.

Clark, C. *Serious Games*. New York: Viking, 1970.

Clark, Jawanza Eric. *Indigenous Black Theology*. New York: Palgrave Macmillan, 2012.

Clay, Elonda. "A Postcolonial Response to Cone's *Black Theology and Black Power* at Forty." *Black Theology: An International Journal* 8:3 (2010): 307–26

Cone, James H. *A Black Theology of Liberation*. Maryknoll, NY: Orbis Books, 1990

Cone, James H. *I Said I Wasn't Gonna Tell Nobody*. Maryknoll, NY: Orbis Books, 2018.

Copeland, M. Shawn *Enfleshing Freedom: Body, Race and Being* Minneapolis, MN: Fortress, 2009

Crumpton, Stephanie M. *A Womanist Pastoral Theology against Intimate and Cultural Violence*. New York: Palgrave Macmillan, 2014.

Dyson, Michael Eric. *Holler If You Hear Me: Searching for Tupac Shakur*
　Pittsburgh: University of Pennsylvania Press, 2002
Dyson, Michael Eric. *I May Not Get There with You: The True Martin Luther King, Jr.*
　New York: Simon and Schuster, 1999.
Dyson, Michael Eric. *Reflecting Black: African American Cultural Criticism*. Minneapolis,
　MN: University of Minnesota Press, 1993.
Erskine, Noel L. *Decolonizing Theology: A Caribbean Perspective*. Maryknoll, NY: Orbis
　Books, 1983
Forrester, Duncan B. *Truthful Action: Explorations in Practical Theology*. Edinburgh: T&T
　Clark, 2000.
Graham, Elaine L. *Transforming Practice: Pastoral Theology in Age of Uncertainty*. Eugene,
　OR: Wipf and Stock, 2002.
Groome, Thomas H. *Sharing Faith: A Comprehensive Approach to Religious Education and
　Pastoral Ministry*. San Francisco, CA: HarperCollins, 1991.
Harris, Melanie L. *Ecowomanism: African American Women and Earth-Honoring Faiths*.
　Maryknoll, NY: Orbis Books, 2017.
Hopkins, Dwight N. *Being Human: Race, Culture and Religion*. Minneapolis, MN:
　Fortress, 2005.
Hopkins, Dwight N., and Marjorie Lewis, eds. *Another World Is Possible: Spiritualities and
　Religions of Global Darker Peoples*. London: Equinox, 2009.
Howard, Charles Lattimore. *Black Theology as a Mass Movement*. New York: Palgrave
　Macmillan, 2014.
Irizarry, Jose. "The Religious Educator as Cultural Spec-Actor: Researching Self in
　Intercultural Pedagogy." *Religious Education [The Vocation of the Religious Educator]*
　98:3 (Summer 2003): 365–81.
Joy, David, and Joseph Duggan, eds. *Decolonizing the Body of Christ: Theology and Theory
　after Empire*. New York: Palgrave Macmillan, 2012.
Julien, Isaac. "Black Is, Black Ain't: Notes on De-essentializing Black Identities." In *Black
　Popular Culture*, edited by Gina Dent, 255–63. Seattle, WA: Bay, 1992.
Lightsey, Pamela R. *Our Lives Matter: A Womanist Queer Theology*. Eugene, OR:
　Pickwick, 2015.
Mercer, Kobena *Welcome to the Jungle: New Positions in Black Cultural Studies*
　London: Routledge, 1994
Mitchem, Stephanie Y. *Introducing Womanist Theology*. Maryknoll, NY: Orbis
　Books, 2002.
Parris, Peter J. *The Social Teaching of the Black Churches*. Philadelphia, PA: Fortress, 1985.
Reddie, Anthony G. *Acting in Solidarity: Reflections in Critical Christianity*.
　London: DLT, 2005.
Reddie, Anthony G. *Black Theology in Transatlantic Dialogue*: New York: Palgrave
　Macmillan 2006.
Reddie, Anthony G. *Dramatizing Theologies: A Participative Approach to Black God-Talk*
　London: Equinox 2006
Reddie, Anthony G. "An Interactive Odyssey." In *Pulpit Journeys*, edited by Geoffrey
　Stevenson, 149–65. London: DLT, 2006.
Reddie, Anthony G. *Is God Colour Blind?* London: SPCK, 2010
Reddie, Anthony G. *Reddie Working against the Grain*. London: Equinox, 2008
Reddie, Anthony G. *SCM Core Text: Black Theology* London: SCM, 2012
Swinton, John, and Harriet Mowat. *Practical Theology and Qualitative Research*.
　London: SCM, 2006

Turman, Eboni Marshall. *Towards A Womanist Ethic of Incarnation: Black Bodies, the Black Church and the Council of Chalcedon*. New York: Palgrave Macmillan, 2013

Wafula, R. S., and Joseph F. Duggan. *Knowledge Activism—Beyond Theory: A Worldwide Call to Action*. Alameda, CA: Borderless, 2016.

Willows, David. *Divine Knowledge: A Kierkegaardian Perspective on Christian Education* Aldershot: Ashgate, 2001.

Woodward, James, and Stephen Pattison, eds. *The Blackwell Reader in Pastoral and Practical Theology*. Oxford: Blackwell, 2000.

Wright, Almeda M. "Image Is Everything? The Significance of the *Imago Dei* in the Development of African American Youth." In *Albert Cleage Jr. and the Black Madonna and Child*, edited by Jawanza Eric Clark, 171–87. New York: Palgrave Macmillan, 2016.

Part III

Postcolonial Reconstructions

8

Starting with the Land under Our Feet

Laurie Cassidy

Jesus took bread, gave thanks, and broke it, and gave it to them saying ... "Do this in memory of me."

—*Luke 22:19*

What if Christians in America can't remember Jesus in our breaking of the bread because we have amnesia? This is an urgent question for theology in a land where the official story is "Indians are dead," slavery is in the past, and immigrants are all criminals. Political theology suggests that collective amnesia is an avoidance of memories that prove dangerous to the status quo.[1] The "dangerous memories" of our history on this land call into question this official story. Christian theology undertakes the responsibility to remember and interpret the life and message of Jesus, but as political theology attests, this is possible only to the extent that we undertake the responsibility to face the suffering human beings in history.[2] But how do we as American Christians remember the death of Jesus when amnesia is a critical epistemic, cultural, and political activity in white supremacist ideology, which made and continues to make possible the United States of America?

My chapter develops a political theology in America, starting with the land, the land right under our feet.[3] A land called Turtle Island by its original inhabitants.[4] Many people living in America do not even know the original name of this place. Our settler

---

[1] Johann Baptist Metz defines "dangerous memory" as one of the basic categories of political theology. See his "Communicating a Dangerous Memory," in *Communicating a Dangerous Memory: Soundings in Political Theology*, Lonergan Workshop 6, ed. Fred Lawrence (Atlanta, GA: Scholar's Press, 1987), 37–53.
[2] M. Shawn Copeland, "Chattel Slavery as Dangerous Memory," in *Tradition and the Normativity of History*, ed. Lieven Boeve and Terrence Merrigan (Leuven: Uitgeverji Peters, 2013), 169.
[3] The land under my feet was stolen from the Ute. The Ute understood the Brunot Treaty of 1874 as protecting four million acres of their tribal land from gold and silver mining. "However, they ended up forcibly relinquishing the lands to the U.S. government." See the history of the Southern Ute at https://www.southernute-nsn.gov/history/ (accessed March 8, 2020).
[4] Turtle Island refers to the Haudenosaunee origin story in which Grandmother Turtle gave her back as a safe landing place and home for Sky Woman. "On the body of Grandmother Turtle earth-island is formed." Paula Gunn Allen, *The Sacred Hoop: Recovering the Feminine in American Indian Traditions* (Boston, MA: Beacon, 1992), 15.

colonizing past blotted out these origins and through violence constructed a new story. I demonstrate that the starting point of this land creates conditions of possibility to re-member our history in America from "the ground up." The land calls us to explore how our stories and our very existences are interconnected. As historian David Chang explains, "Nation, race, and class converged in the land."[5]

Settler colonialism aids Christian theology in how we understand the connections among nation, race, class, and land. This interdisciplinary scholarship explores "a fundamentally triangular system of relationships, a system comprising metropolitan, settler, and indigenous agencies."[6] In this triangular system of relationships the settlers act as barrier and buffer between the colonial metropolitan and the "frontier" indigenous communities. They enact the violent removal of indigenous people on behalf of the colonial metropolitan. This removal in America, as Walter Hixson explains, "is the most sweeping, the most violent, and most significant example of settler colonialism in world history."[7] Settlers who came to this land were victims of the very colonial powers they served. European settlers came to America for land as they were denied land in their home country. As I illustrate, because of the Highland Clearances Scots coming to America had more in common with Native peoples than with the British. However, the violence perpetrated against the Highlanders is what they in turn enacted upon Native people as settlers in America.

Scholars of settler colonialism reveal that this land trauma is at the root of a psychosocial pathology and ideology that is critical to understanding collective historical amnesia in America. The settlers' repression of the trauma of being removed from their homeland makes possible a peculiar disavowal of violence. Settlers come to this land to create a secure future characterized by a lack of violence. As Lorenzo Veracini explains, "As 'settler society' can thus be seen as a fantasy where a perception of a constant struggle is juxtaposed against an ideal of 'peace' that can never be reached, settler projects embrace and reject violence *at the same time*."[8] This disavowal is not simply a past event, but rather is part of the very structure of our life on this land. As Patrick Wolf states, "The colonizers came to stay—invasion is a structure not an event."[9]

Building upon the work of Johann Baptist Metz and M. Shawn Copeland, I further their insight by arguing that settler colonialism, as "dangerous memory," is integral to the development of political theology in America. The dangerous memories of American colonization demand we begin with the land because "everything in US history is about the land—who oversaw it and cultivated it, fished its waters, maintained its wildlife; who invaded it and stole it; how it became a commodity."[10] I demonstrate

---

[5] David Chang, *The Color of the Land: Race, Nation, and the Politics of Landownership in Oklahoma, 1832-1929* (Chapel Hill: University of North Carolina Press, 2010), 7.
[6] Lorenzo Veracini, *Settler Colonialism: A Theoretical Overview* (New York: Palgrave, 2010), 6.
[7] Walter Hixson, *American Settler Colonialism: A History* (New York: Palgrave, 2013), 1.
[8] Veracini, *Settler Colonialism*, 77; emphasis in the original.
[9] Patrick Wolfe, "Settler Colonialism and the Elimination of the Native," *Journal of Genocide Research* 8, no. 4 (December 2006): 387-409, at https://www.tandfonline.com/doi/full/10.1080/14623520601056240 (accessed November 28, 2018).
[10] Roxanne Dunbar-Ortiz, *An Indigenous Peoples' History of the United States* (Boston, MA: Beacon, 2014), 1.

that the land as a methodological starting point for political theology in America creates conditions of possibility for authentic anamnesis in a nation built on amnesia.

"Our" Land

In October 2018 at a rally in Texas President Donald Trump declared he was a nationalist.[11] For a president of the United States to claim this term is shocking, because the term "nationalism" conjures the ideological connection of blood and soil, *blunt und boden*.[12] This most recent conjuring of nationalism has made us come face to face with how integral the land is to the ongoing reproduction of white supremacy in the United States. For example, white nationalists chanted "blood and soil" in the 2017 demonstrations in Charlottesville, Virginia.[13] Settler colonialism challenges us to see the land, and our specific place upon it, as the path to understanding the responsibilities of our coexistence and interrelationships. To begin with the land as a starting point for political theology in America is to "dig" more deeply into the ideology that justified colonizing this land and how that worldview continues to justify multiple and interlocking systems of white supremacy.

Settler colonial theory enables political theology to make intelligible how systems of white supremacy are interlocking and also challenges the false separation of fields of knowledge within the academy.[14] For example, to speak of the land can be read as developing an environmental ethic, to raise issues about indigeneity can be interpreted as postcolonial or a turn to Native American studies, and mentioning chattel slavery is read as scholarship on racism. Settler colonialism draws us as white people back to the very foundations of what we call "America" and enables us to see that to understand contemporary events requires seeing the integral connection of systems of oppression.

By way of illustration, as I was writing these words, people were mourning the deaths of Maurice Stallard and Vickie Lee Jones murdered because they were Black. On Wednesday, October 24, 2018, the shooter, a white man, had tried to break into the First Baptist Church in Louisville before entering the Kentucky Kroger grocery store and shooting these two victims dead. Sam Rogers, the police chief of Jeffersontown, declared the shooting to be motivated by racism. He contends that the racist motivation of this shooting is hard to talk about and to acknowledge.[15] Three days later, on Saturday, as people celebrated Shabbat, a white man entered the Tree of Life

---

[11] This is a paraphrase of a speech given by President Donald Trump at a rally in Houston, Texas, in October 2018. This speech can be viewed at https://www.youtube.com/watch?v=sazitj4x6YI.

[12] See the 1933 film *Blunt und Boden*, a Nazi propaganda film, at https://archive.org/details/1933-Blut-und-Boden (accessed February 6, 2019).

[13] See Meg Wagner, "'Blood and Soil': Protesters Chant Nazi Slogan in Charlottesville," *CNN*, Saturday, August 17, 2017, at https://www.cnn.com/2017/08/12/us/charlottesville-unite-the-right-rally/index.html. (accessed February 6, 2019).

[14] For more on this, see Walter Mignolo, *The Darker Side of Western Modernity: Global Futures, Decolonial Options* (Durham, NC: Duke University Press, 2011).

[15] Thomas Novelly, "Police Chief Calls Kroger Shooting in Louisville a Hate Crime," *USA TODAY*, October 29, 2018, at https://www.usatoday.com/story/news/nation-now/2018/10/29/louisville-police-calls-kroger-shooting/1807654002/ (accessed November 3, 2018).

Synagogue in Pittsburg and opened fire, killing eleven people and injuring six others.[16] On November 2, 2018, a white man who had identified himself as a misogynist walked into a Florida yoga studio and fatally shot two women and wounded five others before killing himself.[17] This week of anguish and horror began on Monday, October 22, 2018, at the political rally in Houston with President Trump declaring that he is a nationalist. He claimed in the speech that his being a nationalist was simply in contrast to being a globalist.[18]

There is debate about what Trump meant by "nationalist," but the dead and broken bodies of that week defined this nationalism, and their deaths declared the truth that "nationalism" defined American on this land as white, Christian, and male. Settler colonialism opens a way forward to understand how violence against all who are not white, male, and Christian is foundational to the concept and reproduction of the United States of America. The "Dangerous Memory" of Jesus calls into question the way things are because his death teaches us to face the crucified people in our past and present.[19]

> The Christian memory of suffering is dangerous because it warns us where things have gone wrong and challenges our comfort in the official story. The memory of suffering, our own and especially that of others, connects each with the other and provides a practical warning system about distorted relationships, institutions, and situations.[20]

The dangerous memory of these most recent victims is a warning about what is wrong in the official story of the United States, and more importantly how the official story continues to distort all our relationships in America. As Roberto Goizueta observes, "The global eruption of a racist, xenophobic, and misogynist 'whitewash' has made palpably manifest the violence inherent in the European (and North American) Enlightenment project."[21]

---

[16] Ralph Iannotti, "Pittsburgh Synagogue Identified As Robert Bowers, Yelled 'All Jews Must Die' As He Opened Fire, Now Facing Federal Charges," *CBS Pittsburgh*, October 27, 2018, at https://pittsburgh.cbslocal.com/2018/10/27/pittsburgh-synagogue-shooting-suspect-identified/ (accessed November 3, 2018).

[17] Gary Fineout, "Man Who Appears to Have Made Racist, Misogynistic Videos Kills 2 Women in Tallahassee Yoga Studio Shooting," *Chicago Tribune*, November 3, 2018, at https://www.chicagotribune.com/news/nationworld/ct-florida-yoga-studio-shooting-20181103-story.html (accessed November 4, 2018).

[18] Aaron Blake, "Trump's Embrace of a Fraught Term—'Nationalist'—Could Cement a Dangerous Racial Divide," *Washington Post*, October 23, 2018, at https://www.washingtonpost.com/politics/2018/10/23/trumps-embrace-fraught-term-nationalist-could-cement-dangerous-racial-divide/?noredirect=on&utm_term=.9d6dd5c5bd54 (accessed November 23, 2018).

[19] James Matthew Ashley, *Interruptions: Mysticism, Politics and Theology in the Work of Johann Baptist Metz* (Notre Dame: Notre Dame University Press, 1998), 161.

[20] John Downey, "Introduction: Risking Memory: Political Theology as Interruption," in *Love's Strategy: The Political Theology of Johann Baptist Metz* (Harrisburg, PA: Trinity Press International, 1999), 8.

[21] Roberto Goizueta, "'A Body of Broken Bones': Shawn Copeland and the New Anthropological Subject," in *Enfleshing Theology: Embodiment, Discipleship, and Politics in the Work of M. Shawn Copeland*, ed. Robert J. Rivera and Michele Saracino (New York: Lexington Books, 2018), 3.

Donald Trump's declaration of nationalism is not a new phenomenon but is rather the most recent iteration of white supremacy in the United States.[22] As Roxanne Dunbar-Ortiz explains, "The history of the United States is a history of settler colonization—the founding of a state based on the ideology of white supremacy, the wide spread practice of African slavery, and a policy of genocide and land theft."[23] Does our history of genocide of Native Americans and enslavement of Africans reveal that these declarations of equality, dignity, and respect are for "just us"—land-owning white people? This question is not to trivialize, minimize, or normalize these horrific current events but to interrogate the present moral and spiritual crisis from the dangerous memories of the land right under our feet.

Under the crust of that portion of Earth called the United States of America— "from California … to the Gulf Stream Waters"—are interred the bones, villages, fields, and sacred objects of American Indians. They cry out for their stories to be heard through their descendants who carry the memories of how this country was founded and how it came to be as it is today.[24]

To understand the current suffering in relation to the dangerous memories of our history on this land, my chapter will proceed in three parts.

First, drawing on the work of Joe Feagin and Patrick Wolfe, I demonstrate historical amnesia as a critical epistemic practice of settler colonialism expressed through the white racial frame.[25] Wolfe demonstrates that settler colonialism was not an event, which we can claim is over and done with. But rather, settler colonialism is a structure that enables the ongoing process of destroying to replace.[26] The exploration of memory is not new to theology. Why turn to this concept of "settler colonialism" to address memory in the task of political theology? Taken together, the works of Feagin and Wolfe provide a theoretical framework to understand memory and forgetting as political and cultural strategies within the worldview of white supremacist ideology that made and continues to make possible white settler colonization.

Moreover, drawing on this scholarship prevents us from exploring history and "dangerous memories" in the abstract and distant from contemporary existence. In America we have been taught to deny our relationship to history and responsibility in such phrases as "I was not born yet" or "My ancestors arrived later." This "presentism"

---

[22] For example, see Tyler G. Anbinder, *Nativism and Slavery: The Northern Know Nothings & the Politics of the 1850s* (New York: Oxford University Press, 1994); John Higham, *Strangers in the Land: Patterns of American Nativism, 1860–1925* (New Brunswick, NJ: Rutgers University Press, 1983).
[23] Dunbar-Ortiz, *An Indigenous Peoples' History of the United States*, 2.
[24] Ibid., 1.
[25] Joe Feagin, *The White Racial Frame: Centuries of Racial Framing and Counter-framing* (New York: Routledge, 2013), x.
[26] Wolfe, "Settler Colonialism and the Elimination of the Native," 387–409. This article is considered essential to the development of the field of settler colonialism. See also J. Kēhaulani Kaunui, *Hawaiian Blood: Colonialism and the Politics of Sovereignty and Indigeneity* (Durham, NC: Duke University Press, 2008); Jean M. O'Brien, *Firsting and Lasting: Writing Indians out of Existence in New England* (Minneapolis: University of Minnesota Press, 2010); Veracini, *Settler Colonialism*; Mark Rifkin, *Settler Common Sense: Queerness and Everyday Colonialism in the American Renaissance* (Minneapolis: University of Minnesota Press, 2014).

trivializes the past and distorts our moral relationship to the past—and present.[27] In contrast, to situate our approach to history within what Feagin describes as the "white racial frame" challenges us to confront how we are socialized. For Wolfe the process of settler colonization is structured into our systems as a nation and is an ongoing process. Settler colonialism theorists contend that we do not live in a postcolonial era, but rather, as Lorenzo Veracini argues, in "the settler colonial present."[28]

Second, I will explore how the starting point of the land furthers the work of Johann Baptist Metz and M. Shawn Copeland. Starting with the land will enable dangerous memories in America to be a "subversive factor in our society, the ferment for that new political life we are seeking on behalf of our future."[29]

Metz and Copeland articulate the theological necessity of facing the disastrous consequences of modernity for being followers of Jesus. For Metz, facing the suffering victims of the Holocaust is to interrogate the rationality that legitimized such horror; for Metz, this rationality is prejudiced against memory. Building on Metz in an American context, Copeland writes that remembering is not simply the regaining of lost information, but recognition of relationship. "Authentic memory … 'is not a type or degree of knowledge, but a relationship to what is known.'"[30] To face chattel slavery in America rejects the Modern insistence that to abolish slavery "denotes progress." Rather anamnestic reason recognizes slavery's continued reproduction in the surveillance, violence, and control of black bodies in today's America.[31] To face the suffering produced by the logic of Modernity in our context requires facing the ongoing settler colonization of America. To interrogate the historical, political, and cultural colonization of America invites political theology on this land to connect bodies, places, and histories, the connections of which have been torn asunder by the process of European colonization.[32]

Finally, I explore how the land as starting point generates three questions. First, how does the land we live on call us into relationship? Second, how do we listen to the stories of the first people who live on this land? Third, how do our ancestors make us understand our life on this land? I explore these questions by uncovering practices, dispositions, and patterns of relating that create conditions of possibility of healing the amnesia of settler colonization. These questions explore the boundaries between interior and exterior, personal and collective, change and transformation. This starting point of the land may contribute to what Copeland describes as coaxing "forward a different sociality." "We do political theology because we want to collaborate in a most fundamental way in healing and creating relations in history and society."[33]

---

[27] Copeland, "Chattel Slavery as Dangerous Memory," 169.
[28] See Lorenzo Veracini, *The Settler Colonial Present* (New York: Palgrave, 2015).
[29] Johann Baptist Metz, *Faith in History and Society: Toward a Practical Fundamental Theology*, trans. David Smith (New York: Seabury, 1980), 119.
[30] Copeland, "Chattel Slavery as Dangerous Memory," 169.
[31] Ibid., 171.
[32] Ibid., 191.
[33] M. Shawn Copeland, "Memory, #BlackLiveMatter, and Theologians," *Political Theology* 17, no. 1 (March 17, 2016), at https://politicaltheology.com/memory-blacklivesmatter-and-theologians-m-shawn-copeland/ (accessed December 1, 2019).

This Land Is My Land

A recent Supreme Court decision requires voters to show identification with a residential address not a post office box.[34] Gregg Deal, a member of Pyramid Lake band of Paiute, highlights the irony of this ruling. He points out that original inhabitants may be stopped from voting in their own land if their residency is called into question.[35] This unveils the interplay of past and present on this land.

Many Native Americans argue that this decision not only violates tribal sovereignty but also disenfranchises Native American voters.[36] Many Native Americans living on reservations do not have street addresses, and therefore mail is delivered to a post office box.[37]

How could the *original* inhabitants of this land be denied their right to vote because they are judged not to have proper residency on their own homelands? I began this section with this recent Supreme Court decision because it is a stark reminder of the constant interplay of past and present in American life. Our historical amnesia prevents us from seeing how we are involved in the interplay that reproduces systems of domination. "Political theology calls for all theology to be political, to engage the concrete human world with its social relations, cultural justifications, economic positioning, and all the rest."[38] And to engage in this task Copeland has called on white theologians in America to utilize analytic tools adequate to the depth and complexity of white supremacy.[39] She explains that we must have an ability to clearly see and to interpret the interplay of past and present. "Past and present compenetrate, for the past is never a fixed reality."[40] What is at stake in maintaining our epistemologies of ignorance is that such ignorance "jeopardizes that which makes us most human—our capacity for relationships."[41]

A way of understanding this interplay of past and present is exploring whiteness as a racial frame, an internalized worldview that makes possible the settler colonial creation of the United States. As Joe Feagin explains,

---

[34] Gabriel Pogrund and Felicia Sonmez, "In Senate Battleground, Native American Voting Rights Activists Fight Back against Voter ID Restrictions," *Washington Post*, October 12, 2018, at https://www.washingtonpost.com/politics/in-senate-battleground-native-american-voting-rights-activists-fight-back-against-voter-id-restrictions/2018/10/12/7bc33ad2-cd60-11e8-a360-85875b-ac0b1f_story.html?utm_term=.e9e9854274a3 (accessed November 16, 2018).

[35] Gregg Deal (Pyramid Lake Paiute) tweeted this comment on October 14, 2018, in response to a court ruling. https://www.instagram.com/p/Bo64BjXAHQB/ (accessed November 15, 2018).

[36] For more on the intersection of the civil rights of Native Americans and issues of sovereignty of tribal governments, see Kristen Carpenter, Matthew L. M. Fletcher, and Angela Riley, *The Indian Civil Rights Act at Forty* (Los Angeles: UCLA American Indians Studies Center, 2012).

[37] Jean Schroeder and Melissa Rogers, "What Keeps Native Americans from Voting—and What Could Change This," *Washington Post* (October 18, 2018) at https://www.washingtonpost.com/news/monkey-cage/wp/2018/10/18/what-keeps-native-americans-from-voting-and-what-could-change-this/?noredirect=on&utm_term=.22591cdee5a3 (accessed November 16, 2018).

[38] John Downey, "Introduction: Risking Memory," 1.

[39] M. Shawn Copeland, "Racism and the Vocation of the Christian Theologian," *Spiritus* 2 (2002): 21.

[40] Copeland, "Chattel Slavery as Dangerous Memory," 170.

[41] Copeland, "Racism and the Vocation of the Christian Theologian," 21.

The white racial frame is more than just one significant frame among many; it is one that has routinely defined a way of being, a broad perspective on life, and one that provides the language and interpretations that help structure, normalize and make sense out of society.[42]

Feagin documents how this frame shapes the everyday life of whites. Far from simply latent unconscious material, the white racial frame "directly shape[s] everyday scripts whites and others actually act on." As Feagin points out, this everyday enactment is how the white racial frame "re-creates, maintains, and reinforces the racially stratified patterns and structures of society."[43]

Collective memory and collective forgetting have a critical place in the everyday scripts of the white racial frame. Feagin points out that in the United States major groups of people have significantly different collective memories. But the most powerful groups control the society-wide institutional memories, such as in school textbooks, films, laws, and public monuments.[44]

Feagin contends that collective forgetting is as important as collective remembering, "especially in regard to the prevailing narratives of this country's developmental history."[45] He explains that the powerful will suppress the history of social oppression and often create "fictional memories of that history."[46] Feagin concretizes the central category of dangerous memory.

> Over nearly four hundred centuries, a critical part of the dominant framing of whites' unjust enrichment at the expense of American's of color—for example, killing off Native American populations and enslavement and segregating African Americans—has included much collective forgetting and mythmaking in regard to these often bloody historical realities.
>
> Significant portions of North American histories about centuries of racial oppression have been allowed to disappear from public consciousness, or to be downplayed and mythologized in scattered societal portrayals.[47]

How does the work of Feagin generate "accurate understandings" of the decision of the Supreme Court on October 10, 2018? First, this decision is not an isolated event but the ongoing reproduction of settler colonization in America, where Native people were not (and it appears are still not) considered citizens. The *Harvard Law Review* recently detailed the ongoing struggle to secure Native American voting rights. In this historical survey legal scholars detail that since the Indian Citizenship Act (1924) and the Voting Rights Act (1965) differing strategies have continually been perpetrated to disenfranchise Native American voters. The strategies include variations of gerrymandering, making it geographically challenging to register to vote and or cast

---

[42] Joe Feagin, *The White Racial Frame: Centuries of Racial Framing and Counter-framing* (New York: Routledge, 2013), 11.
[43] Ibid., 16.
[44] Ibid., 17.
[45] Ibid.
[46] Ibid.
[47] Ibid.

a ballot, and also creating barriers between tribal membership and US citizenship. This history reveals a transmuting of strategies "from the uses by states of Indians' 'distinctive status within the American political' to justify disenfranchisement, to the new techniques of vote dilution and vote denial that prevent Indians' full political participation."[48]

Drawing on the work of Patrick Wolfe enables us to see the history of the suppression of Native American voting rights as a continuation of settler colonialism. Wolf coined the following phrase: "The colonizers came to stay—invasion is a structure not an event."[49] For Wolfe, to view colonization as "a structure not an event" is to understand colonization as an ongoing process. "Taking settler colonization as a structure seriously allows US scholars, for example, to challenge [land] dispossession as a "done deal" relegated to the past rather than ongoing."[50]

One element that is critical to Wolfe's theorizing is that land dispossession is made possible by elimination of Native peoples. He writes, "Where they are is who they are, and not by their own reckoning."[51] This process of elimination does not necessarily involve overt genocidal war, but includes practices such as forced assimilation through systems such as boarding schools, child abduction and adoption, coerced religious conversion, and citizen bestowal.[52]

The current Supreme Court ruling is part of the ongoing settler colonizing myth that *Native* people are not truly American and therefore should not vote. In his infamous 1823 ruling Chief Justice John Marshall declared the right of settler colonizers to Native peoples' lands because of "our discovery" of America.[53] In light of this "landmark" ruling by Marshall it does not seem a coincidence that the recent Supreme Court ruling is a response to the 2017 North Dakota House Bill 1369.[54] North Dakota is the very state where the Standing Rock Nation organized an unprecedented protest against

---

[48] "Securing Indian Voting Rights," *Harvard Law Review* 129, no. 1731 (April 8, 2016), at https://harvardlawreview.org/2016/04/securing-indian-voting-rights/ (accessed November 25, 2018). See also Stephen L. Pevar, *The Rights of Indians and Tribes* (New York: Oxford University Press, 2012).

[49] See *Settler Colonialism and the Transformation of Anthropology* (London: Continuum International, 1998), 2.

[50] J. Kēhaulani Kauanui, "'A Structure, Not an Event': Settler Colonialism and Enduring Indigeneity," *Lateral: Journal of the Cultural Studies Association* 5, no. 1 (Spring 2016), at http://csalateral.org/issue/5-1/forum-alt-humanities-settler-colonialism-enduring-indigeneity-kauanui/#fn-351-3 (accessed November 28, 2018).

[51] Patrick Wolfe, "Settler Colonialism and the Elimination of the Native," *Journal of Genocide Research* (December 2006), at https://www.tandfonline.com/doi/full/10.1080/14623520601056240 (accessed November 28, 2018).

[52] Ibid.

[53] See Jeanine Hill Fletcher, *The Sin of White Supremacy: Christianity, Racism, and Religious Diversity in America* (Maryknoll, NY: Orbis, 2017), 51. This ruling is part of the Marshall Trilogy. See Frank Pommersheim, "The Marshall Trilogy: Foundational but Not Fully Constitutional?," in *Broken Landscapes: Indians, Indian Tribes and the Constitution* (New York: Oxford University Press, 2009), 87–124.

[54] North Dakota House Bill 1369 was signed into law by Governor Doug Burgum on April 24, 2017. "This restrictive voter ID law put North Dakota beyond the norms of vote ID laws and violates the constitutional rights of the state's citizens. Just like North Dakota's previous law, which was found unconstitutional by a federal court, this law makes it harder for some citizens—specifically Native American citizens—to exercise their right to vote." https://www.narf.org/cases/nd-voter-id/ (accessed November 29, 2018). The Native American Rights Fund documents the history of this legislation in North Dakota.

the Dakota Access Pipeline (DAPL).⁵⁵ It is almost as if the US government is sending a message to Native people, "How dare you treat this land like your own!" John Trudell explains clearly the stakes at work in the struggle to vote.

> When they got off the boat they didn't recognize us. They said "who are You?" and we said "we are the people, the human beings." "Oh Indians," [they said], because they did not recognize what it means to be a human being … but the predatory mentality shows up and starts calling us Indians and committing genocide against us as the vehicle for erasing the memory of being a human being.⁵⁶

Memoria passionis in a Land with No History

I return to the opening question of this chapter: what if Christians in America can't remember Jesus in our breaking of the bread because we have amnesia? In this section, I argue that our collective historical amnesia is rooted in the consciousness that made settler colonizing possible in America. The dynamic of settler colonizing rests on the ideology of removal in order to set up the ideal society. As Patrick Wolfe has argued, settler colonialism's dynamic of removal is founded upon the dispensability of Indigenous people.⁵⁷

In order to occupy this land settler colonizers viewed it as wilderness; a place without a history inhabited by a people with no history. John Trudell's words that end the previous section powerfully illustrate this intersection of forgetfulness, othering, and the land for political theology in America. Trudell declares that as the settler colonizers arrived on this land, "the predatory mentality shows up and starts calling us Indians and committing genocide against us *as the vehicle for erasing the memory of being a human being.*"⁵⁸ With this structure to our forgetting, how can white Christians in America claim to remember Jesus?

The anamnesis of Eucharist is not merely mental recall, or religious nostalgia, but an empowering participation in the relationships and events celebrated.⁵⁹ Such remembering made Jesus dangerous. As he broke the bread of Seder in Jerusalem, "Rome had taken the place of Egypt."⁶⁰ Pilate's presence in Jerusalem at Passover signaled the recognition of the subversive power of collective remembrance.⁶¹ As Metz

---

⁵⁵ Jeff Brady, "2 Years after Standing Rock Protests, Tensions Remain but Oil Business Booms," *National Public Radio*, November 29, 2018, at https://www.npr.org/2018/11/29/671701019/2-years-after-standing-rock-protests-north-dakota-oil-business-is-booming (accessed November 29, 2018). See also the Water Protector Legal Collective at https://waterprotectorlegal.org/.
⁵⁶ Dunbar-Ortiz, *An Indigenous Peoples' History of the United States*, 7.
⁵⁷ Cited in Veracini, *Settler Colonialism*, 8–9.
⁵⁸ Dunbar-Ortiz, *An Indigenous Peoples' History of the United States*, 7; emphasis my own.
⁵⁹ Bruce T. Morrill, SJ describes anamnesis as the dynamic of remembrance of the paschal mystery, anticipation of Christ's return, and the present "call to ritual and ethical praxis." *Anamnesis as Dangerous Memory: Political and Liturgical Theology in Dialogue* (Collegeville, MN: Liturgical Press, 2000), xv.
⁶⁰ Jose A. Pagalo, *Jesus: An Historical Approximation* (Miami, FL: Convivium, 2009), 339.
⁶¹ Ibid. Pagalo explains that Josephus documents a series of violent conflicts that occurred in Jerusalem during Passover feasts. See Flavius Josephus, *The Jewish War*, trans. Betty Radice (New York: Penguin Books, 1959).

has pointed out Christians have forgotten the danger of Jesus's time and actions and have systematically disregarded the subversive character of *memoria passionis*.[62]

What makes Jesus's action so dangerous is his celebration of Passover does not relegate God's liberating activity to the past. This concept of time and the ritual that awakens this experience of God is dangerous because it challenges the notion that God's liberating action is in the past, over and done with, and consigned to a different epoch than Roman occupation. In the commemorative feast of Passover remembering the past makes possible a liberating encounter with God in the present.[63] In contrast, amnesia is a disordered condition of memory loss and also "the selective overlooking or ignoring of events or acts that are not favorable or useful to one's purpose or position."[64] The promotion of amnesia as a political strategy is a concept of temporality in which the present is the only reality. The past is over and the future does not exist. From within this framework of time Rome's occupation is absolute, and Jesus's action is simply a religious fabrication or reenactment rendering the story of liberation a failed trope.

From within this context of Jesus's action Copeland has persuasively and consistently argued that "chattel slavery as a site of dangerous memory for the church and for theology in the United States, although such reflection need not be confined to the United States alone."[65] In relationship to contemporary anti-black violence in America she confronts us with the question, "Have theologians reasoned away these black bodies piling up?"[66] She insists our collective inability to meaningfully respond to the anti-black violence in contemporary America is rooted in our conspiracy to forget, "we repress and erase; we edit and delete. The result is a peculiar and unsettling, even puerile, ignorance that seeks to pass off as political ignorance."[67]

Copeland is inviting all Christians to explore *our* collective experience and responsibility on this land "to recognize ourselves and each other in our stories, our memories, our hopes; to grapple with our collective and intersecting pasts" in America.[68] How do white people experience, understand, and claim the collective and intersecting pasts on this land *as truly our own* when the very structures of our settler colonial consciousness deny the history of others? Theoretically how as Christian theologians could we deny human interdependence? However, on a practical level, do we, white people, genuinely experience the memory of lynching as our memories? Aren't these the memories of "other people" and a history that is not our own? Of course we would not deny the horror of lynching or chattel slavery. To denounce slavery is easy, it is a verbal condemnation of a historical reality, which remains on the level of linguistic assertion. Which is to say, as Copeland explains, to speak as if chattel slavery is fixed in

---

[62] Johann Baptist Metz, "Communicating a Dangerous Memory," in *Love's Strategy: The Political Theology of Johann Baptist Metz* (Harrisburg, PA: Trinity Press International, 1999), 144.
[63] Morrill, *Anamnesis as Dangerous Memory*, 177.
[64] Merriam Webster's Dictionary at https://www.merriam-webster.com/dictionary/amnesia (accessed November 3, 2018).
[65] Copeland, "Chattel Slavery as Dangerous Memory," 159.
[66] Copeland, "Memory, #BlackLiveMatter, and Theologians."
[67] Ibid.
[68] M. Shawn Copeland, "Memory, Emancipation, and Hope: Political Theology in the 'Land of the Free,'" *Santa Clara Lectures* 4 (November 9, 1997): 6.

the past and does not condition our relations and the unfolding of current events today is a kind of denial. Essentially, to denounce chattel slavery as merely an institution of the past is to imply the past has no bearing on today, as if it is hermetically sealed off from the present by our denouncing. As a white person, by denouncing slavery I affirm a linguistic anti-racist position. However, by defining chattel slavery as only in the past, I am insulating myself from my/our individual and "collective role(s) in the perpetuation of racism."[69]

To see slavery as only historical fact, events from the past, is to trivialize the reality of chattel slavery. For Copeland this trivialization of chattel slavery has profound epistemological and moral consequences. In drawing on the work of Michel-Rolph Trouillot, Copeland amplifies these consequences.

> The denunciation of slavery in a presentist mode is easy. Slavery was bad, most of us would agree. But presentism is by definition anachronistic. To condemn slavery alone is the easy way out … What needs to be denounced here to restore authenticity is much less slavery than the racist present within which representations of slavery are produced.[70]

At the heart of Copeland's challenge is a connection of temporality and otherness, which we must critically engage. She is uncovering for us an implicit assumption that is structured into our conspiracy to forget, which is that identity and time are static and fixed. Settler colonialism pushes forward Copeland's insight by enabling us to explore how otherness and forgetfulness are inherently connected. For example, this connection can be seen in Hegel's theorizing that Africans reside outside of history and therefore could not make a contribution to the development of humanity.[71] From work in the Congo, anthropologist Johannes Fabian has pointed out this connection in relationship to the settler colonizing mindset of determining the primitive character of indigenous populations.

> We tend to think about both identity and time in fixed categories: we are different from *them*, and the past is different from the present. But in fact, we perceive otherness and time as being fundamentally connected. We often differentiate ourselves by thinking about some kinds of others as belonging to the past—*they* are primitive and irrational, and *we* are not like them. *We* have progressed beyond their ways of thinking and behaving. We *used* to be like that, but we have left that past behind.[72]

---

[69] Alice McIntyre, *Making Meaning of Whiteness: Exploring Racial Identity with White Teachers* (Albany: State University of New York Press, 1997), 45.

[70] This quotation is from Michel-Rolph Trouillot, *Silencing the Past: Power and the Production of History* (Boston, MA: Beacon, 1995), n.4, 148. Cited in Copeland, "Chattel Slavery as Dangerous Memory," 169.

[71] Santiago Slabodsky, "*It's the Theology Stupid*: Coloniality, Anti-Blackness, and the Bounds of 'Humanity,'" in *Anti-Blackness and Christian Ethics*, ed. Vincent Lloyd and Andrew Prevot (Maryknoll, NY: Orbis, 2017), 35.

[72] Joyce Dalsheim and Gregory Starrett, "Racism and Anti-Semitism Are Not Intrusions of a Dark Past into Our Present," Rewire.News, December 5, 2018, at https://rewire.news/religion-dispatches/2018/12/05/its-a-big-mistake-to-see-racism-and-anti-semitism-as-an-eruption-of-a-dark-past/ (accessed

To use settler colonialism to contribute to Copeland's work is not to displace the dangerous memory of chattel slavery. We can never avoid the fact that capitalism in the United States developed by reducing "human beings to *living property*."[73] As Copeland vividly explains, living black bodies today signify the dangerous memory of chattel slavery and "signify the nation's unexamined questions and unresolved anxieties, disturb the nation's aesthetics, and curb the nations quest for the putative and unreflective postracial."[74] Drawing on settler colonialism deepens our understanding of the problem of forgetting within the white racial frame. Settler colonialism offers a mirror for us to see the very "structures of forgetting" inherent in the white supremacist worldview, in which time and others are defined.[75]

Lorenzo Veracini points out that the settler political formation of the United States is based on a declaration that this land called "America" was wilderness, and as such its people and land had no history. He cites the work of Alexis de Tocqueville in *Democracy in America* as clearly explicating this amnesic reasoning.

> Tocqueville narrates the unique combination between a land that is unframed social relations (a "wilderness" waiting to be cultivated) and a settler collective (which is also assumed to be divested of any prior social determination). Tocqueville thus describes a people without a history in a place without a history, a recurring trope in many settler colonial formations.[76]

The settler colonization of America is made possible by a denial of Native people's presence—and shared humanity. Adam Dahl has argued that confronting this history means confronting the reality of democracy on this land.[77] The dangerous memory of genocide and chattel slavery in America confronts us with who has the right to "life, liberty and the pursuit of happiness." Dahl explains that ignoring the settler colonizing foundation and structure of America prevents us from seeing it being used to justify policies today. He cites the political theorizing of Samuel Huntington, who has specifically claimed the United States as a settler democracy.[78]

Drawing on Tocqueville, Huntington argues for more restrictive immigration policies because he claims a stable democracy is founded upon shared national identity.[79] According to Huntington this identity precludes Hispanic immigrants, who

---

December 11, 2018). See Johannes Fabian, "Forgetting and Remembering," in *Memory against Culture: Arguments and Reminders* (Durham, NC: Duke University Press, 2007), 65–120; emphases in the original.

[73] M. Shawn Copeland, *Knowing Christ Crucified: The Witness of African American Religious Experience* (Maryknoll, NY: Orbis, 2018), 82; emphasis in the original.

[74] Ibid., 83.

[75] This phrase "structures of forgetting" come from the work of Paul Ricouer, "Forgetting and Manipulating Memory," in *Memory, History, Forgetting*, trans. Kathleen Blamey and David Pellauer (Chicago: University of Chicago Press, 2004), 450.

[76] Veracini, *Settler Colonialism*, 79.

[77] Adam Dahl, *Empire of the People: Settler Colonialism and the Foundations of Modern Democratic Thought* (Lawrence: University Press of Kansas, 2018).

[78] See Samuel P. Huntington, *Who Are We?: The Challenges to America's National Identity* (London: Simon and Schuster UK, 2004).

[79] Dahl, *Empire of the People*, 185.

he believes "have largely retained their traditional cultural values rooted in Hispanophone culture and Catholic religion at the expense of forming deep attachments to American national identity."[80]

Will understanding this history enable authentic anamnesis as Christians in America gather for Eucharist? I do not believe that more information alone will solve the deeply imbedded structure of settler colonization. As Copeland has argued, what is at stake is our capacity for relationship, not "mastery" of information. However, I do believe that taking up these insights can enable political theology to explore what conditions of possibility open Christians to the grace to take up the dangerous memories of our history in America. Gathering at the table of Eucharist with this question makes us open to transformation of our capacity to love. As Copeland declares, "Only Divine Love can save us. Only Divine Love knows how."[81] What practices, dispositions, and patterns of relating on this land enable us to be open to this transforming love of God?

Starting Place: Two Feet on Land

Robin Wall Kimmerer describes the settler descendants who reside in this land, all these generations since settler colonists first arrived:

> The problem with these people is that they don't have both feet on the shore. One is still on the boat. They don't seem to know whether they are staying or not.[82]

Kimmerer observes the ravages of the land and wonders if a nation of immigrants have yet to call this land home. With the present rush to exploit public lands for extractive industry Kimmerer's perspective is particularly poignant.[83] She asks us to consider the following question: "What happens when we truly become native to place, when we finally make it a home?"[84]

Kimmerer's powerful question orients this final section. Throughout this chapter, I have demonstrated that the ideology of white supremacy demands amnesia of those of us who benefit from and reproduce America's settler colonization. Only through this forgetting could we dominate the land and its inhabitants and continue these processes throughout US history. What would it be like if we treated this land as our home and all its inhabitants as our relatives?

---

[80] Ibid.

[81] M. Shawn Copeland, "God Among the Ruins: Companion and Co-sufferer," in *Violence, Transformation and the Sacred: "They Shall Be Called Children of God,"* ed. Margaret R. Pfeil and Tobias Winright (Maryknoll, NY: Orbis, 2012), 27.

[82] Robin Wall Kimmerer, *Braiding Sweet Grass: Indigenous Wisdom, Scientific Knowledge, and the Teachings of Plants* (Minneapolis, MN: Milkweed Editions, 2013), 207.

[83] Charlotte Simmonds, Gloria Dickie, and Jen Byers, "Lost Lands? The American Wilderness at Risk in the Trump Era," *Guardian*, December 5, 2018, at https://www.theguardian.com/environment/2018/dec/05/american-wilderness-trump-energy-threat (accessed December 6, 2019).

[84] Kimmerer, *Braiding Sweet Grass*, 207.

For Metz, political theology is a fundamental theology, which is to say it is an orientation that shapes our inquiry. As John Downey adeptly explains the power of Metz's method,

> He wants to lay the foundations for doing theology … to remind us of the questions that ground systematic reflection. Questions are an essential mark of theology, which is today more about questioning than answering … He offers vectors of thought that readers draw into their own particular circumstances. Political theology as a foundational theology, is then, a portable perspective and a pattern of questioning.[85]

For political theology in America, the land is a starting point generating questions that draw us into history that has been suppressed, but is right under our feet.

One dimension of fundamental theology is the task of exploring "the conditions which dispose human beings to receiving [God's] revelation."[86] What conditions of possibility enable white people living in America to know and practice what it means to be Christian, here in this place and on this land? A land we have been disposed by settler colonization to experience as something we "destroy to replace." Though we may not be conscious of this collective approach to the land, we may approach the land as simply a backdrop or stage for our human-centered activity. To explore what conditions may dispose Christians in America to a deeper appropriation of God's revelation, I propose three questions. First, how does the land we live on call us into relationship? Second, how do we listen to the stories of the first people who live on this land? Third, how do our ancestors make us understand our life on this land?

How Does the Land We Live on Call Us into Relationship?

In the book *Being Together in Place*, Soren Larsen and Jay Johnson explore how place constitutes self and community. Drawing on both Indigenous scholars and settler colonialism theorists they describe the agency of place, as calling humans and nonhumans together in coexistence. Larsen and Johnson explain that this call of place is to relationship, it is a summons to dialogue, with the humans and nonhumans who share the place.

> Place is forcing these coexistents to acknowledge one another however reluctantly or awkwardly, often in dialogue born of conflict, protest, and activism, calling humans and nonhumans to their inevitable, ongoing entanglement in these lands and making their struggle for co-existence at once a political and a spiritual issue.[87]

---

[85] Downey, "Introduction: Risking Memory," 2.
[86] Morrill, *Anamnesis as Dangerous Memory*, 17.
[87] Soren C. Larsen and Jay T. Johnson, *Being Together in Place: Indigenous Coexistence in a More than Human World* (Minneapolis: University of Minnesota, 2017), 2.

In this understanding the land radically decenters the modern subject as protagonist of history. This is not a settler colonist self who maps, names, invades, and domesticates place. Rather land is "guiding human and nonhuman beings along the knotted paths of responsibility."[88] In addition, this understanding of place includes the political, which is to say place is not taken out of history as romanticized location of "nature."[89]

Larsen and Johnson describe place as guiding humans on a journey of responsibility, and their description generates an understanding of mutual responsibility between place and human beings. I have been fascinated with witnessing how this relationship of mutual responsibility can emerge in attending to a specific place, even through very simple practices of attention. In 2008 I taught an undergraduate class on water ethics. One of the weekly class assignments involved each student finding a place outdoors that they would visit three times a week. Each visit would be for ten minutes and involve a recording of simple observations. The outcome was surprising and thought provoking for me. Students reported being disturbed by seeing their place "trashed." One student in outrage wrote to me, "Why would someone do this!" A number of students were worried that as the semester ended, "who will take care of my place." Sustained presence and attention had made these students "be of place" and demonstrated how they began to experience place as guiding them into relationships of responsibility.

In her essay "Speaking of Nature" Robin Wall Kimmerer describes how her Potawatomi language affirms kinship with the natural world. The word "it" is never used in relationship to creation. Kimmerer explains that "birds, bugs, and berries are spoken of with the same respectful grammar as humans are, as if we are members of the same family. Because we are."[90]

Kimmerer explains how settler colonization stamped out this language of kinship in forbidding her grandfather to speak his native language at the Carlisle Indian Boarding School.

> Linguistic imperialism has always been a tool of colonization, meant to obliterate history and the visibility of the people who were displaced along with their languages. But five hundred years later, in a renamed landscape, it has become a nearly invisible tool ... Beyond the renaming of places, I think the most profound act of linguistic imperialism was the replacement of a language of animacy with one of objectification of nature, which renders the beloved land as lifeless object, the forest as a board feet of timber.[91]

A botany professor, Kimmerer challenges students to learn and write about plants through the grammar of relationship and kinship. She describes walking with her students through a local cemetery to engage in the practice of relating to plants as

---

[88] Ibid.
[89] See this concern articulated in J. Matthew Ashley, "Environmental Concern and the 'New Political Theology,'" in *Missing God? Cultural Amnesia and Political Theology*, ed. John Downey, Jürgen Manemann, and Steven Ostovich (Berlin: Lit Verlag, 2006), 153.
[90] Robin Wall Kimmerer, "Speaking of Nature: Finding Language That Affirms Our Kinship with the Natural World," *Orion Magazine*, March/April 2017, 17.
[91] Ibid.

kin. Caroline, one of Kimmerer's students, says, "Isn't it funny ... that we think it is disrespectful to walk over the dead, but it is perfectly okay to disrespect the other species who actually live here?"[92]

Kimmerer's writing and teaching connect back and illustrate Larsen and Johnson's idea of "being together in place." She offers one example of how non-native and native people can walk together on the land and engage together with all creation as subjects.

How Do We Listen to the Stories of the First People Who Live on This Land?

Larsen and Johnson describe the learning we see in Kimmerer's teaching as a spiritual process. "Walking-with one another is ultimately a spiritual process" and relationships emerge as we struggle together over the land we share.[93] Struggling with Native peoples to relate to the land as subjects leads us more deeply into the dangerous memories of America, which means to learn the suppressed history of the people whose land we live on, in the here and now in our specific location.

Roxanne Dunbar-Ortiz and Dina Gilio-Whitaker, who have detailed the "official history" of Native peoples in America, illustrate the myth of the "vanishing Native." They write, "The myth of the vanishing Native can be traced precisely to the impulse of the state to eliminate the Native."[94] Contemporary Hollywood films such "Island of the Blue Dolphins" and "the Last of the Mohicans" popularize and perpetuate this myth,[95] which is patently false. There are 567 federally recognized Native nations in the United States, and the 2010 census documented "5.2 million people identified as Native American or Alaska Native, either alone or combined with other races. About 2.9 million people identified as Native American or Alaska native alone."[96]

Growing up in New England I did not know that I was living on Nipmuc land and that my Irish immigrant ancestors had also settled on stolen Nipmuc land in central Massachusetts. In *Firsting and Lasting: Writing Indians Out of Existence in New England* Jean O'Brien documents how the myth of the "vanishing Native" has been deeply entrenched within American consciousness.[97] Her work gives an account of how settler colonizers in New England wrote local histories that erased out Native peoples. Even though Native peoples were living among the colonists, this erasing was a way of refuting their claim to the land.

For example, we see this erasure in the history of the Nipmuc. As Christopher Thee describes, originally the Nippiemook land covered area that

> currently spans central Massachusetts, Connecticut, and Rhode Island and historically occupied homelands bounded by New Hampshire border stretching

---

[92] Ibid., 14.
[93] Larsen and Johnson, *Being Together in Place*, 49.
[94] Roxanne Dunbar-Ortiz and Dina Gilio-Whitaker, *"All the Real Indians Died Off" and 20 Other Myths about Native Americans* (Boston, MA: Beacon, 2016), 11.
[95] For an excellent history of this myth, see Brian W. Dippie, *The Vanishing American: White Attitudes and US Indian Policy* (Lawrence: University of Kansas Press, 1991).
[96] Dunbar-Ortiz and Gilio-Whitaker, *"All the Real Indians Died Off,"* 13.
[97] Jean O'Brien, *Firsting and Lasting: Writing Indians Out of Existence in New England* (Minneapolis: University of Minnesota Press, 2010).

from Sudbury, Massachusetts to the Connecticut River, extending south toward Hartford along the river, incorporating northeastern Connecticut and Northern Rhode Island, and looping back to Sudbury, Marlborough, and Concord area.[98]

Thomas L. Doughton details how this strategy of writing Native people out of New England impacted the Nipmuc's existence on the land. In contrast to the stereotypes of any remaining Indians as poor and homeless, in the 1800s the Nipmuc were living in central Massachusetts and raising families, involved in community life, and working as farmers, plumbers, railroad engineers, bakers, stage-coach drivers, shoemakers, and barbers. For Doughton, ironically, the Nipmuc being employed would have made them appear—disappeared—because they were not acting according to the prevailing stereotypes. He explains that through intermarriage and not acting "as Indians should" white New Englanders claimed Nipmuc to be disappeared.[99]

In 1980 the Nipmuc began the arduous process of gathering seventy thousand documents to apply for federal recognition to prove "that this group exists as an Indian tribe."[100] And in 2004 the Nipmuc were denied their quest for recognition because they did not meet the criteria created by the US government. In a series of YouTube videos jointly produced by Bay Path College and the Nipmuc Tribe, tribal members explain their history and declare, "We exist!"[101]

A public practice that originated in Australia may be instructive for Americans attempting to interrupt the erasure of Native history and peoples. In 2008 the Australian government officially adopted a practice called "Welcome to County."[102] This practice involves Indigenous elders welcoming all present at a gathering to their traditional land. When Indigenous elders are not available to attend the public gathering nonindigenous people may begin the meeting with "Acknowledgment." In this acknowledgment, the name of the ancestral people who lived on the land is declared.

Inspired by this practice of public acknowledgment, Hannah Graf Evans describes how Friends Committee has begun this practice in America. During Columbus Day weekend in 2015 Friends who work in the capital gathered in Washington, DC, to acknowledge the ancestral people of the land, the Nacotchtank tribe. In this ritual

---

[98] Christopher J. Thee, "Massachusetts Nipmucs and the Long Shadow of John Milton Earl," *New England Quarterly* LXXIX:4 (December 2006): 636, fn.1.

[99] Thomas L. Doughton, "Unseen Neighbors: Native Americans of Central Massachusetts, a People Who Had Vanished," in *After King Philip's War: Presence and Persistence in Indian New England*, ed. Colin Calloway (Hanover, NH: University Press of New England, 1997), 207–30.

[100] This is the working from the document that denies the Nipmuc's claim. https://www.bia.gov/sites/bia.gov/files/assets/as-ia/ofa/petition/069A_npmcna_MA/069a_fd.pdf (accessed November 30, 2018).

[101] For the first in the series of these videos, see https://www.youtube.com/watch?v=pcrQABPSZNQ.

[102] Prime Minister Kevin Rudd opened parliament with the first official "Welcome to Country." See http://www.abc.net.au/local/stories/2008/02/12/2160380.htm (accessed November 30, 2018). The practice has historical roots in Indigenous Australia. See Natsumi Penberthy, "An Indigenous Australian Tradition Millennia-Old, Welcome to Country's Mainstream Popularity Began to Snowball 40 Years Ago," *Australia Geographic*, March 3, 2016, at https://www.australiangeographic.com.au/topics/history-culture/2016/03/richard-walleys-welcome-to-country/ (accessed November 30, 2018).

of "acknowledgment" they also recounted the Nacotchtank's history since conquest, including their present struggle to be recognized by the US government.

> For centuries, indigenous cultures have been erased, forgotten, or devalued through naming and re-naming; through the privileging of European survival and dismissal of Indigenous resilience ... European settlers even changed Native names to European—often biblical—names, citing that traditional names were too difficult to remember and were antithetical to civilized peoples.[103]

Graf does not describe such an act as an answer or solution to settler colonization. She believes this as "a first step, not a final one." And she makes a powerful description, which is instructive for a political theology that starts with the land. "First, we must join together with Indigenous communities in acknowledging our true shared history, including honoring Indigenous contributions, sorrows, and names."[104]

How Do Our Ancestors Make Us Understand Our Life on This Land?

The addition of the role of "settler" to "colonialism" is critical to understanding our history in America. The logic of this process involves a triangle consisting of settlers, the colonial power, and indigenous populations. The settlers came for land unavailable to them in their home countries in Europe. "Settlers sought to remove and replace the indigenous population and in the process to cast aside the authority of the 'mother' country." As Walter Hixson explains, the American Revolution is an example of this settler colonizing dynamic.[105] Therefore the compounded term itself helps the inquiry into history on this land. Who are these settlers? Why did they come to this land? How are we living the stories of these settlers today? These questions are just the start of an inquiry into who we are as descendants of settlers.

For example, many settlers from Scotland came here as a result of the Highland Clearances. My own ancestors came to America as a result of this land eviction. My family is of the clan McNaughton, and we are recorded as having fought on the side of Prince Charles Edward Stuart who lost at the Battle of Culloden in 1746. After this battle the people and lifestyle of the Scottish Highlands were called into question, because "the Highlands were regarded as the outer edge of civilization—remote, uncouth and dangerously anarchic."[106] In the 1750s the British government attempted to civilize the Highlands, and brutal methods were used to subjugate the people and their way of life. Entire communities were evicted from their land, there were violent removals, expulsions, and forced resettlement from 1740 to 1900. Some historians consider these actions to be ethnic cleansing and even genocide.

---

[103] Hannah Graf Evans, "We Begin with Acknowledgement," Friends Committee on National Legislation, October 15, 2015, at https://www.fcnl.org/updates/we-begin-with-acknowledgement-197 (accessed November 30, 2018).
[104] Ibid.
[105] Walter Hixson, *American Settler Colonization: A History* (New York: Palgrave, 2013), 5.
[106] Eric Richards, *The Highland Clearances* (Edinburgh: Edinburgh University Press, 2007), 8.

In *White People, Indians and the Highlanders: Tribal People and Colonial Encounters in Scotland and America*, Colin Calloway draws parallels between what happened to the Highlanders in Scotland and to Native people in America. The Scots coming to America had more in common with Native peoples than with the British. However, Calloway clearly demonstrates the violence perpetrated against the Highlanders is what they in turn enacted upon Native people as settlers in America.

> Patterns, practices, policies, and philosophies of conquest and colonization that developed in the British Isles were repeated in North America. Highland Scots, many of whom had experienced defeat and dispossession themselves, In turn took a heavy toll on American Indian life, land and culture. They were "the poor foot soldiers of the empire of emigration" in the words of Eric Richards, but "they were as heavily implicated in the quasi (*sic*) genocidal aspects of American and Australian empire as any other groups from the British Isles."[107]

If settler colonialism is a structure not an event, we should ask how this violent reproduction is being enacted today. And how could our openness to this land under our feet be a way of acknowledging this trauma and opening to the dangerous memories in our history?

What I have proposed is a way forward for political theology on this land. This is not a systematic approach, but rather practices and dispositions that create the possibility for new patterns of relating to one another, to ourselves, and to God as the land calls us into relationship. The land as a starting point will resonate with "political theology's efforts to interrogate and repair, reweave and restore the fraying webs of relations that comprise the U.S. cultural and social ... matrices."[108] Authentic memory of Jesus in his breaking of the bread entails contending with the suppressed layers of dangerous memory in our own land. It is only through acknowledging this history that we will be open to who Christ is in our reality today.

Bibliography

Anbinder, Tyler G. *Nativism and Slavery: The Northern Know Nothings & the Politics of the 1850s*. New York: Oxford University Press, 1994.

Ashley, J. Matthew. "Environmental Concern and the 'New Political Theology.'" In *Missing God? Cultural Amnesia and Political Theology*, edited by John Downey, Jürgen Manemann, and Steven Ostovich, 153. Berlin: Lit Verlag, 2006.

Ashley, James Matthew. *Interruptions: Mysticism, Politics and Theology in the Work of Johann Baptist Metz*. Notre Dame: Notre Dame University Press, 1998.

Blake, Aaron. "Trump's Embrace of a Fraught Term—'Nationalist'—Could Cement a Dangerous Racial Divide." *Washington Post*, October 23, 2018. https://www.washingtonpost.com/politics/2018/10/23/

---

[107] Colin Calloway, *White People, Indians and the Highlanders: Tribal People and Colonial Encounters in Scotland and America* (New York: Oxford University Press, 2008), 21. In contrast to Calloway I see settler colonization as an on going form of genocide of Native peoples, not 'quasi genocide'.

[108] Copeland, "Memory, #BlackLiveMatter, and Theologians."

trumps-embrace-fraught-term-nationalist-could-cement-dangerous-racial-divide/?noredirect=on&utm_term=.9d6dd5c5bd54.

Brady, Jeff. "2 Years after Standing Rock Protests, Tensions Remain but Oil Business Booms." *National Public Radio*, November 29, 2018. https://www.npr.org/2018/11/29/671701019/2-years-after-standing-rock-protests-north-dakota-oil-business-is-booming.

Calloway, Colin. *White People, Indians and the Highlanders: Tribal People and Colonial Encounters in Scotland and America*. New York: Oxford University Press, 2008.

Chang, David. *The Color of the Land: Race, Nation, and the Politics of Landownership in Oklahoma, 1832–1929*. Chapel Hill: University of North Carolina Press, 2010, 7.

Copeland, M. Shawn. "Chattel Slavery as Dangerous Memory." In *Tradition and the Normativity of History*, edited by Lieven Boeve and Terrence Merrigan, 155–73. Leuven: Uitgeverji Peters, 2013.

Copeland, M. Shawn. "God among the Ruins: Companion and Co-sufferer." In *Violence, Transformation and the Sacred: "They Shall Be Called Children of God,"* edited by Margaret R. Pfeil and Tobias Winright, 27. Maryknoll, NY: Orbis, 2012.

Copeland, M. Shawn. *Knowing Christ Crucified: The Witness of African American Religious Experience*. Maryknoll, NY: Orbis, 2018.

Copeland, M. Shawn. "Memory, #BlackLiveMatter, and Theologians." *Political Theology* 17:1 (March 17, 2016). https://politicaltheology.com/memory-blacklivesmatter-and-theologians-m-shawn-copeland/.

Copeland, M. Shawn. "Memory, Emancipation, and Hope: Political Theology in the 'Land of the Free.'" *Santa Clara Lectures* 4 (November 9, 1997).

Dahl, Adam. *Empire of the People: Settler Colonialism and the Foundations of Modern Democratic Thought*. Lawrence: University Press of Kansas, 2018.

Dippie, Brian W. *The Vanishing American: White Attitudes and U.S. Indian Policy*. Lawrence: University Press of Kansas, 1991.

Dippie, Thomas L. "Unseen Neighbors: Native Americans of Central Massachusetts, a People Who Had Vanished." In *After King Philip's War: Presence and Persistence in Indian New England*, edited by Colin Calloway, 207–30. Hanover, NH: University Press of New England, 1997.

Dalsheim, Joyce, and Gregory Starrett. "Racism and Anti-Semitism Are Not Intrusions of a Dark Past into Our Present." *Rewire.News*, December 5, 2018. https://rewire.news/religion-dispatches/2018/12/05/its-a-big-mistake-to-see-racism-and-anti-semitism-as-an-eruption-of-a-dark-past/.

Downey, John. *Love's Strategy: The Political Theology of Johann Baptist Metz*. Harrisburg, PA: Trinity Press International, 1999.

Dunbar-Ortiz, Roxanne. *An Indigenous Peoples' History of the United States*. Boston, MA: Beacon, 2014.

Dunbar-Ortiz, Roxanne, and Dina Gilio-Whitaker. *"All the Real Indians Died Off" and 20 Other Myths about Native Americans*. Boston, MA: Beacon, 2016.

Evans, Hannah Graf. "We Begin with Acknowledgement." Friends Committee on National Legislation, October 15, 2015. https://www.fcnl.org/updates/we-begin-with-acknowledgement-197 (accessed November 30, 2018).

Fabian, Johannes. *Memory against Culture: Arguments and Reminders*. Durham, NC: Duke University Press, 2007.

Fineout, Gary. "Man Who Appears to Have Made Racist, Misogynistic Videos Kills 2 Women in Tallahassee Yoga Studio Shooting." *Chicago Tribune*, November 3, 2018.

https://www.chicagotribune.com/news/nationworld/ct-florida-yoga-studio-shooting-20181103-story.html.

Fletcher, Jeanine Hill. *The Sin of White Supremacy: Christianity, Racism, and Religious Diversity in America*. Maryknoll, NY: Orbis, 2017.

Gunn Allen, Paula. *The Sacred Hoop: Recovering the Feminine in American Indian Traditions*. Boston, MA: Beacon, 1992.

Hixson, Walter. *American Settler Colonization: A History*. New York: Palgrave, 2013.

Huntington, Samuel P. *Who Are We?: The Challenges to America's National Identity*. London: Simon and Schuster UK, 2004.

Iannotti, Ralph. "Pittsburgh Synagogue Identified as Robert Bowers, Yelled 'All Jews Must Die' as He Opened Fire, Now Facing Federal Charges." CBS Pittsburgh, October 27, 2018. https://pittsburgh.cbslocal.com/2018/10/27/pittsburgh-synagogue-shooting-suspect-identified/.

Josephus, Flavius. *The Jewish War*. Translated by Betty Radice. New York: Penguin, 1959.

Larsen, Soren C., and Jay T. Johnson. *Being Together in Place: Indigenous Coexistence in a More Than Human World*. Minneapolis: University of Minnesota, 2017.

McIntyre, Alice. *Making Meaning of Whiteness: Exploring Racial Identity with White Teachers*. Albany: State University of New York Press, 1997.

Metz, Johann Baptist. "Communicating a Dangerous Memory." In *Communicating a Dangerous Memory: Soundings in Political Theology*, Lonergan Workshop 6, edited by Fred Lawrence, 37–53. Atlanta, GA: Scholar's Press, 1987.

Mignolo, Walter. *The Darker Side of Western Modernity: Global Futures, Decolonial Options*. Durham, NC: Duke University Press, 2011.

Morrill, Bruce T., SJ. *Anamnesis as Dangerous Memory: Political and Liturgical Theology in Dialogue*. Collegeville, MN: Liturgical Press, 2000.

Novelly, Thomas. "Police Chief Calls Kroger Shooting in Louisville a Hate Crime." *USA Today*, October 29, 2018. https://www.usatoday.com/story/news/nation-now/2018/10/29/louisville-police-calls-kroger-shooting/1807654002/.

O'Brien, Jean. *Firsting and Lasting: Writing Indians Out of Existence in New England*. Minneapolis: University of Minnesota Press, 2010.

O'Collins, Gerald. *Fundamental Theology*. New York: Paulist, 1981.

Penberthy, Natsumi. "An Indigenous Australian Tradition Millennia-Old, Welcome to Country's Mainstream Popularity Began to Snowball 40 Years Ago." *Australia Geographic*, March 3, 2016. https://www.australiangeographic.com.au/topics/history-culture/2016/03/richard-walleys-welcome-to-country/.

Pogrund, Gabriel, and Felicia Sonmez. "In Senate Battleground, Native American Voting Rights Activists Fight Back against Voter ID Restrictions." *Washington Post*, October 12, 2018. https://www.washingtonpost.com/politics/in-senate-battleground-native-american-voting-rights-activists-fight-back-against-voter-id-restrictions/2018/10/12/7bc33ad2-cd60-11e8-a360-85875bac0b1f_story.html?utm_term=.e9e9854274a3.

Richards, Eric. *The Highland Clearances*. Edinburgh: Edinburgh University Press, 2007.

Ricouer, Paul. *Memory, History, Forgetting*. Translated by Kathleen Blamey and David Pellauer. Chicago: University of Chicago Press, 2004.

Schroeder, Jean, and Melissa Rogers. "What Keeps Native Americans from Voting—and What Could Change This." *Washington Post*, October 18, 2018. https://www.washingtonpost.com/news/monkey-cage/wp/2018/10/18/what-keeps-native-americans-from-voting-and-what-could-change-this/?noredirect=on&utm_term=.22591cdee5a3.

Simmonds, Charlotte, Gloria Dickie, and Jen Byers. "Lost Lands? The American Wilderness at Risk in the Trump Era." *Guardian*, December 5, 2018. https://www.theguardian.com/environment/2018/dec/05/american-wilderness-trump-energy-threat.
Slabodsky, Santiago. "*It's the Theology Stupid*: Coloniality, Anti-blackness, and the Bounds of 'Humanity.'" In *Anti-blackness and Christian Ethics*, edited by Vincent Lloyd and Andrew Prevot, 35. Maryknoll, NY: Orbis, 2017.
Trouillot, Michel-Rolph. *Silencing the Past: Power and the Production of History*. Boston, MA: Beacon, 1995.
Veracini, Lorenzo. *The Settler Colonial Present*. New York: Palgrave, 2015.
Veracini, Lorenzo. *Settler Colonialism: A Theoretical Overview*. New York: Palgrave, 2010.
Wolfe, Patrick. "Settler Colonialism and the Elimination of the Native." *Journal of Genocide Research* 8:4 (December 2006): 387–409.
Wolfe, Patrick. *Settler Colonialism and the Transformation of Anthropology*. London: Continuum International, 1998.

9

Ransomed by Money? Toward an African Constructive Theology

Lawrence N. Nwankwo

Introduction

The following troubling experience crystallized the ideas in this chapter. Two priest colleagues of mine in Nigeria were kidnapped on their way to a wedding ceremony. When the kidnappers made contact, they demanded the equivalent of $300,000 per head as ransom for the release of the priests.[1] This was beyond the means of the parish whose annual total cash inflow is less than $3,000. Even if the parish could afford the money, the Diocese of Awka, to which we belong, has a policy of not paying ransom for a kidnapped priest.[2] Our community and others prayed hard. The political leaders in Anambra State got involved. Fortunately, the priests were released after four days of harrowing experiences. Maybe, God answered our prayers through the significant role played by the political authorities. But not many Nigerians have such social capital to draw from. They and their friends would also pray fervently as we did. But sometimes, they would either have to pay up and be released or be "wasted" and left to rot in the forest.

Since kidnapping became routine "business" in Nigeria, "ransom" has evolved into a household word. Ransom is paid in money, lots of it. It buys people back from imminent death. It is a means of salvation. This raises the question of the relationship between salvation from the kidnappers' den and salvation preached by Christians, on the one hand, and ransom by money and ransom paid with the blood of the Lamb (Rev. 12:11), on the other.

While still struggling with this knotty soteriological issue, a member of my community informed me of his inability to avail himself of good medical care for his diabetic condition because of lack money. With the majority of the people not having

---

[1] Zenit Staff, "Two Nigerian Priests Kidnapped on December 6 Released," https://zenit.org/articles/two-nigerian-priests-kidnapped-on-december-6-released/ (accessed December 15, 2019).
[2] This is in solidarity with the many poor people who cannot pay any ransom and lose their lives at the hands of kidnappers. It is also a way of making priests unattractive to kidnappers. Priests are indeed soft targets. The schedule for Eucharistic celebration in the different churches is public knowledge, and the roads are often rough and one cannot afford to speed up.

any health insurance, the hospitals run a policy of collecting a substantial percentage of the cost of treatment as deposit before the patient is even "touched." Again, it boils down to money being key to one's life or death. Yet, as Christians, we confess that Jesus has come that all may have life in abundance (Jn 10:10). Is this abundance of life only related to the many mansions that Jesus is going to His father to prepare for us (Jn 14:2)? Prosperity theology, a dominant strand of popular religiosity in many parts of Africa, answers in the negative. It postulates prosperity as an intrinsic part of salvation. Prosperity is wider than money. It includes health, fertility, longevity, upward social mobility, and so on. But money can be used as a synecdoche for it. The implication of this shift is that money is not only seen as a means of salvation, of paying the ransom for people's lives, but also as an intrinsic element in the salvation won by Jesus Christ. The Jesus event is thus seen as the condition for the possibility of prosperity in this world.

As will be shown, prosperity theology resonates with as well as recomposes the African traditional religious worldview. While contributing to the reconstruction of personal identity and providing a scheme of hope for many, this theological construct does not engage the source of the brokenness in the lifeworld of contemporary Africans because these are externalized and projected onto the spirit world. Lines of response are therefore fashioned in terms of mobilizing divine power to dislodge the evil spirits in the context of a spiritual warfare. The result is that while the continent is brimming with religious faith and fervor—Christianity, Islam, and also traditional religion—it remains marked by many elements that negate the abundance of life projected in these religions. This makes it imperative to theologically open up new ways of being Christian and being church that engage the African lifeworld toward a kind of transformation that holds out the promise of fullness of life for Africans, one and all.

A constructive theological approach is suited to this task. This approach recognizes that the Christian tradition is composite. It seeks to retrieve strands of the tradition that it considers best suited for enhancing love and life and weaves these into a tapestry that addresses the challenges of everyday life thrown up by particular contexts. Because the constructive theological approach is concerned with social change, it tries to listen empathetically to the context in order to ferret out the taken-for-granted schemes and frames of understanding that undergird the production and reproduction of social practices. Similarly, while communicating its insights, the approach strives to remain in continuous exchange with the operative scheme and principle in order to harness and channel the energy from any dissonance toward new and more wholesome practices. This implies a threefold attentiveness: to the underlying schemes operative in a context, to the theological underpinnings of such contextual dynamics and in the light of the latter, to the strands of Christian tradition that could foster the desired change.

Construction of a house usually starts with visiting the site, making a survey, and building plans. Theology is about life, and the site is never a virgin area. Every effort at constructive theology has to reckon with a theological edifice already serving life, even if inadequately. Some elements of this edifice have to be salvaged for the new project. This is not simply for the sake of continuity between the old and the new but more importantly because these elements are like pillars sunk deep into the soil of the context whose strength can be harnessed for the new design. Put simply, we set out in this constructive venture by engaging Emmanuel Katongole's mapping of the African site in his three books, *The Sacrifice of Africa: A Political Theology for Africa*,[3] *A Future for Africa: Critical Essays in Christian Social Imagination*,[4] and *Born from Lament: The Theology and Politics of Hope in Africa*.[5]

Though I appreciate Katongole's analysis, we differ in terms of emphasis and approach. The difference in emphasis seems to derive from our social location and the primary audience we are addressing. Experiences in the Great Lake Region of East Africa, a region that has witnessed protracted and violent conflicts, shape Katongole's analysis. Mine is shaped by my experiences in Nigeria. My audience includes Africans for whom Africa's continued underperformance has drawn attention to the question of "how Africa underdeveloped Africa."[6] The difference in approach rests on our different views on the dynamics of intercultural contact and the impact of colonialism. In distinction from Katongole, I argue that despite the huge impact of the contact with Europe through slave trade, in colonialism and Christianization, the agency of Africans was never suspended. They exercised and continue to exercise situated creativity—creativity within the context thrust on them by their colonial and postcolonial social history. On this creativity hangs the hope of social transformation.

Katongole's emphasis on social imagination is in the right direction. But in his analysis, the dominant components of this imagination are violence and exploitation borne out of Africa's social history of colonialism. The State in Africa is a prolongation of colonial violence and plunder. Therefore, a future for Africa entails evolving alternative social arrangements inspired by different social imagination. Mine is a more modest attempt to aid Africans in understanding why the existing social arrangement—the state and the capitalist system that undergirds it, imperfect as they are—shortchange Africans, and to engage in transforming and making them more life-giving for all. At the background of my analysis is what Jean-François Bayart calls the reciprocal assimilation and mutual entanglement of the state and the society in Africa.[7] The same dysfunctional social imagination operates both in and through the state and in the society at large. This imagination focuses on accessing, accumulating, and leveraging resources of various kinds to escape the constraints of everyday life. The title of this chapter is an interrogation of this imagination captured as "ransomed by money." This social imagination paradoxically is present in a dominant strand of popular religiosity—prosperity theology, which makes prosperity part and parcel

---

[3] Emmanuel Katongole, *The Sacrifice of Africa: A Political Theology for Africa* (Grand Rapids, MI: William Eerdmans, 2011).
[4] Emmanuel Katongole, *A Future for Africa: Critical Essays in Christian Social Imagination* (Eugene, OR: Wipf & Stock, 2017).
[5] Emmanuel Katongole, *Born from Lament: The Theology and Politics of Hope in Africa* (Grand Rapids, MI: William Eerdmans, 2017).
[6] This is the title of a book by Stanley Chinedu Igwe, published in 2010 in Port Harcourt, Nigeria, by Professional Printers & Publishers. This title calls to mind Walter Rodney's *How Europe Underdeveloped Africa* and the dependency theory. Although Igwe does not assail some of Rodney's arguments, he implicates Africans in the continued underdevelopment of the continent.
[7] Jean-François Bayart, *The State in Africa: The Politics of the Belly*, trans. Elizabeth Harrison (London: Longman, 1993).

of salvation. This theology succeeds in presenting a soteriological vision that has a strong innerworldly component and, on this count, resonates with traditional African cosmologies. However, it is captive to the same imagination at the root of Africa's underdevelopment that celebrates individualism rather than solidarity, love of power instead of the power of love, glorification of violence and disorder in place of enthronement of respect and orderliness, among others. The category of *theosis*, used in prosperity theology for the reconstitution of the subjectivity of the "born-again," helps us reappropriate the vision of the human being as temple of the Holy Spirit with the task of building up other temples of the Holy Spirit. This vision, while in continuity with prosperity theology, broadens its scope and redirects its energy by prioritizing solidary love, care, respect, and compassion in interpersonal and social relationship. This is what I have called "ransomed for money." Here, money stands not for resources as in the title, but for integral well-being, abundance, fulfillment, flourishing. Constructive theological reflection in Africa gives rise to a prepositional shift from "ransomed *by* money," in which money (resources) seems to be the source of salvation, to "ransomed *for* money," in which the salvation won by Jesus makes it possible for all to be clothed with and empowered by the Holy Spirit to commit themselves to the well-being of others.

The Sacrifice of Africa: Katongole's Analysis

Emmanuel Katongole's political theology for Africa can be read as a riposte to the theology of Reconstruction, according to which the oppressors are gone, exile is over, and it is time to reconstruct.[8] For Katongole, the opposite is true. The oppressors are not gone yet; only their complexion has changed. The African elite, the inheritors of the nation-state, are the new oppressors, trapped in a colonial imagination in which Africans are seen as mere bodies to be used, mere masses to be exploited and disposed of. In other words, the nation-state handed over to the African nationalists, according to Katongole, continues to perform the colonial script of plunder and violence. For him, the nation-state is thus at the heart of the woes of Africa. Consequently, he argues, "a new future in Africa requires much more than strategies and skills to solve the problems of nation-state politics. It requires a different story that assumes the sacred value and dignity of Africa and Africans, and is thus able to shape practices and policies, or new forms of politics, that reflect this sacredness and dignity."[9]

Katongole tells stories of exemplary people whose lives embody an alternative vision for Africa and for Christianity. These include those who commit themselves to the path of reconciliation, tribal harmony, defense of the poor, taking care of and restoring dignity to those traumatized by war, and so on. Retelling the stories of such people is meant to inspire action and practices in communities that "in turn

---

[8] See Julius Gathogo, "Genesis, Methodologies and Concerns of African Reconstruction Theology," *Theologia Viatorum, Journal of Religion and Theology in Africa* 32, no. 1 (2008): 23–62.
[9] Ibid., 21.

make possible a new sacrifice of Africa (in the sense of the Latin root of sacrifice, which is to 'make sacred': *sacra+facere*) and is thus able to interrupt the wastage (sacrificing) of Africa assumed within the founding narratives and institutions of modern Africa."[10]

A Critique of Katongole's African Political Theology

Katongole focuses on an Africa of warlords who visit terror and violence on the people. First, as already seen, his experiences in the Great Lake Region of East Africa could be responsible for this tunnel vision. There are parts of Africa, equally colonized, that have known relative peace. This calls to mind the challenge and pitfall of any reflection with Africa as a whole as the area of study. Second, Katongole's presentation of the rapid and positive transformation brought to Burkina Faso by Thomas Sankara's purposeful leadership[11] shows that the problem may not simply be the nation-state but the quality and style of leadership.

The diversity of experiences in postcolonial Africa exposes the inadequacy of the mono-causal link established by Katongole between colonialism, on the one hand, and the nation-state, on the other, and the situation in Africa. If colonial experience triggered incessant wars in some parts of Africa but not in others, and if the nation-state afforded Thomas Sankara a platform for transforming Upper Volta to Burkina Faso (land of the incorruptibles), a more discriminating analysis is needed to find out what contingent elements are conducive to situations of war and underdevelopment rather than one of relative peace and progress.

The rediscovery of the contingency of African history exposes the inadequacy of the social theory that undergirds Katongole's analysis. Karl Marx wrote, "Men [sic] make their own history, but they do not make it as they please; they do not make it under self-selected circumstances … The tradition of all dead generations weighs like a nightmare on the brains of the living."[12] Katongole's social imagination, which he describes as specific habits and patterns of life,[13] are like Marx's traditions from the past that weigh on the present. But Katongole glosses over the fact that these habits or structural elements of social life enable as well as constrain actors making their history. It is this agency and the differences in circumstances brought about by colonialism that explains the contingency of African history.

Disappointingly, the initiatives he highlights as alternative politics can be understood in analogy to field hospitals taking care of war casualties. What is needed however is the transformation of the source of the negative experience, which necessitates a transformative engagement with the nation-state.

---

[10] Katongole, *The Sacrifice of Africa*, 25.
[11] Ibid., 87–101.
[12] Karl Marx, "The 18th Brumaire of Louis Bonaparte, 1852," https://www.marxists.org/archive/marx/works/1852/18th-brumaire/ch01.htm (accessed February 9, 2020).
[13] Katongole, *A Future for Africa*, xiv.

The Inadequacy of Katongole's Theological Scheme

In addition to the inadequacy of Katongole's social analysis, his choice of theological scheme leaves much to be desired. He proposes a kenotic vision to excuse God from the tragedies in Africa and to make room for Africans to exercise transformative agency. According to him,

> The notion of a vulnerable/hidden/crucified God needs to play a far more central role in African theological exploration than it has played until now. That it hasn't can be attributed to a number of things, but one suspects that the traditional African religious cosmology makes the idea of a "weak" or "suffering" god impossible to grasp. Within a traditional understanding, Africans do not expect a god to be just another "one of us." They expect their god to be bigger, stronger, more powerful, and more enduring than humans.[14]

Even though he understands this, Katongole goes ahead to recommend this kenotic vision. This makes his approach worse than that of the early missionaries. For someone who has criticized the colonial mentality to display similar insensitivity to the African vision of the world is incomprehensible.

The point being made is not that African traditional vision of the world must be preserved at all cost. It is that Katongole's manner of engagement with the African religious tradition is dismissive rather than constructive. A more constructive approach entails engaging the tradition, retrieving helpful elements therein, and reimagining it in the light of the retrieved elements. This ensures continuity in discontinuity. Another point is that Katongole is not sensitive to the transformation that African traditional religious cosmology has undergone. He misinterprets the traditional vision because he equates what is translated as god in traditional African cosmology with God in Christianity.[15] But Elochukwu Uzukwu has amply shown that what is translated in literature as gods in African traditional religion corresponds to a multiplicity of spirit beings who are in a complex relationship with the One God. These spirit beings are vicegerents of the one God.[16] Thus the one God in African traditional religious cosmology is not directly involved in running the affairs of the world. Even then, the vicegerents are not defined by sovereign power as Katongole claims. According to him, in traditional Africa, it is expected that "their god to be bigger, stronger, more powerful, and more enduring than humans." This assertion is immediately deconstructed by Katongole's reference to Chinua Achebe's account of how the people of Aninta "who when their god failed them, carried him to the boundary between their village and their neighbor's village and set him on fire."[17] This does not show a vision

---

[14] Katongole, *Born from Lament*, 120. This reminds me of a popular song in Nigeria, "I have a very big God who is always by my side, a very big God by my side by my side."

[15] Raymond C. Arazu, *Our Religion—Past and Present* (Awka: Spiritan Centre for Self Realization, 2005), 10.

[16] Elochukwu Eugene Uzukwu, *God, Spirit, and Human Wholeness: Appropriating Faith and Culture in West African Style* (Eugene, OR: Pickwick, 2012), 50.

[17] Katongole, *Born of a Lament*, 120.

of spirit beings sovereignly more powerful and more enduring than humans. Rather it shows a relationship of mutual obligation between human and this class of spirit beings. Contact with Christianity, however, brought the one God to the center stage and assimilated the spirit beings into the horde of demons opposed to God. This is the basis of the warfare scheme that has become dominant in popular Christianity.

Katongole's kenotic scheme forms the basis for his call for new stories to forge a new social imagination for a new Africa. The approach I am sketching seeks to discern the theology implicit in the operative social imagination in contemporary Africa and cross-match it to the scheme in popular religiosity. This social imagination invests money with salvific value, and our aim is to foster new practices that are more conducive to solidary love, care, compassion, and commitment to the integral well-being of all.

Ransomed by Money: Mapping the Social Imagination in Postcolonial Africa

The social imagination is composed of many elements. The task in this section is to highlight the prevalent one.

The kidnap and release of the two priests from my diocese narrated earlier brought home to me the "salvific" value of money and its pervasiveness. Money is used here as a synecdoche, a placeholder for whatever can be exchanged for the achievement of a purpose. In this sense, it includes any resource that can be drawn upon or thrown around in order to get one's desired result. Such resources include financial capital, social capital, sociopolitical clout, physical endowment, and so on. Mobilization of such resources secured the release of my colleagues from the kidnappers. Those who can access and activate such resources leverage them to escape many constraints while making life miserable for others less able to do so.

An incident, in which I became a victim, brought to my attention how the vision of the salvific value of money links up the individual, the society, and the institutions of state in postcolonial Africa. Many people from southeastern Nigeria travel back to their villages of origin during the Christmas season, and the number of vehicles on the road at this time increases astronomically. A long queue usually develops before the traffic light turns from red to green. We were in such a queue waiting for the light to turn green when a police vehicle escorting an SUV with tinted glass sped past. At the intersection, a policeman jumped out of the police vehicle and stopped oncoming vehicles already given right of way by the traffic light. Immediately, the SUV drove through the intersection. The policeman jumped back into the police vehicle and they sped off. Meanwhile, other vehicles had joined the convoy and were taking advantage of the disruption of the order established by the traffic light to drive through the intersection when they should not have. As this went on, the drivers that had been given the right of way by the traffic light sought to reclaim their right. They inched their way forward to block the interlopers. Then, the inevitable happened. One of the interloping buses ran into another. All hell broke loose. The intersection was blocked followed by a total breakdown of law and order. The traffic light was completely ignored.

Every driver became a law unto himself or herself, seeking to escape the confusion as a siren-blaring convoy of vehicles arrived. In the end, it took me two hours to get beyond this intersection.

To imagine the scope of chaos, confusion, and pollution occasioned by the action of one police officer performing from a script normalized in Nigeria makes it even more frustrating. It is reported that 80 percent of Nigerian police officers are engaged in the provision of security for "prominent people"[18] and indeed for anyone rich enough to pay for their services. People reason that it is cheaper to pay for this service than risk being kidnapped, with the attendant trauma. This is the meaning of this chapter's title, "ransomed by money." Wealth is deployed by many in Nigeria to smoothen as far as possible the everyday challenges faced by them. Agents of the state undermine other institutions of the state to achieve this. The police officer used the authority conferred on him by his uniform to undermine the authority of the traffic light. Such personalization of the apparatuses of state is a daily occurrence, celebrated rather than repudiated by such popular figures as the late Nigerian highlife music maestro Oliver Akanite, aka Oliver de Coque, who claimed that some people "own" the community and by extension the society—*a na-enwe obodo enwe*.[19]

Michel de Certeau's distinction between strategy and tactics brings another element in the social imagination to view. For de Certeau, strategy is the modality of action of the powerful who are able to produce, tabulate, and impose on the space their rule, while tactics is the modality of action of the weak who are only able to subvert and manipulate a situation to their advantage.[20] In the event narrated, however, one also sees the deployment of tactics. If the action of the policeman and whoever he was escorting was to be an isolated case, the disruption would have been a glitch that would have been easily resolved. But other commuters took advantage of the disruption thereby endorsing the (dis)value that informed the action of the police officer and his patron. This (dis)value is opportunism—taking advantage of every situation to maximize one's personal good, even at the expense of others and the society at large. The patron of the policeman took advantage of his wealth to "buy" the (dis)service of the policeman, who in turn used the power conferred on him by the state to subvert the principle of order regulated by the traffic light. The motorists, who joined their convoy, also took advantage of the disruption to shorten their wait for the traffic light to turn green. The motorists, whose right of way had been usurped, tried to reclaim their right because they know that life is about fending off opportunists. The total breakdown of order and the deepening of peoples' suffering at that intersection intensified the crisis of assurance that one's life and convenience can be secured by the agencies entrusted with that.

---

[18] As Rasheed Akintunde, the assistant inspector general of police (AIG), zone 5, is reported to have said on February 18, 2018. https://www.premiumtimesng.com/news/more-news/258024-80-of-nigerian-police-officers-provide-personal-security-for-prominent-people-aig-laments.html (accessed December 22, 2019).

[19] For an engagement of this vision, see Lawrence N. Nwankwo, "'A na-enwe obodo enwe?'—A Socio-theological Reflection on a Track in Oliver de Coque's Album," *Ministerium: Journal of Contextual Theology* 2, no. 1 (2016): 26–40.

[20] Michel de Certeau, *The Practice of Everyday Life*, originally published as *Arts de faire*, trans. Steven Rendall (Berkeley: University of California Press, 1984, 1988), 29–31.

Opportunism and the effort to escape the reach of the constraints of the society are the cause as well as the effect of social disorder. Social disorder makes all kinds of violence legitimate. It leaves the individual, both the highly and the lowly placed, at the mercy of arbitrary and predatory forces. It cheapens life and makes it precarious as various people deploy violence, extortion, and exploitation to subjugate the society and establish themselves as the strong men and women. What is described is the outcome of a system in which individuals struggle to "save" themselves. This, as the Psalmist (49/48:7) can be interpreted to say, is an exercise in futility: "no one can ever redeem himself or pay his own ransom to God, the price for himself is too high."

In contrast, order in society requires the emergence of a system of organization that stands above the individuals to ensure justice and fairness for all irrespective of social standing. This is what in the contemporary context, the nation-state, theorized as based on a social contract,[21] is supposed to do. It becomes clear therefore that the problem of order in Africa is related to the failure of the state to be the supra-individual structure that plans and regulates life for the good of all. This is because of what, following Jean-François Bayart, has been termed the reciprocal assimilation of the state and society. Thus, instead of the state and its institutions holding society accountable in line with accepted principles, the apparatus and institutions of the state are appropriated and manipulated by individuals for personal benefit.[22] In these areas, African nation-states have underperformed due to a combination of the enormity of the challenges and bad leadership.

The Nation-State in Africa: Challenge of Leadership

In agreement with Katongole, we recognize that the nation-state is key to addressing the quest for wholeness of life in the African context. With him too, one recognizes the colonial origin of the state. However, it has to be noted that many exogenous elements have been indigenized. Cassava, a root crop that has become staple food in some parts of Africa, for example, is not indigenous to the continent.[23]

Africa has produced great empires.[24] So, there have been social and political systems of a grand scale in the continent. However, the colonial state was in the service of the capitalist economic system that was industrializing. The trans-Atlantic slave trade flourished to provide labor for colonial plantations. Manpower was in short supply and had to be addressed. Industrialization replaced manpower with machine power.

---

[21] Dennis H. Wrong, *The Problem of Order: What Unites and Divides Society* (Cambridge, MA: Harvard University Press, 1994), 9.
[22] See Lawrence N. Nwankwo, "Corruption, the State and Social Stability in Nigeria," *Unizik Journal of Arts and Humanities* 14, no. 3 (2013): 45–64.
[23] A saying among the Igbo can be understood as documenting this history. *Akpu biara igbo ogu di n'etiti ji na ede, wee bute onu mme.* Literally, it means that the cassava came to stop the fight between yam and cocoyam and got bloodied lips. This is a way of indicating that once introduced, cassava displaced yam and cocoyam as the staple food.
[24] Cheikh Anta Diop, *Precolonial Black Africa: A Comparative Study of the Political and Social Systems of Europe and Black Africa from Antiquity to the Formation of Modern State*, originally published as *L'Afrique Noire précoloniale*, trans. Harold J. Salemson (Westport, CT: Lawrence Hill, 1987).

This created the need for a steady supply of raw materials in industrial quantities and market for finished products. At first, trading companies went about organizing these. The Royal Niger Company was granted a royal charter that authorized it to administer the Niger Delta and the areas around the Rivers Niger and Benue. The company manipulated the terms of trade to its advantage with force and subterfuge as seen in how King Jaja of Opobo was exiled. It was indeed from the company that the British bought the area that was to become Nigeria and set up the colonial administration.[25]

The economic relationship with Europe profoundly transformed the African lifeworld.[26] It introduced money and substituted locally available goods with imported ones. Gold dust or cowries, as Cheikh Anta Diop[27] has shown, were used as the medium of exchange in precolonial Africa. With the triangular trade arrangement[28] during the transatlantic slave trade, luxury items such as mirrors, canons, liquor, and so on were used as the medium of exchange. The colonial state fostered the wide use of money whose value was fixed in the metropolis in Europe. The "civilizing" mission involved changing the taste of Africans, making them consumers of industrial products from Europe. This opened up the African market leading to the substitution of locally available materials and techniques with foreign goods and services. Houses of cement, bricks, and corrugated sheets were substituted for traditional architecture made out of locally available material and with labor drawn from one's account in the labor bank. This account was built up by the help one had offered to others in the community in their construction endeavor. The new building materials and technique however were obtained through the market via monetary transaction. This made money making an imperative and gradually led to the emergence of a class of wage earners, those who exchanged their labor and competence for money. Job creation thus became a critical element in society. Yet because of the low level of industrialization in Africa, most of the goods had to be imported. With a low level of production, the challenge of growing the economy and creating jobs deepened. This was a quandary that operators of the state in Africa faced on a daily basis. Neoliberal vision had relieved the state of the duty of creating jobs and moved this onto entrepreneurs.

Identity management is another challenge that the sovereign territorial state system bequeathed to Africans. This came about through the "containerization" of identity.

---

[25] Kenneth Onwuka Dike, *Trade and Politics in Niger Delta 1830–1885: An Introduction to the Economic and Political History of Nigeria* (Oxford: Clarendon, 1956).

[26] The transatlantic slave trade went on for three centuries. The number of human cargo from Igboland shipped out across the Atlantic is put at 18,500 per annum. This lasted for three centuries, probably with ebbs and flows in the trade. One can only say that the total number who suffered this ordeal is staggering. This trade also brought about widespread insecurity. There were slave hunters out to seize any prey. Those caught were exchanged for as little as mirrors and bottles of liquor. Life was indeed cheapened. The spirit world was also compromised. What became known as the Long Juju of Arochukwu was used as a front for capturing and selling people into slavery. Elizabeth Isichei, *A History of the Igbo People* (London: Macmillan, 1976).

[27] Diop, *Precolonial Black Africa*, ibid., 134.

[28] Britain shipped goods to West Africa in exchange for slaves who would be shipped to West Indies in exchange for sugar, rum, and other goods that would then be shipped back to Britain. See Chibuike Rotimi Amaechi, "The Igbos in the Politics of Nigeria," Twelfth Convocation Lecture, March 24, 2018, https://unizik.edu.ng/page/12th-unizik-convocation-lecture-the-igbos-in-the-politics-of-nigeria/ (accessed December 15, 2019).

In precolonial times, empires rose and fell and areas of influence were easily redrawn. Among the Igbo, with decentralized political system, a whole community or a part of a community could migrate and settle in another area by conquest or by agreement with earlier settlers.[29] The colonial state came up with maps and territorial delimitation of communities. Thus, more challenging than the arbitrary partitioning of Africa by the European powers in terms of its continuing effect is the hardening of these boundaries. Civil wars have been fought because groups who wanted to opt out of the unions created by the colonialists have had diplomatic, military, and economic obstacles put on their way by the international community in defense of the sovereignty of the state. This does not reduce the agitation. Katongole is therefore right to speak of the fight for political spoil by the elite but wrong in spotlighting the elite when these are seen as champions and heroes, even if wrongly, by their people.

The enormous resources—allocative and authoritative—at the command of the operators of the nation-state and the intensity of their reach[30] make the capture and retention of the apparatuses of the state a worthwhile project among the constituent groups. Such struggles for power were not unknown in precolonial Africa as reported by Cheikh Anta Diop about the Songhai of the Askias.[31] In postcolonial Africa, such struggles have been heightened not only because of the outworking of some decisions taken by the colonialists but also because of events in the history of these nation-states. In Nigeria, for example, the colonialists limited the penetration of Western education into the northern part with a predominantly Muslim population. This delayed the granting of self-rule to the nationalists as the politicians from the northern part felt marginalized in the civil service and other vital institutions of the state. To assuage this fear, political leadership was ceded to the north and the population figures manipulated to give them more numerical strength. Over the years, the political system has rewarded them with more constituencies and representatives. This has created the feeling that issues of national interest could thus be trumped in order to preserve their historic advantage.

Corrupt leadership has also affected the performance of the state in Africa. Ngozi Okonjo-Iweala has shown how the oil boom in Nigeria turned her economy into a monoculture one based on oil. Interestingly, she explains the phenomenon termed "consuming foreign"—the preference for foreign goods over locally produced ones—in terms of what is called the Dutch Disease.[32] This provides an alternative to the

---

[29] It is documented that the founder of Ndiowu, my community of origin, migrated from Aro and settled first at Omogho, then at Ndikelionwu, before settling among the Mgbom people in the present location. See Okeke B. Ndukuba, *The Story of Ndiowu* (Lagos: Purity Ventures, 2012), 27.

[30] Anthony Giddens, *The Nation-State and Violence, Volume Two of a Contemporary Critique of Historical Materialism* (Cambridge, UK: Polity, 1985), 7–13.

[31] Diop, *Precolonial Black Africa*, 50–8.

[32] See this passage from Ngozi Okonjo-Iweala, *Reforming the Unreformable: Lessons from Nigeria* (Cambridge, MA: MIT Press, 2012), 181.

> The term "Dutch Disease" refers to the repercussions to an economy of a sharp and/or sudden rise in the inflow of foreign currency, resulting from—for example—the discovery and exploration of natural resources such as oil or precious metals. The currency inflows lead to currency appreciation, making the country's other products (usually in the agriculture and manufacturing sectors) less price-competitive on the export market. As a result, productivity

explanation of the phenomenon as evidence of mental colonization. Some bad leaders have also abused the enormous powers and resources of the state. In the five years of General Sani Abacha's rule, Ngozi Okonjo-Iweala reports "an estimated US$3 billion to US$5 billion of Nigeria's public assets were looted and sent abroad by Abacha, his family and their associates."[33] Okonjo-Iweala comments that at the upper end of the range, the amount stolen is larger than the 2006 education and health federal budgets combined. What is frightening about this phenomenon is not simply the critical sectors of the economy and of society being denied funds, but also the ripple effect of such ill-gotten wealth on the polity. The predictable move by such beneficiaries of ill-gotten wealth is to enter into politics or become godfathers to some politicians. This is to protect themselves and extend their influence. It muddies the water all the more. Notwithstanding the critical importance of statecraft, this is handed over to those with less competence and less loyalty to the aspirations of the people. Paradoxically, these are often adopted by their community as champions not because members of the community are confident that they will work for the good of all but because they are seen as the community's best chance of having their own (wo)man close to or actually in charge of the state resources. Whatever crumbs may fall from their table, they reason, will somehow get to their community.

All Hope Is Not Lost: An Interlude

The picture painted in the earlier sections is gloomy. But there have been bright stars lightening up the gloom and bringing about some shifts. One such star is Mr. Peter Obi, governor of Anambra State from 2006 to 2014. The courts declared him winner in 2006 of an election conducted in 2003. Despite other travails, he won a second term in office. The contribution of Mr. Peter Obi is not limited to his landmark victories in court, significant though these are. It is rather what he has brought to governance. He came to office with a vision to transform the state for the better. He cut down the cost of governance by his simple lifestyle and used the money saved and others for the provision of critical infrastructure. He brought about a mental shift by restoring confidence in governance. Under his watch, Anambra State, in which students were out of school for ten months in 2001, promptly paid teachers' salaries and renovated the schools. He demonstrated that governance is about deploying and managing the funds of the state for the good of the people, as well as contributing to the sanitization of the electoral process.

Obi's emergence was a response not only to the challenge of governance in Anambra State but also to the denominational politics between Anglicans and Catholics in the state. The rivalry between these two groups has existed since the advent of Christianity in Igboland.[34] However, unlike in other states in Igboland, this rivalry has entered

> in these other sectors declines rapidly, and their contribution to national income falls. The term was coined in 1977 by *The Economist* to describe the decline of the manufacturing sector in the Netherlands after the discovery (in 1959) and exportation of large quantities of natural gas.

[33] Ibid., 84–5.
[34] F. K. Ekechi, *Missionary Enterprise and Rivalry in Igboland, 1857–1914* (London: Cass, 1972).

politics in Anambra State. Denominational affiliation has become a feature of the local politics. This has not helped ecumenical relations and exposes the churches to manipulation by the political class by compromising church leaders and reducing the efficacy of their prophetic witness. Instead, I argue that "the politics of Jesus"[35] needs to guide the action and ministry of the churches.

Popular Religiosity as Theological Locus

There is always already a theological construct informing peoples' lives and practices. This is especially true in Africa where the intimate connection between religion and life is still strong and palpable.[36] Lived experiences impact on people's faith, their religious ideations, and practices. This can make them grow in their openness and commitment to a theological vision. Thus, it behooves academic theology to take seriously the faith as understood and lived out by the people. In this way, the theologian fulfills his or her role as a member of God's family in a particular location listening and responding to the Word that continues to speak in the life situation of the community. This is why it is important to pay attention to popular religiosity[37] as a *locus theologicus*.

Popular religiosity does not imply a hierarchy or an evaluation as regards what is more authentically Christian. The extensive and intensive reach of modern means of advertising and communication implies that the ideas that are popularized sometimes depend on the power differential with regard to access to and control of the media outlets. The theologian has therefore to be discerning, as with everything else, in his or her engagement with popular religiosity. This is because what is popularized may resonate with elements of the endogenous culture, which in the changed context of life may no longer be very helpful. Attention to popular religiosity ensures the contextuality of one's theologizing. Popular religiosity puts one in touch with the aspirations and the operative universe of meaning in one's community. Without denying that the natural world has its laws, a religious dimension permeates all facets of African life, and it is drawn upon for making sense of the experience of the everyday world. The theologian

---

[35] Lawrence N. Nwankwo, *The Politics of Jesus: Towards Building on the "Successes" of the Involvement of the Awka Diocsan Presbyterium in Party Politics in Anambra State* (Awka: Fab Anieh, 2015).
[36] Malidoma Patrice Somé writes that "nothing happens here [physical world] that did not begin in that unseen world." Malidoma Patrice Somé, *The Healing Wisdom of Africa* (New York: Penguin Putnam, 1998), 23. See also Diop, *Precolonial Black Africa*, 60. This is the context for understanding Chinwoke Mbadinuju, the former governor of Anambra State, who includes as part of his achievement while in office the fact that "I started prayers every Monday morning in all government establishments, I used to go to the Onitsha Market and town halls to conduct prayers and God kept answering the prayers and performing miracles." Sarah Adoyo, "Mbadinuju: I Was Forced to Pay Godfather N10 Million Monthly as Anambra Governor," https://www.legit.ng/54814.html (accessed December 14, 2019).
[37] This refers to a set or sets of ideas, images, and practices that are common or widespread in the people's understanding of themselves in relation to the divine. Popular religiosity is distinguished but not separated from traditional forms of Christianity, that is, Christianity propagated in the mainline churches with their regulatory bodies.

From the African Initiatives in Christianity to Prosperity Theology

Pentecostalism in the form of prosperity theology is the most popular form of religiosity in Africa, spreading in leaps and bounds. Although Pentecostalism is a global phenomenon with a transnational flow of images and meanings, its manifestation in Africa can be read as the reception of Christianity into the categories of the African traditional religion. This started with the emergence of the African Initiatives in Christianity (AICs), called at various times African Independent Churches, African Indigenous Christianity, and African Initiatives in Christianity. These groups separated from the mainline churches and incorporated elements of the traditional religious vision into Christianity. Being Africans, they did their best to build bridges between the traditional and the Christian worldviews.[38]

Popular faith experience, as will soon become clear, provides people with a scheme for making sense of and responding to their situation. There are, however, forms of African popular religiosity that in my view are inadequate. For example, it is believed that, through manipulations in the spirit world, people could cause cars to crash, people to fall sick, women's wombs to be tied making them incapable of conceiving and bearing children, people's destinies to be blocked and their progress stalled, and so on. All these negative experiences are therefore externalized to the world of spirits and consequently abstracted from the socioeconomic, cultural, and political processes. This line of conceptualization also implies that the search for remedy bypasses the socioeconomic, cultural, and political processes. The challenge for the theologian is to "dismantle" the "edifice" of popular religiosity by understanding more deeply the planks or bricks and how these are being put together in order to clearly select what materials are to be reused in a new edifice.

A profitable way to go about prying loose the building blocks of popular religiosity is to see popular religiosity as the outcome of a reception of elements of Christianity into the traditional religious categories in a transformed African context. This transformation came about, as we have seen earlier, through the introduction of the nation-state and by plugging African societies into the World Order, with new social, economic, financial, and diplomatic components.

As seen earlier, the conceptualization of negative experiences in terms of the interference of spirit forces can be traced to the traditional religious conception. Contact with Christianity and the resulting changes in the lifeworld of the Africans brought about new challenges and closed off some traditional lines of response. For example, urbanization brought about changes in human settlement, and other

---

[38] See Matthew A. Ojo, "Historical Overview of Christianity in Nigeria," in *Na God: Aesthetics of African Charismatic Power*, photography by Andrew Esiebo, ed. Annalisa Buttici (Padova: Dipartimento di Filosofia, Sociologia, Pedgogia e Psicologia Applicata, 2013), 13–14.

lifestyle changes have resulted in new health challenges, which cannot be effectively addressed by traditional medical practice and are heightened due to poor healthcare delivery. Poor road and vehicular maintenance as well as reckless driving have increased the number of those killed or maimed on the roads. This has resulted in the reduction both of life-expectancy and of the quality of life. Other examples are unemployment and underemployment. These had been unknown in the traditional economic system. Presently, this is the fate, especially of many young people. Those who profess Christianity, choose from the different interpretive strands in Christianity. In the mainline churches, people are encouraged to see events as the unfolding of the will of God. Negative experiences are seen as meant for their training, and they are encouraged to unite their suffering with that of Jesus Christ on the cross. In prosperity theology, what is recognized is God's will to bless God's people. This amounts to a view that it is never God's will for believers to suffer. This is closer to the African traditional cosmology although transformed.

African traditional cosmology has no place for the will of God and no narrative of a fall.[39] God is not directly involved in the day-to-day running of the world having entrusted to the deities and spirit forces various departments of life to oversee. It is expected that people live in abundance, a fulfilled life characterized among others by health, wealth, fertility, and longevity. The absence of any of these signals a break in the cosmic harmony occasioned by oneself or by one's forebears. This is why Herman Beseah Browne, the Liberian theologian, advances the victim as culprit thesis as what captures the traditional African response to negative experience.[40] The victim or sufferer of the negative experience is implicated as culprit in the genesis of his or her problems. That is why the first response of the Igbo of southeastern Nigeria in the face of negative experience is to protest his or her innocence—*aka m dikwa ocha*. But because the person is not understood simply as an individual but as a nodal point in a vast network extending into the past, the sufferer may be expiating for infringements of the cosmic order by his or her forebears. Recourse is made to diviners for information on the infringement and the sacrifices that are to be performed to appease the offended deity, spirit force, or ancestor and restore the precarious cosmic balance that guarantees protection, safety, and flourishing.

Contact with Christianity put in motion the effort to bring the one God into the center of the African universe. This displaced and demonized the deities and spirit forces, made the African world more insecure, and legitimized the vision of spiritual warfare. Instead of the restoration of cosmic equilibrium through appeasement of the offended spirit, such spirits are driven out by the power of the Holy Spirit. Access to this Holy Spirit and its powers is being projected as the new resource for stepping beyond the constraints of life conceptualized as due to the interference of evil spirits.

---

[39] Uzukwu notes an exception with the Dogon of Mali in whose creation myth something analogous to the Fall is seen. An error led to the abandonment of the first creation. See Uzukwu, *God, Spirit, and Human Wholeness*, 64–5.
[40] Herman Beseah Browne, *Theological Anthropology: A Dialectical Study of the African and Liberation Traditions* (London: Avon Books, 1996).

"Ransomed by Money," "Ransomed for Money"

Ransom refers to what is paid to secure someone's freedom and, by extension, abundance of life. Its use as a soteriological metaphor goes back to the Scriptures where, with other metaphors like redemption, it presents the event of Jesus's life, especially his death and resurrection, as an exchange that effected a definitive transformation of humanity's/creation's relationship with God. St. Paul writes that "Christ ... offered himself a ransom for all" (1 Tim. 2:5). In 1 Pet. 1:18-19, the ransom is said to be paid not in anything perishable but in the precious blood of Christ. Questions were raised whether the ransom was paid to God or to the devil. Gregory of Nazianzus denied the payment of any ransom while SS. Gregory of Nyssa and Augustine argued that the ransom in the blood of Jesus was the means through which Jesus became victorious over the devil.[41]

Ransom was paid to free slaves and the kidnapped. This exchange of resource for human freedom and well-being opened up a vista into the social imagination that functions even in the popular religiosity. The genius of prosperity theology is that it lodges prosperity, abundant life, and human well-being and flourishing at the heart of its soteriological vision. This is worked out with reference to the Deuteronomistic theology of history summed up in Deuteronomy 28.[42] Here, prosperity and blessedness articulated in the context of an agrarian community facing the threat of invasion by more militarily powerful neighbors is made to depend on the covenant faithfulness of the Israelites. Covenant infidelity results in the opposite state of affairs—being accursed and exploited and plundered by others. The evidence of blessedness in Deuteronomy is transposed onto the combined registers of the traditional African vision of abundance—health, wealth, fertility, and longevity—and that of the neoliberal consumerist culture—conspicuous consumption.[43] Conversely, negative experiences are accounted for as consequences of covenant infidelity, which leaves one open to attack by evil forces.

Being born again, that is, accepting Jesus as one's personal lord and savior, is presented as the gateway to covenant blessedness and *theosis*. It brings about a radical reconfiguration of one's identity and entrance into a new affective community. This community is defined over and against others that one had hitherto belonged to. Being born again implies a translation from these communities into the new one. It also involves a transformation of the self.

Thus, David Oyedepo writes, "I want you to know that the prosperity God has planned for you has nothing to do with your profession, your career or your family background ... Your covenant alignment is the issue."[44] This covenant alignment or

---

[41] See Stephen Finlan, *Problems with Atonement: The Origins of, and Controversy about, the Atonement Doctrine* (Collegeville, MN: Liturgical Press, 2005), 67–72.

[42] Lawrence N. Nwankwo, "'Cursed Is Anyone Who Hangs on a Tree' (Deut. 21:23): The Hermeneutics of the Prosperity Message in the Nigerian Context," in *Mentoring Grace: Exploring the Confluence of the Arts and Humanities*, ed. Alaribe Gilbert and Okwuosa Lawrence (Owerri: Divine Favor, 2018), 203–13.

[43] Lawrence N. Nwankwo, "African Christianity and the Challenge of Prosperity Gospel," *Ministerium: Journal of Contextual Theology* 5 (2019): 11–27.

[44] David Oyedepo, *Understanding Financial Prosperity* (Lagos: Dominion, 1997), 11–12.

realignment, as the case may be, comes through being born again. It not only grafts one into a new community of believers, guarantees access to covenant blessings spelt out in Deuteronomy 28, but also enables one to become "rooted in the supernatural" with the attendant discovery that one is "a spirit after the order of God."[45] According to Oyedepo, sons of God "can operate like God," with the ability "to exercise total dominion over all issues of life, bringing deliverance to many. They will think, talk, and live in the realm of dominion where, all things shall be possible with them. They will have it, the way they want it, according to the word of God."[46] More succinctly, Oyedepo claims that "the cardinal mark of sonship is power, power to reign, power to exercise authority. … Understanding your sonship power, rights and privileges is the master key to freedom and a life of fulfilment. That is what puts you over and puts the enemy on the run."[47] Pastor Chris Oyakhilome, another prosperity preacher, asserts that if someone dying of cancer were only to touch a born-again Christian, he or she would be healed because of the tremendous power in such Christians.[48]

The theological vision of the prosperity preachers makes one ask, tongue in cheek, why they have not used their power to empty the hospitals of the patients. In defense, however, it has to be noted that Jesus did not solve all the problems of his time; neither was he spared of all challenges and constraints nor did he deploy his miraculous powers to his advantage. Concretely, Jesus lived out the eschatological proviso—the kingdom has come. But its fullness will be at the eschaton. Prosperity theology works with realized eschatology but to the advantage of a few powerful leaders. This notwithstanding, the fact that such preachers attract followings from all strata of society is indicative that their theological vision resonates with something in the culture. In my view, it resonates with the felt need to live above the constraints of African society; the need to be sovereign, be "winners,"[49] and have "dominion"[50] over all life's challenges. As seen earlier, money in the sense of the first formulation ensures such freedom. Money is, however, unevenly distributed. This uneven distribution and the inequality that arises therefrom is what prosperity preachers seek to do away with by equalizing access to opportunity. One only needs to be born again. This is within the reach of everyone. However, this equality of access is only in theory because the inequality within the group is sometimes scandalous. The preachers consume conspicuously as evidence of divine blessing. The successful ones among them own private jets and fleets of exotic cars. Many of their followers, however, who "sow seed" (contribute money) in the hope of their own upward social mobility, remain at the lower rungs of the social ladder. In sum, prosperity theology places human earthly fulfillment at the heart of soteriology. By repristinating the inequality in the society and recommending an exclusive reliance on miraculous powers for the solution of

---

[45] David Oyedepo, *Releasing the Supernatural: An Adventure into the Spirit World* (Lagos: Dominion, 1993), xi.
[46] Ibid., 45.
[47] Ibid., 48.
[48] Chris Oyakhilome, "The Christian Cannot Have Cancer," https://www.youtube.com/watch?v=tiMq990TlIo (accessed September 19, 2019).
[49] This is the sobriquet of Living Faith Church Worldwide, one of the leading megachurches, founded by Bishop David Oyedepo in 1983.
[50] Dominion City Church is the name of a Pentecostal group founded by Pastor David Ogbueli.

society's problems, prosperity theology shows itself incapable of making good its promise of an indigenous theological synthesis for ensuring abundance of life for all or, at least, for the "born again." This is irrespective of the caritative activities of some of the prosperity preachers. Paying attention to the involvement of the Holy Spirit helps in redirecting this vision.

Building Temples of the Holy Spirit

One piece of block or brick to be salvaged from the edifice of prosperity theology is its reconstitution of the subject. Being born again is seen as a momentous event that puts one in touch with the divine. Faced with existential insecurity from the spirit world and precariousness in society, this vision is powerful. Prosperity theology, however, overreaches itself by ascribing to the born again the qualities of divinity. This brings it closer to the New Age spirituality. This excess can be curbed while retaining the gem of its insight through the notion of the indwelling of the Holy Spirit. Through baptism, Christians are indwelt by the Holy Spirit such that they become temples of the Holy Spirit. This demands that they treat themselves as well as others with respect as they fan into flames the gift they have received.

The vision that people are temples of the Holy Spirit provides a basis for overcoming individualism. All who have received the Spirit are sons and daughters of God (Rom. 8:14) and thus brothers and sisters in the Lord. The challenge is for all Christians and all ecclesial communities to become signs and instruments of God's love and unity of humanity.

An emphasis on the indwelling of the Spirit has direct implication for the mainline churches and indeed for all Christians. Presently, churches and ecclesial communities see themselves primarily as institutions competing against each other for membership. This does not make for ecumenical understanding. Building temples of the Holy Spirit can provide an overarching vision for the ministries of the churches and ecclesial bodies. This will hopefully soften the denominational rivalry and focus attention primarily on bringing Christians into contact with the mystery of God who is Emmanuel, who abides with us in the power of the Holy Spirit. Above all, it will focus attention again on evangelization, bringing people to an acknowledgment of the love of God made manifest in Jesus Christ in the power of the Holy Spirit rather than what seems to be the present situation of teaching dry doctrines to those who have not yet had an encounter with the living God.

The emphasis on the indwelling of the Holy Spirit and on building the temple of the Holy Spirit is liable to being hijacked by the residual idea from popular religiosity that presents the world as a battlefield between good and evil forces. The Holy Spirit is then seen as a form of weapon, a divine missile ready to be launched by Christians in prayer by the shout "Holy Ghost Fire!!!" As already seen, the warfare view abstracts from personal and structural factors that diminish life and project these onto the cosmic stage as enemies to be feared and shot down with the Holy Ghost missile. The vision of the indwelling of the Holy Spirit honors while engaging this vision. The Holy Spirit provides a mantle of protection. It is the fire of God's love directed against anything that enslaves and diminishes life in oneself and in others—guilt, shame, resentment, greed, hate, and other cultural frames of understanding that diminish life for oneself and others. The indwelling Spirit is God's empowering presence, a helper toward self-purification of mind, heart, and body to be able to see, love, and act toward others as God, who is love, does.

Finally, there is need to extend the temple imagery. In the second book of Samuel (7:1-2) one reads of King David's desire to build a temple to God. This was realized by King Solomon and the prayer of dedication of the first temple in Jerusalem underscored the spiritual value placed on temple building. St. Paul extends the imagery of a temple and applies it to the human being. He speaks of the human being as a temple of the Holy Spirit (1 Cor. 3:16). Churches spend enormous energy and resources to erect temples in concrete and steel. But the human temples whom these concrete edifices are meant to serve are drained of life and hope on a daily basis. Would that these churches and ecclesial bodies use the enormous resources they can mobilize to provide quality and affordable primary and secondary education in order to raise a new generation of Africans to run the institutions of society so that they can be focused on fostering and sustaining abundant life for one and for all. This is the way to move from being societies where people are ransomed by money to societies where Jesus ransomed all for abundant and fulfilled life and where all share in the task of fostering integral life, human flourishing, and well-being of one and of all.

Bibliography

Adoyo, Sarah. "Mbadinuju: I Was Forced to Pay Godfather N10 Million Monthly as Anambra Governor." https://www.legit.ng/54814.html (accessed December 14, 2019).

Agency Report. "80% of Nigeria Police Officers Provide Private Security for 'Prominent People.'" *Premium Times*, February 18, 2018. https://www.premiumtimesng.com/news/more-news/258024-80-of-nigerian-police-officers-provide-personal-security-for-prominent-people-aig-laments.html (accessed on December 22, 2019).

Amaechi, Chibuike, Rotimi. "The Igbos in the Politics of Nigeria." 12th Convocation Lecture, March 24, 2018. https://unizik.edu.ng/page/12th-unizik-convocation-lecture-the-igbos-in-the-politics-of-nigeria/ (accessed December 15, 2019).

Arazu, Raymond C. *Our Religion—Past and Present*. Awka: Spiritan Centre for Self Realization, 2005.

Bayart, Jean-François. *The State in Africa: The Politics of the Belly*. Translated by Elizabeth Harrison. London: Longman, 1993.

Browne, Herman Beseah. *Theological Anthropology: A Dialectical Study of the African and Liberation Traditions*. London: Avon Books, 1996.

de Certeau, Michel. *The Practice of Everyday Life*. Originally published as *Arts de faire*, translated by Steven Rendall. Berkeley: University of California Press, 1984, 1988.

Dike, Kenneth, Onwuka. *Trade and Politics in Niger Delta 1830–1885: An Introduction to the Economic and Political History of Nigeria*. Oxford: Clarendon, 1956.

Diop, Cheikh Anta. *Precolonial Black Africa: A Comparative Study of the Political and Social Systems of Europe and Black Africa from Antiquity to the Formation of Modern

State. Originally published as *L'Afrique Noire précoloniale*, translated by Harold J. Salemson. Westport, CT: Lawrence Hill, 1987.

Ekechi, F. K. *Missionary Enterprise and Rivalry in Igboland, 1857–1914*. London: Cass, 1972.

Finlan, Stephen. *Problems with Atonement: The Origins of, and Controversy about, the Atonement Doctrine*. Collegeville, MN: Liturgical Press, 2005.

Gathogo, Julius. "Genesis, Methodologies and Concerns of African Reconstruction Theology." *Theologia Viatorum, Journal of Religion and Theology in Africa* 32:1 (2008): 23–62.

Giddens, Anthony. *The Nation-State and Violence, Volume Two of a Contemporary Critique of Historical Materialism*. Cambridge, UK: Polity, 1985.

Igwe, Stanley Chinedu. *How Africa Underdeveloped Africa*. Port Harcourt: Professional Printers & Publishers, 2010.

Isichei, Elizabeth. *A History of the Igbo People*. London: Macmillan, 1976.

Katongole, Emmanuel. *Born from Lament: The Theology and Politics of Hope in Africa*. Grand Rapids, MI: William Eerdmans, 2017.

Katongole, Emmanuel. *A Future for Africa: Critical Essays in Christian Social Imagination*. Eugene, OR: Wipf & Stock, 2017.

Katongole, Emmanuel. *The Sacrifice of Africa: A Political Theology for Africa*. Grand Rapids, MI: William Eerdmans, 2011.

Marx, Karl. "The 18th Brumaire of Louis Bonaparte, 1852." https://www.marxists.org/archive/marx/works/1852/18th-brumaire/ch01.htm (accessed on February 9, 2020).

Nwankwo, Lawrence N. "'A na-enwe obodo enwe?'—A Socio-theological Reflection on a Track in Oliver de Coque's Album." *Ministerium: Journal of Contextual Theology* 2:1 (2016): 26–40.

Nwankwo, Lawrence N. "African Christianity and the Challenge of Prosperity Gospel." *Ministerium: Journal of Contextual Theology* 5 (2019): 11–27.

Nwankwo, Lawrence N. "Corruption, the State and Social Stability in Nigeria." *Unizik Journal of Arts and Humanities* 14:3 (2013): 45–64.

Nwankwo, Lawrence N. "'Cursed Is Anyone Who Hangs on a Tree' (Deut. 21:23): The Hermeneutics of the Prosperity Message in the Nigerian Context." In *Mentoring Grace: Exploring the Confluence of the Arts and Humanities*, edited by Alaribe Gilbert and Okwuosa Lawrence, 203–13. Owerri: Divine Favor, 2018.

Nwankwo, Lawrence N. *The Politics of Jesus: Towards Building on the "Successes" of the Involvement of the Awka Diocsan Presbyterium in Party Politics in Anambra State*. Awka: Fab Anieh, 2015.

Ojo, Matthew A. "Historical Overview of Christianity in Nigeria." In *Na God: Aesthetics of African Charismatic Power*, photography by Andrew Esiebo, edited Annalisa Buttici, 13–15. Padova: Dipartmento di Filosofia, Sociologia, Pedgogia e Psicologia Applicata, 2013.

Okeke, Ndukuba B. *The Story of Ndiowu*. Lagos: Purity Ventures, 2012.

Okonjo-Iweala, Ngozi. *Reforming the Unreformable: Lessons from Nigeria*. Cambridge, MA: MIT Press, 2012.

Oyakhilome, Chris. "The Christian Cannot Have Cancer." https://www.youtube.com/watch?v=tiMq 990TlIo (accessed September 19, 2019).

Oyedepo, David. *Releasing the Supernatural: An Adventure into the Spirit World*. Lagos: Dominion, 1993.

Oyedepo, David. *Understanding Financial Prosperity*. Lagos: Dominion, 1997.

Somé, Malidoma Patrice. *The Healing Wisdom of Africa*. New York: Penguin Putnam, 1998.

Uzukwu, Elochukwu Eugene. *God, Spirit, and Human Wholeness: Appropriating Faith and Culture in West African Style*. Eugene, OR: Pickwick, 2012.

Wrong, Dennis H. *The Problem of Order: What Unites and Divides Society*. Cambridge, MA: Harvard University Press, 1994.

Zenith Staff. "Two Nigerian Priests Kidnapped on December 6 Released." https://zenit.org/articles/two-nigerian-priests-kidnapped-on-december-6-released/ (accessed December 15, 2019).

10

The Evidence of Ghosts: Constructive Theology as Apologetic Theology in the Making

Judith Gruber

Searching for a Methodological Framework after the Loss of Theological Self-Evidence

In his review of Katherine Sonderegger's *Systematic Theology, Vol. 1*,[1] Brad East starts off with a short, but vivid sketch of the disciplinary history and current state of systematic theology. In just a few words, he succinctly sketches some of the major epistemological, political, and institutional changes that academic theology has been subjected to since the rise of modernity:

> Academics love stories of decline, especially about themselves. But academic theologians may love them most of all (owing, perhaps, to the lapsarian character of their own narrative). So let us begin with such a tale. Once there was systematic theology. But because of a combination of serpentine factors, each tempting theology away from the comprehensive character of its object and method—whether by the allure of liberalism, the disenchantment of modernity, the fragmentation of postmodernism, the modifiers of emancipation, the crisis of authority, or the professionalization of academe—systematic theology lost its way, fell from grace, and scattered, confused, in the Babel of the modern university. Systematic theology is no more. So, at times, the story goes.[2]

These shifts have been profoundly unsettling indeed for the (self-)understanding of theological reflection: The modern emergence of historical thinking has already called for major theological reconfigurations, whose development and reception have been a long and painful process for the churches and their theological discourses to make. And yet, with Virginia Burrus, we can argue that the resulting developmental paradigm

---

[1] Katherine Sonderegger, *Systematic Theology. Volume 1: The Doctrine of God* (Minneapolis, MA: Fortress, 2015).
[2] Brad East, "Renewing the Heart of Systematic Theology," *Marginalia: Los Angeles Review of Books*, August 1, 2016, https://marginalia.lareviewofbooks.org/renewing-heart-systematic-theology-brad-east/.

has, ultimately, not yet meant a radical departure from traditional ecclesial identity constructions and their theological imaginations. Instead, it has allowed theologians to continue to think inside "the Eusebian box"[3] by subjecting historical changes of tradition and inner-Christian polyphony to a historically modified theological paradigm of stability and coherence. Established theological imaginations of an absolute foundation and a teleological orientation of Christian tradition were thus left intact. More recently, a power-critical relecture of Christian traditions through the lens of critical cultural theories has presented a more radical challenge to established paradigms of theological reflection. It has shown that these theological orienting principles are not absolute (i.e., detached from historical contingencies) either. Instead, it has exposed them to be the effects of contingent negotiations of power/knowledge in ecclesial traditions. Drawing on Judith Butler's Foucauldian power critique, Karen King succinctly points to the profound challenges at stake. She argues that an established theological

> ordering system appears obvious and self-evident only insofar as its mechanisms conceal "the genealogy of power relations that constitute its effects." As Butler explains: "Insofar as power is successful by constituting an object domain, a field of intelligibility, as a taken-for-granted ontology, its material effects are taken as … primary givens. These material positivities appear outside discourse and power, as its incontestable referents, its transcendental signifieds. But this appearance is precisely the moment in which the power/discourse regime is most fully dissimulated and most insidiously effective. [When this material effect is taken as an epistemological point of departure, a sine qua non of some political argumentation, this is a move of … foundationalism that, in accepting this constituted effect as a primary given, successfully … masks the genealogy of power relations by which it is constituted.]"[4]

Through a power-critical lens, the established normative orienting principles of theological reflection have thus lost their self-evidence. While they might have served in the past as a supposedly absolute foundation to settle conflict over theological interpretations, we now see that they themselves are not free from contestation. On the contrary, it becomes clear that theological orienting principles create their self-evidence by concealing their contingent emergence and masking their entanglement into relations of power. Christian faith and its theological reflections find themselves robbed of an absolute foundation and teleological accounts of their history. Such a profoundly unsettling loss of self-evidence, of course, turns theology into an intellectually and politically precarious endeavor—as East has dramatically concluded: "Systematic theology [as we knew it] is no more." The efforts of twentieth-century liberal theology to demonstrate the rationality of Christian faith and its theological reflection have been deprived of their modern epistemological presuppositions and

---

[3] Virginia Burrus, "History, Theology, Orthodoxy, Polydoxy," *Modern Theology* 30, no. 3 (2014): 7.
[4] Karen King, "Nicht länger marginal. Vom Diskurs über Orthodoxie und Häresie zur Kritik der Kategorien und darüber hinaus," in *Antike christliche Apokryphen: Marginalisierte Texte des Frühen Christentums*, ed. Outi Lehtipuu and Silke Petersen (Stuttgart: Kohlhammer, 2019).

their historical-theological credibility. Instead, the risky—perhaps foolish (cf. 1 Cor. 1:23)?[5]—decision to hold on to a faith perspective regains importance as an explicit point of departure for theological reflection. Such a faith-full continuation of theology after the radical loss of the self-evidence of its orienting principles is currently being pursued in a variety of methodological approaches.

First, there are approaches that make a choice for a theological perspective over against its power critique. The passage quoted here serves for Brad East as a foil to present Katherine Sonderegger's book as an approach that heroically and unapologetically defies theology's histor(iograph)y of decline[6] and instead strives to continue directly, albeit under modern conditions, the tradition of reflecting on God as a reality that is given to us as Universal, Eternal, One. In Sonderegger's own words, her monumental tome aims to outline a contemporary theological approach that "shake[s] off its Critical slumbers" and overcomes the "wariness, born of a chastened intellect, to grand schemes that set out high truths and peer into deep seas." While she observes that waves of critique in the wake of enlightenment have triggered "methodological discussions and second or third order analyses of prolegomena" in contemporary theology, she still "believe[s] that theology must simply begin: it speaks of and before Almighty God." This is possible because the "Almighty God is One who gives Himself to be known, and is willing, in great humility, to be laid down as Object of our thought."[7] Sonderegger presents us with a theological approach that reestablishes the self-evidence of (its foundation in) God's revelation—and hence the conditions of its possibility—by way of a methodological omission of post/modern critique. The time has come for theology, she holds, to withdraw from investigations into the conditions of its possibility in view of post/modern critique and to re/turn to its proper foundation in God's revelation. Then, an overarching representation of a positive doctrine of God will, on principle, be possible again.

The contributions to this volume choose to respond differently to the theological challenges that arise from a power-critique of the Christian tradition. In contrast to Sonderegger, they do not eschew these questions "from outside" in order to develop their theological proposals. On the contrary, they seek to make the loss of self-evidence the very point of departure for their practice of theology—both the processes and the products of constructive theology are in/formed by a proactive reception of the questioning of theological evidences in the wake of modernity.[8] Accordingly, it

---

[5] Cf. M. Grau, *Refiguring Theological Hermeneutics: Hermes, Trickster, Fool* (New York: Palgrave Macmillan, 2014).
[6] Echoing reviews of Karl Barth's Commentary on Paul's Letter to the Romans as a "bombshell dropped in the playground of the theologians," East describes Sonderegger's volume as "a surprise attack on a divided battalion in retreat." East, "Renewing the Heart of Systematic Theology."
[7] Katherine Sonderegger, "An Interview with Katherine Sonderegger," http://fortresspress.com/content-wysiwyg/interview-katherine-sonderegger.
[8] Jason Wyman, for example, describes this loss of self-evidence as a foundational challenge that has motivated the collaborative publication projects of the Workgroup on Constructive Theology:

> [It] begins with the claim that doing theology today is a fundamentally different task than it has been in the past; doing theology can no longer take many of the claims and beliefs of the past "for granted." Reasons for this include Enlightenment challenges, discursive challenges, and the recognition that things that seem innate are in fact "constructed," and a critique of the normative position from which theology is to be done.

proceeds with an interdisciplinary methodology that seeks to reframe theological practice within a power-critical epistemology in order to reformulate the loci of Christian tradition such that they can speak effectively to and from the "signs of our times."

Thus, if Sonderegger withdraws from the questioning of theology through post/modern critique and returns "unapologetically"[9] to God's revelation as the proper, self-evident foundation of theological practice, then we could argue, in contrast, that constructive theologies engage in a theological project of *apologetics*. That is to say, with Paul Tillich, they perform the "art of answering"[10] and fulfill the biblical mandate to "be ready always to give an answer [απολογιαν] to every man that asketh you a reason of the hope that is in you with meekness and fear" (1 Pet. 3:15).[11] Theology as the practice of apologein, of course, has often been understood as the "defense" of a given deposit of religious truth that can be applied invariably to a range of different challenges and situations.[12] At first sight, few constructive theologians would thus describe their projects as "apologetic." In this contribution, however, I will argue that the methodological approach of constructive theology offers us resources to reconceive of apologetics not as a mere application, but as the very constitution of Christian tradition. As I hope to show, such a reconfiguration of theology as "apologetic" (1) offers an apt conceptual lens to capture the methodological cornerstones of the constructive-theological project and (2) allows to explicate the epistemo-theological presuppositions that undergird the interdisciplinary methodology with which constructive theology seeks to respond to the loss of self-evidence in the wake of power/knowledge critique. I will develop conceptual resources for building this argument by way of a constructive-theological case study that rereads New Testament narratives of cross and resurrection through the lens of postcolonial trauma studies. My goal in this interdisciplinary relecture is to sketch a soteriological imagination that is sensitive to a power-critique of theological orienting principles. Like many projects in constructive theology, it proceeds in faithful dis/continuation with theological traditions, that is, it applies a power-critical

---

Jason Wyman, "Interpreting the History of the Workgroup on Constructive Theology," *Theology Today* 73, no. 4 (2017): 321. Cf. Serene Jones and Paul Lakeland, "Introduction: Theology as Faith in Search for Understanding," in *Constructive Theology: A Contemporary Approach to Classical Themes*, ed. Serene Jones and Paul Lakeland [Nachdr.]. (Minneapolis, MN: Fortress, 2008), 1–10, 1.

[9] Cf. also Philip Ziegler, "Properly Preoccupied with God: Katherine Sonderegger's Systematic Theology Volume 1," *Pro Ecclesia* 17, no. 1 (2018): 38: "The work is stylistically unapologetic, offering no argument for its own possibility and propriety beyond that divine call to which [it] is a reasoned response." Sonderegger is also a contributor to a volume that is described by its editors as of "unapologetic dogmatics": Oliver Crisp et al., eds., *Christology, Ancient and Modern: Explorations in Constructive Dogmatics* (Grand Rapids, MI: Zondervan, 2013), 18.

[10] Paul Tillich, *Systematic Theology: Three Volumes in One* (Chicago: University of Chicago Press, 1967), vol. 3, 195. This contribution follows Tillich's argument that systematic theology can be understood as "apologetic," that is, as the "art of answering." It will do so under different epistemo-theological presuppositions and within a framework of radical hermeneutics.

[11] This is the translation according to the *King James Bible*. The *New Revised Standard Version Catholic Edition* translates απολογιαν as "make your defense."

[12] For a disciplinary history and evaluation of contemporary approaches, cf. Avery Dulles, *A History of Apologetics*, new updated and revised ed. (San Francisco, CA: Ignatius, 2005). For an analysis of postmodern adaptions, cf. Christina M. Gschwandtner, *Postmodern Apologetics? Arguments for God in Contemporary Philosophy*, 1st ed., Perspectives in Continental Philosophy (New York: Fordham University Press, 2013).

hermeneutics of suspicion to established patterns of theological interpretation in order to free them for new textures of meaning-making. While it desires to hold on to a liberative thrust of theological knowledge production, it is, as we will see, also painfully aware of the profound ambiguity that marks any production of meaning and prevents all of our interpretative endeavors from ever becoming "safe,"[13] or ultimately and unambivalently liberative. In order to accentuate these methodological choices and conceptual presuppositions, and to highlight the soteriological ramifications that they entail, I will use Johann Baptist Metz's new political theology[14] as a foil against which the methodological shifts and theological reconfigurations of a constructive theological approach can be clearly brought to the fore.

Metz's theological oeuvre has deeply influenced the development of liberation theologies,[15] and the cornerstones of his approach continue to inform the work of constructive theologians, which, too, is concerned with a re/presentation of God's presence in salvation history via a *memoria passionis* that hopes to grant justice to the victims of history.[16] For Metz, the political practice of remembering the suffering is a constitutive dimension of Christian faith, and such a consideration of the fundamental-theological status of the political also remains a formative element of contemporary constructive theological work.[17] Yet, after the entanglement of theological orienting principles into power/knowledge regimes has been exposed, Metz's dialectical constellations of suffering and healing, of memory and justice, have lost their straightforwardness and self-evidence. Donald Trump's victory in the 2016 election for the American presidency is symptomatic of the pressing need to reconsider the theological relations between a *memoria passionis* and the hope for salvation. After all, Trump's campaign was successful, also and predominantly because it succeeded in portraying him as a savior figure for those who consider themselves victims of the complex economic, demographic, and political situation in the contemporary United States.[18] He ran with the promise to give a voice to those who felt unheard and excluded.[19] Many would argue that we can unmask Trump as a false

---

[13] Marion Grau, *Of Divine Economy: Refinancing Redemption* (New York: T&T Clark International, 2004), 165.

[14] Johannes Baptist Metz, *Glaube in Geschichte und Gesellschaft: Studien zu einer praktischen Fundamentaltheologie*, 5th ed. (Mainz: Matthias Grünewald, 1992).

[15] The historical relations between new political theology in Europe and Latin American liberation theologies are complex and fraught. There are contested narratives over origins and trajectories of influence between the two fields. Cf. Kim Christiaens, ed., *Progressive Catholicism in Latin America and Europe 1950s–1980s: Social Movements and Transnational Encounters* (Leuven: Leuven University Press, forthcoming).

[16] For the reception of specifically black liberation theologies in constructive theological approaches, cf. Jason Wyman, "Constructive Theology, Black Liberation Theology and Black Constructive Theology: A History of Irony and Resonance," *Black Theology: An International Journal* 15, no. 3 (2017): 4–21.

[17] Mark L. Taylor, *The Theological and the Political: On the Weight of the World* (Minneapolis, MN: Fortress, 2011).

[18] Joel Baden, "The 'Trump Prophecy' Includes Troubling Parallels for American Democracy," *Religion News Service*, October 4, 2018, https://religionnews.com/2018/10/04/the-trump-prophecy-includes-troubling-parallels-for-american-democracy/.

[19] This topos is picked up very explicitly in Trump's inauguration speech:

messiah,[20] but before we engage in any such political-theological evaluation, we have to register that his victory is an assault on the very foundations of the epistemo-theological framework of political theology as proposed by Metz. Trump's success, after all, is not told as a straightforward victory story, against which we can pitch a remembrance of the victims in order to call for justice. Rather, it was possible for him to co-opt a plea for the suffering in order to maintain and reinforce white male privilege.[21] This marks the foundations of political theology with ambivalence. The remembrance of the victims of history has lost its self-evident liberative quality. The belief that justice takes place when the voiceless are given a voice has lost its innocence. Instead, the clear soteriological fronts of new political theology are beginning to blur; its straightforward account of salvation history as unfolding in opposition to a history of injustice is starting to waver. As Michael Schüssler argues, Metz still held on to the faith in a teleological unilinearity of (salvation) history that allowed him to identify a history of suffering—dialectically broken, by way of "interruption"[22]—as the history of salvation: Metz, Schüssler says, embedded his interpretation of Christian faith as *memoria passionis* in

> a theology of history that strived to salvage a meaningful unity of salvation history as a history of suffering; his goal, ultimately, was to restore a "Christian continuum." His theology is a defense of Christian faith as an ultimately stable framework that can salvage the human promises of modernity in the very moment of their fading, because it finds an absolute anchoring in God. In the end, he did not question [the modern proposition of] a final meaning of history, even if he no longer located this final meaning in the history of progress toward a world becoming more and more humane, and instead postulated it, through a negative lens, in the interruptions of modern pathologies through the Christian memory of suffering.[23]

> Today's ceremony, however, has very special meaning. Because today we are not merely transferring power from one Administration to another, or from one party to another—but we are transferring power from Washington, D.C. and giving it back to you, the American People. For too long, a small group in our nation's Capital has reaped the rewards of government while the people have borne the cost ... That all changes—starting right here, and right now, because this moment is your moment: it belongs to you ... This is your day. This is your celebration. And this, the United States of America, is your country ... January 20th 2017, will be remembered as the day the people became the rulers of this nation again. The forgotten men and women of our country will be forgotten no longer. Everyone is listening to you now.
>
> Donald Trump, *Inaugural Speech* (Washington DC, 2017), https://www.whitehouse.gov/briefings-statements/the-inaugural-address/.

[20] Miguel A. de La Torre, ed., *Faith and Resistance in the Age of Trump* (Maryknoll, NY: Orbis Books, 2017).

[21] Diana Mutz, "Status Threat, Not Economic Hardship, Explains the 2016 Presidential Vote," *PNAS* 115, no. 19 (2018), https://www.pnas.org/content/pnas/115/19/E4330.full.pdf.

[22] Johann Baptist Metz, *Unterbrechungen: Theologisch-politische Perspektiven und Profile,* Gütersloher Taschenbücher Siebenstern 1041 (Gütersloh: Gütersloher Verlagshaus Mohn, 1981).

[23] Michael Schüssler, "Praktische Wende der Politischen Theologie? Von der schöpferischen Kraft des Evangeliums im Risiko der Ereignisse," in *Extra ecclesiam ... zur Institution und Kritik von Kirche,* Jahrbuch politische Theologie Band 6/7, ed. Henning Klingen, Peter Zeillinger, and Michael Hölzl (Münster: Lit-Verlag, 2013), 286–307, 294; my translation.

However, once this orienting framework has lost its self-evidence and innocence, major theological reconfigurations are in order: We have to reconsider how we can account for the Christian hope for resurrection through a *memoria passionis in the very midst* of ambivalence. We have to confront the question if, and how, it is possible to imagine salvation history past any soteriological unambivalence, beyond historiographical unilinearity and without a teleological theology of history.

Re/membering History, Imagining Salvation in Post/colonial Belgium

Let us start our search for such soteriological reconfigurations in a perhaps unexpected place: the Royal Museum for Central Africa (RMCA) in Brussels, Belgium, which was founded in 1897 by King Leopold II to promote his colonial efforts in Central Africa. Up until recently, the museum served as a powerful framework for colonial knowledge production that told the history of the Belgian–African encounter from the perspective of the colonizers, in a glorifying and triumphant way that remained silent on the extremely violent and exploitative nature of this colonial project. Describing the history of the permanent exhibition at the RMCA, Patrick Hoenig argues that the "erasure of trauma in public memory seems to have been one of the main organizing principles"[24] of its politics of imagination. He outlines how the exhibition has, by representing "colonial history as 'geography of the other,'"[25] contributed to the production of selective, sanitized memories of the Belgian colonial past in public consciousness that oscillate "between glorification, acknowledgement and avoidance of any mention of wrong-doing."[26] From 2013 to 2018, the RMCA was closed for renovation. Concomitant with an architectural overhaul, the museum administration also worked on new modes for the representation of the country's colonial past and how it lives on in contemporary society.[27] The goal was to develop an exhibition that makes the former colonial power accountable for its violent history and also paves

---

[24] Patrick Hoenig, "Visualizing Trauma: The Belgian Museum for Central Africa and Its Discontents," *Postcolonial Studies* 17, no. 4 (2014): 346. Hoenig quotes Murat Aydemir, "Staging Colonialism: The Mise-en-Scene of the Africa Museum in Tervuren, Belgium," in *Migratory Settings*, Thamyris/Intersecting: Place, Sex and Race 19, ed. Murat Aydemir and Alex Rotas (Amsterdam: Rodopi, 2008), 123–52, 147–8.
[25] Hoenig, "Visualizing Trauma," 356.
[26] Ibid., 353.
[27] "The permanent exhibition had ... become extremely dated," the museum's homepage declares; its "presentation ... did not take a critical enough eye of the colonial image that reigned in the 20th century." February 22, 2018, http://www.africamuseum.be/museum/renovation/renovate/index_html.

> Bambi Ceuppens, researcher at the RMCA, noted that many Belgians still had [the] image, fed by colonial propaganda, of Belgium bringing civilization to the Congo, building boats and hospitals, infrastructure and industry, and that "Congolese were actually better off during the colonial era than after independence." Investigating the "link between colonialism and the discrimination and racism that people of African origin suffer in Belgium nowadays" ... constituted not only a "very important perspective that we [as a museum] have to take on board" but was also "part of our moral responsibility." (Hoenig, "Visualizing Trauma," 351, 356)

the way for new relationships between Belgium and the Congo. The museum aimed to divest itself of its colonial gaze that served to legitimize the colonial exploitation of the Congo. Instead, it wanted to shift its focus to a portrayal of the natural and cultural diversity of Central Africa in order to allow for a representation of Africa from non-European perspectives.

I believe we can trace thematic parallels between these reorientations of the museum's post/colonial memory politics and the project of new political theology. Both aim for a retelling of history from the perspective of those that have hitherto been excluded from the authoritative master narrative. Both believe that such a relecture serves to acknowledge historical guilt and bring about justice. In both discourses, hence, historiographical revisions are linked to promises of healing and redemption. Given these parallels, I suggest therefore that the RMCA can serve as a "locus alienus" in order to examine the implications of various historiographical and soteriological imaginations. Starting from the question of how the museum stages healing and redemption in the wake of post/colonial trauma, I aim to develop conceptual resources for a reconfiguration of Christian soteriology after the loss of self-evidence of theological orienting principles. I will proceed in an interdisciplinary manner that intersects postcolonial trauma studies with theological perspectives on New Testament narratives of cross and resurrection.

A particular rich site for such an investigation is the museum's former entrance hall. Entering the grand rotunda, visitors used to be greeted with statues of white men and women in gilded robes cradling naked African children, above plaques that extol Belgium for bringing "civilisation," "security," and "well-being" to the Congo. They represented the colonial discourse through the gaze of the colonizer. The renovation committee decided to reshape this space through an artistic intervention: it commissioned a new statue by a sculptor from the Congo, Aimé Mpane.[28] It is entitled "Congo Nouveau Souffle" and is placed in addition to the colonial statues, near the center of the rotunda. In which ways can we read the relation between these statues old and new—and which historiographical and soteriological conceptions underpin each of these interpretations of the rotunda's new spatial configuration?

I encountered a first possible reading of the RMCA's new post/colonial memory politics during a tour through the museum in October 2017, before it was reopened to the public. The renovations were still in full swing, and Mpane's statue had not yet been installed in the rotunda. I thus got my first impression of the new arrangements in the rotunda through our guide's description. A desire to construct an unambivalent story line from wounding to healing underpinned his imagination of the future redesigned hall. In his account, the new statue would provide a sharp contrast to the colonial representation of the older statues—a vision that allowed him to build a linear story line from past colonialism to contemporary independence, from African subjugation to African agency. Based on our guide's account, I imagined Mpane's statue to represent

---

[28] For an interview with the artist and a picture of the statue, cf. Lise Coirier, "Aimé Mpane—Between Shadow and Light: Sculpting and Painting Humanity," *TL Magazine*, June 30, 2018, https://tlmagazine.com/aime-mpane-between-shadow-and-light-sculpting-and-painting-humanity/.

an unblemished black body, adorned with traditional African embellishments, telling a story about the beauty and resilience of African life that has left the colonial past behind. Colonial death, the statue signaled for him, has been overcome; it has lost its sting. Under his eyes, Mpane's sculpture became part of an overarching story of hope that leads from wounds to healing, from marginalization to self-representation, from debt to reparation, from death to new life. Our guide put forth a reading of the future spatial arrangements in the rotunda that speaks to complete restoration and an orderly transfer of power, both political and epistemic, telling a story of wounds fully healed, leaving no scars.

The Historiography of the Cure: Decolonizing or Recolonizing?

Yet, is this story of healing the only story that these statues allow us to tell about the post/colonial history of Belgium and the Congo? Is this the only narrative into which we can texture the artifacts of post/colonial history? Gayatri Spivak has succinctly pointed to the epistemo-political pitfalls of such a historiography of "the cure"[29] that constructs a linear narrative from wounding to healing. She argues that it actually reinscribes the authority of the master narrative and reiterates the violent exclusions on which this narrative is built. The historiography of the cure creates "predictable chronologies ... that seduce the subject into pure repetition ... [by] imagin[ing] history as 'a genealogy of the historian' thus repeating the colonial practice of constructing the self by constructing the other."[30] It reestablishes white sovereignty of interpretation over the colonial past and reinscribes hegemonic authority in order to establish a "simulacrum of continuity"[31] in the contested construction of history. The "cure" is thus a mode of historiography that runs the risk of "fetishiz[ing] African art and other native resources with the eye of an imperial overlord."[32] In a story of healing, the white gaze, which now wants to leave colonialism behind, remains the organizing principle in the telling of colonial history. It utilizes seemingly unblemished black flesh to absolve the post/colonizers from their historical guilt, and it conceals the powerful asymmetries into which representations of the past are inextricably entangled: by ostensibly shifting agency in post/colonial representation to the subaltern, it continues to instrumentalize black bodies and black voices for the self-definition of the post/colonial masters. The discourse of colonial healing builds an overarching narrative of liberation, reparation, and reconciliation that, first, conceals the suppressed shares of colonial death on which

---

[29] Cf. Gayatri Chakravorty Spivak, *A Critique of Postcolonial Reason: Toward a History of the Vanishing Present*, 4th ed. (Cambridge, MA: Harvard University Press, 1999), 206f.
[30] Mayra Rivera, "Ghostly Encounters: Spirits, Memory, and the Holy Ghost.," in *Planetary Loves: Spivak, Postcoloniality, and Theology*, Transdisciplinary Theological Colloquia, ed. Stephen D. Moore and Mayra Rivera (New York: Fordham University Press, 2011), 118–35, 122, referencing Gayatri C. Spivak, "Ghostwriting," *diacritics* 25, no. 2 (1995).
[31] Spivak, *A Critique of Postcolonial Reason*, 207.
[32] Gert Buelens and Stef Craps, "Introduction: Postcolonial Trauma Novels," *Studies in the Novel* 40, nos. 1&2 (2008): 6.

contemporary post/colonial societies are built and that, second, reiterates the violent exclusions of the colonial gaze. The discourse of healing thus appears to give voice to the voiceless and remember the forgotten victims of a violent history. Yet, as Sam Durrant asserts, it ultimately has a "counter-intuitively amnesiac effect"[33] that conceals the victims of history and perpetuates the lethal logic of imperial power. It subscribes to an amnestic memory politics that perceives colonialism as an "unapproachable, even 'unhomely' concept"[34] and meets it with the desire to put an end to a "dark chapter" of history.

And indeed, with Valerie Rosoux and Laurence Van Ypersele, we can argue that such amnesia is the prevalent mode of remembering the colonial past in Belgium[35]—the RMCA's new discourse of healing aligns with a suppression of the traumatic effects of colonialism in Belgian society. German Vietnamese political studies scholar Kien Nghi Ha highlights that such, as any, societal practice of commemoration is imminently political: "Silence is deliberate amnesia, and amnesia is a political expression of collective memory. Therefore, consensual silence is a dominant enunciation of power that actively resists a reckoning with imperial practices and images."[36] The taboo on colonial history serves as a political tool to reinscribe a societal "infra- and power-structure"[37] that continues to be shaped by the colonial logics of subjugation, racialization, and exploitation. Amnestic memory politics finds its manifestation in hegemonic power differentials that perpetuate colonial politics in postindependence Europe. The power of amnesia "can, in its totalizing dimensions, condense into secondary colonization."[38] With its amnesiac side effects, the discourse of healing thus has a recolonizing underbelly—an unambivalent story line from wounding to healing effectively conceals and reinscribes the ongoing psycho-political effects of colonialism in today's society, which live on in the form of neocolonial exploitation and racism. Ultimately, by establishing a "simulacrum of continuity," the cure does not bring transformation, but continues to erase the victims of history. It does not interrupt, but perpetuates the logic of hegemonic power.

---

[33] Sam Durrant, "Undoing Sovereignty: Towards a Theory of Critical Mourning," in *The Future of Trauma Theory: Contemporary Literary Criticism*, ed. Gert Buelens, Sam Durrant, and Robert Eaglestone (New York: Routledge, 2014), 91–110, 95.

[34] Kien Nghi Ha, *Unrein und Vermischt: Postkoloniale Grenzgänge durch die Kulturgeschichte der Hybridität und der kolonialen »Rassenbastarde«*, Postcolonial Studies 6 (Transcript-Verlag, 2015), 71; my translation. The German original for "unhomely" is "unheimlich"; Freud's concept "unheimlich" refers to the estranged sense of encountering something familiar yet threatening that lies within the bounds of the intimate. It is usually translated as "uncanny." Homi Bhabha retains a more literal meaning by using "unhomely." Cf. Homi Bhabha, "The World and the Home," *Social Text* 31, no. 32 (1992): 141.

[35] Valerie Rosoux and Laurence van Ypersele, "The Belgian National Past: Between Commemoration and Silence," *Memory Studies* 5, no. 1 (2012): 115–27.

[36] Kien Nghi Ha, *Unrein und Vermischt*, 71; my translation.

[37] Ibid.; my translation.

[38] Ibid.; my translation.

Ghost Stories: The Transformative Power of the Refusal to Be Cured

Willie Jennings succinctly points to the question that the critique of the historiography of the cure poses for us: "How does one remember horror when *every* work of remembering is being drawn inside the ideological uses of memory?"[39] At stake is a mode for telling history that resists the violent temptations built into an overarching narrative of healing, liberation, justice, and redemption. At stake is a framework for dangerous memory that challenges a teleological imagination of past, present, and future. Spivak suggests ghost stories as such an alternative historiographical mode: "I pray instead to be haunted, bypassing the arrogance of the cure."[40] Why Ghosts? With Gregor Hoff, we can approach ghosts as "figures of social memory"[41] that help us to negotiate the challenge of resisting the amnestic effects of the cure: Ghosts are "archetypes of the symbolic work of interpretation"[42] that open "a perspective on the suppressed shares of death in life, especially in societal processes of marginalization."[43] "The talk of ghosts connects ... life and death. It answers to guilt and articulates the desire for redemption."[44] Ghosts are narrative figures that "signify ... the simultaneity of past and present ... by identifying time as debt"—they are an "emblem of the ... unredeemed and perhaps the irredeemable."[45]

Ghost stories, then, give a different account of history. The historiographical mode of haunting, too, like the cure, is concerned with death and life, guilt and justice, suffering and redemption. Yet, it strikes a different, more complex, balance between a history of suffering and a hopeful future. Haunting engages in a redescription of time through wounds that register the desire for a time without suffering but does not subject wounding and healing to the violence of a linear narrative that reiterates exclusion by silencing the shameful shares of death in histories. Haunting, instead, is the occupation with a troubled past that opens the imagination for a fragile future, knowing that the experience of suffering, but also the hope for healing, disarrays time. Ghosts represent wounding and healing, life and death in ways that disrupt the self-evidence of a linear sequence, and instead embody healing, justice, reparation by way of a fleeting absence, a painful incompleteness, a hopeful yearning. As "this figure of interruption, of a rupture"[46] in cohesive, linear narratives, therefore, Hoff points out,

---

[39] Willie J. Jennings, "War Bodies: Remembering Bodies in a Time of War," in *Post-traumatic Public Theology*, ed. Stephanie N. Arel and Shelly Rambo (Cham: Springer International; Imprint: Palgrave Macmillan, 2016), 23–36, 25; emphasis added.
[40] Spivak, *A Critique of Postcolonial Reason*, 207.
[41] Gregor Maria Hoff, *Religionsgespenster: Versuch über den religiösen Schock*, 1 (Paderborn: Schöningh, 2017), 18; here and later, my translation.
[42] Ibid.
[43] Ibid., 24.
[44] Ibid., 17.
[45] Ibid.
[46] Ibid., 51.

the metaphor of haunting, crucially, "signifies a problem of observance ... How can we perceive absence?"[47]

Sam Durrant suggests that such a ghostly historiography will take the form of "critical ... recalcitrant ... anti-therapeutic mourning"[48] that "comes to be transformative ... [by] foreground[ing] ruptured temporalities, or else the temporality of ruptures, as an integral aspect of the redemption of history."[49] With David Lloyd we can argue that such "a non-therapeutic relation to the past, structured around the notion of survival or living on rather than recovery, ... [can] ground *a different mode of historicization*"[50] that will disrupt the linear, teleological temporality of amnestic healing by "making *other* sense of the event and the narratives that congregate around it."[51]

Haunting the Museum

Through the lens of haunting and mourning, we begin to see that Aimé Mpane's statue can tell a more complex story of postcolonial African life. Such a spectral approach informed by the "refusal to be cured" allows us to texture the spatial arrangements in the rotunda into a ghost story that disrupts the predictable chronology of healing. In such an alternative, ghostly reading of the RMCA's postcolonial historiography, "Congo Nouveau Souffle" does reclaim Africa for black bodies. It is shaped in form of the African continent that bears the facial features of a black person—and yet, its color is white. Here, black and white are inextricably entangled, for better or for worse. Black agency does not replace the white invasion of the continent, but is at work within it, telling a story about resilience in which chronologies of death and life, wounds and healing, subjugation and agency appear convoluted. Mpane's statue presents us with a wounded resurrection body that is (irredeemably?) marked by the lethal violence of empire, and yet reinterprets signs of death for the purpose of life: a hesitant plant is sprouting from what looks like a barren landmass that has been systematically mined, exploited, and marred by the violent mapping of the colonial scramble for Africa. This sign of new life is tied to a colonial history: it mirrors the crown of palms that surrounds the portrait of Leopold II, which has dominated the rotunda before the renovation. What was a spectacle of colonial sovereignty becomes a spectral presence of postcolonial living-on in the wake of lethal violence, while the wounds, from which this new life hesitantly grows, remain visible and continue to haunt Africa. The statue

---

[47] Ibid., 48. Shelly Rambo similarly suggests that this question is at the heart of trauma studies: "What kind of presence can witness to an absence?" Shelly Rambo, "Between Death and Life: Trauma, Divine Love and the Witness of Mary Magdalene," *Studies in Christian Ethics* 18, no. 2 (2005): 8.

[48] Sam Durrant, "Undoing Sovereignty: Towards a Theory of Critical Mourning," in *The Future of Trauma Theory: Contemporary Literary Criticism*, ed. Gert Buelens, Sam Durrant, and Robert Eaglestone (New York: Routledge, 2014), 91–110, 94.

[49] Norman S. Nikro, "Situating Postcolonial Trauma Studies," *Postcolonial Text* 9, no. 2 (2014): 9. Summarizing Durrant's reading of Chinua Achebe's *Things Fall Apart* in Sam Durrant, "Surviving Time: Trauma, Tragedy and the Postcolonial Novel," *Journal of Literature and Trauma Studies* 1, no. 1 (Spring 2012): 95–117.

[50] David Lloyd, "Colonial Trauma/Postcolonial Recovery?," *Intervention* 2, no. 2 (2000): 219f.; italics mine.

[51] Ibid., 215; emphasis in the original.

represents new life not by relegating colonial wounds to the past, but by reappropriating the tools of colonial subjugation. The cure, we have seen, feigns an end of colonial subjugation in an instrumentalization of seemingly unblemished black flesh that repeats and reinscribes colonial politics of representation. Mpane's reappropriation of colonial significations, in contrast, resists the fetishization of native resources and thus interrupts the power of the colonial gaze: "Traces of the past live on, but without classical references."[52] In this ghostly reading, Mpane's statue takes on a nontherapeutic relation to the past, structured around the notion of living-on rather than recovery. It disrupts the teleological temporality of amnestic healing by "making *other* sense of the event and the narratives that congregate around it."[53] Not by concealing the suppressed shares of colonial death, but by ad/dressing the festering wounds on a traumatized body can truly transformed life, hesitantly, take place—like a tender plant that sprouts from barren land against all odds, like a fickle shadow on the wall.[54]

Our visit to the RMCA thus allows us to differentiate between two historiographical paradigms in postcolonial memory politics: a *memoria passionis* in the wake of historical trauma can be performed by way of the cure, on the one hand, or in ghost stories, on the other. Each has distinct soteriological implications that can inform our constructive search for new theological constellations between memory and justice, suffering and redemption. Linear soteriologies, we have seen, do not effect real transformation. Agency, further, is inextricably entangled with politics of representation that are potentially recolonizing. The ideal to turn victims into subjects of history (one of the most crucial presuppositions of Metz's political theology)[55] thus remains ambivalent and can, again, become a discourse of subjectification. These insights from a critique of the historiography of the cure call for a careful revision of the theology of history that informs Metz's new political theology: it has tried to build an anamnesis of suffering into an overarching narrative of salvation; however, in constructing such a "predictable chronology," it runs the risk of continuing to conceal the victims of history and perpetuate the logic of hegemonic power. Ghost stories, we

---

[52] Coirier, "Aimé Mpane—Between Shadow and Light."
[53] Lloyd, "Colonial Trauma/Postcolonial Recovery?," 215; emphasis in the original.
[54] Another art installation interrupts the museum's established narrative of Belgium's colonial past and its practices of commemoration in a similar way: the original museum had a wall devoted to the thousands of Belgians killed in the country, but remained silent on the millions of unknown, unnamed, and disremembered Congolese victims. The curators looked for ways of exposing these asymmetries in visibility in the politics of memory that resist "breaking the discussion of colonialism down to guesstimating the death toll of Leopold II's 'red rubber' regime, which … [would] reinforce an ambiguous and apologetic attitude towards colonial rule of the Congo and undercut current debates on the structural underpinnings of the colonial project, its inherent disregard for human life and its entrenchment in contemporary political structures" (Hoenig, "Visualizing Trauma," 350). Instead, an art installation breaks into the anonymity of colonial violence that has made its black victims invisible. It commemorates the six Congolese men and women who died during the cold winter they spent as viewing objects in the "human zoo" in the opening year of Leopold's exhibition (1897), by etching their names into a window opposite the commemorative wall; the shadows of these etchings fall, like a haunting, onto the officially established narrative about the victims of Belgian colonial history. The fact that this artistic intervention depends on Belgium's hesitant sunshine only underlines the fragility and precarity that inscribes itself into any efforts of remembering those who have been written out of the master narrative of history.
[55] For an analysis, cf. Philipp Geitzhaus, "Karl Marx grüßt die Politische Theologie: Zur Kritik der neuesten politischen Theologie," *Ethik und Gesellschaft* 1–39 (2018).

have seen, offer an alternative historiographical mode for soteriological imaginations. They perform a reinscription of time through wounds within a normative framework that registers the desire for a time without suffering, but resists a reification of hope. By engaging in a scrutiny of wounds, they present us with convoluted temporalities that unsettle the powerful simulacra of continuity. *Memoria passionis* here becomes a "continuing process of reckoning with the past"[56] that interrupts narratives of temporal linearity and instead triggers a critical investigation of the epistemologies and politics of historiography. With Michel Foucault we can argue that such a critique of epistemo-political conditions effects "kinds of virtual fracture which open up a space of concrete freedom, i.e., of possible transformation."[57] Ghost stories, therefore, can be read as an act of resistance that underpins melancholia with political agency: they express a "refusal to be cured"[58] that has subversive, transformative potential.[59] They offer a radicalized *memoria passionis* that does not subject a remembrance of the victims to a totalitarian promise of salvation, but seeks transformation in spectral reconfigurations of memory and justice, suffering and healing.

Cross and Resurrection: Healing or Haunting?

This outcome challenges us to rethink the political practices of remembrance with which theology pursues its goal of doing justice to the victims of history—and it has a profound impact on how we understand central soteriological concepts of the Christian tradition: Can we tell the Christian story of new life without giving in to the powerful temptations of the cure? Can we frame soteriology in a way that does not succumb to a teleological triumphalism, which conceals suffering and silences the victims? Can we register the desire for healing without subjecting it to the simulacrum of a (Christian) continuum? Can we kindle hope beyond "predictable chronologies ... that seduce the subject into pure repetition"[60] and do not bring real transformation? Can the story of cross and resurrection become a narrative for resisting the violent linearity inherent to the historiography of the cure? Can we tell it as a ghost story that unsettles sovereign discourses of agency and healing and, like Mpane's statue, makes space for new life by reappropriating and reinterpreting instruments of colonial oppression?

The critique of feminist theologians has asserted that the story of cross and resurrection, too, is a narrative of wounding and healing that has often been subjected to a triumphalist teleology of life defeating death, thus making us blind to ongoing suffering and the asymmetries of power on which it rests.[61] Linear soteriologies have

---

[56] Shelly Rambo, "Introduction," in *Post-traumatic Public Theology*, ed. Stephanie N. Arel and Shelly Rambo (Cham: Springer International; Imprint: Palgrave Macmillan, 2016), 1–21, 9.
[57] Michel Foucault, "Structuralism and Post-structuralism: An Interview with Michel Foucault," *Telos* 55 (Spring 1983); 195–211, 206.
[58] Lloyd, "Colonial Trauma/Postcolonial Recovery?," 219.
[59] Cf. also Emmanuel Katongole, *Born from Lament: The Theology and Politics of Hope in Africa* (Grand Rapids, MI: Eerdmans, 2017).
[60] Rivera, "Ghostly Encounters," 118–35, 123, referencing Spivak, "Ghostwriting."
[61] Margaret D. Kamitsuka, *Feminist Theology and the Challenge of Difference*, Reflection and Theory in the Study of Religion Series (New York: Oxford University Press, 2007); Grace Jantzen, "Feminism

nourished the commitment of new political and liberation theologies to the struggle for justice, but they have also served to reestablish hegemonic power structures in theological memory politics; theological tradition has not been immune to the powerful temptations of the cure in the wake of cross and resurrection. Yet, drawing on postcolonial trauma studies, Bennie Liew, and others, have shown that the gospels' stories of cross and resurrection are also open to other readings that complicate linear soteriological imaginations. Their haunting relecture uncovers profound ambiguities at the heart of these stories that disrupt a straightforward narrative from cross to resurrection.

Liew's postcolonial rereadings show that the cross is simultaneously a spectacle of Roman imperial power that demonstrates its sovereignty by disposing of killable people *and* a spectre of death that hauntingly reveals that Pax Romana builds on lethal violence.[62] Jesus died as an instrument for the demonstration and maintenance of colonial sovereignty, and his traumatized resurrection body continues to tell a story about the might, reach, and supremacy of his masters. The wounds that remain on Jesus's resurrection body, therefore, present us, first and foremost, with a spectacle of imperial power. Yet, at the very same time, these wounds have the power to destabilize the sovereignty of the hegemonic narrative of the empire about itself. Wounds and scars are a powerful way to make the empire accountable for the lethal ways in which it brings peace and civilization. They expose the unacknowledged shares of death on which it rests and make the spectacle of power also a specter of death. Wounds—and the tears by which they are remembered—thus cannot but give rise to haunting, and a spectral hermeneutics of critical mourning reveals a moment of undecidability in the significance of the cross that paves the way for re/signing death and life. The refusal to be cured thus wrests the hope for resurrection from the traumatic history of colonial power. A remembrance of wounds develops a narrative in the mode of yearning, which believes that "something remains to be seen"[63] beyond the colonial regimes of in/visibility of spectacle and spectrality that relies on suppressing the shares of death on which they are built.

Resurrection, in these haunting relectures, therefore, is not a straightforward, linear, and self-evident triumph of life over death. Instead, it emerges from semantic undecidabilities and is confirmed only through a hermeneutics of wounds and tears. The resurrection narratives of the New Testament appear as ghost stories, populated by absent presences and present absences—haunting figures that identify time as debt and stand for the desire for change, transformation, redemption. And here, too, it might be a "refusal to be cured" that carries seeds for salvation: Thomas has to touch gaping wounds in order to believe.[64] It is through Mary's mourning at the empty tomb

---

and Flourishing: Gender and Metaphor in Feminist Theology," *Feminist Theology* 81, no. 4 (1995): 81–101.

[62] Tat-siong B. Liew, "The Gospel of Bare Life: Reading Death, Dream and Desire through John's Jesus," in *Psychoanalytic Mediations between Marxist and Postcolonial Readings of the Bible*, Semeia Studies 84, ed. Tat-siong B. Liew and Erin Runions (Atlanta, GA: SBL, 2016), 129–71.

[63] Natalie J. Baloy, "Spectacles and Spectres: Settler Colonial Spaces in Vancouver," *Settler Colonial Studies* 6, no. 3 (2016): 210.

[64] Shelly Rambo, *Resurrecting Wounds: Living in the Afterlife of Trauma* (Waco, TX: Baylor University Press, 2017).

that a vision for new life emerges.[65] It is the traumatized witness of the women at the tomb that silently voices recalcitrant memories of the founding violence of imperial power that cannot be fully buried.[66] It is Jesus's initiative in his own death on the cross that reinterprets death for the purposes of life by reclaiming a subversive sovereignty from within bare life.[67] A relecture of cross and resurrection as a story of haunting and mourning thus breaks with a triumphant narrative from death to life, but does open our eyes to life that emerges from the midst of suffering that remains. A story about the scars that remain from the crucifixion unsettles and displaces the sovereignty of healing. It turns to wounds and tears as the organizing principles of Christian soteriology and wrests hope for resurrection from the lethal logic of colonial politics by assigning a different significance to the spectacle of political death. In a haunting relecture that resists the powerful temptations of the cure, Jesus's wounded resurrection body epitomizes a convoluted chronology of death and life that reveals afterlife in the mode of mourning and yearning. Together, these spectral relectures show that the refusal to be cured is of profound soteriological relevance—and they reveal the irresolvable ambiguity of salvation history. Ghost stories manifest the potentially redemptive effects of an anamnesis of suffering—but they do not operate with given self-evidences and in teleological temporalities. Instead, they are performances of reinterpretation that reveal a moment of undecidability in the meaning of discourses that may—*perhaps*[68]—make space for possible transformations.

Epistemo-theological Shifts: Haunting Theology

Ghost stories thus entail profound epistemo-theological reconfigurations. They derange linear accounts of salvation history and blur clear soteriological fronts. No longer here a history of suffering, there a history of justice. Instead, in ghost stories, salvation history takes places as interpretation of irreducibly ambiguous events and narratives. "Haunting," Spivak says, "is a way of reading."[69] She therefore also suggests that the ghost dance will never be quite successful.[70] Ghost stories are always supplementary and remain inconclusive, emerging from and remaining inextricably entangled with the contingencies of (salvation) history. In ghost stories, we "surrender to undecidability … as the condition of possibility of responsible decision."[71] They emerge by way of a political practice of remembering that makes "*other* sense of the

---

[65] Rambo, "Between Death and Life."
[66] Tat-siong B. Liew, "Haunting Silence: Trauma, Failed Orality, and Mark's Messianic Secret," in *Psychoanalytic Mediations between Marxist and Postcolonial Readings of the Bible*, Semeia Studies 84, ed. Tat-siong B. Liew and Erin Runions (Atlanta, GA: SBL, 2016), 99–128.
[67] Rambo, *Resurrecting Wounds*, 148.
[68] Cf. John D. Caputo, *The Insistence of God: A Theology of Perhaps*, Indiana Series in the Philosophy of Religion (Bloomington: Indiana University Press, 2013), 3–24.
[69] Cf. Gayatri C. Spivak, "Extempore Response to Susan Abraham, Tat-siong Benny Liew, and Mayra Rivera," in *Planetary Loves: Spivak, Postcoloniality, and Theology*, Transdisciplinary Theological Colloquia, ed. Stephen D. Moore and Mayra Rivera (New York: Fordham University Press, 2011), 136–48, 141.
[70] Spivak, "Ghostwriting," 71.
[71] Ibid.

event and the narratives that congregate around it."⁷² A spectral theology, therefore, can no longer expect God's life-giving presence to be continuously available for Christian hope, to be grasped in dialectic negation to a history of suffering. Instead, this presence happens as interpretative meaning-making *in the midst of* ambivalent biopolitics.

Michael Schüssler is succinct in outlining the epistemo-theological shifts that such a disarray of soteriological imaginations entails: such a theology "also knows the miraculous 'point of view of salvation' (Adorno), but it does not expect to find it in eschatological fulfilment at the end of days, but instead in a limited event of an opening within the present—not in opposition to society, but in the midst of it."⁷³ Such a soteriological understanding, he argues, has deep roots in many interpretations of Christian tradition, which recognize "revelation … as revealed mystery" and therefore understand that it "does not offer a religious anchor, from which we can consider the world as if we were not part of it. For the world doomed and the world redeemed are one."⁷⁴ With Walter Benjamin, Dietrich Bonhoeffer, and Giorgio Agamben, Schüssler brings the provocative ambivalence of such soteriological disarrays to the fore: it calls followers of the resurrected crucified to

> know that … the redeemed world is identical to the irredeemably lost world; that they now must, in Bonhoeffer's words, indeed live in a world without God, and that in no way are they to conceal their Being-without-God in the world; and that the God who saves them is the God who abandons them; that redemption cannot claim to also redeem the appearance of redemption. [They] do not envision the world as if it has been redeemed. Rather, in Benjamin's words, they envision redemption by losing themselves in the irredeemable.⁷⁵

A spectral soteriology thus escapes the violent temptations of the cure that ultimately does not bring transformation. Yet, it also finds itself deprived of epistemo-theological imaginations of God's self-evident presence in history. Ghost stories do not allow for an anchoring of salvation history in a given, unambiguous foundation and they resist imaginations of its unfolding toward a self-evident telos. Instead, they reveal undecidabilities that can be read as manifestations of God's salvific presence, by way of a fleeting absence, through unfulfilled desire, in hopeful yearning. When we abandon teleological frameworks of theological understanding, we are deprived of imaginations of self-evidence in discerning God's salutary presence. Left with the loss of self-evidence as the orienting principle of our theological practice, we encounter God in the mode of missing, yearning, desiring. As Mayra Rivera aptly puts it: "Remaining faithful to 'dangerous memories' entails acknowledging their plurality and irreducible ambiguity. … Witness, we must ever remind ourselves, is the result of being haunted by spirits, rather than possessing them."⁷⁶ Ulrich Engel, a student of Metz, therefore, proposes to supplement the "three classic methodical steps *see—judge—act* with the moment

---

[72] Lloyd, "Colonial Trauma/Postcolonial Recovery?," 215; emphasis in the original.
[73] Schüssler, "Praktische Wende der Politischen Theologie?," 286–307, 298.
[74] Ibid.
[75] Ibid.
[76] Rivera, "Ghostly Encounters," 118–35, 133.

of (unfulfilled) desire."⁷⁷ In his political theology "nach der Postmoderne,"⁷⁸ written explicitly in continuation of new political theology, he thus ruptures the predictable chronology of theological knowledge production: "seeing world, thinking the political ... living (in) discipleship" are built on the shaky epistemo-theological grounds of "missing God."⁷⁹

In his seminal essay "How Is Christianity Thinkable Today?,"⁸⁰ Michel de Certeau offers trajectories to think about this absent presence of God with theological depth. His text is a theological reflection on the loss of epistemic authority and political sovereignty that the church(es) are confronted with in the wake of post/modernity. Drawing on incarnation theology to develop a theological interpretation of this historical experience, Certeau points to a peculiar predicament that arises because Christian tradition finds its foundation in a historical event. The origin of Christian tradition in God's self-revelation in Jesus the Christ can be grasped only through its manifold witnesses that efface this event by representing it.

> We can not observe anything outside of a plurality of practices and discourses that neither conserve nor replicate it ... The founder disappears; it is impossible to grasp and "detain" him to the degree that he takes shape and meaning in a plurality of Christian experiences and acts ... An ... immediately given "essential" is missing. On the contrary, a kenosis of presence gives rise to a plural and communitarian scripture.⁸¹

As any account of a historical event, so is Christian tradition therefore faced with the problem that reiterating this event cannot but erase its originality:

> The event is lost precisely in what it authorizes. It somehow dies to its own historical specificity, but this happens in the very discoveries which it provokes. The process of death (the absence) and the survival (the presence) of Jesus continues in each Christian experience: What the event makes possible is different each time, as a new remoteness from the event and a new way of erasing it.⁸²

The relation of Christian tradition to its founding event thus has the form of a loss: "The reference to 'origin' is a process of absence. Our relation to the origin is in the function of its increasing absence. The beginning is more and more hidden by the multiple creations which reveal its significance."⁸³ A fundamental lack of self-evidence, Certeau

---

⁷⁷ Ulrich Engel, *Politische Theologie "nach" der Postmoderne: Geistergespräche mit Derrida & Co*, 2nd ed. (Ostfildern: Matthias-Grünewald, 2016), 24; emphasis in the original.
⁷⁸ Engel explains the two possible meanings of the German "nach": it can either mean "after" or "according to." Ibid., 13.
⁷⁹ Ibid., 24.
⁸⁰ Michel de Certeau, "How Is Christianity Thinkable Today?," in *The Blackwell Companion to Postmodern Theology*, ed. Graham Ward (Oxford: Blackwell, 2001), 142–58.
⁸¹ Ibid., 145.
⁸² Ibid.
⁸³ Ibid., 146f.

thus argues, is not only a historical experience of Christian tradition in post/modern times; rather, it can be understood as its basic theological condition:

> This "lack" is not something missing that needs to be obtained but a limitation by which every witness can openly confess their relation to the "author" of faith, his internal law (which requires a death in order to become a place for others) and the nature of his connection to the unexpected or unknown spaces, which God opens up *elsewhere* and *in different ways*.[84]

How, by which procedures, can we theologize in view of this fundamental lack of Christianity's self-evidence? Which theological methods correspond with the epistemo-theological modes of missing, yearning, and desire? As Certeau puts it, "How do we generate a language of believers"[85] that reflects the absent presence of God? Because it is built on a fundamental loss, Certeau argues, Christian theology does not have a language of its own. Because it erases its subject in the very moment it reiterates it, it does not have a permanent place that it can inhabit and from which it can speak. Its foundation in a historical event does not manifest into a deposit of theological knowledge, nor does it translate into a clearly definable Christian proprium. Instead, theology is performed by way of a specific "modus loquendi"[86] that Certeau describes as "displacement" or "conversion"[87] of existing discourses: because Christian tradition has no original narrative at its disposal, it has developed a strategy of drawing on other discourses and establishing a difference within them. Certeau finds resources for explicating this distinct practice of theological knowledge production in his analysis of mystic language: it is a linguistic practice that "has no language of its own, but it is marked (as a 'wound,' the mystics say) in theological discourse; it inscribes itself, through the labor it effects, inside the discourse which it received from another ... tradition."[88] It "produce[s] otherness, but within a field that didn't belong to [it] any more than that other language did, a field in which [it] had no right of authorship. [It] produce[s], but without any place of [its] own, in that no-man's-land ... mystics' manners of speaking are the product of that drifting operativity that has no domain proper."[89] Theology thus is "the production of otherness"[90]—it is dislocation and disarticulation: "It cannot be reduced to a fact that just needs to be confirmed. It arises out of an act of differentiation that fixes a place and at the same time it is beyond, a 'now' and a 'later,' a 'here' and an 'elsewhere.'"[91] The *loci proprii* of Christian

---

[84] Michel de Certeau, *Glaubensschwachheit* (Stuttgart: Kohlhammer Verlag, 2009), 180; translation and italics mine.
[85] Ibid., 216; translation mine.
[86] "[Christian] discourse is a modus loquendi. It is the outcome of an entire set of operations on and in the shared social text. It is an artefact (a production) created by the labor of putting language to death." Michel de Certeau, *Heterologies: Discourse on the Other*, Theory and History of Literature 17 (Minneapolis: University of Minnesota Press, 2010), 159.
[87] Certeau, "How Is Christianity Thinkable Today?," 142–58, 153.
[88] Certeau, *Heterologies*, 250.
[89] Michel de Certeau, *The Mystic Fable*, Religion and Postmodernism (Chicago: University of Chicago Press, 1992), 118f.
[90] Ibid., 118.
[91] Certeau, *Glaubensschwachheit*, 181; my translation.

theology—the sites that inform and normatively orient its knowledge production—hence do not exist independently from and prior to theological practice. Rather, they are forged through acts of differentiation from *other* discourses. They emerge from the performance of theology that establishes differences in other sites and "disturbs"[92] existing languages.[93] Here, it appears "like a wound." In them, it is at work by staging a difference, by hauntingly making "*other* sense of ... event[s] and the narratives that congregate around [them]."[94]

The precise nature of this difference, however, remains undefinable and fleeting. It emerges from and within particular sites and is inextricably tied to and informed by their languages. It provides us only with transient definitions of Christian God/talk. In its foundational dependence on other discourses, theological knowledge production is principally inconclusive and provisional. It cannot follow a politics of appropriation that accumulates theologies made elsewhere into ever greater knowledge of God. It cannot, as Certeau asserts, follow a logic of both/and that "pretends to overcome the differences [and] to reconcile all the former positions within a new and particular truth."[95] Rather than such a summatic, teleological theo-logics of fulfilment and abundance, Christian theology requires a language textured into lack and loss in order to adequately re/present its founding event as elusive. It is to be performed by way of a kenotic language that, like mystics, makes "out of [their] I the representation of what was lacking—a representation that found the place of that which it did not replace"[96] and becomes a "sign of ... what ... it lacks."[97]

Certeau describes this kenotic theology first and foremost as an ongoing practice; theology is a performance of difference, it is a particular "way [literally: method] of reading"[98] *elsewhere*—a "perpetual departure"[99] from established (Christian) traditions. Yet he also shows that reflections of this theological approach can still be traced within the positive bodies of knowledge that have been forged through this kenotic practice. It has given shape, Certeau argues, to the central normativized text of the Christian tradition[100] and finds expression in some of its most influential metaphors and tropes, such as the empty tomb or the ascension of Christ. With Certeau, we can thus read the *loci proprii* of Christian tradition such that they provide us with methodological

[92] Cf. Michel de Certeau, *The Writing of History* (New York: Columbia University Press, 1988), 244–68.
[93] Cf. Judith Gruber, "Religious Language in 'Other' Places: Cano's De Locis Theologicis—a Case Study in Mapping the Religious and the Secular," in *God in Question: Religious Language and Secular Languages*, ed. Martin M. Lintner (Brixen: A. Weger, 2014), 179–92.
[94] Lloyd, "Colonial Trauma/Postcolonial Recovery?," 215; emphasis in the original.
[95] Certeau, "How Is Christianity Thinkable Today?," 142–58, 154.
[96] Certeau, *The Mystic Fable*, 119.
[97] Certeau, *Glaubensschwachheit*, 180; my translation.
[98] Cf. Spivak, "Extempore Response to Susan Abraham," 136–48, 141.
[99] Certeau, *The Mystic Fable*, 299.
[100] See Certeau, "How Is Christianity Thinkable Today?," 142–58, 154:

> By [this] movement alone it conforms to the way in which the entire Christian faith is articulate in the conversion of the Old Testament into the New Testament ... Jesus does not cease to hold on to the uniqueness of the Jewish institution, while he creates the beginning of another meaning for it. His brings about a displacement which gives birth to a new law ... This type of conversion inaugurated by the act of Jesus is to be continued indefinitely ... The essential here is not a new content ... but the conversion of relationships.

instructions to produce theological knowledge "elsewhere," in order to develop a theological language that "represents what it lacks" by performing "a perpetual departure." With him, we can argue that the epistemo-theological mode of yearning and desire translates into an interdisciplinary methodological approach that performs theology by way of a principally inconclusive de/construction of Christian tradition that may have transformative effects—and this brings us surprisingly close to an astute description of the methodological program of constructive theology as discussed in this volume.

Toward an Apologetic Theology

These methodological considerations bring us full circle. In my introductory remarks, I have posited that constructive theology takes an interdisciplinary, de/constructive approach in order to respond to the epistemological and political challenges of theology in the wake of its critique as a power/knowledge regime. We can now see that these methodological choices imply and perform a profound theological statement that re/presents God's salutary presence in the mode of desire. They are the mode of theological knowledge production that rests on the epistemo-theological assumption that it cannot dispose of God's self-evident presence. They allow for a performance of theological knowledge production that does not maintain sovereignty and independence for Christian God-talk (read both: *revelation* and *theology*). They, instead, offer the hermeneutical tools with which theology can be pursued as interpretative labor in the midst of irreducible ambivalence. These methodological choices tell us that, in contrast to Brad East and Katherine Sonderegger, constructive theology does not simply read the contemporary condition of systematic theology as the tragic finale in a history of decline. Rather, it grasps the lack of theological self-evidence as the constitutive condition of Christian God-talk—and can thus reclaim East's vivid narrative as an apt description of its own methodological program: Indeed, contemporary systematic theology "lost its way, fell from grace, and [finds itself now] scattered, confused, in the Babel of the modern university"[101]—responding theologically to the challenges of a power critique, it departs from teleological frameworks, it employs a radically hermeneutical approach in view of the irreducible ambivalence of (salvation) history, and it proceeds with interdisciplinary methods that resist final systematization and closure. By way of this methodological program, constructive theology reconceives of the loss of theological self-evidence as the constitutive condition of theological knowledge production. It thus responds to its epistemological and political challenges by performing profound epistemo-theological shifts.

Earlier, I have indicated that its distinct approach allows us to understand constructive theology as an "apologetic" project. Pursuing this thought a little further, I will conclude by arguing that understanding constructive theology as apologetic does indeed enable us to conceptualize the epistemo-theological shifts that undergird its methodological program. The Greek prefix ἀπό- translates into English as "from, away

[101] East, "Renewing the Heart of Systematic Theology."

from," "without, or lacking," and "derived from, or related to." It is used both temporally and spatially, and generates a relation between two entities by establishing a distance between them. ἀπό- indicates derivation and dependence, rather than autonomy and self-evidence. Apology is, literally, speech that comes from somewhere else. With Franz Gmainer-Pranzl, we can elaborate:

> As a genre, apologetics has a juridical background and adapted the "topology and structure of forensic defense speeches." It is a speech form that starts with the objections made by an other person. In the original sense of the word, "apologists" re-act with intellectual alertness and hermeneutical sensitivity to challenges that they do not choose themselves. Their argumentation does not originate from the "inner realm" of their own plausibility, but starts from outside, with a challenge that calls them to reformulate their convictions.[102]

With these semantics in mind, we can part with an understanding of apologetics as the defense of a given, self-evident proprium of Christian tradition. Rather, we can reconceive of apologetic theology as "responsive"[103] theology. It is theology that is in-formed by its others, that emerges in reaction to challenges from outside. It is theology that is indeed public, multilingual, and interdisciplinary—not, as we have seen earlier, because it has a specifically Christian proprium to defend in public space, but because it cannot but find sources for re/presenting God's *absent* presence *elsewhere*, in other languages and places. As such a speech "from elsewhere," apologetic theology is kenotic performance that resists ultimate closure. It is theology that continues to take its shape in haunting relectures that "produce otherness"[104] in established texts— but cannot be consolidated into a solid body of (self-)evidence. Apologetic theology is de/constructive theology that embraces the lack of theological self-evidence as its epistemo-theological point of departure.

Bibliography

Arel, Stephanie N., and Shelly Rambo, eds. *Post-traumatic Public Theology*.
    Cham: Springer International; Imprint: Palgrave Macmillan, 2016.
Aydemir, Murat. "Staging Colonialism: The Mise-en-Scene of the Africa Museum in
    Tervuren, Belgium." In *Migratory Settings*, Thamyris/Intersecting: Place, Sex and Race
    19, edited by Murat Aydemir and Alex Rotas, 123–52. Amsterdam: Rodopi, 2008.
Aydemir, Murat, and Alex Rotas, eds. *Migratory Settings*. Thamyris/Intersecting: Place, Sex
    and Race 19. Amsterdam: Rodopi, 2008.
Baden, Joel. "The 'Trump Prophecy' Includes Troubling Parallels for American Democracy."
    Religion News Service, October 4, 2018. https://religionnews.com/2018/10/04/
    the-trump-prophecy-includes-troubling-parallels-for-american-democracy/.

---

[102] Franz Gmainer-Pranzl, "Interversalität des Hoffnungslogos. 1 Petr 3,15 als Beanspruchung theologischer Erkenntnislehre," *Zeitschrift für Katholische Theologie* 134 (2012): 203.
[103] Ibid.
[104] Certeau, *The Mystic Fable*, 118.

Baloy, Natalie J. "Spectacles and Spectres : Settler Colonial Spaces in Vancouver." *Settler Colonial Studies* 6:3 (2016): 209–34.
Bhabha, Homi. "The World and the Home." *Social Text* 31:32 (1992): 141–53.
Buelens, Gert, and Stef Craps. "Introduction: Postcolonial Trauma Novels." *Studies in the Novel* 40:1&2 (2008): 1–12.
Buelens, Gert, Sam Durrant, and Robert Eaglestone, eds. *The Future of Trauma Theory: Contemporary Literary Criticism*. New York: Routledge, 2014.
Burrus, Virginia. "History, Theology, Orthodoxy, Polydoxy." *Modern Theology* 30:3 (2014): 7–16.
Caputo, John D. *The Insistence of God: A Theology of Perhaps*. Indiana Series in the Philosophy of Religion. Bloomington: Indiana University Press, 2013.
Certeau, Michel de. *Glaubensschwachheit*. Stuttgart: Kohlhammer Verlag, 2009.
Certeau, Michel de. *Heterologies: Discourse on the Other*. Theory and History of Literature 17. Minneapolis: University of Minnesota Press, 2010.
Certeau, Michel de. "How Is Christianity Thinkable Today?" In *The Blackwell Companion to Postmodern Theology*, edited by Graham Ward, 142–58. Oxford: Blackwell, 2001.
Certeau, Michel de. *The Mystic Fable*. Religion and Postmodernism. Chicago: University of Chicago Press, 1992.
Certeau, Michel de. *The Writing of History*. New York: Columbia University Press, 1988.
Christiaens, Kim, ed. *Progressive Catholicism in Latin America and Europe 1950s–1980s: Social Movements and Transnational Encounters*. Leuven: Leuven University Press, forthcoming.
Coirier, Lise. "Aimé Mpane—Between Shadow and Light: Sculpting and Painting Humanity." *TL Magazine*, June 30, 2018. https://tlmagazine.com/aime-mpane-between-shadow-and-light-sculpting-and-painting-humanity/.
Crisp, Oliver, Fred Sanders, George Hunsinger, Peter J. Leithart, Katherine Sonderegger, and Alan J. Torrance, eds. *Christology, Ancient and Modern: Explorations in Constructive Dogmatics*. Grand Rapids, MI: Zondervan, 2013.
Dulles, Avery. *A History of Apologetics*, new updated and revised ed. San Francisco, CA: Ignatius, 2005.
Durrant, Sam. "Surviving Time: Trauma, Tragedy and the Postcolonial Novel." *Journal of Literature and Trauma Studies* 1:1 (Spring 2012): 95–117.
Durrant, Sam. "Undoing Sovereignty: Towards a Theory of Critical Mourning." In *The Future of Trauma Theory: Contemporary Literary Criticism*, edited by Gert Buelens, Sam Durrant, and Robert Eaglestone, 91–110. New York: Routledge, 2014.
East, Brad. "Renewing the Heart of Systematic Theology." *Marginalia. Los Angeles Review of Books*, August 1, 2016. https://marginalia.lareviewofbooks.org/renewing-heart-systematic-theology-brad-east/.
Engel, Ulrich. *Politische Theologie "nach" der Postmoderne: Geistergespräche mit Derrida & Co*, 2nd ed. Ostfildern: Matthias-Grünewald, 2016.
Foucault, Michel. "Structuralism and Post-structuralism: An Interview with Michel Foucault." *Telos* 55 (Spring 1983): 195–211.
Geitzhaus, Philipp. "Karl Marx grüßt die Politische Theologie. Zur Kritik der neuesten politischen Theologie." *Ethik und Gesellschaft* 1–39 (2018): 1–39.
Gmainer-Pranzl, Franz. "Interversalität des Hoffnungslogos. 1 Petr 3,15 als Beanspruchung theologischer Erkenntnislehre." *Zeitschrift für Katholische Theologie* 134 (2012): 202–17.
Grau, M. *Refiguring Theological Hermeneutics: Hermes, Trickster, Fool*. New York: Palgrave Macmillan, 2014.

Grau, Marion. *Of Divine Economy: Refinancing Redemption*. New York: T&T Clark International, 2004.

Gruber, Judith. "Religious Language in 'Other' Places. Cano's De Locis Theologicis—a Case Study in Mapping the Religious and the Secular." In *God in Question: Religious Language and Secular Languages*, edited by Martin M. Lintner, 179–92. Brixen: A. Weger, 2014.

Gschwandtner, Christina M. *Postmodern Apologetics? Arguments for God in Contemporary Philosophy*, 1st ed. Perspectives in Continental Philosophy. New York: Fordham University Press, 2013.

Hoenig, Patrick. "Visualizing Trauma: The Belgian Museum for Central Africa and Its Discontents." *Postcolonial Studies* 17:4 (2014): 343–66.

Hoff, Gregor M. *Religionsgespenster: Versuch über den religiösen Schock*, 1. Paderborn: Schöningh, 2017.

Jantzen, Grace. "Feminism and Flourishing: Gender and Metaphor in Feminist Theology." *Feminist Theology* 81:4 (1995): 81–101.

Jennings, Willie J. "War Bodies: Remembering Bodies in a Time of War." In *Post-traumatic Public Theology*, edited by Stephanie N. Arel and Shelly Rambo, 23–36. Cham: Springer International; Imprint: Palgrave Macmillan, 2016.

Jones, Serene, and Paul Lakeland, eds. *Constructive Theology: A Contemporary Approach to Classical Themes* [Nachdr.]. Minneapolis, MN: Fortress, 2008.

Jones, Serene, and Paul Lakeland. "Introduction: Theology as Faith in Search for Understanding." In *Constructive Theology: A Contemporary Approach to Classical Themes*, edited by Serene Jones and Paul Lakeland [Nachdr.], 1–10. Minneapolis, MN: Fortress, 2008.

Kamitsuka, Margaret D. *Feminist Theology and the Challenge of Difference*. Reflection and Theory in the Study of Religion Series. New York: Oxford University Press, 2007.

Katongole, Emmanuel. *Born from Lament: The Theology and Politics of Hope in Africa*. Grand Rapids, MI: Eerdmans, 2017.

Kien Nghi Ha. *Unrein und Vermischt: Postkoloniale Grenzgänge durch die Kulturgeschichte der Hybridität und der kolonialen »Rassenbastarde«*. Postcolonial Studies 6. Bielefeld: Transcript-Verlag, 2015.

King, Karen. "Nicht länger marginal: Vom Diskurs über Orthodoxie und Häresie zur Kritik der Kategorien und darüber hinaus." In *Antike christliche Apokryphen: Marginalisierte Texte des Frühen Christentums*, edited by Outi Lehtipuu and Silke Petersen, 18–33. Stuttgart: Kohlhammer, 2019.

Klingen, Henning, Peter Zeillinger, and Michael Hölzl, eds. *Extra ecclesiam … zur Institution und Kritik von Kirche*. Jahrbuch politische Theologie Band 6/7. Münster: Lit-Verlag, 2013.

La Torre, Miguel A. de, ed. *Faith and Resistance in the Age of Trump*. Maryknoll, NY: Orbis Books, 2017.

Lehtipuu, Outi, and Silke Petersen, eds. *Antike christliche Apokryphen: Marginalisierte Texte des Frühen Christentums*. Stuttgart: Kohlhammer, 2019.

Liew, Tat-siong B. "The Gospel of Bare Life: Reading Death, Dream and Desire through John's Jesus." In *Psychoanalytic Mediations between Marxist and Postcolonial Readings of the Bible*, Semeia Studies 84, edited by Tat-siong B. Liew and Erin Runions, 129–71. Atlanta, GA: SBL, 2016.

Liew, Tat-siong B. "Haunting Silence: Trauma, Failed Orality, and Mark's Messianic Secret." In *Psychoanalytic Mediations between Marxist and Postcolonial Readings of*

the Bible, Semeia Studies 84, edited by Tat-siong B. Liew and Erin Runions, 99–128. Atlanta, GA: SBL, 2016.
Liew, Tat-siong B., and Erin Runions, eds. *Psychoanalytic Mediations between Marxist and Postcolonial Readings of the Bible*. Semeia Studies 84. Atlanta, GA: SBL, 2016.
Lintner, Martin M., ed. *God in Question: Religious Language and Secular Languages*. Brixen: A. Weger, 2014.
Lloyd, David. "Colonial Trauma/Postcolonial Recovery?" *Intervention* 2:2 (2000): 212–28.
Metz, Johann B. *Glaube in Geschichte und Gesellschaft: Studien zu einer praktischen Fundamentaltheologie*, 5th ed. Mainz: Matthias Grünewald, 1992.
Metz, Johann B. *Unterbrechungen: Theologisch-politische Perspektiven und Profile*. Gütersloher Taschenbücher Siebenstern 1041. Gütersloh: Gütersloher Verlagshaus Mohn, 1981.
Moore, Stephen D., and Mayra Rivera, eds. *Planetary Loves: Spivak, Postcoloniality, and Theology*. Transdisciplinary Theological Colloquia. New York: Fordham University Press, 2011.
Mutz, Diana. "Status Threat, Not Economic Hardship, Explains the 2016 Presidential Vote." *PNAS* 115:19 (2018). https://www.pnas.org/content/pnas/115/19/E4330.full.pdf.
Nikro, Norman S. "Situating Postcolonial Trauma Studies." *Postcolonial Text* 9:2 (2014): 1–21.
Rambo, Shelly. "Between Death and Life: Trauma, Divine Love and the Witness of Mary Magdalene." *Studies in Christian Ethics* 18:2 (2005): 7–21.
Rambo, Shelly. "Introduction." In *Post-traumatic Public Theology*, edited by Stephanie N. Arel and Shelly Rambo, 1–21. Cham: Springer International; Imprint: Palgrave Macmillan, 2016.
Rambo, Shelly. *Resurrecting Wounds: Living in the Afterlife of Trauma*. Waco, TX: Baylor University Press, 2017.
Rivera, Mayra. "Ghostly Encounters: Spirits, Memory, and the Holy Ghost." In *Planetary Loves: Spivak, Postcoloniality, and Theology*, Transdisciplinary Theological Colloquia, edited by Stephen D. Moore and Mayra Rivera, 118–35. New York: Fordham University Press, 2011.
Rosoux, Valerie, and Laurence van Ypersele. "The Belgian National Past: Between Commemoration and Silence." *Memory Studies* 5:1 (2012): 45–57.
Schüssler, Michael. "Praktische Wende der Politischen Theologie? Von der schöpferischen Kraft des Evangeliums im Risiko der Ereignisse." In *Extra ecclesiam … zur Institution und Kritik von Kirche*, Jahrbuch politische Theologie Band 6/7, edited by Henning Klingen, Peter Zeillinger, and Michael Hölzl, 286–307. Münster: Lit-Verlag, 2013.
Sonderegger, Katherine. "An Interview with Katherine Sonderegger." http://fortresspress.com/content-wysiwyg/interview-katherine-sonderegger.
Sonderegger, Katherine. *Systematic Theology. Volume 1: The Doctrine of God*. Minneapolis, MN: Fortress, 2015.
Spivak, Gayatri C. *A Critique of Postcolonial Reason: Toward a History of the Vanishing Present*, 4th ed. Cambridge, MA: Harvard University Press, 1999.
Spivak, Gayatri C. "Extempore Response to Susan Abraham, Tat-siong Benny Liew, and Mayra Rivera." In *Planetary Loves: Spivak, Postcoloniality, and Theology*, Transdisciplinary theological colloquia, edited by Stephen D. Moore and Mayra Rivera, 136–48. New York: Fordham University Press, 2011.
Spivak, Gayatri C. "Ghostwriting." *diacritics* 25:2 (1995): 65–84.
Taylor, Mark L. *The Theological and the Political: On the Weight of the World*. Minneapolis, MN: Fortress, 2011.

Tillich, Paul. *Systematic Theology: Three Volumes in One*. Chicago: University of Chicago Press, 1967.
Trump, Donald. *Inaugural Speech*. Washington DC, 2017. https://www.whitehouse.gov/briefings-statements/the-inaugural-address/.
Ward, Graham, ed. *The Blackwell Companion to Postmodern Theology*. Oxford: Blackwell, 2001.
Wyman, Jason. "Constructive Theology, Black Liberation Theology and Black Constructive Theology: A History of Irony and Resonance." *Black Theology: An International Journal* 15:3 (2017): 4–21.
Wyman, Jason. "Interpreting the History of the Workgroup on Constructive Theology." *Theology Today* 73:4 (2017): 312–24.
Ziegler, Philip. "Properly Preoccupied with God: Katherine Sonderegger's Systematic Theology Volume I." *Pro Ecclesia* 17:1 (2018): 37–42.

Contributors

Editors:

Marion Grau is Professor of Systematic Theology, Ecumenism, and Missiology at MF Norwegian School of Theology, Religion and Society, in Oslo, Norway. From 2001 until 2015, she taught theology at the Graduate Theological Union in Berkeley, California, United States. Her areas of interest include theology and climate change, theological hermeneutics, ecology and economy, and pilgrimage. Her current research project has the working title *Anointed with Oil: A Critique of Petro-Religion*.

Jason Wyman received his PhD from Union Theological Seminary in the City of New York. He is a constructive theologian and Christian social ethicist. His first book, *Constructing Constructive Theology: An Introductory Sketch* (2017), recounts the history of constructive theology and describes its key methodological features and themes. He is also a member of the Workgroup on Constructive Theology.

Contributors:

Laurie Cassidy is a theologian and spiritual director. She teaches in the Christian Spirituality Program at Creighton University. Most recently, she was Associate Professor in Religious Studies Department at Marywood University in Scranton, Pennsylvania, United States, and her other appointments include Trinity College in Hartford, Connecticut, and Loyola University/Chicago. Her first volume coedited with Alex Mikulich is *Interrupting White Privilege: Catholic Theologians Break the Silence* (2007). Her latest book, coauthored with Alex Mikulich and Margie Pfeil, is *The Scandal of White Complicity in US Hyper-Incarceration: A Non-Violent Spirituality of White Resistance* (2013). Her research and writing explore the political and cultural impact of Christian mysticism in personal and social transformation.

Judith Gruber received her PhD in systematic theology from the University of Salzburg, Austria, in 2012. From 2012 to 2017, she was Assistant Professor of Systematic Theology at Loyola University, New Orleans, United States. She is Research Professor of Systematic Theology and Director of the Centre for Liberation Theologies at KU Leuven, Belgium. Her research brings Catholic theology into conversation with critical cultural theories, focusing on intercultural theology and postcolonial theology. Her recent publications include *Intercultural Theology: Exploring World Christianity after the Cultural Turn* (2017).

Holly Hillgardner is Associate Professor of Religious Studies at Bethany College in Bethany, West Virginia. Her publications include *Longing and Letting Go: Hindu and Christian Practices of Passionate Non-Attachment* (2016), and her research interests involve Hindu-Christian comparative theology as well as critical pedagogies. She is currently working on a comparative theology of pilgrimage, which attends to the lived contexts of pilgrims as they journey.

Lawrence N. Nwankwo is a Catholic priest, theologian, and Lecturer at the Department of Religion and Human Relations, Nnamdi Azikiwe University, Awka, Nigeria. He specializes in African Christianity with special interest in the ongoing reception of Christianity on the continent and how Christianity can contribute more fully to addressing the challenges faced on the continent. He completed his doctorate in theology and religious studies in 2004 at KU Leuven, Belgium. He was the Moderator of the Liberation Theology Forum and a collaborator at the Centre for Liberation Theologies, KU Leuven. Since 2004, he has placed his theological expertise at the service of his diocesan bishop. Presently, he is the chancellor of his diocese and a parish priest. He has published numerous works on African Christianity, with a special focus on the mission of the church in the context of Africa's (Nigeria) present socioeconomic, political, and cultural challenges.

Heike Peckruhn is Assistant Professor of Religious Studies at Daemen College, New York, United States. Her scholarly interests in religious studies, Christian theology, and ethics are at the intersections of gender, sexuality, race, disability, and colonialism. How we make meaning and engage in meaningful communal action toward increased social justice are at the heart of her research. She was recently named cochair of the Religion and Disability Studies Unit of the American Academy of Religion.

Shelly Rambo is Associate Professor of Theology at Boston University School of Theology, Massachusetts, United States. A theologian working in the Christian tradition, her research and teaching interests focus on religious responses to suffering, trauma, and violence. Her book *Spirit and Trauma: A Theology of Remaining* (2010) develops a theology of the Spirit in response to the interdisciplinary study of trauma. Her work brings together postmodern literary theory, biblical hermeneutics, and contemporary Christian theology. Her most recent book project, *Resurrecting Wounds: Living in the Afterlife of Trauma* (2017), explores the significance of resurrection wounds within the Christian tradition and as it meets contemporary expressions of post-traumatic life in the broader culture.

Anthony G. Reddie is the Director of the Oxford Centre for Religion and Culture at Regent's Park College, at Oxford University. He is also an Extraordinary Professor of Theological Ethics with the University of South Africa. He is the editor of *Black Theology: An International Journal*. His latest book is entitled *Theologizing Brexit: A Liberationist and Postcolonial Critique* (2019), the first postcolonial and intercultural exploration of the phenomenon. His research interests straddle black liberation theology and practical theology, the combination of the two giving rise to a hybrid form of theological reflection he describes as "participative black theology."

John J. Thatamanil is Associate Professor of Theology and World Religions at Union Theological Seminary in the City of New York. He is the author of *The Immanent Divine: God, Creation, and the Human Predicament. An East-West Conversation* (2006) and *Circling the Elephant: A Comparative Theology of Religious Diversity* (2020). His research and teaching include comparative theology, philosophical theology, and theologies of religious diversity. He is currently at work on a book provisionally titled *The Quest for Interreligious Wisdom*.

Index

Althaus-Reid, Marcella 62, 68, 80–2, 87
anti-Judaism 33, 43–4
apologetic 69, 216, 233–4
apophatic 59, 69

Barth, Karl 19
bible 22–3, 41, 60, 70, 148
body/embodiment 23, 79–89, 94–6, 98, 128

climate change 53, 67, 70–1
colonialism 26, 81, 92, 136, 168–71, 175, 181, 185–6, 193, 195, 219–24
comparative theology 49–50, 65
Cone, James 1, 26, 150, 154, 156, 158
conscientization 146–9
contextual theology 57, 63, 145
Copeland, M. Shawn 26–7, 168, 172

dangerous memory/ies 167–8, 170–2, 174, 177–80, 183, 186, 223, 229
disability 61–2, 83, 129

ecotheology 33, 43
epistemology 77, 148, 157, 216
ethics 23, 33, 129, 146
ethnography 49–50, 123, 132–5
eucharist 153, 176, 180

Farley, Edward 19–22, 35, 47, 104
feminism/feminist theology 2, 22, 42, 58, 64, 106–8, 111, 123–4, 127–9, 132, 140, 226

haunting 223–8, 232–4
hermeneutics 4, 28, 58–9, 77, 82, 103, 104–9, 217, 227
Heyward, Carter 85–6, 88
holy spirit 194, 205, 208–9
house of tradition 33

imagination/imaginative 18, 32, 35, 37, 40, 42, 44, 89, 110, 113
imperialism 125, 136, 182
indigenous 50, 53, 60, 66–73, 108, 125, 134, 168, 176–85, 199, 204, 208
interdisciplinary 3, 11, 16, 25, 28–9, 69, 124–5, 131, 136–8, 141, 161, 168, 216, 220, 233–4
intersectionality 27, 63

Kaufman, Gordon 13, 19–24, 32, 35, 45–7
Keller, Catherine 35, 37–8, 42, 58–60, 63, 109, 111
kenotic 196–7, 232–4
Kimmerer, Robin Wall 53, 56, 180, 182–3

liberation 1, 4, 9–10, 23, 26–9, 70–1, 80, 82, 86–8, 106–10, 147–50, 158, 177, 217, 221, 227

marginalization 34, 80, 221, 223
McFague, Sallie 13, 19–25, 35, 47, 58, 67, 82, 87, 106, 127
Metz, Johann Baptist 168, 172, 176–7, 181, 217–18, 225, 229
ministry 147–9, 152, 203
myth 18, 22, 45, 53–6, 174–5, 183

nationalism 92–3, 151, 169–71

pedagogy/pedagogical 67, 147, 152, 155
pluralism 1, 21–3, 62
political theology 167–73, 176–7, 180–2, 186–8, 193–5, 217–20, 225, 230
polydoxy 42, 62, 132
popular religiosity 192–3, 197, 203–6, 208
postcolonialism 62, 65, 68, 109, 111, 123–7, 131–4, 136, 153, 169, 172, 193, 195, 197, 201, 216, 220, 224–5, 227

practical theology 64, 148–9, 161–2
process theology 37
prosperity theology 192–4, 204–8

queer/queer theory 34, 81, 92–4, 154

revelation 32, 40, 78–80, 86, 104–5, 108, 181, 215–16, 229–30, 233
Ruether, Rosemary Radford 45, 105

soteriology 138, 207, 220, 226–9

Tanner, Kathryn 41

theological anthropology 78–9, 96, 124, 128, 147
theological liberalism 16, 18–19, 24, 55, 213
theosis 37–9, 41, 194, 206
Tillich, Paul 19–22, 40, 55, 216
Tracy, David 1, 21–4, 47

Williams, Delores 61, 84, 87, 158
womanism 157–8
Workgroup on Constructive Theology 1, 11, 19–29, 61, 64–7, 103–4

www.ingramcontent.com/pod-product-compliance
Lightning Source LLC
Chambersburg PA
CBHW072146290426
44111CB00012B/1991